ECONOMIC AND SOCIAL RIGHTS AFTER THE GLOBAL FINANCIAL CRISIS

Edited by

AOIFE NOLAN

The University of Nottingham

CAMBRIDGE
UNIVERSITY PRESS

CAMBRIDGE
UNIVERSITY PRESS

University Printing House, Cambridge CB2 8BS, United Kingdom

Cambridge University Press is part of the University of Cambridge.

It furthers the University's mission by disseminating knowledge in the pursuit of education, learning and research at the highest international levels of excellence.

www.cambridge.org
Information on this title: www.cambridge.org/9781107618428

First published 2014
First paperback edition 2015

A catalogue record for this publication is available from the British Library

Library of Congress Cataloguing in Publication data
Economic and social rights after the global financial crisis / edited by Aoife Nolan.
pages cm
Includes bibliographical references and index.
ISBN 978-1-107-04325-1 (hardback)
1. Economic policy. 2. Basic needs–Law and legislation. 3. Human rights–Economic aspects. 4. Social rights. 5. Global Financial Crisis, 2008–2009. I. Nolan, Aoife, editor of compilation.
K3820.E26 2014
330–dc23
2014013616

ISBN 978-1-107-04325-1 Hardback
ISBN 978-1-107-61842-8 Paperback

This book is dedicated to my parents, Úna and David, with love and thanks.

CONTENTS

FIGURES

CONTRIBUTORS

RADHIKA BALAKRISHNAN is Executive Director of the Center for Women's Global Leadership, and Professor, Women's and Gender Studies at Rutgers University. She has a PhD in Economics from Rutgers University. Previously, she was Professor of Economics and International Studies at Marymount Manhattan College. She has worked at the Ford Foundation as a programme officer in the Asia Regional Programme. She is on the Board of the Center for Constitutional Rights and the International Association for Feminist Economics. She is the co-editor with Diane Elson of *Economic Policy and Human Rights: Holding Governments to Account* (2011). She edited *The Hidden Assembly Line: Gender Dynamics of Subcontracted Work in a Global Economy* (2001), co-edited *Good Sex: Feminist Perspectives from the World's Religions*, with Patricia Jung and Mary Hunt (2000), and also authored numerous articles that have appeared in books and journals.

CHRISTIAN COURTIS is a human rights officer with the Office of the United Nations High Commissioner for Human Rights, where he coordinates the working team on economic, social and cultural rights. He is a law professor at the University of Buenos Aires Law School (Argentina) and invited professor at ITAM Law School (Mexico). He has been a visiting professor and researcher at various universities in Europe, Latin America and the United States. He has served as a consultant for the World/Panamerican Health Organization, UNESCO, the UN Department for Economic and Social Affairs (DESA), the Economic and Social Commission for Latin America and the Caribbean (ECLAC) and the Inter-American Institute for Human Rights. He was previously the coordinator of the Economic, Social and Cultural Rights Project of the International Commission of Jurists (Geneva). He has written various books and articles (many of them published in Mexico) on human rights, constitutional theory and legal theory and sociology. He is author of the ground-breaking *Courts and the*

Legal Enforcement of Economic, Social and Cultural Rights: Comparative Experiences of Justiciability (2008).

OLIVIER DE SCHUTTER is a professor at the Catholic University of Louvain and at the College of Europe (Natolin). From 2008–14, he was the United Nations Special Rapporteur on the right to food. He is also a member of the Global Law School Faculty at New York University and is a visiting professor at Columbia University. In 2002–6, he chaired the EU Network of Independent Experts on Fundamental Rights, a high-level group of experts which advised the European Union institutions on fundamental rights issues. He has acted on a number of occasions as an expert for the Council of Europe and for the European Union. From 2004, and until his appointment as the UN Special Rapporteur on the right to food, he was the General Secretary of the International Federation of Human Rights (FIDH) on the issue of globalisation and human rights.

JAMES HEINTZ is Research Professor at the Political Economy Research Institute of the University of Massachusetts, Amherst. He has collaborated with numerous UN agencies, including the United Nations Development Program, the International Labour Organization, the UN Research Institute for Social Development, the UN Economic Commission for Africa, and UN Women. He has published in the areas of employment and labour markets, macroeconomic alternatives, the distributive effects of monetary policy, and development strategies in sub-Saharan African countries.

HELEN HERSHKOFF is the Herbert M. and Svetlana Wachtell Professor of Constitutional Law and Civil Liberties at New York University School of Law, where she co-directs the Arthur Garfield Hays Civil Liberties Program. She joined the NYU faculty in 1995, after having practiced law in New York for almost 20 years, first at a private law firm, then at The Legal Aid Society of New York, and finally at the American Civil Liberties Union. She is the author of numerous articles about socio-economic rights that are published in journals that include the Harvard, Stanford and New York University law reviews, and is a co-author of several books involving United States civil procedure. She is a graduate of Harvard College and Harvard Law School, and studied Modern History at St Anne's College, Oxford University, as a Marshall Scholar.

DAVID LANDAU is Associate Dean for International Programs and Assistant Professor of Law at The Florida State University College of Law. He holds an AB and JD from Harvard University, and is currently completing his

PhD in Government there. His main research interests are in comparative constitutional law and politics, with a particular focus on Latin America. He has recently done work on the enforcement of social rights and on constitution-making processes, and is completing a book (with Manuel José Cepeda) containing translations and commentary on major decisions of the Colombian Constitutional Court. He has also served as a consultant on constitutional issues for the Truth and Reconciliation Commission of Honduras. His work has appeared in the *Harvard International Law Journal* and the *Alabama Law Review*, among other fora.

STEPHEN LOFFREDO is Professor of Law and Director of the Economic Justice Project at the City University of New York School of Law. After graduating from Harvard Law School and clerking for the New Jersey Supreme Court, he entered practice in 1982 as a staff attorney with The Legal Aid Society in the South Bronx, where he provided neighbourhood legal services and conducted law reform litigation, including actions that secured the rights of homeless families in New York to safe and adequate shelter and established the right of single, homeless shelter residents to public assistance and Medicaid. He has continued to practise poverty law through the clinical programme at CUNY and as counsel to the Urban Justice Center. He has written and spoken widely on the constitutional dimensions of economic rights and the role of wealth in a constitutional democracy, and served as consultant to the late Senator Paul Wellstone on the constitutional aspects of federal welfare legislation.

NICHOLAS J. LUSIANI is Director of the Human Rights in Economic Policy Program at the Center for Economic and Social Rights, where his work focuses on developing alternative human rights-centred economic and development policies. He received a Master's degree in International Affairs from the School of International and Public Affairs at Columbia University, where he specialised in international human rights law and macroeconomics. Niko has published extensively in the areas of human rights, economic analysis and fiscal policy, including, most recently, *Maximum Available Resources and Human Rights: Analytical Report* (2011) and 'Human Rights in the "Great Regression": Towards a Human Rights-centred Economic Policy in Times of Crisis' in Reidel *et al.*, *Economic, Social and Cultural Rights: Contemporary Issues and Challenges* (2014) (co-authored).

GUSTAVO MAURINO is Founder and Co-director of Asociación Civil por la Igualdad y la Justicia (ACIJ). He holds a JD from the National

University of Córdoba and a postgraduate degree in tort law, University of Belgrano, Buenos Aires. He is a professor (undergraduate and postgraduate level) in civil law, constitutional theory and legal philosophy at the University of Palermo, Buenos Aires. He coordinates the professional practice section of the Department of Clinical Education, University of Palermo, is a visiting lecturer in the Political Science and International Studies Department of Di Tella University, and lectures in the Human Rights Master's Programme at Lanús National University. Maurino is co-author of *Las Acciones Colectivas, Análasis Conceptual, Constituticional, Procesal, Jurisprudencial y Comparado* (2006) (with Martin Sigal and Ezeqiuel Nino) and a book on medical malpractice, co-authored with Alfredo Kraut. He is the editor of *Los Escritos de Carlos Nino* (2007).

EZEQUIEL NINO holds a JD from Universidad de Buenos Aires and a BA in Journalism from Taller Escuela Agencia, Buenos Aires. He earned his Master of Laws (LLM) from New York University and a Masters in International Relations from the University of Pompeu Fabra and the University of Barcelona. He is the founder and co-director of Asociación Civil por la Igualdad y la Justicia (ACIJ) and teaches Constitutional Law and Professional Practice at Universidad de Palermo. He participates annually in the Seminar in Latin America on Constitutional and Political Theory (SELA) organised by Yale Law School and several Latin American universities. He has been appointed to the UNCAC (UN Convention against Corruption) Coalition Coordination Committee. He is co-author of *Las Acciones Colectivas, Análasis Conceptual, Constituticional, Procesal, Jurisprudencial y Comparado* (2006) (with Martin Sigal and Gustavo Maurino) and several articles on economic, social and cultural rights, access to information and anti-corruption issues.

AOIFE NOLAN is Professor of International Human Rights Law at Nottingham University School of Law. She has published extensively in the areas of human rights, particularly in relation to children's rights and economic and social rights, as well as on constitutional law. She is the founding coordinator of the Economic and Social Rights Academic Network, UK and Ireland (ESRAN-UKI). She has worked with and acted as an expert advisor to a wide range of international and national organisations and bodies working on human rights issues, including the Council of Europe, a range of UN Special Procedures, ESCR-Net, the Northern Ireland Bill of Rights Forum and the International NGO Coalition for an Optional Protocol to the International Covenant on Economic, Social and Cultural Rights. Her recent books on economic and social rights include

Children's Socio-economic Rights, Democracy & the Courts (2011) and *Human Rights & Public Finance: Budgets and the Promotion of Economic and Social Rights* (2013) (co-edited with R. O'Connell and C. Harvey).

COLM O'CINNEIDE is a Reader in Law at University College London. He has published extensively in the field of human rights and anti-discrimination law, and is currently Vice-President of the European Committee on Social Rights of the Council of Europe. He has also acted as a specialist legal advisor to the Joint Committee on Human Rights of the UK Parliament and as UK *rapporteur* for the European Commission's network of independent legal experts on anti-discrimination law.

ANASHRI PILLAY is a Lecturer in Law at Durham University, where she teaches international law and international human rights law. She has held academic posts at Leeds University and the University of Cape Town. Anashri's research interests lie in the field of comparative constitutional law, particularly the adjudication of economic and social rights by national courts. Her publications focus on principles of judicial restraint; implementation of economic and social rights; and judicial review for unreasonableness. Anashri is a member of the Economic and Social Rights Academic Network, UK and Ireland (ESRAN-UKI), the International Association of Constitutional Law (IACL) and the African Network of Constitutional Lawyers (ANCL).

LIDIA RABINOVICH is a human rights lawyer and academic researcher. She currently serves as Head of Legal Aid Child Representation at the Israeli Ministry of Justice. She previously headed the legal division of the United Nations High Commissioner for Refugees (UNHCR) office in Tel Aviv and served as a human rights officer in the Special Procedures Branch at the Office of the United Nations High Commissioner for Human Rights (OHCHR) in Geneva. Prior to joining the UN, she served as State Attorney at the Israeli Ministry of Social Affairs and at the Israeli Ministry of Justice, dealing mainly with children's rights and child protection, juvenile justice and rights of persons with disabilities. She holds an LLB from the Hebrew University in Jerusalem and an LLM, magna cum laude, from Tel Aviv University. She has taught child rights and welfare law at Tel Aviv University. Areas of expertise include welfare law and international human rights law, particularly the rights of the child and economic and social rights.

RAQUEL ROLNIK is an architect and urban planner, with over 30 years' experience in planning and urban land management. She has extensive experience in the implementation and evaluation of housing and urban policies. Based in São Paulo, she is a professor at the Faculty of Architecture and Urbanism of the University of São Paulo and is the author of several books and articles on the urban issue. In her career, she has held various government positions, including Director of the Department of Planning of the city of São Paulo (1989–92) and National Secretary for Urban Programs of the Brazilian Ministry of Cities (2003–7), as well as NGO activities (she was Urbanism Coordinator of the Polis Institute (1997–2002)). She has advised national and local governments on policy reform and institutional development as well as on planning and management of housing and local development programmes. Between May 2008 and June 2014, she held the mandate of Special Rapporteur on adequate housing, appointed by the United Nations Human Rights Council.

MAGDALENA SEPÚLVEDA CARMONA was the United Nations Special Rapporteur on extreme poverty and human rights from 2008 to 2014. She is a Visiting Fellow at the United Nations Research Institute for Social Development (UNRISD). Since 2013, she has been a member of the High Level Panel of Experts on Food Security and Nutrition of the UN Committee on World Food Security (CFS). Ms Sepúlveda is a Chilean lawyer who holds a PhD in International Law from Utrecht University in the Netherlands and an LL.M in human rights law from the University of Essex in the United Kingdom. She has worked as a researcher at the Netherlands Institute for Human Rights, as a staff attorney at the Inter-American Court of Human Rights, and as the Co-Director of the Department of International Law and Human Rights of the United Nations-mandated University for Peace in San Jose, Costa Rica. She has also served as a consultant to several intergovernmental and non-governmental organisations such as the Office of the United Nations High Commissioner for Refugees, the Office of the United Nations High Commissioner for Human Rights, the Economic Commission for Latin American and the Caribbean, the Norwegian Refugee Council and the Inter-American Institute for Human Rights. More recently she was Research Director at the International Council on Human Rights Policy in Geneva and Research Fellow at the Norwegian Center for Human Rights.

MURRAY WESSON completed his LLB at the University of KwaZulu-Natal in Durban, South Africa, before studying at the University of Oxford as a Rhodes Scholar. There he completed a Bachelor of Civil Law, MPhil in Law and DPhil in Law. He is currently an associate professor at the Faculty of

Law, University of Western Australia. He was previously a lecturer at the School of Law, University of Leeds, and a visiting lecturer at the Central European University in Budapest, Hungary. His teaching and research are in the areas of constitutional and human rights law, with a particular interest in socio-economic rights.

ACKNOWLEDGEMENTS

This book would not have been possible without the generous contributions of a considerable number of scholars. Huge thanks are owed to Daniel Brinks, Manuel José Cepeda, Rosalind Dixon, Alice Donald, Mary Dowell-Jones, Conor Gearty, Jessie Hohmann, Benjamin Mason Meier, Paul O'Connell, Rory O'Connell, Marius Pieterse and Sigrun Skogly. Their extensive advice and feedback contributed enormously to the quality of the book. I am also grateful to Finola O'Sullivan and Elizabeth Spicer of Cambridge University Press for their excellent advice and support throughout the process. Pei-Lun Tsai provided outstanding research assistance.

The support of colleagues at the School of Law, University of Nottingham is much appreciated. Thanks are due to the Socio-economic Rights and Administrative Justice Project, Faculty of Law, Stellenbosch University, the Children's Rights Centre, Queen's University Belfast and the Project on Economic, Social and Cultural Rights at the Geneva Academy of International Humanitarian Law and Human Rights, where I spent time while working on the book. As always, I owe enormous thanks to my family and friends for their love and support, especially Kevin, Helen, Emer, Katie, Oisín, JJ and the KT Collective.

CASES

National Cases

Argentina

Colombia

Germany

Hungary

Latvia

Portugal

South Africa

Spain

United Kingdom

United States (Federal)

United States (State)

Arizona

California

Colorado

Connecticut

Indiana

Maryland

Massachusetts

New Hampshire

New Jersey

New York

Ohio

Washington

Regional Cases

European Committee of Social Rights

European Court of Human Rights

European Court of Justice

Inter-American Commission on Human Rights

Inter-American Court of Human Rights

LEGISLATION

National legislation

Argentina

Belgium

Canada

Colombia

Finland

France

Germany

Greece

Ireland

Kenya

Netherlands

Poland

Portugal

Slovenia

South Africa

Spain

United Kingdom

United States

Legislation (Federal)

Legislation (State)

Massachusetts

Regional instruments

International instruments

ABBREVIATIONS

ACP	African, Caribbean and Pacific Group of States
CESCR	United Nations Committee on Economic, Social and Cultural Rights
CFS	Committee on World Food Security
CSJN	Corte Suprema de Justica de la Nación (Argentina)
CSM	International Food Security and Nutrition Civil Society Mechanism
CSO	civil society organisation
ECB	European Central Bank
ECHR	European Convention on Human Rights and Fundamental Freedoms
ECSR	European Committee of Social Rights
ECtHR	European Court of Human Rights
ESCR	economic, social and cultural rights
ESR	economic and social rights
EU	European Union
FAO	United Nations Food and Agricultural Organization
FRA	European Union Agency for Fundamental Rights
FTT	financial transaction tax
GDP	gross domestic product
GNP	gross national product
GSF	Global Strategic Framework on Food Security and Nutrition
HLPE	High-Level Panel of Experts
ICESCR	International Covenant on Economic, Social and Cultural Rights
ILO	International Labour Organization
IMF	International Monetary Fund
LDC	least developed country
NGO	non-governmental organisations
ODA	official development assistance
OECD	Organisation for Economic Co-operation and Development
OHCHR	Office of the United Nations High Commissioner for Human Rights
PPP	Purchasing Power Parity
SCN	Standing Committee on Nutrition
UNCTAD	United Nations Conference on Trade and Development
UNDP	United Nations Development Programme

UNHCR	United Nations High Commissioner for Refugees
UNRISD	United Nations Research Institute for Social Development
UNICEF	United Nations Children's Fund
VAT	Value Added Tax
WB	World Bank
WHO	World Health Organization
WTO	World Trade Organization

Introduction

AOIFE NOLAN

Economic and social rights are at a critical juncture. The burst of the US housing bubble and the subsequent financial and economic crises have impacted severely on human rights realisation globally.[1] This is particularly so with regard to economic and social rights (ESR),[2] the enjoyment of which has been grievously affected by the crises and the domestic and supranational responses thereto.

The financial and economic crises have created, and exacerbated, jobs, food and housing crises. According to the International Labour Organization, in the 51 countries for which data were available, at least 20 million jobs were lost between October 2008 and the end of the following year.[3] Almost 43 million further workers were deemed to be at risk of exclusion from the labour market.[4] While the global food prices crisis had

[1] This book does not seek to explain the origins and evolution of the crises in any detail but it is necessary to provide a short overview of the approach adopted to the crises herein. While definitions and perceived root causes of the financial and economic crises vary, this volume treats them as separate but strongly interrelated entities. The global financial crisis, the start of which was signalled by the American sub-prime mortgage collapse, effectively resulted from a combination of a failure of risk models to assess financial products underpinned by serious long-term shortcomings related to the financial system such as financialisation, inadequate regulation and mismanagement of intentionally abstruse institutions. The economic crisis, which goes beyond crises in relation to the financial system per se (albeit that the latter contributed to the former) has had a number of causes, including recessions caused by housing bubble collapses in the US, Ireland and Spain, recessions partially caused by retrenchment in banks leading to a cut in credit in the economy, as well as sovereign debt crises, some of which stemmed from States taking on banking losses in order to shore up their banks and/or socialise losses.

[2] The terms economic and social rights, socio-economic rights and social rights are used interchangeably by authors in this collection. The term 'human rights' is used to denote the full spectrum of human rights, including civil, political and cultural rights – not simply economic and social rights. In this introduction, the terminology used to describe rights reflects that employed by authors in their specific chapters.

[3] International Labour Organization/International Institute for Labour Studies, *World of Work Report 2009: The Global Jobs Crisis and Beyond* (Geneva: International Institute for Labour Studies, 2009), p. vii.

[4] *Ibid.*, p. 1.

peaked by June 2008 its effects were still being felt when the financial system went into turmoil; an estimated 40 million people were pushed into hunger in 2008, bringing to 963 million the number of hungry people worldwide at the end of that year.[5] As of June 2009 that number had risen to 1.02 billion.[6] With regard to the right to adequate housing, there is mounting evidence of increases in homelessness and reduced access to housing finance.[7]

The financial and economic crises have had a devastating and disproportionate effect on already vulnerable groups, including women, children, people with disabilities, ethnic minorities and migrants.[8] Emerging research demonstrates that the poorer, more powerless and less visible populations, those who already experienced lower levels of economic and social rights enjoyment than other social groups, have been hit especially hard by the job losses, poverty and economic and political upheaval that have followed the global financial collapse.[9] While the financial crisis effectively originated in the US, and has had a direct effect on the economic stability and performance of that country (as well as a large number of European States), there is growing evidence of severe impact on developing countries too. With regard to the Millennium Development Goals, 2010 data suggested that in numerous countries the crises resulted in progress towards many of the Goals either stalling or going into reverse.[10]

[5] Special Rapporteur on the Right to Food, 'The Right to Food and the Financial and Economic Crisis: Submission to the UN Conference on World Financial and Economic Crisis, UN General Assembly, 24–26 June 2009', www2.ohchr.org/english/issues/food/docs/NoteCrisisFinal26062009.pdf, last accessed 22 January 2014.

[6] *Ibid.*

[7] See, e.g., in the US context, National Coalition for the Homeless, the National Health Care for the Homeless Council, the National Alliance to End Homelessness, the National Association for the Education of Homeless Children and Youth, the National Law Center on Homelessness & Poverty, the National Low Income Housing Coalition and the National Policy and Advocacy Council on Homelessness, 'Foreclosure to Homelessness 2009: The Forgotten Victims of the Subprime Crisis' (2009), www.nationalhomeless.org/advocacy/ForeclosuretoHomelessness0609.pdf, last accessed 22 January 2014; National Law Center on Homelessness and Poverty, 'Indicators of Increasing Homelessness Due to the Foreclosure and Economic Crises' (2010), www.nationalhomeless.org/advocacy/ForeclosuretoHomelessness0609.pdf, last accessed 23 January 2014.

[8] M. Sepúlveda, 'Report of the Independent Expert on the Question of Human Rights and Extreme Poverty on the Human Rights Based Approach to Recovery from the Global Economic and Financial Crises, with a Focus on Those Living in Poverty' (17 March 2011) UN Doc. A/HRC/17/34, para. 23.

[9] See, e.g., R. Heltberg, N. Hossain and A. Reya (eds.), *Living through Crises: How the Food, Fuel, and Financial Shocks Affect the Poor* (Washington, DC: World Bank, 2012).

[10] *Global Monitoring Report 2010: The MDGs after the Crisis* (Washington, DC: World Bank, 2010), pp. 6–7.

The damage done to ESR realisation is not only attributable to specific crises-related outcomes such as turmoil on markets and labour opportunities but also results from a 'creeping' of austerity measures and excessive economic contraction in terms of public expenditure beyond those countries/economies (e.g. the US, Spain, Greece, Ireland, Portugal and Italy) that have dominated the financial headlines since 2008.[11] While most governments affected by the crisis introduced fiscal stimulus programmes (fiscal expansion) and ramped up public spending in 2008–9, by 2010, premature expenditure contraction – in the form of 'austerity' measures – became widespread, and this public expenditure consolidation is now expected to intensify at least into 2016.[12] And, far from being exclusively a Eurozone or North American issue, fiscal contraction has been most severe in the developing world.[13]

Together with growing awareness on the part of human rights scholars and advocates of the role that non-rights-centric neoliberal, supranational and domestic economic policies and structures have played in causing (or at least not preventing) the crises,[14] there is mounting concern about the implications of the national and supranational responses just described for the human rights enjoyment of the most vulnerable in

[11] See, e.g., I. Ortiz, J. Chai and M. Cummins, *Austerity Measures Threaten Children and Poor Households: Recent Evidence in Public Expenditures from 128 Developing Countries* (New York: UNICEF, 2011). This study found that 70 developing countries (or 55 per cent of the study sample) reduced total expenditures by nearly 3 per cent of gross domestic product (GDP), on average, during 2010, and 91 developing countries (or more than 70 per cent of the sample) were expected to reduce annual expenditures in 2012. Moreover, comparing the 2010–12 and 2005–7 periods suggested that nearly one-quarter of developing countries appeared to be undergoing excessive contraction, defined as cutting expenditures below pre-crisis levels in terms of GDP. The study also highlights that the scope of austerity measures under consideration in developing countries seems to have widened considerably since 2010.

[12] See I. Ortiz and M. Cummins, 'Age of Austerity; A Review of Public Expenditures and Adjustment Measures in 181 Countries' (Initiative for Policy Dialogue and the South Centre Working Paper, May 2013), i.

[13] *Ibid.*

[14] Neoliberalism is a contested term that has been accorded multiple definitions. However, frequently identified elements of neoliberalism as an economic theory include an emphasis on deregulation, economic liberalisation and market reforms. These will be understood as constituting fundamental elements of neoliberalism for the purposes of this chapter. For considerations of the history and evolution of neoliberalism as a political and economic movement and a philosophy, see D. Stedman Jones, *Masters of the Universe: Hayek, Friedman and the Birth of Neoliberal Politics* (Princeton University Press, 2012) and P. Mirowski & D. Plehwe, *The Road from Mont Pèlerin: The Making of the Neoliberal Thought Collective* (Harvard University Press, 2009).

society.[15] Notably, 'austerity'-focused national and supranational policies have generally operated to exacerbate and entrench pre-existing disadvantage. As Saiz noted in 2009, 'despite the obvious human rights dimensions of the crisis, human rights have barely figured in the diagnoses or prescriptions proposed by the international community'.[16] Far from putting an end to the dominance of anti-statist unregulated free market liberalism that predated and contributed to the crises,[17] it is strongly arguable that by rescuing the financial markets (through taxpayer money), mainstream neoliberalism has actually contrived an opportunity to *intensify* the dominance of individualistic, anti-statist unregulated free market liberalism, and that this has been at the expense of other, more potentially 'human rights-friendly' models. That is not to suggest that international human rights law, including ESR, requires States to adopt a specific economic model – indeed, the United Nations Committee on Economic, Social and Cultural Rights (CESCR) has emphasised that it does not.[18] However, international human rights law has a crucial role to play as an analytical framework for evaluating (and, if necessary, critiquing) and recalibrating the processes, inputs, outputs and outcomes of the models that have been chosen, albeit that there is very limited evidence that States are prepared to employ it in such a way.[19]

[15] See, e.g., ESCR-Net, AWID, Center for Economic and Social Rights, Center for Women's Global Leadership and Center for Concern, 'Bringing Human Rights to Bear in Times of Crisis: A Human Rights Analysis of Government Responses to the Economic Crisis' (March 2010), 1–3, www.escr-net.org/usr_doc/HRResponsestoEconCrisis_Final.pdf, last accessed 22 January 2014.

[16] I. Saiz, 'Rights in Recession? Challenges for Economic and Social Rights Enforcement in Times of Crisis', *Journal of Human Rights Practice*, 1 (2009), 277–93, 280.

[17] See, e.g., Grant and Wilson who note the ongoing dominance of what they term 'neoliberal Washington consensus policies' following the global financial crisis, and contrast this with earlier financial crises which resulted in major shifts in policy paradigms. (W. Grant and G. Wilson, 'Introduction' in W. Grant and G. Wilson (eds.), *The Consequences of the Global Financial Crisis: The Rhetoric of Reform and Regulation* (Oxford University Press, 2012), pp. 1–14, p. 6). See also D. Persendorfer, 'Good-Bye Neoliberalism? Contested Policy Responses to Uncertain Consequences of the 2007–2009 Financial Crisis' in K. Alexander and R. Dhumale (eds.), *Research Handbook on International Financial Regulation* (Cheltenham: Edward Elgar, 2012), pp. 414-434; John Quiggin, *Zombie Economics: How Dead Ideas Still Walk among Us* (Princeton University Press, 2010).

[18] UN Committee on Economic, Social and Cultural Rights (CESCR), 'General Comment No. 3' in 'Note by the Secretariat, Compilation of General Comments and General Recommendations Adopted by Human Rights Treaty Bodies' (27 May 2008) UN Doc. HRI/GEN/1/Rev.9 (Vol. I), para. 8.

[19] An ongoing critique of State responses to the crisis has been the widespread failure on the part of many States to carrying out human rights impact assessment and equality impact

In sum, while the financial and economic crises have heightened awareness of ESR as an advocacy tool at the domestic and international levels, responses to them have largely served to shore up existing power distributions and inequalities, to the detriment of ESR.[20] In short: ESR were largely ignored by economic policymakers prior to the financial meltdown and resultant economic turmoil,[21] have been seriously affected by both, and appear largely to be being ignored in past and current state responses to such.

I. Painting the big (global) picture: the crises and economic and social rights protection internationally

This collection is motivated by two key questions: what have the crises meant in terms of ESR enjoyment? What is the alternative(s)? With other than a few notable exceptions,[22] the crises and their interrelationship with and impact upon ESR have not yet been subjected to adequate academic, policymaker or activist attention or analysis. Even the Committee on Economic, Social and Cultural Rights – the body with pre-eminent

assessments that would evaluate the potential and actual ESR impact of State responses to the crises. This has been highlighted by the CESCR in its review of a number of States who have enacted post-crisis austerity measures. See, e.g., CESCR, 'Concluding Observations on Spain' (6 June 2012) UN Doc. E/C.12/ESP/CO/5, para. 23.

20 Paul O'Connell has argued that the undermining of ESR protection and enjoyment associated with the contemporary age of austerity is not an anomaly, but rather the necessary fate of ESR in the current social and economic order; the recent push for austerity is motivated not by objective, economic necessity but is driven by an ideological and political project to further entrench neoliberal capitalism. See P. O'Connell, 'Let Them Eat Cake: Socio-Economic Rights in a Time of Austerity' in A. Nolan, R. O'Connell and C. Harvey (eds.), *Human Rights and Public Finance: Budgets and the Promotion of Economic and Social Rights* (Oxford: Hart Publishing, 2013), pp. 59–76.

21 See, e.g., S. Way and S. Stanton, *Human Rights and the Global Economic Crisis: Consequences, Causes and Responses* (New York: Center for Economic and Social Rights, 2009); S. Way, N. Lusiani and I. Saiz, 'Economic and Social Rights in the "Great Recession": Towards a Human Rights-Centered Economic Policy in Times of Crisis' in E. Riedel, G. Giacca and C. Golay (eds.), *Economic, Social and Cultural Rights: Contemporary Issues and Challenges* (Oxford University Press, 2014), pp. 86–110, p. 86.

22 See, e.g., Sepúlveda, 'Report on the Human Rights Based Approach to Recovery'; R. Rolnik, 'Report of the Special Rapporteur on Adequate Housing as a Component of the Right to an Adequate Standard of Living, and on the Right to Non-Discrimination in this Context on the Financial Crisis and Its Causes' (4 February 2009) UN Doc. A/HRC/10/7; Office of the Council of Europe Commissioner for Human Rights, 'Safeguarding Human Rights in Times of Economic Crisis' (Council of Europe Commissioner for Human Rights Issue Paper, November 2013), www.enetenglish.gr/resources/article-files/prems162913_gbr_1700_safeguardinghumanrights_web.pdf, last accessed 10 December 2013.

responsibility for interpreting international ESR standards – has been slow to engage in a consistent, coherent way from an ESR perspective with the events leading up to, and the responses that have followed, the 2008 collapse.[23]

This collection of essays seeks to fill the gap, identifying not only the various impacts of the crises on economic and social rights but also how rights standards can be used to frame a different set of responses to the situation in which rights-flouting neoliberalism has left the world.

Challenging this 'radio silence' on the rights impact of the Great Recession, Magdalena Sepúlveda opens this volume by providing a clear-eyed overview of the impact of the post-2007 turmoil and austerity policies on ESR. In exploring the concept of a human rights-based approach to dealing with the crises, Sepúlveda argues that by designing and implementing recovery policies taking into account human rights obligations, States can prevent a steep rise in poverty levels, and ensure that the most disadvantaged groups in society are not disproportionately impacted by the crises. While the chapter provides a key evidence base in terms of the potential of regional and national responses to the economic collapse, including austerity policies, to threaten the enjoyment of economic, social and cultural rights of the poorest sectors of society, Sepúlveda also makes a set of important, pragmatic recommendations with regard to how States can facilitate a human rights-based recovery from the crises.

In their contributions, Raquel Rolnik and Lidia Rabinovich and Olivier De Schutter further develop the theme of the need for a human rights-centric response to the economic crisis. So far as the first of these chapters is concerned, Rolnik and Rabinovich highlight the key elements of the neoliberal approach to housing, demonstrating the way in which the commodification of housing, as well as the increased use of housing as an investment asset integrated in a globalised financial market, have resulted in public policies that have abandoned the conceptual meaning of housing as a social good. They argue that this approach has deeply impacted upon the enjoyment of the right to adequate housing. In doing so, Rolnik and Rabinovich discuss the relationship between this non-rights-centric approach to housing and

[23] The Committee has appeared reluctant to address issues arising in relation to the economic crisis, failing, for instance, to produce a General Comment that could serve as guidance to States and advocates with regard to economic and social rights protection in a time of financial and economic crisis. Indeed, the Committee has limited itself to a May 2012 open letter to States Parties, in which it sought to clarify a set of criteria by which to judge the lawfulness of austerity measures. It has subsequently applied this letter in its review of state reports. For more on this point, see Nolan *et al.*'s contribution to this volume.

the financial and economic crises, including the degree to which the former constituted both a cause and a response to the latter. In considering the effect of that approach on the enjoyment on the right to housing of the poorest and most disadvantaged in different contexts and across time, they analyse the three main housing finance policies directed at low income households (mortgage finance, demand side subsidies and housing micro-finance) from a human rights perspective. Ultimately, Rolnik and Rabinovich call for a paradigm shift from prevalent housing policies that focus on the financialisation of housing over to a rights-based approach to housing policies.

De Schutter also addresses the notion of ESR relating to, or constituting, social or public goods. He argues that the global food price crisis of 2008, and the financial and economic crises which followed, have led to a reassessment of the complementarity between actions to be undertaken at the domestic level to protect and fulfil the right to food, as well as of the measures that need to be adopted at the supranational level to create an international environment 'enabling' such efforts. In his view, given the growing interdependency between States, and because national efforts are doomed to fail unless supported by measures at the international level. ESR, including the right to adequate food, have become global public goods, As such, the delivery of food security requires new forms of collaboration and cooperation between States, rather than the 'beggar thy neighbour' policies that have tended to be a feature of domestic governmental policy in times of crisis. Highlighting the problem of what he terms 'the fragmentation of global governance', De Schutter argues that the reform of the global governance of food security following the global food crisis – instituted in order to ensure that sectoral policies in the areas of trade, investment and food aid converge towards the realisation of the right to food – should serve as a source of inspiration for the global governance reforms that, in De Schutter's view, are essential if ESR are to be realised at the domestic level as we move forward.

Both contributions emphasise both the critical impact of the crises on ESR enjoyment and the need for the reformulation of policy approaches at the local, national and supranational level. Taking up the second key question addressed in this book, the authors identify ways in which an ESR-oriented approach can provide an effective pathway through the current financial and economic turmoil – one that, in contrast to the current predominant model, aims to minimise damage to, indeed prioritise, the poor and the socially excluded and marginalised.

II. Teasing out obligations in a time of crisis

It is clear that a number of key challenges arise in relation to using ESR to guide post-crisis recovery approaches and global governance reforms. Probably the most fundamental of these is the fact that the substantive content of ESR duties (such as 'maximum available resources' and 'minimum core obligation') is itself complex and subject to contestation. Arguably the most pressing example of this is Article 2(1) of the International Covenant on Economic, Social and Cultural Rights (ICESCR),[24] the foundational obligation-related provision in terms both of that instrument and ESR law more generally.[25] The supposed difficulties with the obligations imposed by this provision, as well as the other duties set out in ICESCR or identified by the CESCR, have been much discussed.[26] There are undoubtedly definite advantages to having ESR and the obligations that they impose phrased or conceptualised sufficiently broadly to ensure that they are capable of general application to a variety of individual circumstances and different contexts over time.[27] However, it is obvious that where the scope of obligations is uncertain, this will have implications for the use of ESR as a framework for evaluating state action (or inaction). Fundamentally, how can one evaluate state responses in terms of compliance with ESR

[24] International Covenant on Economic, Social and Cultural Rights, 993 UNTS 3 (ICESCR). Article 2(1) provides that: 'Each State Party to the present Covenant undertakes to take steps, individually and through international assistance and co-operation, especially economic and technical, to the maximum of its available resources, with a view to achieving progressively the full realization of the rights recognized in the present Covenant by all appropriate means, including particularly the adoption of legislative measures.'

[25] This is evidenced, for instance, by the way in which the Committee on the Rights of the Child has shaped its interpretation of Article 4 and the obligations imposed by the substantive economic and social rights provisions under the Convention on the Rights of the Child in light of the Committee on Economic, Social and Cultural Rights' construal of Article 2(1). See, e.g., Committee on the Right of the Child, 'General Comment No. 5' in 'Note by the Secretariat, Compilation of General Comments and General Recommendations Adopted by Human Rights Treaty Bodies' (27 May 2008) UN Doc. HRI/GEN/1/Rev.9 (Vol. II), para. 6.

[26] There is a wealth of literature on this point. For two key discussions of the obligations imposed by Article 2(1), see M. Sepúlveda, *The Nature of the Obligations under the International Covenant on Economic, Social and Cultural Rights* (Antwerp: Intersentia, 2003); R. O'Connell, A. Nolan, C. Harvey, E. Rooney and M. Dutschke, *Applying an International Human Rights Framework to State Budget Allocations: Rights and Resources* (London: Routledge, 2014).

[27] A. Nolan, M. Langford and B. Porter, 'The Justiciability of Social and Economic Rights: An Updated Appraisal' (NYU Centre for Human Rights and Global Justice Working Paper Series No.15, 2007), 14.

standards if those standards are themselves not clear? Always a difficulty, this becomes especially problematic during a time of economic tumult of the sort that the world has been witnessing since 2008.

ESR frameworks are certainly not without tools to resist the rights-related damage of the kind that has arisen following the crises. Possibly the most important obligation in terms of constraining – or critically evaluating – governmental action that might impact negatively on ESR achievement is the prohibition on 'deliberate' retrogressive measures in terms of ESR other than in very limited circumstances.[28] Such a measure can be defined as a backward step in the level of ESR enjoyment as a consequence of an intentional decision(s) by the State.[29] However, as Aoife Nolan, Nicholas Lusiani and Christian Courtis highlight in their contribution, the scope of this obligation remains nebulous, a fact that has made ESR advocacy and litigation in a time of financial and economic crisis more difficult than would otherwise have been the case. These authors seek to explain the CESCR's reticent approach towards non-retrogression and the main conceptual issues posted by such. Having provided conceptual clarification of the obligation, they outline the 'state of play' with regard to the specification of operative legal standards capable of assessing state compliance with the general prohibition of retrogression.

Another important issue arising in relation to ESR obligations in a time of financial and economic turmoil is the scope and enforceability of extraterritorial obligations, which have an ever greater role to play in a globalised economy.[30] This is particularly so with regard to monetary policy formulation and financial regulation, which are the central foci of Radhika Balakrishnan and James Heintz's chapter. These authors argue that the global economic crisis has demonstrated that the operation of financial markets and the management of the global macroeconomy have direct implications for human rights across national borders. In considering the largely ignored issue of the scope of extraterritorial obligations with regard to economic policy, Balakrishnan and Heintz document the nature of economic interdependence in terms of financial markets,

[28] See Committee on Economic, Social and Cultural Rights, 'General Comment No. 3' in 'Compilation of General Comments', para. 9.

[29] Sepúlveda, *The Nature of the Obligations*, p. 323.

[30] For more on extraterritorial obligations and economic and social rights more generally, see M. Gibney and S. Skogly (eds.), *Universal Human Rights and Extraterritorial Obligations* (University of Pennsylvania Press, 2010), chs. 5–9; M. Langford, W. Vandenhole, M. Scheinin and W. van Genugten (eds.), *Global Justice, State Duties: The Extraterritorial Scope of Economic, Social and Cultural Rights in International Law* (Cambridge University Press, 2013).

financial regulation and monetary policy, and draw out the implications of such for the realisation of human rights. They assert that an effective response requires international economic policy coordination across countries, and they consider the implications of this for global institutions such as the International Monetary Fund and the World Bank.

In addressing significant obligation-related gaps that go to the very heart of developing a clear, convincing ESR framework in the context of financial and economic crisis, these chapters identify and scrutinise a wide range of actions and actors that have played a central role in causing and ameliorating (or not) the financial and economic turmoil. Furthermore, they outline the implications that ESR obligations – properly conceptualised – can and should have for the development of responses to the recent crises and the avoidance of future ones.

III. Exploring responses to financial and economic crises

The third part of the collection focusses on regional and national experiences in relation to current and past financial and economic crises. Colm O'Cinneide opens this section with a consideration of Europe, a region in which ESR remain better protected in practice than almost anywhere else. Having reviewed the national and supranational legal and policy dimensions of the European social model, O'Cinneide argues that the formal embrace of the idea of 'social Europe' is not necessarily reflected in law and policy; the 2008 economic crisis and the intensification of austerity measures across much of the continent have demonstrated that the European commitment to social rights is essentially rhetorical in nature, and, what he terms, their 'partial constitutionalisation' remains an incomplete project. While O'Cinneide criticises the limits of European social rights law, he also identifies elements of European law and political practice that point the way towards how the concept of a social Europe could be given new vitality. These include the fact that the welfare state remains alive and well in parts of Europe, the existence of the constitutional principle of the *Sozialstaat* which gives legal expression to the concept of 'social citizenship' that originally underpinned the historical development of the European social model, and the possibility that international human rights law may yet influence the development of European Union (EU) law in the social field, and by extension national law and policy.

Moving from the broad European regional context to a specific European jurisdiction that has been hit particularly hard by the crises, Lusiani's chapter addresses the effect of government austerity policies that 'continue to unravel the social contract' in Spain. Having opened with a discussion of Spain's international obligations related to the human right to health, Lusiani outlines the socio-economic outcomes of the first and second waves of the current economic crisis in terms of the enjoyment of the right to health in Spain. He proceeds to use Spain's international obligations related to the right to health to analyse Spain's austerity-driven policy responses to the economic crisis, before reflecting on the opportunities and remaining challenges in using international human rights law to contest austerity policies in Spain.

The remaining four chapters in this Part focus extensively on the use of litigation and the role of courts in times of crisis. They reflect experiences from countries in a variety of global regions, with very divergent levels of economic development, and with different frameworks and mechanisms for ESR protection.

The first of the four contributions centres on the contemporary context. Helen Hershkoff and Stephen Loffredo examine the effect of the 2008 meltdown on judicial willingness to enforce socio-economic rights in the United States. Focusing on US state court-based efforts to secure quality public schooling for children, to provide health care to immigrants and to protect homeowners from mortgage foreclosure, Herskoff and Loffredo draw a number of key lessons about the role that courts can play in times of recession. They find that the cases under examination interrogate the emerging dichotomy between 'weak' and 'strong' judicial review and suggest instead a complementarity that has theoretical significance for assessing judicial legitimacy, for informing public discourse about taxing and spending, and for encouraging governmental implementation of socio-economic programmes. The decisions under consideration also underscore the interdependence between socio-economic rights and classical liberal rights to equal protection and due process, as well as the importance of statutory and common-law baselines in judicial attitudes toward socio-economic claims. The authors ultimately conclude that US state courts have played a countercyclical role with regard to socio-economic rights, by preventing legislators from reneging on social-welfare commitments during times of fiscal crisis and economic distress.

The current financial and economic crises did not arise out of the blue. Nor are they or their ESR implications unprecedented. Despite that, there has been a persistent failure to analyse the lessons that previous regional or domestic crises may have for our contemporary international political and economic circumstances, and the impact of such on ESR. This collection addresses this through a consideration of two important domestic experiences of financial and economic tumult, those undergone by Colombia and Argentina in the late 1990s and 2000s.

David Landau considers the response of the Colombian Constitutional Court to two different economic crises – the very deep financial crisis of 1999–2000 and the shallower, but still harmful one that followed global financial and economic developments in 2008. At first, the Court responded with sweeping interventions in the housing and public sector salary sectors. These interventions were spectacular in scope, he argues, but may ultimately have benefitted relatively affluent groups and provoked substantial political backlash because of their significant budgetary and macroeconomic effects. However, after a turnover in terms of the Court's personnel in 2000, new justices shifted to a more targeted approach; while maintaining a robust review of austerity measures on socio-economic grounds, this new Court focused especially on preventing harm to the poorest through a renewed focus on the vital minimum. Landau argues that the Court's jurisprudence demonstrates the viability and attractiveness of a judicial review model that emphasises the minimum core of socio-economic rights within the broader framework of the principle of a social state of law. He asserts that, in comparative terms, the Colombian experience should at least give us some optimism that courts can play an effective and sustainable role in protecting and expanding safety nets during times of crisis.

In the next chapter, Gustavo Maurino and Ezequiel Nino assess the work of the Supreme Court of Argentina pertaining to ESR over the last decade or so. In doing so, they focus in particular on the way in which the Court dealt with the extreme socio-economic and political crisis of 2001–3. Maurino and Nino argue that the cyclical dynamics of the Argentine economy over that period, together with the reconstitution of the Court in 2003–4, provide an interesting backdrop for this study, permitting an exploration of the way in which an evolving judiciary adapted to the shifting economic and political context when adjudicating ESR. The chapter centres on two key aspects of the Court's jurisprudence: first, ESR violations affecting low-income groups, which were more harshly affected by the crisis than anyone else; and, second, economic restrictions on ownership and other rights of an economic nature which were affected by regulations relating to salaries, pensions, personal savings and private contracts ordered by Congress and the executive branch in response to crisis-caused resource constraints. The authors assert that the Argentine example may be relevant to countries which are currently in the throes of responding to the post-2007 crises, as it depicts an experience where many of the conflicts arising from a situation of economic emergency were 'judicialised', under the framework of a Constitution that accords strong recognition to ESR.

In the final chapter in this part of the collection, Anashri Pillay and Murray Wesson discuss the economic effects of the global financial crisis on South Africa and the government's response. They also assess whether the crisis has had any impact on the judicial enforcement of ESR. South Africa provides an interesting case study for two main reasons. First, because its transformative Constitution includes directly enforceable ESR and, second, because the Constitutional Court has produced an influential body of case-law giving effect to these rights. It is not that simple, however: as the authors note, South Africa had high levels of economic deprivation and inequality prior to 2007. Thus, the global recession has served mainly to highlight and exacerbate these pre-existing problems. Furthermore, the recession in South Africa has been relatively shallow compared to that experienced by some other countries. The result is that it is difficult to discern a distinct turn in the Constitutional Court's case-law in 2009 (the year in which the South African economy entered recession) or to establish a direct causal link between the global financial crisis and any developments in the Court's jurisprudence. As the authors argue, however, given that all of the South African cases have been decided in circumstances of deprivation, inequality and resource constraint – problems now gripping many other parts of the world to various degrees – a consideration of that jurisdiction can serve to shed some light on the role that the judicial enforcement of ESR can play in times of economic crisis.

Viewed together, the chapters in this Part paint a wide-ranging and intriguing picture of judicial responses to ESR claims in a time of financial and economic turmoil. Do (or have) courts serve(d) as a countercyclical or counterhegemonic force in relation to the crises, the economic policies that caused them and the measures introduced in their wake? The answer to that question varies from court to court,[31] jurisdiction to jurisdiction[32] and over time.[33] The national experiences described here make it clear that it is very much not a case of 'one size fits all' – whether in

[31] See, e.g., the different approaches adopted by the lower and superior South African courts to ESR cases discussed in Pillay and Wesson's contribution to this volume.

[32] See, e.g., the difference in approaches by United States state courts to litigation seeking to secure ESR in a post-crisis context in Hershkoff and Loffredo's contribution to this volume.

[33] See, e.g., Maurino and Nino's account of the evolving approach of the Argentine Supreme Court to ESR from 2001 to 2013.

terms of forms of review,[34] adjudicative interpretive approaches to ESR obligations,[35] implementation and enforcement strategies[36] or explicit judicial engagement with the crisis context in decision-making.[37]

Furthermore, several contributions demonstrate the importance of non-ESR legal avenues to those seeking to bring crisis-related challenges – this is true not just in terms of the rights that such litigation is based on, but also the use of different branches of the law. Procedural protections, rule of law principles, property rights and other civil and political rights norms have all been put to use effectively by actors seeking to legally constrain – or mandate – post-crisis action on the part of the State.[38] A focus on equality and non-discrimination is evident throughout all of the chapters. This is not only due to author concerns in terms of unequal impacts of the crises but also due to the potential use of equality and non-discrimination protections as key standards to challenge and recalibrate state responses to such.[39] Indeed, equality and non-discrimination norms have been employed by numerous courts and quasi-judicial bodies finding post-crisis austerity measures to be contrary to ESR.[40] Furthermore, just as ESR protection does not begin and end with constitutional ESR

[34] Compare, e.g., the 'weak-form' models of review discussed in the contributions of Hershkoff and Loffredo and Pillay and Wesson with those described by Nino and Maurino and Landau in the Argentinian and Colombian contexts, respectively.

[35] Contrast, e.g., the willingness of the Colombian Constitutional Court to recognise the right to have at least the minimum level of satisfaction of social needs to be able to live a dignified existence (discussed by Landau), with the South African Constitutional Court's refusal to construe ESR as imposing a minimum core obligation (considered by Pillay and Wesson).

[36] See, e.g., the discussions of the different mechanisms/strategies used by courts to ensure enforcement in the US (e.g. retaining jurisdiction to monitor enforcement post-judgment), South Africa (e.g. meaningful engagement) and Colombia (e.g. issuing follow-up orders with deadlines for political action on discrete issues, and using public hearings and civil society groups to monitor compliance) in the context of crisis-related litigation.

[37] Contrast the 'silence' of the Argentine Supreme Court in its crisis-related ESR jurisprudence with the explicit engagement with concerns about economic crisis and resource constraints by other courts considered in the collection. (See, e.g., Hershkoff and Loffredo's discussion of the Massachusetts Supreme Judicial Court's ruling *Finch v. Commonwealth Health Insurance Connector Authority*, 959 NE 2d 970 (Mass 2012); Landau's discussion of the Colombian Constitutional Court decision C-288 pf 2012.)

[38] For more on these points, see in particular the contributions of O'Cinneide, Hershkoff and Loffredo and Maurino and Nino to this volume.

[39] See in particular the contributions of Sepúlveda and Rolnik and Rabinovich to this volume.

[40] See, e.g., O'Cinneide's discussion of the 2012 decisions of the European Committee of Social Rights against Greece; Nolan *et al.*'s discussion of the Portugal Constitutional Court jurisprudence; Hershkoff and Loffredo's discussion of US state courts' employment of equality norms to protect health care for immigrants.

adjudication, the same is true in relation to the use of constitutional law mechanisms. While the *amparo* and *tutela* actions have been vital to the protection of constitutional ESR in Argentina and Colombia,[41] there is also clear scope for the use of common law[42] and EU consumer protection law,[43] amongst other avenues, to pursue ESR protection.

Finally, the crisis has also thrown into sharp relief the 'political' nature of ESR adjudication and the interrelationship between judicial approaches to ESR and different stakeholder perceptions of the institutional legitimacy of the judicial branch of government. At different points, the courts discussed in this collection were criticised both by the public for being inadequately responsive in the face of ESR erosion[44] and by politicians, economists and others for being too assertive in their ESR-based responses to crisis-related litigation.[45]

IV. Conclusions and new post-crisis frontiers

A number of key messages emerge from this collection. First, austerity measures are hitting those who were already disadvantaged hardest; inequality and discrimination have been exacerbated in all of the jurisdictions discussed in this volume. Second, while global newspaper headlines focus on the impact of the Great Recession on the developed world, the creeping impact of the crises on developing economies – and the adoption of austerity measures by such States – are of enormous concern from a human rights perspective.

Furthermore, the crises and their direct and indirect impacts have highlighted long-standing academic and political debates on ESR. These

[41] For more on this point, see the contributions of Landau and Maurino and Nino to this volume.

[42] For more on this point, see Hershkoff and Loffredo's contribution to this volume.

[43] See Case C-415/11 *Mohamed Aziz* v. *Caxias d'Estalvis de Catalunya, Tarragona i Manresa (Catalunyacaixa)* (ECJ 14 March 2013) (where the European Court of Justice found that Spanish legislation infringed EU law to the extent that it precluded a court which has jurisdiction to declare unfair a term of a loan agreement relating to immovable property from staying the mortgage enforcement proceedings initiated separately).

[44] See, e.g., the contributions of Landau and Maurino and Nino to this volume.

[45] See, e.g., Landau's discussion of state official and economist criticisms of the crisis jurisprudence of the Colombian Constitutional Court. See also the Portuguese Government's response to the 2013 decision of the Constitutional Court of Portugal, Judgment no. 187/2013 (5 April 2013) discussed by O'Cinneide and Nolan, Lusiani and Courtis: T. Wagner, 'Court Blocks Reform in Portugal, Government Says', *Deutche Welle* (7 September 2013), www.dw.de/court-blocks-reform-in-portugal-government-says/a-17073147, last accessed 23 January 2014.

include: the obligations imposed by ESR; the challenges posed by such rights for traditional conceptions of democratic and constitutional theory as advanced by courts and scholars; the relative desirability of different adjudicative models; the impact of ESR litigation and adjudication; the role of the legislature and the executive with regard to ensuring the implementation of ESR; the appropriate scope of judicial monitoring and enforcement vis-à-vis such rights; and the linkage between micro and macroeconomic decision-making and human rights attainment. Although these topics are neither new nor limited to a crisis context, that context renders them particularly pressing. Where government measures are presented as required by a financial, economic or social emergency accompanied by severe State resources constraints, a lack of an authoritative approach to these 'general' considerations in terms of ESR theory and practice can result in ESR being brushed aside in the pursuit of more politically palatable – and prioritised – economic policy objectives.

Fourth, another element of human rights discourse and scholarship that is strongly underlined in this collection is the interdependence and indivisibility of human rights. While much of the attention focused on the crises and their impacts has been focused on ESR, this volume makes clear that they also have major implications for the rights to life,[46] fair trial[47] and freedom from inhuman or degrading treatment,[48] and the principle of human dignity.[49] Cuts to legal aid and increases in legal fees, reductions in access to mental and physical health care goods and services, savage drops in living standards – these involve and have implications for both ESR and civil and political rights. Indeed, inter-right connections have been expressly highlighted by a number of judicial bodies addressing crisis-related litigation discussed in this volume, including the Colombian Constitutional Court[50] and the Argentine Supreme Court.[51] Furthermore, the targeting of programmes focused on specific minority

[46] See e.g., the contributions of Sepúlveda and Lusiani to this volume.

[47] See Sepúlveda's contribution to this volume.

[48] See O'Cinneide's contribution to this volume.

[49] One area that has not been explored in this collection is the impact of the Great Recession on the right to protest. On this point, it is important to note that after widespread anti-austerity demonstrations in a number of countries, States have proposed introducing strict anti-protest laws. For more details on this from a Spanish perspective, see A. Kassam, 'Spanish government drafts strict anti-protest laws', *The Guardian*, 21 November 2013, www.theguardian.com/world/2013/nov/21/spain-government-strict-anti-protest-laws, last accessed 23 January 2014.

[50] See Landau's contribution to this volume.

[51] See Maurino and Nino's contribution to this volume.

groups will have an inevitable knock-on effect on cultural rights.[52] Thus, despite the title of this volume, it is clear that it would be inappropriate – and, indeed, impossible – to conceptualise the post-2007 developments under consideration solely in terms of their impacts on ESR.

Moving from conclusions to new frontiers, the collection raises a number of key questions about ESR that have not yet been accorded adequate attention by ESR scholars, advocates and practitioners.

First, this book focusses heavily on the courts and legal frameworks. This is unsurprising given ESR status as legal norms (and ESR commentators' long-standing concern with the effective recognition of such). It is evident from the various chapters that rights – both domestic and international – have played an important role in relation to legal challenges to the crises' effects, particularly on the part of national and international civil society. However, it is notable that although rights have formed part of the discourse of political and social protest in some countries affected by the Great Recession, such as that of the *Indignados* in Spain, this has not been the case in others, such as Ireland or Portugal (where, indeed, such protest has been much more muted).[53] Indeed, the contributions to this collection suggest that, in some (if not many) countries, there appears to only be limited societal and political awareness and absorption of ESR as concepts that should direct and constrain state action.[54] In turn, this has prevented societies impacted by financial and economic turmoil and state responses to such from conceptualising those impacts in terms of rights and rights-claims in a political – as opposed to merely a legal – context. It remains to be seen in the long term the role that ESR have played (and will play) in relation to social resistance and, ultimately, social resilience in the context of the current crises.

Second, authors in this collection have consistently noted the role and impact of financial institutions (both international and domestic), international governmental organisations and macroeconomic decision-

[52] A useful example of such an argument in the Irish context is presented in Pavee Point, 'Travelling with Austerity: Impacts of Cuts on Travellers, Traveller Projects and Services' (2012), www.paveepoint.ie/tempsite3/wp-content/uploads/2013/10/Travelling-with-Austerity_Pavee-Point-2013.pdf, last accessed 23 January 2014. Amongst other things, this report highlights the impact that the post-2008 'disinvestment' in the Traveller Community, an Irish ethnic and cultural minority, has had on Traveller education and community development.

[53] For more on this point, see C. Kilpatrick *et al.*, 'Social Rights in Crisis in the Eurozone: The Role of Fundamental Rights Challenges' (European University Institute (EUI) Working Paper Law No. 2014/05).

[54] See, e.g., the discussion of this point in O'Cinneide's contribution to this volume.

making in terms of ESR enjoyment.[55] As such, this work contributes to the growing scholarship around the interrelationship between ESR, macroeconomic policy, financial regulation, bond markets and financial globalisation.[56] However, it is clear from the chapters in this volume that this is an area that undoubtedly merits further exploration – particularly given the central part that such actors and factors played in relation to the causation and the design of responses to both the current and past financial crises. In the post-2007 context, this has been perhaps most strongly evidenced by the role of the International Monetary Fund, European Commission and European Central Bank troika with regard to the bilateral loans or loans from the European Financial Stability Mechanism and the European Financial Stability Facility taken by a (growing) number of Eurozone States. If international financial institutions remain largely 'untouched' (or at least unconstrained) by the existing state-centric human rights framework(s), how can they be expected to accord weight to ESR in their functioning? The same is true of corporations and other private entities whose actions have contributed to, or exacerbated the effects of, the crisis – for example, financial institutions (frequently banks and mortgage loan companies) which have played a significant role in relation to foreclosing on mortgaged properties, thereby negatively impacting on the right to adequate housing.[57] Another group are employer organisations and other members of the business sector which have taken advantage of the current economic context to argue for tax breaks and a weakening of labour protections, resulting in an erosion of work rights.[58] To what extent can a State-focused model of ESR protection serve to effectively protect right-holders from the rights-impacting actions (and omissions) of such actors?

A third and final area that is hinted at in this collection but requires further, urgent consideration from scholars is the issue of intergenerational justice. While the full effects of the crises on intergenerational justice are

[55] See, in particular, the contributions of Balakrishnan and Heintz, Sepúlveda, Rolnik and Rabinovich and De Schutter to this volume.

[56] For discussion of these points, see D. Elson, R. Balakrishnan and J. Heintz, 'Public Finance, Maximum Available Resources and Human Rights' in Nolan *et al.* (eds.), *Human Rights and Public Finance*, pp. 13–40; M. Dowell-Jones, 'Financial Institutions and Human Rights', *Human Rights Law Review*, 13 (2013), 423–68.

[57] For more, see Hershkoff and Loffredo's contribution to this volume.

[58] For an overview of such lobbying activities, see ILO Bureau for Employers' Activities, 'Employers' Organisations Responding to the Impact of the Crisis' (Working Paper No. 2, 2010), www.ilo.org/public/english/dialogue/actemp/downloads/publications/working_paper_n2.pdf, last accessed 23 January 2014.

not yet computable,[59] one cannot avoid the question of how these crises and the responses thereto (the guaranteeing of banks and the socialisation of debt, the taking on of sovereign debt that will take decades to pay off, state decisions to cut social protection programmes rather than raising taxes) will pan out in terms of long-term ESR achievement. How will cuts to education, high levels of youth immigration and an ageing population impact on the maximum resources available to States currently in economic difficulty to give effect to ESR in the future? How will the 'separating out' of economic and environmental sustainability (for instance, through austerity-motivated cuts to programmes aimed at environmental sustainability and the relaxation of environmental regulations) operate in terms of securing the ESR enjoyment of future generations?[60] Given projected demographic changes, does intergenerational justice require suffering in terms of ESR now in order to achieve fiscal sustainability and (it is presumed) more extensive achievement of ESR in future due to an improved global economic context?[61] More fundamentally, how can we conceptualise the impact of the crises on life opportunities and outcomes of current children and young people and future generations in human rights terms? The human rights framework as it stands deals poorly with issues of intergenerational justice in the sense of providing a set of standards that would enable assessment and mediation of competing (and potentially conflicting) rights-related interests of current and future ESR-right-holders. This collection does not proffer a solution to this problem but it is clear that one is required.

And so, in conclusion, what of our two key questions: what have the crises meant in terms of ESR enjoyment? What is the alternative(s)? The first

[59] See, e.g., Bertelsmann Stiftung and Sustainable Governance Indicators, 'Intergenerational Justice in Aging Societies: A Cross-National Comparison of 29 OECD Countries' (2013), www.sgi-network.org/pdf/Intergenerational_Justice_OECD.pdf, last accessed 23 January 2013.

[60] For a discussion of such developments in the UK context, see M. Spencer, 'The green movement must escape the confines of austerity thinking', *The Guardian* (28 February 2012), www.theguardian.com/environment/2012/feb/28/green-movement-austerity-thinking, last accessed 23 January 2014. For an argument against such an approach, see D. J. Thampapillai, 'Economic Fixes Should Not Worsen Environmental Crisis', *YaleGlobal* (19 October 2011), http://yaleglobal.yale.edu/content/economic-fixes-should-not-worsen-environmental-crisis, last accessed 23 January 2014.

[61] For a discussion that the achievement of 'fiscal sustainability' is crucial is vital to ensure intergenerational justice in the face of demographic changes in the Greek context, see Y. Mersch, 'Intergenerational Justice in Times of Sovereign Debt Crises', Speech at the Minsky Conference in Athens, Greece (8 November 2013), www.levyinstitute.org/publications/?docid=1948, last accessed 23 January 2014.

is easy to answer. The chapters in this collection provide ample testimony of the rampant damage inflicted on ESR realisation by the crises and the responses thereto. The second question is the more challenging, however, and – as we move from the post facto to an ex ante context – is arguably more important.

The financial and economic crises served as a brutal 'wake-up call' – initially for governments and subsequently for ESR-holders. A crucial, consistent theme in this collection has been the opportunity provided by the current economic and financial tumult for transformation and improvement – and the role that human rights, including ESR, can play as a 'framework'[62] or a 'signpost'[63] for such transformation. Whether the context is judicial adjudication of crisis-related litigation, the conceptualisation of the role of the State with regard to the social and economic well-being of its citizens, the conduction of international monetary policy or global governance in the broadest sense, this volume makes clear that ESR have an enormous amount to say in terms of what governments – and others – can and should be doing to ensure ESR. This is true with regard to both the national and supranational contexts. Fragmentation in terms of international policy, law, regulation and governance played a key role in the creation of, and reactions to, the financial, economic, food, housing and other crises[64] discussed in this volume. It is therefore unsurprising that there is a clear appetite on the part of the authors for increased coordination and collaboration across countries and global governance frameworks and institutions.

All of the chapters in this book highlight the need to ensure that crisis and post-crisis efforts focus on those whose ESR are at greatest risk. Bringing about the economic, political and social shift that would ensure this would be truly transformative. The authors do not underestimate the huge challenge of effectuating the change in existing power and resource distributions that such a shift would entail. However, they make it clear that it cannot, and must not, be avoided if ESR are to be given effect to in the current context – and in future. Sepúlveda concludes her chapter with the statement that, 'post-crisis economic policy is emphatically a matter of human rights concern, and we must use the human rights law standards and mechanisms at our disposal to combat its worst effects'. This collection is testament to the growing determination of ESR advocates, scholars and practitioners to do just that.

[62] See the contributions of Sepúlveda and Rolnik and Rabinovich to this volume.

[63] See De Schutter's contribution to this volume.

[64] See, in particular, the contributions of Heintz and Balakrishnan, De Schutter and Lusiani to this volume.

PART I

Painting the big (global) picture: the crises and economic and social rights protection internationally

1

Alternatives to austerity: a human rights framework for economic recovery

MAGDALENA SEPÚLVEDA CARMONA

I. Introduction

The onset of the global economic and financial crises, following consecutive fuel and food crises, exacerbated existing deprivations, poverty[1] and inequality,[2] with global ramifications exceeding those of any previous comparable economic downturn.[3] Globally in 2011, 205 million people were unemployed[4] – the highest number since records began. As a result of the crises, at least 55,000 more children are likely to die each year from 2009 to 2015.[5] The prevalence of children dropping out of school has increased, as boys have been propelled into the workforce and girls given an increased burden of household tasks.[6] By 2009, at least 100 million

[1] See, e.g., United Nations Development Programme (UNDP), *Poverty and Social Impact Analysis of the Global Economic Crisis: Synthesis Report of 18 Country Studies* (New York: UNDP, 2010); I. Ortiz and M. Cummins, 'The Age of Austerity: A Review of Public Expenditure and Adjustment Measures in 181 Countries' (Initiative for Policy Dialogue and The South Centre Working Paper, March 2013), 31.

[2] Statistics clearly show that inequality has risen in recent years within wealthy, middle-income and developing countries in nearly every region of the world. See, T. Piketty, *Capital in the Twenty-First Century* (London:The Belknap Press of Harvard University Press, 2014). In OECD countries, for example, the average income of the richest 10 per cent of the population is about nine times that of the poorest 10 per cent, and across most of these countries the household incomes of the richest 10 per cent grew faster than those of the poorest 10 per cent over the past 20 years, so widening inequality (OECD, *Divided We Stand: Why Income Inequality Keeps Rising* (Paris: OECD Publishing, 2011), p. 22).

[3] S. Claessens *et al.*, 'Crisis Management and Resolution: Early Lessons from the Financial Crisis' (IMF Research Paper, August 2012).

[4] International Labour Organization (ILO), *Global Employment Trends 2011: The Challenge of a Jobs Recovery* (Geneva: ILO, 2011), p. 12.

[5] J. Espey and M. Garde, *The Global Economic Crisis: Balancing the Books on the Backs of the World's Most Vulnerable Children?* (London: Save the Children, 2010).

[6] R. Mendoza, 'Inclusive Crises, Exclusive Recoveries, and Policies to Prevent a Double Whammy for the Poor' (UNICEF Social and Economic Policy Working Paper, May 2010), 18.

more people were hungry and undernourished,[7] a situation that continues to deteriorate owing to escalating food prices.

This chapter argues that the effects of the crises themselves are being compounded rather than relieved by the measures that many governments are taking in response. These are seriously threatening the lives and livelihoods of millions of the poorest people,[8] and are having a devastating effect on their enjoyment of economic, social and cultural rights (ESCR). While the human rights framework does not prohibit austerity measures per se, in many instances these have had grave consequences for the enjoyment of human rights, particularly for those living in poverty.

The chapter explores these consequences and suggests alternatives to austerity from a human rights perspective. In Section II, I outline the human rights framework, while in Section III, I analyse some of the austerity measures currently being pursued from the perspective of this framework and States' legal obligations. Lastly, in Section IV, I outline a number of alternative measures that States should consider so as to better respect, protect and fulfil the rights of the poorest sectors of the population. I argue that States should seize the opportunity presented by the crises to adopt a comprehensive long-term strategy for a sustainable recovery aimed at addressing the root causes of poverty and ensuring respect for all human rights, including gender equality, inclusive participation, freedom of association and expression, and equal access to quality public services.

II. Human rights framework

The obligations that States – in particular parties to the International Covenant on Economic, Social and Cultural Rights (ICESCR)[9] – have in relation to ESCR prescribe the ways in which they must behave in order to protect and guarantee substantive rights such as the rights to an adequate standard of living, health, education and social security.[10] In addition to the wording of ICESCR, these obligations have been spelt out by the

[7] Food and Agricultural Organization of the United Nations (FAO), *The State of Food Insecurity in the World: Economic Crises, Impacts and Lessons Learned* (Rome: FAO, 2009), p. 4

[8] Ortiz and Cummins, 'The Age of Austerity'.

[9] International Covenant on Economic, Social and Cultural Rights, 993 UNTS 3 (ICESCR). As at 23 April 2014, 162 States are bound by this treaty.

[10] The evaluation in this section is based primarily on the obligations enshrined in ICESCR. See arts. 11, 12, 13 and 9 respectively.

Committee on Economic, Social and Cultural Rights (CESCR), the body of independent experts that monitors the implementation of ICESCR by States Parties. As will become clear below, States cannot use the economic hardship caused by the crises to justify actions or omissions that amount to violations of basic human rights obligations.

A. *Using the maximum resources available*

States must devote the maximum available resources to ensure the progressive realisation of all ESCR as expeditiously and effectively as possible.[11] This is so even during times of severe resources constraints, whether caused by a process of adjustment, economic recession, or by other factors.[12] This obligation imposes limitations on a State's freedom to allocate available resources, defined not only as in-country resources, but also those available through 'international assistance and cooperation'.[13] States that do not possess the necessary resources are obliged to 'actively seek assistance' to ensure, at the very least, minimum essential levels of enjoyment of human rights.[14]

While several external factors affect the availability of resources, such as the provision of official development assistance (ODA) and the role of international trade, compliance with this principle also depends on how the State generates and mobilises resources to fund compliance with human rights obligations.[15] For example, if a State generates too little revenue or allocates a high proportion of its budget to defence, its ability to provide sufficient levels of public services will be compromised.[16]

11 ICESCR, art. 2(1).

12 UN Committee on Economic, Social and Cultural Rights (CESCR), 'General Comment No. 3' in 'Note by the Secretariat, Compilation of General Comments and General Recommendations Adopted by Human Rights Treaty Bodies' (27 May 2008) UN Doc. HRI/GEN/1/Rev.9 (Vol. I).

13 ICESCR, art. 2(1).

14 CESCR, 'General Comment No. 4', in 'Compilation of General Comments', para. 10; CESCR, 'General Comment No. 5', in *ibid.*, para. 13; CESCR, 'General Comment No. 11', in *ibid.*, para. 11.

15 See R. Balakrishnan, D. Elson, J. Heintz and N. Lusiani, 'Maximum Available Resources and Human Rights' (Rutgers Center for Women's Global Leadership Report, June 2011).

16 See M. Sepúlveda, 'Report of the Special Rapporteur on Extreme Poverty and Human Rights: Taxation and Human Rights' (22 May 2014) UN Doc. A/HRC/26/28.

B. *Ensuring minimum essential levels of ESCR*

States Parties to ICESCR have an immediate minimum core obligation to ensure the satisfaction of, at the very least, minimum essential levels of all ESCR.[17] These minimum essential levels are entitlements that are crucial to securing an adequate standard of living through basic subsistence, essential primary health care, basic shelter and housing, and basic forms of education for all members of society.[18]

Even during times of severe resource constraints, when available resources are demonstrably inadequate, the obligation remains for States to demonstrate that every effort has been made to use all resources that are at their disposal, in an effort to satisfy, as a matter of priority, minimum essential levels.[19] According to the CESCR, any proposed policy change or adjustment should identify the minimum core content of rights and ensure its protection at all times.[20]

In the context of recovery from successive crises, this principle obliges States to ensure that any programmes or policies that are integral to delivering essential services (for example, primary education, basic health care and social assistance programmes) are protected from reduced expenditure to the greatest extent possible. It does not imply that the State may adopt a very narrow approach; States continue to have responsibilities to move as expeditiously and effectively as possible towards the widest possible enjoyment of rights by all, which means maintaining services beyond a basic level.[21]

C. *Avoiding deliberate retrogressive measures*

There is a strong presumption that deliberately retrogressive measures that affect the level of enjoyment of ESCR are in violation of human rights standards.[22] Examples of retrogressive measures might include the adoption of

[17] *Ibid.*; CESCR, 'General Comment No. 3', para. 10.

[18] M. Sepúlveda, *The Nature of the Obligations under the International Covenant on Economic, Social and Cultural Rights* (Antwerp: Intersentia, 2003), pp. 365–70; CESCR, 'General Comment No. 3', para. 10.

[19] CESCR, 'An Evaluation of the Obligation to Take Steps to the "Maximum of Available Resources" under an Optional Protocol to the Covenant' (21 September 2007) UN Doc. E/C.12/2007/1, paras. 4–6. See also CESCR, 'General Comment No. 3', para. 12; CESCR 'General Comment No. 12', in 'Compilation of General Comments', para. 28; CESCR, 'General Comment No. 14', in *ibid.*, para. 18.

[20] CESCR, Letter to States Parties dated 16 May 2012, Reference CESCR/48th/SP/MAB/SW.

[21] CESCR, 'General Comment No. 3', para. 11.

[22] *Ibid.*, para. 9; CESCR, 'General Comment No. 4', para. 11.

policy or legislation with a direct or collateral negative effect on the enjoyment of rights by individuals, or unjustified reductions in expenditures devoted to implementing public services that are critical for the realisation of ESCR, such as those which guarantee basic health care, ensure access to primary education or provide assistance in terms of food and shelter.[23]

If adopting retrogressive measures, States must demonstrate that they have carefully considered all alternatives prior to implementation, and that such measures are duly justified by reference to the totality of the rights provided for in the Covenant, in the context of the full use of the maximum available resources.[24] If a State uses 'resource constraints' as an explanation for any retrogressive measure, the CESCR will assess the situation considering, inter alia, the country's level of development, the severity of the breach, whether the situation concerned the enjoyment of the minimum core content of a right, whether the State has identified low-cost options, or has sought international assistance.[25]

D. *Ensuring non-discrimination and equality*

The requirement that States ensure that rights are enjoyed equally and without discrimination of any kind is a fundamental pillar of the human rights framework.[26] From a rights perspective, in a time of limited resources due to economic crises, vulnerable and disadvantaged groups must be protected as a matter of priority, including through affirmative action measures[27] and, where necessary, the adoption of relatively low-cost targeted programmes.[28]

[23] Sepúlveda, *The Nature of the Obligations*, pp. 323–32.

[24] *Ibid.* See also CESCR, 'General Comment No. 3', para. 9; CESCR, 'General Comment No. 13', in 'Compilation of General Comments', para. 45; CESCR, 'General Comment No. 14', para. 32; CESCR, 'General Comment No. 15', in 'Compilation of General Comments', para. 19; CESCR, 'General Comment No. 17', in *ibid.*, para. 27; CESCR, 'General Comment No. 18', in *ibid.*, para. 34; CESCR, 'General Comment No. 19', in *ibid.*, para. 42; CESCR, 'General Comment No. 21' (21 December 2009) UN Doc. E/C.12/GC/21, para. 65.

[25] CESCR, 'An Evaluation of the Obligation', para. 10. For more on retrogressive measures, see Nolan *et al.*'s contribution to this volume.

[26] See, e.g., ICESCR, arts. 2(2), 3; International Covenant on Civil and Political Rights, 999 UNTS 171 (ICCPR) arts. 2(1), 3, 26; International Convention on the Elimination of All Forms of Racial Discrimination, 660 UNTS 195 (CERD) art. 2(1); Convention on the Elimination of All Forms of Discrimination against Women, 1249 UNTS 13 (CEDAW) art. 2; Convention on the Rights of the Child, 1577 UNTS 3 (CRC) art. 2(1).

[27] See CESCR, Letter to States Parties.

[28] CESCR, 'General Comment No. 3', paras. 11–12. See also, M. Sepúlveda, *The Nature of the Obligations*, pp. 379–407.

Expenditure and entitlements should benefit all social groups equally, and exclusions from public funds based on, for example, citizenship, employment status or economic and social situation[29] may violate the requirement for non-discrimination. These principles also require States to identify vulnerable and disadvantaged groups and to protect them as a matter of priority.[30] States have an obligation to take special and positive measures to diminish or eliminate conditions that cause or help to perpetrate discrimination.[31] Indeed, as the CESCR has noted, eliminating systemic discrimination will frequently require devoting greater resources to traditionally neglected groups.[32]

To ensure substantive equality in the enjoyment of rights, austerity policies should avoid placing a larger burden on certain individuals or groups in society, such as single parents, children and youth, persons with disabilities, ethnic minorities or migrants, and must actively combat any disproportionate impact on them as a consequence of the crises or the spending cuts.[33] If these disproportionate impacts are not addressed and prevented, the cuts will lead to a greater inequality and social exclusion.

Considering that gender inequality can cause and perpetuate poverty, States must evaluate the differential impact of existing and proposed social policies on women and men, ensure gender equality and the protection of women's full range of rights in the design, implementation and evaluation of all policies.[34] States must examine the impact of austerity measures not only in the short and medium term but also in the longer term. The withdrawal or scaling back of some social services has a devastating impact on substantive equality in the long term. For example, cuts in early childhood education, school drop-out prevention and school meal programmes could be a major threat to the equality of opportunity of children throughout their adult lives, particularly for those who have no access to private education.[35]

[29] CESCR, 'General Comment No. 20' (2 July 2009) UN Doc. E/C.12/GC/20, para. 35.

[30] See, e.g., Human Rights Committee (HRC), 'General Comment No. 18', in 'Compilation of General Comments', para. 10; CESCR, 'General Comment No. 20', paras. 9, 39.

[31] See, e.g., CEDAW, art. 4(1); CERD, art. 2(2). HRC, 'General Comment No. 18', para. 10; CESCR, 'General Comment No. 20', para. 39.

[32] CESCR, 'General Comment No. 20', para. 39.

[33] *Ibid.*, para. 38; CESCR, Letter to States Parties.

[34] CESCR, 'General Comment No. 16', in 'Compilation of General Comments'.

[35] I. Ortiz, J. Chai and M. Cummins, 'Austerity Measures Threaten Children and Poor Households' (UNICEF Social and Economic Policy Working Paper, September 2011).

E. Guaranteeing participation

Human rights must not only guide the content of State policies but also the process by which they are formulated and implemented. At the core of the human rights framework is an overarching requirement for public participation in the design, implementation and evaluation of policies that affect their lives.[36] This is crucial for self-determination, empowerment and dignity, and is also a fundamental right enshrined in numerous international human rights instruments.[37]

In formulating policies in response to the crises such as reductions in public expenditure, increases in taxation or entering into conditional loans with donors or financial institutions, States must allow for full transparency and the broadest possible national dialogue, with effective and meaningful participation of civil society, including those who will be directly affected by such policies.[38] To this end, it must provide information in an accessible format to the population[39] and establish inclusive mechanisms to ensure that they are actively engaged in devising the most appropriate policy options.[40]

F. Ensuring accountability

The human rights framework (as set out in human rights treaties that States have themselves agreed to) rests on the principle of accountability, and on the notion that individuals should be able to seek recourse and justice if their rights are violated. In consequence, States have a negative obligation not to block any person's access to justice and a positive obligation to construct institutional arrangements that allow *all*

[36] See, e.g., UN Development Group, 'The Human Rights Based Approach to Development Cooperation, Towards a Common Understanding among UN Agencies' (2003).

[37] See, e.g., ICCPR, arts. 19, 25; ICESCR, arts. 13(1), 15(1). M. Sepúlveda, 'Report of the Special Rapporteur on Extreme Poverty and Human Rights: Participation' (11 March 2013) UN Doc. A/HRC/23/36, paras. 25–30.

[38] I. Ortiz, J. Chai and M. Cummins, 'Identifying Fiscal Space: Options for Socio-Economic Investments in Children and Poor Households', in I. Ortiz and M. Cummins (eds.), *A Recovery for All: Rethinking Socio-Economic Policies for Children and Poor Households* (New York: UNICEF, 2012), pp. 231–301, p. 289; M. Sepúlveda, 'Report of the Independent Expert on the Question of Human Rights and Extreme Poverty: Mission to Ireland' (17 May 2011) UN Doc. A/HRC/17/34/Add.2, paras. 36–8.

[39] Human Rights Committee, 'General Comment No. 34' (12 September 2011) UN Doc. CCPR/C/GC/34, para. 19.

[40] Sepúlveda, 'Report on Participation'.

persons – including disadvantaged groups, whose inclusion is the litmus test of universality – access to accountability mechanisms.[41]

A human rights approach necessitates that recovery measures be open to oversight, including judicial scrutiny, and public officials involved in social and economic policy should be accountable for any policy decisions that endanger the enjoyment of human rights.[42] The democratic accountability of public authorities cannot be satisfied only through periodic elections, but rather should be strengthened at all levels. Citizens should be enabled to better oversee and monitor States' actions and engage in processes such as budgeting, policy-making and expenditure tracking.[43] Courts, national human rights institutions and parliamentary commissions should also be able to monitor and eventually sanction officials for improper conduct in regard to austerity measures. In no case should a State be forced to prioritise accountability to international financial institutions over that to its own people.[44]

III. States' responses to the crises and their potential threat to the realisation of human rights

I now turn to look through a human rights lens at some of the specific measures that States are designing and implementing as part of fiscal austerity packages, and highlight the ways in which they may construct barriers to enjoyment of ESCR for the most vulnerable sectors of societies.

States have responded to the global economic and financial crises in differing ways, but some trends are clear. In 2008–9 many States introduced countercyclical measures (such as fiscal stimulus packages and social protection interventions) as a means of responding effectively to the emerging crises and mitigating some of their most severe effects on

41 See, e.g., ICCPR, art. 2; Basic Principles and Guidelines on the Right to a Remedy and Reparation for Victims of Gross Violations of International Human Rights Law and Serious Violations of International Humanitarian Law, UNGA Res. 60/147 (16 December 2005).

42 M. Sepúlveda, 'Report of the Special Rapporteur on Extreme Poverty and Human Rights: Access to Justice' (9 August 2012) UN Doc. A/67/278.

43 International Budget Partnership, 'Open Budget Survey 2012' (2012).

44 ESCR-Net, AWID, Center for Economic and Social Rights, Center for Women's Global Leadership and Center for Concern, 'Bringing Human Rights to Bear in Times of Crisis: A Human Rights Analysis of Government Responses to the Economic Crisis' (March 2010), 1–3, www.escr-net.org/usr_doc/HRResponsestoEconCrisis_Final.pdf, last accessed 22 January 2014.

their populations.[45] These countercyclical measures proved to be crucial in protecting the poorest. However, starting in 2010, a majority of States began to scale back stimulus programmes and cut public spending, with these 'austerity' measures gaining momentum in 2012 and projected to continue over the coming years, with increased depth and breadth of cuts.[46]

The measures are similar to those that Latin American and African States adopted at the behest of the World Bank and the International Monetary Fund (IMF) after the 1980s debt crises, with devastating consequences for the population of those countries as well as their economies.[47] Instead of learning the lessons from this 'lost decade', the same policies are being implemented today.

Eighty per cent of the global population, or 5.8 billion people, will have been affected by austerity in 2013.[48] Despite media focus on austerity in Europe, recent findings show that fiscal contraction is most severe in the developing world, indicating that the world's poorest are paying the highest price of austerity, in a global sense as well as within countries. Overall, 68 developing countries are projected to cut public spending by 3.7 per cent of gross domestic product (GDP) on average between 2013 and 2015, compared to 26 high-income countries whose average contraction is expected to be 2.2 per cent of GDP.[49] In sub-Saharan Africa, the poorest region in the world, 31 countries were due to contract public expenditure in 2013, affecting 78.3 per cent of the region's population.[50] Much of this contraction results from cutting subsidies, adjusting the wage bill and introducing or expanding sales taxes.[51] Two-thirds of 56 low-income countries surveyed in 2010 were cutting budget allocations to one or more pro-poor sectors, including education, health, agriculture or social protection.[52]

Specific, common austerity measures are examined separately in the text below. However, it is their cumulative impact that is so devastating for people living in poverty and, in many cases, results in a violation of human rights, including the rights to an adequate standard of

[45] I. Ortiz and L. M. Daniels, 'A Recovery with a Human Face? Insights into the Global Crisis', in Ortiz and Cummins (eds.), *A Recovery for All*, pp. 11–57.

[46] Ortiz and Cummins, 'The Age of Austerity', 6.

[47] See, e.g., G. Cornia, R. Jolly and F. Stewart (eds.), *Adjustment with a Human Face* (New York: Oxford University Press, 1987).

[48] Ortiz and Cummins, 'The Age of Austerity', i. [49] *Ibid.* [50] *Ibid.*, 3

[51] *Ibid.*, 22. The negative impact of such measures on human rights will be examined below.

[52] K. Kyrili and M. Martin, 'The Impact of the Global Economic Crisis on the Budgets of Low-Income Countries' (Oxfam Research Report, July 2010), 38.

living, health, education and adequate housing. The resources and coping mechanisms of many families living in poverty are being diminished by several changes: cuts in childcare, restrictive eligibility criteria for social protection benefits, elimination of social care, increasing health care and education costs, restricted unemployment benefit, frozen pensions, lower salaries and increased taxes. Overall, these measures run a real risk of constituting unjustified retrogressive measures contrary to the general obligation to progressively realise all ESCR, and they may also impede States' ability to maintain minimum essential levels of enjoyment of ESCR for their populations.[53]

Ultimately, it is people living in poverty who are bearing the brunt of these measures, as they rely most on the benefits and services that are being cut, being unable to afford private alternatives. Furthermore, in many countries there is evidence that the cuts disproportionately target already-disadvantaged regions and sections of the population. For example, a study in the United Kingdom shows that local councils in northern urban cities and London boroughs with high levels of deprivation have seen their budgets cut by almost ten times the amount lost by local authorities in wealthy, rural southern England.[54] Due to multiple forms of entrenched discrimination, women are especially vulnerable to the detrimental effects of reductions in social services and benefits. Advocates have noted that women face a 'triple jeopardy' in relation to austerity.[55] First, because women are concentrated in public sector jobs, they are being hit hardest by cuts to public sector jobs, wages and pensions. Second, women are being hit hardest as the services and benefits they use and rely on more (such as childcare services, maternal health care and domestic violence services) are cut. Third, women will be left 'filling the gaps' as state services are withdrawn, for example by being forced to take on even more unpaid care responsibilities.[56] Groups such as ethnic minorities and migrants are also suffering disproportionately from the crises. For example, in Spain, the government has removed immigrants' right to public health care, a measure that could affect the right to health of approximately 150,000 persons.[57]

[53] For more on this point, see Nolan *et al.*'s contribution to this volume.

[54] R. Ramesh, 'Council Cuts "Targeted towards Deprived Areas"', *The Guardian* (14 November 2012).

[55] Fawcett Society, 'The Impact of Austerity on Women' (Fawcett Society Policy Briefing, March 2012).

[56] *Ibid.*

[57] For more on this point, see Lusiani's contribution to this volume.

A. *Eroding social protection systems*

Social protection systems play an exceptionally important role in protecting the ESCR of the poorest, especially during economic shocks and other forms of crisis.[58] However, only 20 per cent of the world's working-age population and their families had effective access to social protection[59] at the outbreak of the financial and economic crises in 2007. Unfortunately, since 2008–9 many States have been proposing and implementing reductions in funding to social protection systems, by reducing the level of benefits or narrowing eligibility criteria and reducing coverage.[60] Social protection allocations contracted in 2010 and ended the period more than 0.2 per cent of GDP lower than in 2008, on average.[61]

In Spain, for example, where the social protection expenditure was already relatively low in comparison with other States of the European Union (EU), severe cuts have been implemented in this area. As a consequence, in 2012, 28.2 per cent of the population was considered to be at risk of poverty or social exclusion[62] and inequality has risen.[63] Statistics show that homelessness is rising in many countries where welfare cuts are being implemented. Rough sleeping and statutory homelessness are on a sharp upward trajectory in England, with regions where the new national welfare benefit cap is restricting access to housing for low-income applicants worst affected.[64]

[58] For an assessment of the vital role that social protection systems play in facilitating the enjoyment of multiple ESCR, see, e.g., M. Sepúlveda, 'Report of the Independent Expert on the Question of Human Rights and Extreme Poverty: Cash Transfer Programmes' (27 March 2009) UN Doc. A/HRC/11/9; M. Sepúlveda, 'Report of the Independent Expert on the Question of Human Rights and Extreme Poverty: Social Pensions' (31 March 2010) UN Doc. A/HRC/14/31; M. Sepúlveda, 'Report of the Independent Expert on the Question of Human Rights and Extreme Poverty: Global Financial Crisis' (11 August 2009) UN Doc. A/64/279; M. Sepúlveda, 'Report of the Independent Expert on the Question of Human Rights and Extreme Poverty: Millennium Development Goals' (9 August 2009) UN Doc. A/65/259.

[59] ILO, *World Social Security Report 2010–2011* (Geneva: ILO, 2010), p. 33.

[60] I. Ortiz, J. Chai, M. Cummins and G. Vergara, 'Prioritising Expenditures for a Recovery for All: A Rapid Review of Public Expenditures in 126 Developing Countries' (UNICEF Social and Economic Policy Working Paper, October 2010), 15.

[61] *Ibid.*

[62] See European Social Statistics (Eurostat), available at http://appsso.eurostat.ec.europa.eu/nui/show.do?dataset=ilc_peps01&lang=en, last accessed 9 July 2014.

[63] For more on the impact of austerity policies on ESCR in Spain, see Lusiani's contribution to this volume.

[64] S. Fitzpatrick, H. Pawson, G. Bramley and S. Wilcox, 'The Homelessness Monitor: Great Britain 2012 – Executive Summary' (December 2012), www.crisis.org.uk/data/files/policy_research/TheHomelessnessMonitor_GB_ExecutiveSummary.pdf, last accessed 24 April 2014.

Welfare 'reforms' and cuts to social protection benefits such as unemployment, child support and disability benefits currently being implemented by several States are disproportionately impacting women, persons with disabilities and children. Persons with disabilities have been badly impacted by austerity measures in many countries: in Portugal, disability benefits have been cut by 30 per cent.[65] In the United Kingdom, a gender audit of the 2010 budget found that women would shoulder 70 per cent of the budget cuts, with the cuts falling especially harshly on single mothers.[66] In a climate of rising unemployment and fewer affordable childcare options, these changes in the welfare system will undoubtedly seriously diminish the possibilities of these parents to provide for their children's basic material needs.

The rights of children to an adequate standard of living, education and food may also be violated by the cumulative effect of welfare reforms. Fewer housing benefits, scholarships and school food programmes coupled with lower pensions and reductions to direct child-related support, including pregnancy health services, maternity grants and child benefits, will have a significant effect on child poverty, impacting on their enjoyment of all rights. In London alone, it is estimated that around 63,000 households with children could be left unable to pay their rent due to the cumulative effect of three cuts to social security (caps on local housing allowance, an overall benefit cap and under-occupation penalties for families in social housing), likely leading to an increase in overcrowding, child poverty and homelessness.[67]

Cuts to social protection benefits contravene the obligation of States to take deliberate, concrete and targeted steps towards the full realisation of all ESCR including the right to social security (Article 9 of ICESCR), especially for individuals belonging to the most disadvantaged and marginalised groups.[68] Such cuts may also violate the prohibition of retrogressive measures and seriously compromise the ability of States to ensure minimum essential levels of ESCR for all, particularly the most vulnerable.

[65] European Women's Lobby (EWL), 'The Price of Austerity – The Impact on Women's Rights and Gender Equality' (October 2012), 10.

[66] Fawcett Society, 'Single Mothers: Singled Out – The Impact of 2010–15 Tax and Benefit Changes on Women and Men' (July 2011).

[67] Child Poverty Action Group, 'Between a Rock and a Hard Place: The Early Impacts of Welfare Reform on London' (October 2012).

[68] CESCR, 'General Comment No. 19', paras. 23–40.

B. Cutting spending on public services

Cuts to social protection benefits have often been coupled with funding reductions for social services[69] that are essential for the same vulnerable people – including health and education services, disability, community and voluntary services, domestic violence shelters and drug outreach initiatives. These cuts not only hamper the ability of the State to ensure minimum essential levels of ESCR but also often undermine the principle of equality and non-discrimination by having a disproportionate impact on those living in poverty, in particular children and women. For example, deep cuts in education spending, undertaken in several countries such as Spain[70] and Latvia[71], may imply a severe limitation on the enjoyment of children's rights.

When cuts are made to education spending, there is a higher likelihood that children will drop out of schools, as demonstrated in countries such as Portugal and Spain.[72] Health services have also been weakened in several countries. In Greece, the three-year agreement with the IMF, European Commission and European Central Bank signed in May 2010 stipulated health spending be cut from 9.7 per cent to no more than 6 per cent of GDP. As a consequence, many public hospitals have been closed or merged and those remaining face shortages of staff and materials.[73] Cuts to health services will have a long-term impact on the public health of the population; for example, statistics shows that HIV infections among drug users in Greece jumped more than 20-fold in fewer than two years, fuelled by a lack of needle exchange and methadone programmes.[74] Furthermore, groups such as pregnant women, older persons and persons with disabilities who are more frequent users of health care services will be disproportionately impacted.

69 Ortiz *et al.*, 'Prioritising Expenditures for a Recovery for All', 21.

70 In Spain, where social spending per capita was already low, the government announced budget cuts totalling EUR 27.3 billion in May 2012, with EUR 10 billion coming from health and education.

71 In Latvia, the education budget was cut by 50 per cent in 2009. EWL, 'The Price of Austerity', 10.

72 Center for Economic and Social Rights (CESR), 'Spain' (CESR Fact Sheet No. 12, 2012), 6, http://cesr.org/downloads/FACT%20SHEET%20SPAIN.pdf?preview=1, last accessed 24 April 2014.

73 EWL, 'The Price of Austerity', 10.

74 European Centre for Disease Prevention and Control (ECDC), ' Risk Assessment on HIV in Greece – Technical Report' (November 2012).

In many contexts, the accessibility and availability of childcare and other care services are also being limited, disproportionately impacting women who (due to gender stereotypes) tend to be primary carers. In Greece and Portugal public kindergartens have been closed down, while other countries have limited the hours of kindergartens and schools, tightened eligibility for public day-care and/or reduced the amount of childcare costs covered by the State.[75] At the same time, care services for the elderly and persons with disabilities have also been cut.[76] These cuts have an extremely detrimental impact on care recipients and their carers, who now have to take on extra care responsibilities themselves, often to the detriment of their earning potential and the enjoyment of their rights;[77] more women living in poverty will be forced to forego work or work part-time due to lack of care services.[78] It is therefore likely that the crises and government responses to it will undo progress towards greater equality between the sexes in terms of employment and division of care responsibilities.

In addition, many countries are cutting back on services that are essential for gender equality such as women's refuges and domestic violence prevention programmes. In the United Kingdom, local authority funding to violence against women services was cut by 31 per cent from 2010/11 to 2011/12, while in Greece, local government funding for women's shelters has been cut altogether.[79] Coupled with cuts to social protection that negatively affect the financial independence of women, and cuts to legal aid programmes in cases of domestic violence or divorce, austerity measures are making it harder for women to leave violent relationships and to seek protection.

Taken together, the cuts to social services are not only threatening the principle of equality and non-discrimination but they are also undermining progress towards accessible, affordable and high-quality public services for all. In addition, the cuts may push wealthier people to move to private providers, which can translate in an unequal dual system or deterioration of public service provision in the long term.

C. *Reducing wage bills*

A significant percentage of post-crises austerity budgets have included proposals to limit the public wage bill by reducing the public sector

[75] EWL, 'The Price of Austerity', 8. [76] *Ibid.*

[77] M. Sepúlveda, 'Report of the Special Rapporteur on Extreme Poverty and Human Rights: Unpaid Care Work' (9 August 2013) UN Doc. A/68/293.

[78] *Ibid.* [79] *Ibid.*, 10.

workforce and cutting or freezing wages of public sector employees.[80] Often these cuts have a disproportionate impact on the lowest wage brackets. The United Nations Children's Fund (UNICEF) has expressed concern that wage cuts or caps might translate into the reduction or erosion of the real value of salaries, as living costs continue to rise.[81] As highlighted above, public sector redundancies/wage cuts also have a disproportionate impact on women, who are often concentrated in public sector jobs. For example, women constitute on average 69.2 per cent of the public sector workforce in the EU.[82]

Reductions in the public wage bill are likely to severely impede the delivery of social services, and may cause a damaging 'brain drain' of skilled and educated workers to other countries.[83] Limited or decreased staff numbers may hamper the capacity of social services to respond to public demand, and the removal of allowances or incentive schemes might have an adverse impact on the efficiency of employees. In Romania, where there has been a freeze on employment and a reduction of 25 per cent in the gross income of all personnel in state services, many positions in hospitals and childcare services remain vacant. Low pay means that even where hiring is allowed, applicants are often under-skilled.[84] In Cambodia, after the government announced that it would reduce the number of staff in all ministries (except education and health) by 50 per cent in the 2010 fiscal year, and also that salary supplementation, allowances and incentive schemes for civil servants would be cancelled, site surveys showed increased staff absenteeism and/or reduced working hours.[85]

Salary cuts for primary school teachers and nurses in some States are resulting in their wages being barely sufficient for an adequate standard of living.[86] In about one-sixth of the developing countries surveyed by UNICEF, the salaries of primary school teachers and nurses are barely sufficient to keep them out of poverty (using the international US$2 a day poverty line).[87] The erosion of teachers' wages commonly leads to teacher absenteeism and an increase in informal fees.[88] This has an adverse impact on the right of children to education and increases the likelihood of inter-

[80] Ortiz *et al.*, 'Prioritising Expenditures for a Recovery for All', 20.
[81] *Ibid.* [82] EWL, 'The Price of Austerity', 4.
[83] UNICEF, 'Protecting Salaries of Frontline Teachers and Health Workers' (UNICEF Social and Economic Policy Working Briefs, April 2010).
[84] S. Ruxton, 'How the Economic and Financial Crisis Is Affecting Children and Young People in Europe' (Eurochild Report, December 2012).
[85] *Ibid.* [86] UNICEF, 'Protecting Salaries'. [87] *Ibid.*, 3.
[88] Ortiz *et al.*, 'Prioritising Expenditures for a Recovery for All', 21.

generational and child poverty being perpetuated, particularly in rural areas.[89]

The above measures have a disproportionate impact on people living in poverty, particularly those in rural areas and the most disadvantaged, who already face numerous barriers in accessing health care and education services. Furthermore, these measures run a real risk of constituting unjustified backward steps in ESCR realisation, particularly if they impede the State's ability to maintain minimum essential levels of enjoyment of ESCR.

D. *Implementing regressive taxation measures*

States have an unambiguous responsibility to take steps towards the full achievement of ESCR by using the maximum amount of resources available.[90] In the aftermath of the global economic and financial crises, it has become clear that, in many States, efforts to increase resources for recovery through the whole spectrum of available options have been insufficient, thus impeding States' compliance with human rights. Low levels of domestic taxation revenue, in particular, could be a major obstacle to a State's ability to meet obligations to realise ESCR.[91]

States should be cognisant of their obligations to raise tax revenue in accordance with the principles of non-discrimination and equality. Indirect taxes such as sales tax or Value Added Tax (VAT) may represent an unequal burden for those living in poverty, as they constitute a larger percentage of their income.[92] For example, in Latin America on average the poorest 20 per cent of the population dedicates 13.7 per cent of their income to the payment of VAT, while for the richest 20 per cent it only constitutes 5.8 per cent of their income. Thus, despite exemptions aimed at lowering the burden on lower-income groups, the poor carry a tax burden 2.4 times higher than that of the wealthiest people, relative to income.[93]

Unfortunately, after the crises, a number of States have chosen to increase sales tax rather than pursuing more egalitarian tax measures. For

89 UNICEF, Protecting Salaries', 1.

90 M. Sepúlveda, 'Report of the Special Rapporteur on Extreme Poverty and Human Rights: Taxation and Human Rights' (22 May 2014) UN Doc. HRC/26/28.

91 O. De Schutter, 'Report of the Special Rapporteur on the Right to Food: Mission to Guatemala' (26 January 2010) UN Doc. A/HRC/13/33/Add.4, para. 87(e).

92 See Sepúlveda, 'Report on Taxation and Human Rights', paras. 46–55.

93 Banco Interamericano de Desarrollo, 'Recaudar No Basta: Los impuestos como instrumento de desarrollo' (Inter-American Development Bank, 2013), 247.

example, the Irish Government's Budget 2012 provided for an increase in VAT from 21 to 23 per cent;[94] the same year saw Spain increase sales tax from 18 to 21 per cent;[95] in 2010 Romania increased VAT from 19 per cent to 24 per cent; and Hungary, where a 25 per cent rate had already been in place since 2008, increased it to 27 per cent in 2012.[96]

Taxation reform that comes in the form of cuts, exemptions and waivers may also disproportionately benefit the wealthier segments of society, discriminating against people living in poverty, as well as decreasing available resources for rights fulfilment.[97]

E. *Limiting food subsidies*

Some States have removed or limited food subsidies in recent years, and many more have indicated that they plan to do so.[98] From a human rights perspective, the decision to limit food subsidies at a time when food prices are escalating[99] is extremely worrying. There is still a pressing need for public food and nutrition support: local food prices remained at historic highs at the start of 2012 in a large sample of developing countries, where people are paying on average 80 per cent more for local foodstuff compared to pre-crises price levels.[100]

By providing access to a basic form of food security, food subsidies can limit the prevalence of hunger, increase consumption and improve nutrition in recipient households. Food subsidies also contribute to ensuring price stabilisation and thus create greater food access for all.[101] They thus represent

94 Finance Act 2012, sec. 87, which amended the Value-Added Tax Consolidation Act 2010.

95 Royal Decree Law 20/2012, of 13 July, Measures to guarantee budget stability and promote competitiveness, BOE no 168, 13 July 2012, art. 90, www.boe.es/boe/dias/2012/07/14/pdfs/BOE-A-2012-9364.pdf, last accessed 24 April 2014.

96 Eurostat, 'Taxation Trends in the European Union. Data for the EU Member States, Iceland and Norway'. 2013 Edition (Publications Office of the European Union, 2013), 31.

97 For more on this point, see I. Saiz, 'Resourcing Rights: Combating Tax Injustice from a Human Rights Perspective' in A. Nolan *et al.* (eds.), *Human Rights and Public Finance: Budgets and the Promotion of Economic and Social Rights* (Oxford: Hart Publishing, 2013), pp. 77–104. See also Sepúlveda, 'Report on Taxation and Human Rights'.

98 Ortiz and Cummins, 'The Age of Austerity', 204.

99 I. Ortiz, J. Chai and M. Cummins, 'Escalating Food Prices: The Threat to Poor Households and Policies to Safeguard a Recovery For All' (UNICEF Social and Economic Policy Working Paper, February 2011).

100 Ortiz and Cummins, 'The Age of Austerity', 61.

101 S. Jha and B. Ramaswami, 'How Can Food Subsidies Work Better? Answers from India and the Philippines' (Asian Development Bank Economics Working Paper Series No. 221, September 2010), 4.

one way in which States can move towards meeting their obligations regarding the right to an adequate standard of living, including the right to food.[102]

The recurrent crises have taken a harsh toll on access to adequate food and nutrition for those living in poverty, and limited food subsidies may be a blow that many are unable to bear. Policies that limit or eliminate food subsidies could threaten the ability of States to ensure minimum levels of enjoyment of ESCR, particularly for the most vulnerable. These policies may also undermine other efforts to address the effects of the crises: higher food costs can have an adverse impact on social protection systems as a result of real losses in the value of income received.[103] While commodity prices continue to fluctuate, from a human rights perspective it is imperative that food subsidy schemes remain intact or are replaced with alternative policies that ensure food security for those living in poverty.

IV. Recommendations for a rights-based recovery

While these measures have been presented by governments as unavoidable, many commentators, activists, politicians and economists have noted that there are alternative policy options.[104] Governments could raise or save money in ways that protect the already-disadvantaged and ensure an inclusive recovery, for example by raising taxes on the wealthy, investing in public services or cutting defence budgets.

By imposing austerity measures without exploring these other options – and often even avoiding acknowledgement of alternatives – States are refusing to pursue, to the maximum of their available resources, the progressive realisation of ESCR for their populations, as required by ICESCR. Although in many countries, States have been encouraged or compelled to push ahead with harsh austerity measures by supranational institutions or international financial institutions, such as the European Union or the IMF,[105] it is important to note that States are still responsible for ensuring that human rights are respected, protected and fulfilled.

[102] Universal Declaration of Human Rights (adopted 10 December 1948), UNGA Res. 217 A(III) (UDHR) art. 25; ICESCR, art. 11; CEDAW, art. 12; CRC, arts. 24, 27.

[103] Ortiz *et al.*, 'Escalating Food Prices', 13.

[104] See, e.g., P. Krugman, *End This Depression Now!* (New York: W.W. Norton, 2012); R. Avent, 'There is an Alternative to Austerity', *The Economist* (1 May 2012); CESR, 'Mauled by the Celtic Tiger' (CESR Rights in Crisis Briefing Paper, February 2012).

[105] See, e.g., the role of the EU in Greece. C. Paris and A. Cohen, 'EU Tells Greece Austerity Plan Isn't Enough', *Wall Street Journal* (26 February 2010).

This applies to both their domestic role and their role as a State Party with decision-making power in such institutions. State members of international financial institutions must ensure that their agreements do not impair the ability of another State to comply with its international human rights obligations.[106]

Human rights do not dictate what policy measures States should take. States have the discretion to select and take policy measures according to their specific economic, social and political circumstances.[107] The choice of policy measures must, however, comply with the State's human rights obligations. There is now a growing consensus that austerity measures are violating human rights, demonstrated by statements of the United Nations High Commissioner for Human Rights, the CESCR and, more recently, the Council of Europe Commissioner for Human Rights.[108] Human rights are not a mere policy 'option', dispensable during times of economic hardship. While a human rights response does not stipulate a particular economic system or specific fiscal measures, it nevertheless provides a clear legal framework for the design and implementation of all policies, including economic and fiscal policy.

A comparison of the impact of measures adopted by governments in Iceland and Ireland (both hard hit by the crises) on real disposable earnings of couples by income deciles shows that the poorest tenth of earners in Iceland suffered a drop in earnings of 9 per cent, compared to 26 per cent in Ireland; the richest experienced a drop in earnings of 38 per cent in Iceland compared to 8 per cent in Ireland.[109] This clearly shows that, although in many societies some negative impacts of the crises are inevitable,

[106] See Sepúlveda, *The Nature of the Obligations*, p. 218; Maastricht Principles on Extraterritorial Obligations of States in the Area of Economic, Social and Cultural Rights, Principles 15–17.

[107] See, e.g., CESCR, 'General Comment No. 15', in 'Compilation of General Comments', para. 45.

[108] See Office of the United Nations High Commissioner for Human Rights (OHCHR), 'Austerity Measures May Violate Human Rights' (2 November 2012), www.ohchr.org/EN/NewsEvents/Pages/AusterityMeasures.aspx, last accessed 24 April 2014; CESCR, Letter to States Parties; Office of the Council of Europe Commissioner for Human Rights, 'Safeguarding Human Rights in Times of Economic Crisis' (Council of Europe Commissioner for Human Rights Issue Paper, December 2013), www.enetenglish.gr/resources/article-files/prems162913_gbr_1700_safeguardinghumanrights_web.pdf, last accessed 24 April 2014.

[109] V. Browne, 'Irish Solution Has Been to Make the Most Vulnerable Pay', *The Irish Times* (10 October 2012). The data for Ireland was for the period 2008–2009 and for Iceland 2008–2010.

the impacts can be distributed in different ways. Some distributions are clearly fairer and more rights-compliant than others.

Through a human rights-based recovery, States have the chance to embrace new and ambitious approaches to reducing inequality, eliminating poverty and creating stable societies and economies that will withstand future shocks. There is no space in human rights for a trickle-down approach to the achievement of minimum essential levels of rights or ensuring access to basic services. From a human rights perspective, recovery must start with the most vulnerable and disadvantaged, who are rights-holders rather than burdensome or passive recipients of charity. A human rights approach is the best way for States to rectify the persistent inequalities that have diminished social cohesion and increased feelings of insecurity and exclusion, exacerbated by successive crises. Should these inequalities persist – and moreover be combined with food insecurity, declining availability of natural resources and unpredictable climate changes – social unrest and conflict are likely to increase. What is needed, therefore, is human rights-based reform that directly addresses the long-term structural barriers to equality and sets the foundations for a more equal, inclusive society with a more sustainable and fairly distributive economy.

Acknowledging that no one policy recommendation is a 'silver bullet', there are a number of measures to which States should give serious consideration when formulating their vision for recovery. These are outlined from a human rights perspective below. In some places, examples of positive measures taken by governments along these lines have been included.[110]

A. *Ensuring a social protection floor for all*

Long-term investments in comprehensive social protection systems are necessary to cushion the impact of crises, reduce poverty and contribute to economic growth.[111] A comprehensive rights-based social protection system must therefore be the foundation of any transformative recovery from the global economic and financial crises. Ensuring social protection floors now will ensure greater resilience against future crises and help to prevent the effects of the current crises from transmitting to future generations. Some governments have recognised this; for example, in response

[110] The use of certain examples should not be taken as indicating that the cited policy as a whole is human rights-compliant or wholly successful.

[111] Ortiz and Cummins, 'The Age of Austerity', 16.

to the crisis, the government of Antigua and Barbuda subsidised utilities for pensioners and increased pension payments, and the government of Bolivia spent more than 2 per cent of GDP investing in social protection programmes while raising the minimum wage by 12 per cent.[112]

A national social protection floor[113] is the minimum level of social protection that everyone should enjoy – a basic set of rights and transfers that enables and empowers all members of a society to have access to essential services (such as adequate nutrition, health, education, housing, water and sanitation) and income security (through social transfers). The concept overlaps with the existing notion of 'core obligations' to ensure the realisation of, at the very least, minimum essential levels of ESCR.

Social protection floor initiatives must be implemented through a rights-based approach.[114] In order to ensure that social protection systems are in line with human rights standards, a solid legal and institutional framework for a social protection system at the national level is necessary. For example, India's National Rural Employment Guarantee Act 2005 (NREGA) confers a statutory right to at least 100 days of paid employment for all rural households.[115]

By creating legal entitlements or social protection guarantees, States ensure that beneficiaries are empowered as rights-holders and ensure the continuity of the programme, helping to protect it against political manipulation and to receive lasting commitments from State authorities. The legal and institutional framework regulating social protection should clearly define the role and responsibilities of all stakeholders and must guarantee accessible complaint mechanisms and ensure transparency and access to information. Social protection systems must also incorporate effective and meaningful participatory mechanisms to enable feedback and accountability.

A rights-based approach also requires policymakers to ensure that all persons are protected in an equal and non-discriminatory manner. This principle implies that in the long term, social protection systems should aim at achieving universal coverage. In the meantime, policies should

[112] ESCR-Net *et al.*, 'Bringing Human Rights to Bear', 8.

[113] ILO, 'Recommendation Concerning National Floors of Social Protection' (14 June 2012) R202.

[114] See, e.g., Sepúlveda, 'Report on Cash Transfer Programmes'; Sepúlveda, 'Report on Social Pensions'; Sepúlveda, 'Report on Global Financial Crisis'; Sepúlveda, 'Report on Millennium Development Goals'; M. Sepúlveda and C. Nyst, *The Human Rights Approach to Social Protection* (Helsinki: Ministry of Foreign Affairs Finland, 2012).

[115] India National Rural Employment Guarantee Act 2005 (No.42 of 2005), sec. 3.

prioritise the most vulnerable and disadvantaged in line with human rights standards. States must carefully screen policy choices to avoid the unfair exclusion of disadvantaged and disempowered groups and actively seek out ways to ensure that they are reached (for example, under India's NREGA at least one-third of those employed must be women and child-care should be provided on-site).[116]

B. Promoting employment and supporting decent work

One of the most visible effects of the crises has been the high level of unemployment. Austerity measures have exacerbated unemployment and reduced the quantity and quality of decent work.[117] The ILO estimates that 912 million people and their families were affected by working poverty in 2011, around 30 per cent of the global workforce.[118] These people are employed, but they often work long hours in unsafe conditions and ultimately they are unable to raise their families out of poverty through their efforts.

A key priority for many States in responding to the crises has been the reduction of unemployment, especially among young people. Employment creation is a vital means of providing income security, generating economic growth, restoring social cohesion, preventing social and political instability and enabling individuals to achieve a number of ESCR, including the right to work,[119] which is essential for realising other human rights.[120]

Job creation must be geared towards *sustainable, productive* and *decent* work. Human rights standards require States to ensure just and favourable conditions of work, including reasonably limited working hours and paid annual leave,[121] the right to form and join trade union organisations and engage in collective bargaining.[122] Workers must have access to a social security system that provides for the broadest possible coverage such as health care, sickness compensation, old age pensions, unemployment benefits and compensation for employment-related injuries.[123]

Any form of discrimination – such as that based on sex, race, ethnicity or religion – against workers is prohibited.[124] Workers' remuneration

[116] *Ibid.* Schedule II. [117] ICESCR, arts. 6, 7.
[118] ILO, *Global Employment Trends 2012: Preventing a Deeper Jobs Crisis* (Geneva: ILO, 2012), p. 41.
[119] ICESCR, art. 6. [120] CESCR, 'General Comment No. 16', para. 1.
[121] ICESCR, art. 7. [122] ICESCR, art. 8; ICCPR, art. 2.
[123] ICESCR, art. 9. See also CESCR, 'General Comment No. 19', paras. 12–21.
[124] See, e.g., CEDAW, art. 11; CERD, art. 5.

must allow for a decent standard of living for workers and their family. Equal remuneration for work of equal value must also be ensured without discrimination of any kind; in particular, women must enjoy equal pay with men.[125] To ensure the implementation of these obligations, labour market regulation and mechanisms to strengthen the accountability of private actors will be necessary.

Considering that the majority of people living in poverty work in informal jobs, receiving low and irregular wages, policies should prioritise improving their working conditions, applying labour legislation and extending formal social protection to them.[126] These measures have the potential to reduce labour market inequality and to extend the coverage of labour institutions to groups that were previously excluded.[127]

The obligations of non-discrimination and equality oblige States to ensure that employment creation policies benefit all sectors of society equally.[128] Policies that increase the employability (for example, through demand-driven skills development and vocational training) of groups that face specific barriers in their access to employment, such as persons with disabilities, young people and indigenous populations, will assist States in fulfilling their human rights obligations.[129] For example, in their respective crises response measures, the government of Chile has included support for hiring youth while Japan has directed support towards hiring persons with disabilities.[130] To remove obstacles to employment for women, States should ensure the availability of care services (from the State, the community and the market), and work actively towards the redistribution of paid and unpaid work and the elimination of all forms of gender discrimination.[131] This requires not only legislative and regulatory measures but also measures to modify social and cultural patterns of conduct that perpetuate prejudices and stereotyped gender roles.[132]

[125] ICESCR, art. 7; CEDAW, art. 11.
[126] CESCR, 'General Comment No. 18', para. 10; CESCR, 'General Comment No. 19', para. 34.
[127] Economic Commission for Latin America and the Caribbean (ECLAC), 'Time for Equality: Closing Gaps, Opening Trails' (May 2010), 166.
[128] CESCR, 'General Comment No. 18', para. 31.
[129] *Ibid.*, para. 27. [130] ESCR-Net *et al.*, 'Bringing Human Rights to Bear', 7.
[131] ICESCR art. 6 (in conjunction with art. 2(1)); CEDAW, art. 11(2)(c).
[132] CEDAW, arts. 3, 5(2).

C. Implementing socially responsible taxation policies

In several countries, there is a clear need to identify additional sources of fiscal space to increase resources for social and economic recovery and realise ESCR. Evidence shows that even in developing countries, widening tax bases and improving tax collection efficiency could raise considerable additional revenue.[133]

Human rights principles require tackling tax abuses which include tax evasion, tax fraud and other illegal practices such as bribery, corruption and money laundering.[134] They also require the putting in place of progressive tax systems, preferring direct taxes such as personal income tax over indirect taxes, such as those based on consumption (e.g. Value-Added/sales taxes) which are typically regressive.

Careful consideration must be given to rebalancing the tax contributions of corporations (for example by applying natural resource extraction taxes) and those in high-income brackets. Many least developed countries, for example, offer extremely favourable tax deals to foreign investors in agriculture and mining.[135] These incentives warrant a heightened level of scrutiny in human rights terms, because they restrict the State's revenue, and therefore the resources it is able to devote to rights realisation. The revenue losses to developing countries amount to US$138 billion in revenue per year, by some estimates.[136] Estimates in many African countries show that revenue losses from tax incentives were between 2 and 8 per cent of GDP.[137]

Improving the efficiency of tax collection requires reconsidering tax abatements, exemptions and waivers that disproportionally benefit better-off segments of society. A human rights approach also requires States to take steps effectively to combat tax evasion and illicit financial flows, a problem that reduces the resources available to realise human rights.[138]

133 IMF, 'Revenue Mobilization in Developing Countries', (8 March 2011), 17, www.imf.org/external/np/pp/eng/2011/030811.pdf, last accessed 24 April 2013.

134 International Bar Association's Human Rights Institute Task Force on Illicit Financial Flows, Poverty and Human Rights, 'Tax Abuses, Poverty and Human Rights' (International Bar Association, 2013).

135 United Nations Conference on Trade and Development (UNCTAD), 'The Least Developed Countries Report 2013: Growth with employment for inclusive and sustainable development' (New York: UNCTAD, 2013), 136.

136 ActionAid, *Give Us a Break: How Big Companies are Getting Tax-free Deals*, (June 2013), 9.

137 TJN-Africa and Christian Aid, 'Africa Rising? Inequalities and the Essential Role of Fair Taxation' (February 2014), 43.

138 C. Lumina, 'The Negative Impact of the Non-Repatriation of Funds of Illicit Origin on the Enjoyment of Human Rights: Interim Report by the Independent Expert on the Effects of Foreign Debt' (21 February 2013) UN Doc. A/HRC/22/42.

For example, tax evasion has been estimated to result in annual revenue losses of US$285 billion to developing countries.[139] These types of reforms could help States to achieve a more progressive, equitable and sustainable taxation regime and to comply with international commitments to make tax systems more pro-poor.[140]

A financial transaction tax (FTT) is worthy of serious consideration, especially by G20 countries.[141] It would represent an appropriate contribution by the financial sector to recovering the costs of the crises and provide new and necessary resources to be allocated to poverty alleviation and development.[142] It could help States to mobilise their 'maximum available resources' for the protection of ESCR: if applied across the G20 countries the FTT would yield about US$48 billion at its lowest rate, with higher rates offering up to US$250 billion per year – significant amounts to offset austerity measures.[143]

Consideration should also be given to reprioritising spending on social sectors (such as education and health) over, for example, military expenditures in order to ensure the maximum use of available resources for the realisation of ESCR. As discussed below, a human rights approach requires States to debate fiscal options openly, avoiding technocratic decisions being made behind closed doors, and instead allowing for greater transparency and participation.

D. *Enhancing financial regulation*

The crises have exposed the weaknesses of deregulated financial markets, but States are not using the opportunity to address problems in the architecture of the global financial and monetary systems. States should utilise

[139] Ortiz, Chai and Cummins, 'Identifying Fiscal Space', p. 242.

[140] See, e.g., 'Doha Declaration on Financing for Development: Outcome Document of the Follow-up International Conference on Financing for Development to Review the Implementation of the Monterrey Consensus: Draft Resolution' (9 December 2008) UN Doc. A/CONF.212/L.1/Rev.1; 'Keeping the Promise: United to Achieve the Millennium Development Goals: Draft Resolution' (17 September 2010) UN Doc. A/65/L.1.

[141] Eleven EU countries – accounting for 90 per cent of Eurozone GDP – are planning to introduce an FTT, although in June 2013 it was announced that the introduction would be delayed and it could be watered down. T. Fairless, 'European Financial Transaction Tax Delayed', *Wall Street Journal* (25 June 2013).

[142] See OHCHR, 'G-8/EU: "A Global Transaction Tax, a Human Rights Imperative Now More than Ever"' (14 May 2012), www.ohchr.org/EN/NewsEvents/Pages/DisplayNews.aspx?NewsID=12150&LangID=E, last accessed 24 April 2014.

[143] Righting Financial Regulation Initiative, 'Financial Transaction Tax: A Human Rights Imperative' (Righting Financial Regulation series Issue 3, 2012), 3.

this moment to restructure the global financial system so that it is more equitable and shields vulnerable people from economic shocks.

The human rights framework obliges States to take measures to ensure that individuals under their jurisdiction are protected from infringements of their rights by third parties, and to take all available legal or policy measures to prevent third parties from violating ESCR.[144] Accordingly, regulation of banking and financial sector entities is vital, in order to prevent them from violating or infringing upon human rights. In addition, if adequate resources are to be available for the realisation of ESCR, budgetary resources must be protected from being compromised by bank bailouts. From 2008 to 2011, European countries committed EUR 4.5 trillion (equivalent to 37 per cent of EU economic output) in rescuing their financial institutions.[145]

A human rights approach stipulates that legal and policy measures should be taken to strengthen the accountability and transparency of financial systems, and avoid the risks posed by increasingly sophisticated financial instruments. States should also seek to limit or abolish off-shore tax havens[146] and oblige banking institutions to serve the interests of society by, for example, ensuring access to credit without discrimination and making their financial products more transparent. For example, reforms to Argentina's central bank have added financial stability and economic development to its mandate of monetary stability, empowering it to steer investment capital and loans towards projects that promote productive investment and boost job creation.[147] Those adversely affected by actions of financial sector institutions should have adequate means of redress and States should create accountability mechanisms that penalise risky behaviours and prosecute perpetrators. The functioning and transparency of financial commodity markets must be improved in order to curb financial speculation and excessive commodity price volatility, which directly affect the enjoyment of the right to food.[148]

144 See, e.g., CESCR, 'General Comment No. 12', in 'Compilation of General Comments', para. 27; CESR, 'Human Rights and the Global Economic Crisis: Consequences, Causes and Responses' (2009), 5–6.

145 European Commission, 'New Crisis Management Measures to Avoid Future Bank Bail-Outs' (6 June 2012), http://europa.eu/rapid/press-release_IP-12-570_en.htm?locale=en, last accessed 24 April 2014.

146 See, e.g., Council of Europe Parliamentary Assembly Resolution 1651 (29 January 2009).

147 R. Rowden, 'The Shots Heard Around the World', *Foreign Policy* (3 July 2012).

148 O. De Schutter, Special Rapporteur on the Right to Food, 'Food Commodities Speculation and Food Price Crises: Regulation to Reduce the Risks of Price Volatility' (Special

E. *Adopting a comprehensive national strategy to reduce poverty*

In addition to the crisis response measures that are necessary in the short term, States must adopt a comprehensive long-term strategy for sustainable development aimed at addressing the root causes of poverty.[149] Respect for all human rights – including the rule of law, gender equality and empowerment of women, inclusive participation, freedom of association and expression, and equal access to public services – are essential for poverty reduction. According to the circumstances of each State, national development strategies should also support small-scale farming through land redistribution, equal access to financial services and access to public services and infrastructure in rural areas.

Reducing poverty and promoting social inclusion require not only comprehensive national strategies but also international collective action to ensure equitable international regulatory measures and international assistance and cooperation, particularly with regard to addressing widespread food insecurity and rising food prices.[150]

F. *Conducting human rights impact assessments*

All States must take into account their international human rights obligations when designing policy responses. Before implementing a budget cut or any other policy measure, States must comprehensively assess its social impact, including from an equality and gender perspective, and should only adopt policies that are compatible with their international human rights obligations, including their non-discrimination obligations.[151] Moreover, the findings of these assessments must genuinely influence the final decision.

Rapporteur on the Right to Food Briefing Note No. 2, September 2010), www.srfood.org/images/stories/pdf/otherdocuments/20102309_briefing_note_02_en_ok.pdf, last accessed 24 April 2014. For more on this point, see De Schutter's contribution to this volume.

[149] UN Guiding Principles on Extreme Poverty and Human Rights (2012) UN Doc. A/HRC/21/39, para. 50.

[150] Strategies that support rural development, promote sustainable food production and reduce volatility in commodity markets must be a priority for States at both the national and international levels. FAO, 'Voluntary Guidelines to Support the Progressive Realization of the Right to Adequate Food in the Context of National Food Security' (2005).

[151] ESCR-Net *et al.*, 'Bringing Human Rights to Bear', 190. For a discussion of the use of economic and social rights standards to analyse budget decisions, see R. O'Connell, A. Nolan, C, Harvey, M. Dutschke and E. Rooney, *Applying an International Human Rights Framework to State Budget Allocations: Rights and Resources* (London: Routledge, 2014).

Policymakers must take into account the cumulative impact of different recovery measures on particularly vulnerable and disadvantaged groups and should periodically monitor the implementation and impact of such.[152] They should ensure policy consistency and coherency between various measures to avoid exacerbating the situation of the poorest sectors of society.[153] Cuts in funding to social services that have the greatest impact on the lives of those living in poverty should be a measure of last resort, and should be taken only after serious consideration of all alternative policy options, including how budget allocation to other areas might be otherwise reduced.[154]

G. *Ensuring gender-sensitive policies*

There are several measures that States should take to ensure a gender approach in the design and implementation of recovery measures, including comprehensive and disaggregated gender analyses. In designing social, economic and macroeconomic measures, policymakers should consider their impact on women's unpaid care work, and avoid intensifying women's unpaid care workload.[155] A more equal distribution of unpaid care between men and women and from households to the State can be enabled by investing in care services, social protection measures such as child benefit, and accessible public services. Such policies will have positive social and economic impact, enhancing women's ability to pursue a decent livelihood and enjoy their rights, including their right to work.[156]

Recovery measures should prioritise investments in education and skills development for women and girls, and in sectors where women make up a considerable proportion of the labour force (such as in export manufacturing). Gender budget analysis can monitor whether women benefit equally from public investments.[157] Policymakers must design, implement, monitor and evaluate initiatives through a gender lens, so that

[152] CESR, 'Mauled by the Celtic Tiger', 25.

[153] UN Guiding Principles on Extreme Poverty, para. 61.

[154] CESCR, Letter to States Parties.

[155] D. Elson, *Budgeting for Women's Rights: Monitoring Government Budgets for Compliance with CEDAW* (New York: UNIFEM, 2006), p. 33.

[156] ILO, 'Equal Sharing of Responsibilities between Women and Men, Including Care-Giving in the Context of HIV-AIDS' (Background Paper Prepared for the UN Division for the Advancement of Women Expert Group Meeting, September 2008), 33–4.

[157] See EWL, 'The Price of Austerity', 15.

policies are able to address asymmetries of power and structural inequalities, and enhance the realisation of women's rights.[158]

H. *Increasing participation and creating a national dialogue*

A human rights-based recovery from the successive crises is one in which all segments of society play a significant role. The human rights principles of participation, transparency and accountability require States to create and maintain mechanisms by which individuals and civil society can meaningfully and effectively contribute to and provide feedback on policy measures, including economic policy, and claim redress for those that affect their enjoyment of human rights. States should also take measures to invest in the capacity of those groups to contribute to and participate in policy formulation.[159] For example, the South African government has taken efforts to design its policy response to the crises in a participatory manner by working with the National Economic Development and Labour Council, which brings together constituencies from government, business, labour unions and the community.[160]

Increasing participation in policy-making can enable better assessments of the root causes of deprivation in any given community, the structural challenges to poverty alleviation, the local cultural, ethnic or societal obstacles to successful poverty reduction, and the best means of reaching the most vulnerable. It therefore increases the likelihood that policies will be effective in reaching the poorest members and segments of society.[161] Participation is also a right in itself (see Section II E above) and intrinsically valuable because of its empowerment effect.

I. *Ensuring vulnerable people can effectively challenge policy decisions that threaten their ESCR*

Unfortunately, in some countries ESCR are still not effectively enforceable through courts, political institutions or administrative bodies, impeding access to remedies and accountability. Moreover, many States have created a double jeopardy for human rights by implementing cuts to

[158] M. Sepúlveda, 'Report of the Special Rapporteur on Extreme Poverty and Human Rights: Unpaid care and Human Rights', 9 August 2013) UN Doc. A/68/293.

[159] See Sepúlveda, 'Report on Participation'.

[160] ESCR-Net *et al.*, 'Bringing Human Rights to Bear', 15.

[161] See X. Godinot and Q. Woden (eds.), *Participatory Approaches to Attacking Extreme Poverty* (Washington, DC: World Bank, 2006).

welfare benefits and essential social services, while at the same time limiting access to accountability or complaints mechanisms through funding cuts and eligibility restrictions.

In some countries court fees have been increased and the provision of legal aid has been cut, at a time when the demand for civil legal aid in relation to critical matters such as foreclosure proceedings, welfare review or asylum proceedings is in fact increasing. In Ireland, for example, the resources allocated to legal aid have decreased, while the number of applications for civil legal aid rose by 84 per cent from 2007 to 2011.[162] In the United Kingdom, the Legal Aid Sentencing and Prevention of Offenders Act 2012 was projected to reduce government spending on legal aid by a quarter over three years.[163] The cuts overwhelmingly affect family and social welfare law; areas that are crucial to upholding the rights of people living in poverty. In Spain, a 2012 law increased court fees (now determined at between EUR 100 and 1,200) and attached a cost to many court proceedings which were previously exempted from fees, such as cases related to labour conditions – effectively blocking many people living in poverty from launching claims.[164]

Instead of actions such as these, States should ensure that all individuals, including people living in poverty, have access to effective remedies when their ESCR have been violated. Without such access, many people living in poverty are stuck in a cycle of powerlessness against abuse, exploitation and violence, which exacerbates and perpetuates their poverty, deepens societal inequality and stunts economic development.[165] As emphasised by the EU's Fundamental Rights Agency, 'While financial austerity might require streamlining, it should and need not be to the detriment of access to justice.'[166]

162 Responses by the Minister for Justice and Equality to Parliamentary Questions on 21 March 2012 (Office of the Houses of the Oireachtas, Written Answers – Garda Transport (21 March 2012), http://debates.oireachtas.ie/dail/2012/03/21/00317.asp, last accessed 24 April 2014) and 23 June 2011 (Office of the Houses of the Oireachtas, Priority Questions – Legal Aid Service (23 June 2012), http://debates.oireachtas.ie/dail/2011/06/23/00010.asp, last accessed 24 April 2014).

163 R. Smith. 'After the Act: What Future for Legal Aid?' (JUSTICE Tom Sargant Memorial Annual Lecture, 16 October 2012).

164 Royal Decree Law 10/2012, of 20 November 2012, Regulating certain fees in relation to the Ministry of Justice and the National Institute of Toxicology and Forensic Sciences, BOE no 280, 21 November 2012, www.boe.es/boe/dias/2012/11/21/pdfs/BOE-A-2012-14301.pdf, last accessed 24 April 2014.

165 Sepúlveda, 'Report on Access to Justice'.

166 EU Agency for Fundamental Rights, 'Access to Justice in Cases of Discrimination in the EU: Steps to Further Equality' (December 2012), 11.

J. *Strengthening state institutional and technical capacity and data collection*

To address future crises in an effective and timely manner, ensuring that the most disadvantaged and vulnerable groups are protected, States should improve their technical and institutional capacity to develop evidence-based policy-making. Staff in key government departments must be trained and have the analytical skills to assess the human rights implications of their decisions, and effective coordination mechanisms should ensure communication and information-sharing between government departments on human rights-related issues.

In order to better inform policy debates, more accurate and efficient data is needed to identify people living in poverty and to assess their needs.[167] To this end, States should work towards creating mechanisms that provide better information about the incidence and substance of deprivation and inequality.[168] This includes instituting means of gathering larger quantities of better quality disaggregated data on the impact of the crises and of recovery policies. Data should be disaggregated according to several dimensions, such as gender, age, geographical location, ethnicity and health status.

K. *Enhancing international assistance and cooperation*

To ensure an equitable and sustainable recovery, developed States should redouble their efforts towards long-standing human rights commitments to provide international assistance and cooperation.[169] Increased international aid could help reduce fiscal pressure for many low-income countries, which have limited financial and institutional ability and whose populations are most feeling the strain of fiscal contraction.[170]

Unfortunately, some developed countries are cutting funds for international assistance just when it is most needed,[171] rather than moving

[167] High-Level Panel of Eminent Persons on the Post-2015 Development Agenda, 'A New Global Partnership: Eradicate Poverty and Transform Economies through Sustainable Development' (May 2013), 23.

[168] UN Guiding Principles on Extreme Poverty, para. 105.

[169] ICESCR, art. 2(1); Charter of the United Nations (adopted 26 June 1945, entered into force 24 October 1945) 1 UNTS XVI, art. 1(3).

[170] Ortiz and Cummins, 'The Age of Austerity', i.

[171] In 2011, the ODA provided by members of the Development Assistance Committee (DAC) of the OECD suffered a 2.7 per cent drop in real terms compared to 2010. As it takes several years from the onset of a recession for the full impact to be felt on aid

toward the target of 0.7 per cent of gross national product in ODA that they have repeatedly pledged to meet since 1970.[172] Indeed, 'the justification for meeting the ... target has never been greater' given the staggering levels of global inequality, where the wealthiest fifth of the global population enjoys 70 per cent of the total world income, with only 2 per cent for the poorest fifth.[173] ODA is an important redistributive channel. To ensure that ODA is effective, it should be given under conditions that respect national ownership and be predictable, transparent and harmonised with national priorities.[174]

The international community should look for innovative means of generating financial resources to assist developing countries in taking a human rights response to crises, such as an FTT (see Section IV C, above) or a Global Fund for Social Protection.[175] Consensus and collective action are also essential to address the deficits in the global financial and economic architecture. Given that domestic economies are intertwined with the global economic system, in order for poverty to be reduced, national efforts must be supported by an enabling international environment.[176] In this regard, an open, non-discriminatory, equitable and transparent multilateral trading system is essential. States should honour their commitments to work expeditiously towards a balanced and ambitious, comprehensive and development-oriented outcome of the Doha Development Agenda.[177]

Onerous conditionalities placed on financial support from international financial institutions raise several human rights concerns. Member States should ensure that human rights are prioritised in all

flows, it is expected that from 2013–15 assistance will continue to be decreased. (See OECD, 'Development: Aid to Developing Countries Falls Because of Global Recession' (4 April 2012), www.oecd.org/dac/aidstatistics/developmentaidtodevelopingcountries-fallsbecauseofglobalrecession.htm, last accessed 4 September 2013.) In some developed countries the cuts have been dramatic. For example, in Spain the ODA has dropped 70 per cent since 2009. See Intermón Oxfam, 'La realidad de la ayuda 2013' (2013), www.oxfamintermon.org/sites/default/files/documentos/files/informe_AOD_v05_doble.pdf, last accessed 24 April 2014.

172 For more information, see UN Millennium Project, 'The 0.7% Target: An In-Depth Look', www.unmillenniumproject.org/press/07.htm, last accessed 24 April 2014.

173 Ortiz, Chai and Cummins, 'Identifying Fiscal Space', p. 254.

174 'UN Guiding Principles on Extreme Poverty', paras. 91–8.

175 See O. De Schutter and M. Sepúlveda, 'Underwriting the Poor: a Global Fund for Social Protection: The Right to Food as a Global Goal, (2012), www.ohchr.org/Documents/Issues/Food/20121009_GFSP_en.pdf, last accessed 24 April 2014.

176 UNGA Res. 66/191 (29 August 2011).

177 UNGA Res. 65/1 (22 September 2010), para. 78.

policies and measures and ensure that they do not impede the realisation of human rights.[178] This obligation lies particularly with those States with the greatest powers of participation, voting and decision-making in the institutions. Moreover, major reforms to the governance of these institutions are necessary to make them more inclusive and representative, and to enhance transparency and accountability.

In their negotiations and agreements with international financial institutions, States' obligations under ICESCR should be taken into account to ensure that ESCR are not undermined, and they should not be forced to agree to loan conditions that might compromise their ability to meet their obligations regarding the realisation of human rights.

V. Conclusion – crisis as opportunity: a time for transformative policies

The challenge of recovery from successive crises presents a unique opportunity for States to formulate a transformative vision for the future, aimed at the full realisation of human rights. Unfortunately, even now that the counter-productive and regressive effects of austerity have become clear, some States are failing to take this opportunity, or to learn from previous crises.

In the context of record unemployment worldwide and escalating cost of living, austerity measures are exacerbating inequality and denying enjoyment of ESCR to a significant proportion of the global population. It is clear that in a large number of developed as well as developing countries the trend towards austerity has increased and will continue into 2014 and beyond.[179] The full impact of these measures is still unfolding, but it is already clear that many austerity measures are reducing the dignity, autonomy, equality and rights of people living in poverty, as well as devastating their fragile incomes and livelihoods.

States are not exploring the full range of feasible alternatives to austerity. This failure not only has a devastating impact on human rights enjoyment, but also is likely to entrench and exacerbate inequality and poverty for a long period of time. At this crucial time, we cannot afford a further large-scale deterioration in living standards due to the blind implementation of misguided, ideologically motivated or simply bad

[178] CESCR, 'General Comment No. 14', para. 39.

[179] I. Ortiz, J. Chai and M. Cummins, 'Austerity Measures and the Risks to Children and Poor Households', in Ortiz and Cummins (eds.), *A Recovery for All*, pp. 172–230, pp. 176–8.

policy choices. Basic principles of human rights, social justice and fairness mandate that we should not be asking those who have so little to pay a harsh price – far more than their 'fair share' – to rectify a situation that they did not create.

Human rights obligations require States to move away from the austerity paradigm that prioritises cutting budgets and reducing debt above all else, towards a human-centred framework that places protection of vulnerable persons at its centre. ESCR restrain states from taking measures that would exacerbate poor people's deprivation, require the removal of the obstacles that such persons face in terms of enjoyment of their rights, and mandate the satisfaction of at least minimum essential levels of ESCR. Looking at recovery through a human rights framework orients the discussion away from deficit reduction and towards the reduction of poverty and the eradication of obstacles to the realisation of rights.

Rather than hoping that the benefits of a still-remote recovery will 'trickle down' to the disadvantaged, recovery should be premised on securing the livelihoods, improving rights enjoyment and increasing the social and economic inclusion of people living in poverty. To overcome the impact of economic deprivation and social exclusion, the poor require specific initiatives aimed at enhancing their economic empowerment and political voice. Without this, any recovery is bound to be short-lived and unsustainable. Moreover it will be achieved at a great human cost. In focusing their efforts on human rights, States could instead ensure a recovery premised upon equality, inclusiveness, justice and improved social cohesion, to the benefit of all members of society. International human rights law provides us with a tool to balance asymmetries of power, pursue accountability and protect and empower those who do not have a mainstream political voice. As austerity policies have demonstrated with painful clarity, post-crisis economic policy is emphatically a matter of human rights concern, and we must use the human rights law standards and mechanisms at our disposal to combat its worst effects.

2

Late-neoliberalism: the financialisation of homeownership and the housing rights of the poor

RAQUEL ROLNIK AND LIDIA RABINOVICH

I. Introduction

Housing has been one of the most powerful new frontiers of financial capital during the last few decades. From the outset of the financial crisis, housing was converted into one of the main Keynesian strategies to recover from it. The commodification of housing, as well as the increased use of housing as an investment asset integrated into a globalised financial market, has deeply impacted upon the enjoyment of the right to adequate housing globally.

The belief that markets could regulate the allocation of housing as the most rational means of resource distribution, combined with experiments with 'creative' financial products related to it, have resulted in public policies that have abandoned the conceptual meaning of housing as a social good. Housing policies have shifted from being part of the commonalities that a society agrees to share or to provide to those with fewer resources – a means to distribute wealth – into being a means to accumulate individual wealth and generate financial gain. Inevitably, the people most negatively affected by these policies have been the poorest and most marginalised in developed and developing countries, countries in transition, and in emerging markets.

As with other social fields, housing has been affected by a wave of measures that have dismantled basic institutional welfare, by the mobilisation of a range of policies intended to extend market discipline, by competition and by commodification. Taking the 1990s as a starting point, and the sub-prime crisis as

This article is a revised, updated, extended and edited version of a Thematic Report presented by the Special Rapporteur on Adequate Housing as a Component of the Right to an Adequate Standard of Living, and on the Right to Non-discrimination in this Context (Special Rapporteur on the Right to Adequate Housing), Raquel Rolnik, to the General Assembly at its 67th Session in October 2012 (UN Doc. A/67/286). The views expressed herein are those of the authors and do not necessarily reflect the views of the United Nations.

its first great international collapse, this chapter traces some key elements of the prevalent neoliberal approach to housing. It considers the impact of this approach on the enjoyment of the right to housing by the poorest and most disadvantaged across time and various regions. The chapter concludes with a call for a paradigm shift from the financialisation of housing to a rights-based approach to housing policies.

In terms of structure, Section II will provide the background to the rise of neoliberal doctrine in the housing context in various regions and the emergence of housing finance as the main housing policy in both developed and developing countries. Section III details States' main human rights obligations with regard to the right to adequate housing under the international human rights framework. This is the prism used in this chapter to analyse the various housing finance policies considered. Section IV analyses the three main housing finance policies directed at low-income households (mortgage finance, demand side subsidies and housing micro-finance) from a human rights perspective. Section V summarises the conclusions emerging from this analysis and aims to suggest an alternative – a human rights-based approach to housing policies.

II. The rise of housing finance

When the acute misery of the urban poor began to be revealed by social reformers in Europe and North America in the late nineteenth and early twentieth centuries, governments began to provide housing assistance to individuals and households and to supply housing directly.[1] By the middle of the twentieth century many developing countries in Latin America, Africa and Asia had experienced rapid urbanisation of the rural poor.[2] The absence of urban and housing policies to enable this new urban population to access urbanised land (serviced and developed land in urban areas) led to the creation of self-built informal settlements, characterised by precarious dwellings and a severe lack of basic services and infrastructure.[3]

[1] For example, in the United Kingdom, about 5.5 million social dwellings were constructed between the end of the Second World War and 1981. M. Harloe, *The People's Home: Social Rented Housing in Europe and America* (Hoboken, NJ: Wiley-Blackwell, 1995); D. Fée, 'Le logement social en Angleterre: trente ans de déclin', *Informations Sociales*, 159 (2010), 80–9, 82.

[2] R. Rolnik, 'Report of the Special Rapporteur on Adequate Housing as a Component of the Right to an Adequate Standard of Living, and on the Right to Non-Discrimination in this Context on the Financial Crisis and Its Causes' (4 February 2009) UN Doc. A/HRC/10/7, 11.

[3] *Ibid.*

During the same period, in most formerly planned economies,[4] the State was responsible for providing all citizens with adequate housing and the predominant model applied was centrally planned construction of state rental housing.[5] In the case of public rental housing, the occupants and their families enjoyed extraordinary tenant protection – quasi-ownership tenure and the rents were low, amounting to on average 2–3 per cent of the household budget.[6] Though there were significant differences between countries, in the late 1980s these States often succeeded in meeting their basic housing needs.[7] Although it is now generally acknowledged that substantive differences existed between the housing models in the States, one of the shared characteristics of these economies was the absence of a market-based mortgage lending legal framework and institutions.[8] Lending mechanisms and home ownership tenure were common only in a few States (such as Hungary, Bulgaria, Poland and the former Yugoslavia).[9]

In the late 1970s a dramatic shift occurred in housing policies, starting with North America and Europe, followed later by developing countries in Latin America, Asia, Africa and by formerly planned economies. This shift, supported by hegemonic neoliberal economic doctrine,[10] called for the transfer of activities from state control to the private sector and for unrestricted free markets and free trade. This view gained momentum after the fall of the Berlin Wall, shaping the policies of States, international financial institutions and development agencies. The effects of

[4] Former Soviet Union and Eastern Bloc States and also several Asian countries (such as China and Vietnam).

[5] J. Hegedüs, S. E. Mayo and I. Tosics, 'Transition of the Housing Sector in the East Central European Countries', *Review of Urban & Regional Development Studies*, 8(2) (1996), 101–36; UN Economic Commission for Europe (ECE), *Housing Finance Systems for Countries in Transition: Principles and Examples* (New York and Geneva: United Nations, 2005); M. Stephens, 'Locating Chinese Urban Housing Policy in an International Context', *Urban Studies*, 47 (2010), 2965–82, 2965, 2971.

[6] Hegedüs, Mayo and Tosics, 'Transition of the Housing Sector', 101; UN ECE, *Housing Finance Systems*; Stephens, 'Locating Chinese Urban Housing Policy', 2971.

[7] However, this was achieved by constructing large anonymous housing estates using low-cost high-rise prefab building technologies. The low standard of housing construction quality, low average dwelling space, lack of social and cultural facilities on housing estates and insufficient maintenance of both buildings and common areas led to low levels of habitability.

[8] Hegedüs, Mayo and Tosics, 'Transition of the Housing Sector'.

[9] UN ECE, *Housing Finance Systems*, p. 3.

[10] This approach has been labelled as the 'Washington Consensus' and was strongly promoted by international financial institutions.

this approach on housing policies across the globe have been dramatic and well documented.[11]

A growing consensus developed, according to which governments should renounce their role as suppliers of affordable housing and become facilitators,[12] supporting market demand rather than directly providing outcomes: 'Governments should be encouraged to adopt policies that enable housing markets to work ... and avoid distorting housing markets.'[13] This new role implies creating conditions, institutions and regulations aimed at supporting housing finance systems to promote homeownership under the neoliberal dogma of reliance on private property and market forces.[14] 'Housing finance' in the context of this chapter refers to financial policies and programmes that aim to finance the cost of housing for individuals and families by providing loans (mortgages or micro-loans) or grants (subsidies or tax exemptions) for the purchase, rental, construction or improvement of housing units.[15]

Developed and developing countries have thus been steadily moving away from traditional supply-side assistance to demand-side housing policies. As a result, support for households to take on credit debt, the financial sector and the private housing market became the primary mechanisms for allocating housing solutions. Foreign assistance from international financial institutions greatly influenced the development of market-based housing finance and boosted housing market activity in developing countries.[16] Despite some diversity in housing policy experience,[17] most countries opted for promoting housing markets and

[11] For details of this shift, see, e.g., N. Brenner and N. Theodore, *Spaces of Neoliberalism: Urban Restructuring in North America and Western Europe* (Oxford: Blackwell, 2002); R. Rolnik, 'Late-Neoliberalism: The Financialization of Homeownership and Housing Rights' *International Journal of Urban and Regional Research*, 37 (2013), 1058–66.

[12] United Nations Human Settlements Programme (UN-Habitat), *Quick Guide to Policy Makers, Quick Guide 2 – Housing the Poor in African Cities, Low-Income Housing* (Nairobi: UN-Habitat, 2011), pp. 35–6; M. Atterhög and H. S. Song, 'A Survey of Policies that May Increase Access to Home Ownership for Low-Income Households', *Housing, Theory and Society*, 26 (2009), 248–70.

[13] World Bank, *Housing: Enabling Markets to Work* (Washington, DC: World Bank, 1993), p. 6.

[14] J. Doherty *et al.*, *The Changing Role of the State: Welfare Delivery in the Neoliberal Era* (Brussels: FEANTSA, 2005).

[15] However, broader definitions of housing finance exist, including developer finance and rental finance. See L. Chiquier and M. Lea (eds.), *Housing Finance Policy in Emerging Markets* (Washington, DC: World Bank, 2009), p. xxxii.

[16] UN ECE, *Housing Finance Systems*, p. 7; World Bank Urban Development Division, 'The Emerging Role of Housing Finance' (Report INU 33, November 1988).

[17] Such as Switzerland and Austria. See E. Bauer, 'Housing Finance and Housing Providers in Austria: Performance in the Light of the Financial and Economic Crisis',

individual homeownership, privatising social housing programmes and deregulating housing finance markets.[18]

In some countries, selling publicly owned houses to tenants has been seen as a way to increase homeownership while diminishing state expenditure.[19] Privatisation was also supported by increased stigmatisation of public housing as centres of extreme poverty, crime and marginalisation.[20] In Europe and North America, the privatisation of public housing has taken various forms, including the sale to sitting tenants of public rented housing through right-to-buy policies (the United Kingdom),[21] property transfers to not-for-profit actors (the Netherlands)[22] and, in some cases, to profit-maximising actors (Germany[23] and the United States of America[24]).

During the 1990s, most formerly planned economies also embarked on projects of large-scale privatisation of public housing through 'right to buy' programmes, resulting, in some cases, in the almost complete eradication of public housing. In most countries that adopted this approach,[25] this process led to radical changes in tenure structure; in many formerly

in *Financing Social Housing after the Economic Crisis, Proceedings of the CECODHAS Seminar* (Brussels: CECODHAS Housing Europe, 2009), pp. 38–41; J. Lawson, 'Path Dependency and Emergent Relations: Explaining the Different Role of Limited Profit Housing in the Dynamic Urban Regimes of Vienna and Zurich', *Housing, Theory and Society*, 27 (2010), 204–20.

18 R. Ronald, *The Ideology of Home Ownership* (Basingstoke: Palgrave-Macmillan, 2008).

19 UN-Habitat, *Affordable Land and Housing in Europe and North America* (Nairobi: UN-Habitat, 2011), p. 9.

20 Rolnik, 'Late-Neoliberalism'.

21 H. Premius and F. Dieleman, 'Social Housing Policy in the European Union: Past, Present and Perspectives', *Urban Studies*, 39 (2002), 191–200.

22 D. Czischke and A. Pittini, *Housing Europe 2007: Review of Social, Co-operative and Public Housing in the 27 EU Member States* (Brussels: CECODHAS European Social Housing Observatory, 2007), p. 49.

23 K. Scanlon and C. Whitehead, 'Le logement social en Europe: tendances communes et diversités persistantes', in C. Lévy-Vroelant and C. Tutin (eds.), *Le logement social en Europe au début du XXIe siècle: la revision générale* (Presses Universitaires de Rennes, 2010), pp. 17–44, p. 24.

24 In the United States, the Housing and Community and Development Act of 1974 ended most new construction of public housing and initiated the Housing Choice Voucher Programme (Section 8), shifting funds from public housing authorities to the private sector which was to construct low-income housing. These 'affordable' houses were eventually too costly for many public housing tenants. R. Rolnik, 'Report of the Special Rapporteur on Adequate Housing as a Component of the Right to an Adequate Standard of Living, and on the Right to Non-discrimination in This Context: Mission to the United States of America' (12 February 2010) A/HRC/13/20/Add.4, paras. 10, 25.

25 Only a few countries did not adopt the 'right to buy' for tenants (e.g. the Czech Republic and Poland).

planned economies owner-occupied housing now forms more than 90 per cent of the housing stock (e.g. 96 per cent in Estonia, 77 per cent in Slovenia[26] and more than 80 per cent in China[27]).

Even in countries where massive privatisation did not take place, the ideological transfer of responsibility for provision of housing to the market has been prevalent, accompanied by a homeownership-based model of tenure to be placed at the centre of all housing policies. This process has overshadowed other well-established alternative forms of tenure, such as rental housing (public and private) and different forms of cooperative and collective ownership.[28] Consequently, since the end of the Second World War homeownership rates have been constantly climbing,[29] and by mid-2000 had reached more than 50 per cent in the Member States of the Organisation for Economic Co-operation and Development (OECD), with the exception of Germany and Switzerland.[30]

As previously indicated, 'housing finance' in the context of this chapter refers to financial policies and programmes that aim to finance the cost of housing for individuals and families by providing loans (mortgages or micro-loans) or grants (subsidies or tax exemptions) for the purchase, rental, construction or improvement of housing units. As will be subsequently illustrated, most housing finance policies and strategies currently in place target individuals rather than institutional landlords. They aim to promote ownership and are based on the premise that the housing market, if properly designed and regulated, and provided with the necessary supporting legal and institutional framework, is capable of ensuring access to adequate and affordable homeownership for all.

Housing finance is now perceived not only as a tool for promoting access to adequate housing but also as critical to the development of the financial

[26] Replies from Estonia and Slovenia to the questionnaire sent by the Special Rapporteur on the Right to Adequate Housing to Member States on 5 April 2012 (hereafter 'the questionnaire'). For the State replies to the questionnaire, see 'Submissions by the Governments to the Questionnaire on Housing financing for the poor', www.ohchr.org/EN/Issues/Housing/Pages/HousingFinancingForThePoorAnswerstoQuestionnaire.aspx, last accessed 10 October 2013.

[27] K. T. Rosen and M. C. Ross, 'Increasing Home Ownership in Urban China: Notes on the Problem of Affordability', *Housing Studies*, 15 (2000), 77–88.

[28] J. Lawson, T. Gilmour and V. Milligan, 'International Measures to Channel Investment towards Affordable Rental Housing' (Australian Housing and Urban Research Institute Research Paper, May 2010).

[29] Atterhög and Song, 'A Survey of Policies', 248–9.

[30] Spain and Ireland lead with 83.2 per cent and 91.4 per cent, respectively. D. Andrews and A. Caldera Sánchez, 'Drivers of Homeownership Rates in Selected OECD Countries' (OECD Economics Department Working Paper No. 849, 2011), 9.

sector, and together with other real estate investments has become one of the central pillars of the financial market, expanding the terrain for global capital.[31] The deregulation, liberalisation and internationalisation of finance that started in the 1980s had major implications for housing and urban development. Funds for mortgage lending now derive from national and international capital markets and not solely from existing savings and retail finance. These developments have been characterised as the '"financialization" of housing'.[32] This process has been accompanied by the conceptual transformation of adequate housing from a social good into a commodity and a strategy for household wealth accumulation and welfare security. Housing has become a financial asset ('real estate'), and housing markets are increasingly regulated so as to promote the financial aspects rather than the social aspects of housing.[33]

Yet, market-based housing finance has contributed to a widespread bubble in real estate prices and a decrease in affordability, and has done little to promote access to affordable adequate housing for the poorest. For instance, between 1997 and 2004 average housing prices grew by 149 per cent in Spain, 139 per cent in the United Kingdom, 187 per cent in Ireland, 112 per cent in Australia, 65 per cent in the United States and 227 per cent in South Africa.[34] As real estate prices and rents increased and came to be financed through global instead of local financial surpluses, more households faced difficulties in accessing adequate housing through the market. Several studies have pointed to the negative impacts of housing asset dispersion on social stratification and inequality, and the uneven spatial impact of these processes within cities, regions and globally.[35]

The affordability crisis was compounded by the erosion, neglect and liberalisation of non-market mechanisms for allocating housing resources. Even countries with a long tradition of broad-based social

[31] UN ECE, 'Policy Framework for Sustainable Real Estate Markets: Principles and Guidance for the Development of a Country's Real Estate Sector' (2010) UN Doc. ECE/HBP/147.

[32] M. B. Aalbers, 'The Financialization of Home and the Mortgage Market Crisis', *Competition and Change*, 12 (2008), 148–66.

[33] Chiquier and Lea (eds.), *Housing Finance Policy in Emerging Markets*, p. xxxiv.

[34] UN-Habitat, *Financing Urban Shelter: Global Report on Human Settlements 2005* (Nairobi: UN-Habitat, 2005), p. 1.

[35] See, e.g., R. Forrest, 'Globalization and the Housing Asset Rich: Geographies, Demographies and Policy Convoys', *Global Social Policy*, 8 (2008), 167–87, 178–9; J. P. Ye, J. N. Song and C. G. Tian, 'An Analysis of Housing Policy during Economic Transition in China', *International Journal of Housing Policy*, 10 (2010), 273–300.

rental housing have redefined their systems to promote ownership, 'free market' and competition policies. A significant reduction in the construction of adequate public housing for the poor and most vulnerable groups has occurred along with decreasing national budgets and available public funds for social housing. In the United States, the budget of the Department of Housing and Urban Development was cut from $83 billion in 1978 to $18 billion in 1983.[36] Between 1996 and 2001 no funding at all was allocated to public housing construction.[37] The constant reduction in public housing has resulted in long waiting lists, deterioration of the existing public stock due to lack of maintenance, resulting in a large number of people in inadequate housing conditions.[38] Even in the former Soviet countries, which did not experience a shortage of housing in the short term (following mass privatisation), low-income households were soon faced with a huge affordability problem.[39]

With the decline of state investment in the social housing sector and the increasing focus on homeownership – which also led to a shrinking private rental market[40] – access to housing finance became vital for low-income households. These households were left with no other option for securing shelter than to embark on credit schemes to purchase homes, if, where and when those homes and credit became available, and under the conditions established by real estate and financial markets.

Our concern with the growing centrality of housing finance at the expense of broader and more diverse housing policies led us to focus this analysis on the compatibility of housing finance policies with the promotion of the right to adequate housing of those living in poverty and vulnerable conditions. The right to adequate housing provides a critical prism through which current and previous housing policies can be assessed, alternatives examined and past mistakes rectified. The right to adequate housing is particularly relevant to efforts to address the housing characteristics and needs of the poorest and most marginalised, which are often side-lined in housing policy design and implementation.

[36] Western Regional Advocacy Project, '2012 HUD Budget Fact Sheet' (2011).

[37] *Ibid.*

[38] Rolnik, 'Report: Mission to the United States of America', para. 21; Rolnik, 'Report on the Financial Crisis and Its Causes'.

[39] See, e.g., reply of Slovakia to the questionnaire.

[40] UN-Habitat, *A Policy Guide to Rental Housing in Developing Countries* (Nairobi: UN-Habitat, 2011), p. 1; UN-Habitat, *Rental Housing: An Essential Option for the Urban Poor in Developing Countries* (Nairobi: UN-Habitat, 2003), p. 1.

III. The international human rights framework

Housing finance policies directly affect the affordability component of the right to adequate housing (article 11, paragraph 1, of the International Covenant on Economic, Social and Cultural Rights[41]). The obligation to promote the right to adequate housing requires States to establish laws, policies and programmes to ensure that the percentage of housing-related costs is commensurate with income levels and that the attainment and satisfaction of other basic needs is not threatened or compromised by such costs.[42]

Nonetheless, affordability is only one of the components of the right to adequate housing, and certainly not the only one that has been affected by the financialisation of housing. When designing, implementing and monitoring housing policies, States must ensure that they not only promote access to affordable housing, but also access to housing that is habitable, accessible and adequately located, as well as ensuring the availability of services (such as health, education and welfare), means of livelihood, building materials, facilities and infrastructure, and security of tenure.[43] States must also guarantee that housing policies are non-discriminatory and do not increase existing inequalities. When designing housing finance policies, States must pay particular attention to the rights of the poor and disadvantaged. Policies and legislation should be designed to bridge inequality gaps and to ensure access to affordable housing for the poor and marginalised and not benefit already advantaged social groups at the expense of others.[44]

The obligation to ensure the realisation of the right to adequate housing does not oblige governments to provide publicly built housing for all. Although the Committee on Economic, Social and Cultural Rights (CESCR) expressed the view that in some cases the State is obliged to provide social housing or low-rental units for low-income households,[45]

[41] International Covenant on Economic, Social and Cultural Rights, 993 UNTS 3 (ICESCR).

[42] UN Committee on Economic, Social and Cultural Rights (CESCR), 'General Comment No. 4' in 'Note by the Secretariat, Compilation of General Comments and General Recommendations Adopted by Human Rights Treaty Bodies' (27 May 2008) UN Doc. HRI/GEN/1/Rev.9 (Vol. I), para. 10 (which can also be seen as authoritative guidance for the interpretation of the right to an adequate standard of living referred to in other international human rights instruments such as the Universal Declaration of Human Rights).

[43] *Ibid.*, para. 8. [44] *Ibid.*, para. 11.

[45] See, e.g., CESCR 'Concluding Observations on India' (8 August 2008) UN Doc. E/C.12/IND/CO/5, paras. 30, 70; CESCR 'Concluding Observations on Lithuania'

States are encouraged to employ a variety of housing policies,[46] including 'enabling strategies' and access to credit for low-income groups,[47] provided that 'measures being taken are sufficient to realise the right for every individual in the shortest possible time in accordance with the maximum of available resources'.[48]

States are required constantly to monitor housing policies and assess their compatibility with the progressive realisation of the right to adequate housing. When a policy proves detrimental to the enjoyment of the right to adequate housing (for example, when housing policies lead to land speculation, increase of homelessness, discrimination or affordability crises),[49] States should adjust and rectify their policies and programmes accordingly.[50]

How do prevalent housing finance policies assist States in meeting these basic human rights obligations, particularly in the contemporary crisis context? This is the question we aim to address in this chapter. Although most countries apply a myriad of housing finance policies and programmes, we decided to focus this chapter on three policies that have been implemented most prevalently as a means of facilitating access for the poorest and most disadvantaged to housing finance for homeownership: (1) the increase in the scale of mortgage lending for low-income borrowers; (2) the provision of capital subsidies to low-income groups as a means of supporting entry of households into housing credit markets; and (3) micro-finance for housing construction or improvements. These policies have both influenced and been affected by the recent financial and economic crises in various ways that will be further discussed below.

(7 June 2004) UN Doc. E/C.12/1/Add.96, para. 47; CESCR 'Concluding Observations on Kenya' (1 December 2008) UN Doc. E/C.12/KEN/CO/1, para. 30; CESCR 'Concluding Observations on the United Kingdom of Great Britain and Northern Ireland (12 June 2009) UN Doc. E/C.12/GBR/CO/5, para. 29; CESCR 'Concluding Observations on France' (9 June 2008) UN Doc. E/C.12/FRA/CO/3, para. 44.

[46] CESCR 'Concluding Observations on Cyprus' (12 June 2009) UN Doc. E/C.12/CYP/CO/5, para. 21; CESCR 'Concluding Observations on Nicaragua' (28 November 2008) UN Doc. E/C.12/NIC/CO/4, paras. 24–5.

[47] See CESCR 'Concluding Observations on Cyprus', para. 21; CESCR 'Concluding Observations on Nicaragua', paras. 24–5.

[48] CESCR 'General Comment No. 4', para. 14.

[49] See CESCR 'Concluding Observations on Argentina' (14 December 2011) UN Doc. E/C.12/ARG/CO/3.

[50] CESCR 'General Comment No. 4', para. 11.

IV. Prevalent housing finance policies and their impact on the right to adequate housing of people living in poverty

A. *Mortgage markets*

In recent years market-based housing finance has spread throughout the world at an unprecedented rate. In the United States, European countries, Australia and Japan, residential mortgage markets represent between 50 and 100 per cent of gross domestic product (GDP).[51] Several countries experienced strong growth in mortgage debt in the last decade before the sub-prime mortgage crisis, including Australia, Ireland, Spain, Sweden and the United States.[52] By 2009, the ratio of mortgage debt to GDP had reached more than 100 per cent in Denmark and the Netherlands.[53] Mortgage markets have also been developing in emerging markets.[54] For example, the Chinese mortgage market, which started only in the early 1990s, has been growing at more than 40 per cent annually since 2000, reaching 11 per cent of GDP in less than ten years[55] to become the largest mortgage market in Asia. Similarly, the Indian market has been growing at 30 per cent per year.[56]

However, mortgage lending remains low throughout most transition economies and developing countries, despite intensive efforts to develop mortgage-based finance systems.[57] In 2010, only 5 per cent of the population of Eastern Europe reported having a mortgage,[58] and mortgage lending is negligible (less than 5 per cent) in most of sub-Saharan Africa.[59]

[51] International Monetary Fund (IMF), *Global Financial Stability Report: Durable Financial Stability: Getting There from Here* (Washington, DC: IMF, 2011), pp. 133–4.
[52] *Ibid.* [53] *Ibid.*
[54] H. Zhu, 'The Structure of Housing Finance Markets and House Prices in Asia', *BIS Quarterly Review* (2006), 55–69.
[55] Stephens, 'Locating Chinese Urban Housing Policy', 2975.
[56] Chiquier and Lea (eds.), *Housing Finance Policy in Emerging Markets*, p. xxxi.
[57] Although some transition countries such as Hungary, the Baltic countries and Kazakhstan have seen growth of more than 20 per cent per year. IMF, *Global Financial Stability Report*, p. 134.
[58] This compared with 26 per cent in five Western European comparator countries (Sweden, Germany, Italy, France and the UK). European Bank for Reconstruction and Development (EBRD), *Transition Report 2011: Crisis and Transition: The People's Perspective* (London: EBRD, 2011), p. 56.
[59] The main exceptions being: South Africa, where mortgage debt accounts for just over 40 per cent of GDP, and Namibia, with about 20 per cent, UN-Habitat, *Quick Guide to Policy Makers, Quick Guide 5 – Housing Finance: Ways to Help the Poor Pay for Housing* (Nairobi: UN-Habitat, 2011), pp. 23–5.

Market-based housing finance inevitably targets the more affluent segments of society, which have the necessary capital to take on the initial housing loan and generate profit to lenders through the payment of interest.[60] Mortgage finance has been traditionally considered unattainable for the poor owing to issues such as lack of legally recognised titles, informal and illegal settlements, restrictive zoning and occupancy regulations, low and erratic income and large-scale employment in the informal sector.[61] Banks traditionally focus their marketing on the upper-income groups, tending to adopt an over-collateralised approach to lending (multiple guarantors, low loan-to-value ratio, etc.), which inherently excludes low-income groups.[62] Mortgage markets, therefore, in effect discriminate against low-income borrowers.[63] Research commissioned by the FinMark Trust in 12 countries across Africa found that less than 10 per cent of local populations are eligible for mortgage finance. In Eastern European countries in transition, recent estimates by UN-Habitat indicate that rapid house price increases coupled with high unemployment and higher interest rates on mortgages have excluded more than 80 per cent of new households from the new housing construction market.[64]

With the growing understanding that mortgage finance remains unaffordable for the lower- (and often middle-) income groups in both developed and developing countries, during the past two decades new 'creative' mortgage products have been designed specifically for borrowers with low income and/or a poor credit history, who would not be eligible for regular mortgage finance. The development of this new mortgage finance 'market segment' increased enormously during the 1990s and even more so during the 2000s.[65]

Credit began to be increasingly awarded to households that, in normal circumstances, would not be eligible for loans, generating what is known as 'sub-prime' loans. Although these lending policies were intended to enable access to housing finance for low-income households previously

[60] R. M. Buckley and J. Kalarickal (eds.), *Thirty Years of World Bank Shelter Lending: What Have We Learned?* (Washington, DC: World Bank, 2006), pp. 70–1.

[61] Chiquier and Lea (eds.), *Housing Finance Policy in Emerging Markets*, p. xxxvi.

[62] Council of Europe Development Bank, *Trends and Progress in Housing Reforms in South Eastern Europe (2005)*, pp. 113, 122–3. In in the former Yugoslav republic of Macedonia only 3 per cent of the households were able to borrow in 2005.

[63] S. Leckie, 'Regional Housing Issues Profile, Implementing Housing Rights in South East Europe' (UN-HABITAT Paper presented to the Regional Consultation on Making Cities Inclusive, Belgrade, 2002), 7; UN ECE, *Housing Finance Systems*, p. 9.

[64] UN-Habitat, *Affordable Land and Housing in Europe and North America*, p. 48.

[65] Buckley and Kalarickal (eds.), *Thirty Years of World Bank Shelter Lending*, pp. 39–47.

excluded from the mortgage markets, in practice they are still unaffordable and strongly discriminatory with respect to the poor. Mortgage lenders classify loan applicants according to the risks that they pose to both lenders and investors. Credit scoring facilitates risk-based pricing by allowing lenders to charge higher interest rates for borrowers with low scores (high risks) and lower interest rates for borrowers with high scores (low risks). Lenders became more willing to issue credit at a relatively high price to higher-risk borrowers.[66] Because of their weaker credit profile, low-income clients were charged higher interest rates. For instance, in the United States, a typical sub-prime borrower would pay $5,222 more during the first four years of a $166,000 mortgage than would a similar borrower with a normal mortgage.[67]

Predatory lending has also impacted disproportionally on the most vulnerable. Predatory lending is a form of price discrimination that targets the same groups that were once excluded from mortgage markets. However, the loans offered to these groups are more expensive than their risk profile would warrant, the mortgage insurance is overpriced, and abusive or unnecessary provisions are added to the loan agreements, including balloon payments, large prepayment penalties and underwriting that ignores a borrower's ability to repay.[68]

Once overtly excluded from accessing mortgage loans, from the 1990s on the poor became the target of these more subtle, discriminatory mechanisms. High-interest loans led to ever-increasing household indebtedness and economic insecurity and poor households were forced to reduce expenditure on other basic needs in order to meet their housing debt.[69]

The adverse effects of housing credit growth on affordability have also been visible at the macroeconomic scale. Wider access to mortgage loans resulted in higher house prices. In Spain, between 1995 and 2005 housing prices rose 105 per cent, a result of cheap debt and access to global capital for credit.[70] A 2011 IMF analysis confirms the strong positive relationship between house price movements and household credit growth;[71] on

[66] Aalbers, 'The Financialization of Home', 155–9.

[67] Rolnik, 'Report on the Financial Crisis and Its Causes'. For more on the US experience, see Hershkoff and Loffredo's contribution to this volume.

[68] Aalbers, 'The Financialization of Home', 159.

[69] Chiquier and Lea (eds.), *Housing Finance Policy in Emerging Markets*, p. 133; Forrest, 'Globalization and Housing Asset Rich', 168–9.

[70] M. Kothari, 'Report of the Special Rapporteur on Adequate Housing as a Component of the Right to an Adequate Standard of Living: Mission to Spain' (7 February 2008) UN Doc. A/HRC/7/16/Add.2, para. 44.

[71] IMF, *Global Financial Stability Report*, p. 134.

average, a 10 per cent increase in household credit is associated with an increase in housing prices of about 6 per cent.[72]

Increasing dependence on mortgage credit and the growing interconnection between housing financial markets to global capital markets have overexposed national housing systems to the turbulence of global finance, raising levels of debt and concentrating risks among individual households. Countries that adopted a strongly open system of mortgages – based on sub-prime loans, easily granted credit and the financialisation of mortgages – have seen a serious crisis since 2008, when the US sub-prime mortgage crisis and the subsequent financial crisis spread internationally.[73]

The discrepancy between income levels and soaring housing and rental prices coupled with unemployment led to increased payment default, foreclosures and homelessness. These processes were exacerbated by the adoption of legal and institutional adjustments aimed at facilitating foreclosure, which have been promoted in recent years as 'imperatives for developing a housing finance system'.[74] The paradigm that promoted homeownership as the most secure form of tenure has been proven false, as increasing foreclosure rates have been one of the main results of the recent crises.[75] In Spain, more than 350,000 foreclosures have occurred since 2007 and in 2011, about 212 foreclosures and 159 evictions occurred daily.[76] The sub-prime and financial crises have disproportionately affected the poorest and most vulnerable, who were the last to join the mortgage markets and the first to suffer the consequences of the crises owing to their low resilience to economic shocks and low repayment abilities.[77] Recent research indicates that the majority (70 per cent) of defaults

[72] *Ibid.*

[73] See reports of the Special Rapporteur on the Right to Adequate Housing (A/HRC/7/16/Add.2, A/HRC/10/7, A/HRC/13/20/Add.4 and A/HRC/16/42/Add.3), analysing the impact of mortgage market liberalisation and the sub-prime mortgage system on the economic and financial crises.

[74] Chiquier and Lea (eds.), *Housing Finance Policy in Emerging Markets*, pp. 94–5.

[75] According to the RealtyTrac, a company that maintains a database of foreclosures, in the third quarter of 2009 foreclosures were filed for 1 in every 136 housing units in the United States. See RealtyTrac, National Real Estate Trends & Market Info, www.realtytrac.com/foreclosure/foreclosure-rates.html, last accessed 10 October 2013.

[76] A. Colau and A. Alemany, *Vidas Hipotecadas* (Barcelona: Angle Editoriál-Cuadrilátero Libros, 2012), pp. 21–2.

[77] See, e.g., CESCR 'Concluding Observations on Spain' (6 June 2012) UN Doc. E/C.12/ESP/CO/5, para. 21; Amnesty International, 'Spain: Submission to the UN Committee on Economic, Social and Cultural Rights, 48th session, May 2012' (AI index EUR 41/005/2012, 2012).

in Spain are related to the unemployment crisis and that 35 per cent of the foreclosed properties belong to migrants.[78]

The effect of the sub-prime and subsequent financial crises has been less detrimental for emerging economies where, owing to their structure and performance, mortgage markets remain smaller, more conservative and less connected to capital market flows. Emerging mortgage markets that have made heaviest use of global securitisation (e.g. the Russian Federation, Kazakhstan and the Republic of Korea) were most affected.[79] In 2010, more than 40,000 borrowers in Kazakhstan were waiting for their apartments to be finished while construction companies went bankrupt.[80]

In Eastern Europe an aggravating factor has been the high rate of foreign currency denomination loans in some of the countries in the region. In 2010, 42 per cent of mortgages in emerging Europe were denominated in a foreign currency.[81] For example, by the time the financial crisis hit, some two-thirds of all mortgage loans in Hungary were in Swiss francs. With the onset of the crises, the value of the franc escalated against the Eastern European currencies. Homeowners suddenly found their repayments skyrocketing and in some cases saw the amount of their loans outstrip the value of their houses.[82] Research indicates that mortgage debtors were hit harder by the economic crisis than households without a mortgage in Eastern Europe.[83]

The onset of the housing and the subsequent global financial and economic crises have yet not resulted in a paradigm shift. Government responses to the crisis have concentrated on: (1) adjusting demand-side policies, tightening mortgage market conditions and adopting regulations (in Norway, Sweden, Israel, Canada and the Netherlands); (2) abolishing interest tax deductions (in Poland, Spain and China); and (3) introducing demand-side subsidies to assist mortgage lenders and prevent arrears (in

[78] Colau and Alemany, *Vidas Hipotecadas*, pp. 30, 237.

[79] Chiquier and Lea (eds.), *Housing Finance Policy in Emerging Markets*, p. xxxvii.

[80] R. Rolnik, 'Report of the Special Rapporteur on Adequate Housing as a Component of the Right to an Adequate Standard of Living, and on the Right to Non-Discrimination in this Context: Mission to Kazakhstan' (19 January 2011) UN Doc. A/HRC/16/42/Add.3.

[81] EBRD, *Transition Report 2011*, p. 56.

[82] A. Lovasz and E. Balazs, 'Hungary's Battered Banks Brace for Latest Bad-Debt Cure, Bloomberg News' (10 September 2013), www.bloomberg.com/news/2013-09-09/hungary-s-latest-toxic-debt-plan-rattling-banks-voters.html, last accessed 19 January 2014.

[83] EBRD, *Transition Report 2011*, pp. 55–6.

Spain and Chile).[84] Governments have introduced regulations for responsible lending and financial institutions have tightened their mortgage conditions, again placing mortgage finance out of reach for low-income groups.[85] Following the sub-prime crisis, the supply of housing and household mobility have been significantly curtailed by a shortage of long-term credit for real estate development on the supply side (in both the rental and ownership sectors) as well as by increased rationing of mortgages on the demand side. The housing and financial crises have not led to a shift to supply-side non-market housing policies, and social housing investment remains low in most countries.[86] Recovery measures based on austerity (i.e. cuts in public spending) led in some instances to additional curtailment of social housing programmes, as was the case of the OEK (Workers' Housing Organization) scheme in Greece,[87] while huge public resources were allocated to 'bail-outs' of financial institutions. This has resulted in increased homelessness, indebtedness of families and worsening housing conditions, as we are currently witnessing, for example, in Spain, Ireland and Greece.

B. *Demand subsidies*

A major component of the shift from supply-side to demand-side housing policies has been the promotion of demand subsidies as a means of enlarging the market for privately produced residential units, mobilising public resources and directing them to potential buyers with the idea of reducing government intervention. The rationale behind demand-subsidy programmes is that low-income households will be able to finance their housing through the free market, with their own savings, assisted by a down-payment subsidy or a subsidised loan provided by the state. The main types of household demand subsidies used are: (a) direct payments, either up front (to lower the amount of the loan, the closing costs, the down payment or the insurance premium, or in the form of a capital grant) or on a monthly basis; (b) subsidies tied to savings programmes;

[84] IMF, *Global Financial Stability Report*, pp. 115–16.

[85] In September 2011 the Bank of Lithuania adopted regulations which limit the loan-to-value ratio to 85 per cent. EBRD, *Transition Report 2011*. Also – in the case of Hungary – see J. Hegedüs, M. Lux and P. Sunega, 'Decline and Depression: The Impact of the Global Economic Crisis on Housing Markets in Two Post-Socialist States', *Journal of Housing and the Built Environment*, 26 (2011), 315–33, 327.

[86] IMF, *Global Financial Stability Report*, pp. 115–16.

[87] Reply of Greece to the questionnaire.

(c) interest-rate or interest-payment subsidies; or (d) tax subsidies tied to mortgage payments or real estate taxation.[88]

Most countries employ a combination of these demand subsidies. However, capital-grant subsidies have been popular mainly in Latin America and are relatively rare in developed economies.[89] In Europe, the United States, Canada and Australia, demand subsidy programmes have largely taken the form of tax exemptions, interest rate subsidies or bonuses through savings accounts.[90] Mortgage interest tax relief existed at some point, for example, in Ireland, the Netherlands, Germany, the United States, the United Kingdom, China, Slovakia, Hungary, the Russian Federation, Croatia and the Czech Republic.[91] France promotes a mixture of subsidies, including subsidised savings schemes for newly built and renovated properties and a means-tested interest-free loan granted to first-time buyers.[92]

One of the most common housing subsidies in European countries (influenced by the German and French model) has been the contract-savings scheme. Savers who fulfil their contracts are eligible for mortgage loans at an interest rate that is below the market rate. Since the saving capacity of low-income groups is very limited, they are generally prevented from enjoying the advantages of this model.[93] The favourable tax treatment of households that are related to homeownership (which may take the form of tax relief or tax credit for the mortgage repayment, tax advantages related to capital gains for owner-occupiers and reduced property tax or imputed tax) are also used in developed countries, emerging markets and countries in transition and favour those better-off households that can afford a mortgage loan.[94] Mortgage interest rate subsidies that reduce the interest paid

[88] See R. Rolnik, 'Report of the Special Rapporteur on Adequate Housing as a Component of the Right to an Adequate Standard of Living and on the Right to Non-discrimination in this Context' (10 August 2012) UN Doc. A/67/286. There is a critical distinction between subsidies that work through the financial system and those that do not, e.g. the construction and operation of rental housing or the payment of housing allowances to help renters meet their rent. This section focuses on demand subsidies aimed at increasing homeownership through the financial market. UN-Habitat, *Guide to Preparing a Housing Finance Strategy* (Nairobi: UN-Habitat, 2009), p. 45.

[89] Council of Europe, *Housing Policy and Vulnerable Social Groups* (Strasbourg: Council of Europe, 2008), p. 31.

[90] H. M. Katsura and C. T. Romanik, 'Ensuring Access to Essential Services: Demand Side Housing Subsidies' (World Bank Social Protection Discussion Paper Series No. 0232, December 2002), 6; replies of Canada and Australia to the questionnaire.

[91] UN-Habitat, *Financing Urban Shelter*, p. 63.

[92] Reply of France to the questionnaire.

[93] Chiquier and Lea (eds.), *Housing Finance Policy in Emerging Markets*, p. 35.

[94] Council of Europe, *Housing Policy and Vulnerable Social Groups*, p. 38.

by the borrower have been implemented in Denmark, the United States, Norway, Greece, Mexico, Portugal, Croatia and Indonesia.[95]

Demand subsidies linked to mortgage finance or savings usually do not target the poor and in effect benefit the better-off (middle- and even upper-middle-income households). Income tax deductions of interest payments or a broad-based interest rate subsidy for mortgage loans tend to be regressive, as they increase with the amount of the loan and benefit those who can afford larger loans more than those with smaller loans.[96] In the Philippines, interest rate subsidies account for 90 per cent of the value of housing subsidies; however, 77 per cent of the country's population cannot afford a formal-sector loan even at subsidised interest rates.[97] Part of these subsidies may also leak out to benefit others in the housing systems and raise the value of existing dwellings and land.[98]

Although the rationale for the implementation of subsidised mortgage markets is supposedly to reduce state intervention in the housing sector, support for savings banks, interest rate subsidies and tax allowances mobilise a large amount of public money. The government implementing these policies is committed to long-term subsidy payments, which are hard to control during the contract period. For example, in Spain and Hungary, tax-exemption schemes were recently cancelled owing to serious fiscal problems.[99]

A State's sole reliance on mortgage subsidies may be considered incompatible with its obligation to employ the maximum available resources to promote the right to adequate housing without discrimination. This is particularly the case where States devote the majority of their budgets to these policies while at the same time dismantling or failing to promote social housing programmes or other alternatives that specifically target the poor. A stark example of this is Spain where governmental housing policy focused for more than two decades, up to 2008, on mortgage

[95] N. C. Martins and E. Villanueva, 'The Impact of Interest-Rate Subsidies on Long-Term Household Debt: Evidence from a Large Program' (October 2003), http://repositori.upf.edu/bitstream/handle/10230/510/713.pdf?sequence=1, last accessed 10 October 2013. Also replies of Croatia, Indonesia, Mexico and Portugal to the questionnaire.

[96] A. Ridenour, L. Weld and E. J. Raymond, 'The Mortgage Interest Deduction: The Regressive Tax Benefit', *Journal of Business, Society and Government*, 4 (2012), 16–28.

[97] UN-Habitat, *The Role of Government in the Housing Market: The Experiences from Asia* (Nairobi: UN-Habitat, 2008), pp. 39–40.

[98] J. Pollard, 'Soutenir le marché: les nouveaux instruments de la politique du logement', *Sociologie du travail*, 52 (2010), 323–39, 333.

[99] Hegedüs, Lux and Sunega, 'Decline and Depression', 321.

subsidies while neglecting assistance to social rental housing.[100] This resulted in a huge burden being placed on the state budget, while assisting only a limited number of beneficiaries from higher income brackets.

Capital-grant subsidies have been promoted to particularly target low-income households and therefore warrant further analysis. The capital-grant subsidy approach has been promoted to target low-income households in particular and the Chilean experience has been considered the model that inspired other countries.[101] The model emphasises: (a) the shift of responsibility for housing provision from the State to the private sector; (b) provision of one-time grants for home purchase while curtailing all indirect subsidies; and (c) transparent qualifying mechanisms based on household income and a savings contribution. Programmes aim to increase housing affordability by offering a cash subsidy to cover part of the purchase price of a formally constructed dwelling offered for sale in the market by private companies. Subsidies may be combined with mortgage or micro-finance loans and/or household savings. Capital grants are perceived to encourage the integration of lower-income households into conventional housing markets, leading to financial market expansion.[102]

The Chilean model has been praised as a best practice for its transparency, the scale of its shift of housing provision to private market providers (which were seen as more efficient and effective than the State in addressing the diversity of housing demand) and its targeting of the poor.[103] The model has been widely replicated in Latin America (Brazil, Colombia, Costa Rica, Ecuador, El Salvador, Guatemala, Mexico, Panama, Peru and Venezuela).[104] Outside Latin America, the capital-

[100] See J. Hoelkstra, I. H. Saizarbitoria and A. E. Etxarri, 'Recent Changes in Spanish Housing Policies: Subsidized Owner-Occupancy Dwellings as a New Tenure Sector?', *Journal of Housing and the Built Environment*, 25 (2010), 125–38, 130.

[101] A. Gilbert, 'Power, Ideology and the Washington Consensus: The Development and Spread of Chilean Housing Policy', *Housing Studies*, 17(2) (2002), 305–24.

[102] D. Mitlin, 'New Directions in Housing Policy' in A. M. Garland, M. Massoumi and B. A. Ruble (eds.), *Global Urban Poverty: Setting the Agenda* (Washington, DC: Woodrow Wilson International Center for Scholars, 2007), pp. 151–79, 163.

[103] UN-Habitat, *Affordable Land and Housing in Latin America and the Caribbean* (Nairobi: UN-Habitat, 2011), p. 57.

[104] See, e.g., replies of El Salvador, Guatemala, Mexico and Venezuela to the questionnaire. Some 20 per cent of the Inter-American Development Bank lending for shelter has been allocated to capital-subsidy programmes. Inter-American Development Bank, 'Sharpening the Bank's Capacity to Support the Housing Sector in Latin America and the Caribbean: Background Paper for the Implementation of the Social Development Strategy' (Inter-American Development Bank Sustainable Development Department Technical Papers Series No. SOC-142, February 2006), Foreword.

grant approach has been implemented on a large scale in South Africa since 1994.[105]

However, in the absence of land management policies, a large amount of subsidies available in the housing market has led to significant increases in land and housing prices, a general problem of affordability for low-income households and long waiting lists. The combination of land shortages and irregular budgetary expenditure, high housing deficits and fast population growth (characteristics of most developing countries which implemented capital subsides) has led to limited coverage of subsidies programmes in the face of growing demand.[106] In South Africa, although the government has delivered more than 3 million fully subsidised housing units over the past 17 years, the country is still experiencing a backlog of over 2 million houses.[107]

Problems also soon emerged with regard to the location of these programmes (location constituting another key element of the right to adequate housing). In Chile, planning regulations were loosened and city limits expanded on the premise that a freely operating land market would automatically contribute to providing access to adequate housing through the market.[108] Unlike in the case of housing markets for higher-income families, in which suppliers have to be sensitive to demand requirements and therefore to the trilogy of product–price–location as they operate in a competitive context, operators that supply social housing have a captive demand, particularly when it is fully subsidised.[109] In a context of housing deficit, beneficiaries of housing subsidies will simply 'buy' what is available for them at the moment, because they do not have any other options. Suppliers of social housing can therefore be insensitive to, or simply ignore, demand preferences, as there is no competition.[110]

It is thus not surprising that subsidised housing developments have been built primarily in the urban periphery where land costs are lowest. In Chile, the majority of housing built through the subsidy scheme between 1978 and 2000 has been concentrated in peripheral locations, lacking sufficient or adequate infrastructure, schools, health facilities and employment opportunities. Poor public transport and road quality

[105] South Africa Financial and Fiscal Commission, 'Building an Inclusionary Housing Market: Shifting the Paradigm for Housing Delivery in South Africa' (January 2012).

[106] In Chile, in 1998 the estimated waiting time for a housing subsidy was over 20 years. UN-Habitat, *Affordable Land and Housing in Latin America and the Caribbean*, p. 55.

[107] South Africa Financial and Fiscal Commission, 'Building an Inclusionary Housing Market', 6.

[108] Pablo Trivelli and Company, Ltd., 'Urban Structure, Land Markets and Social Housing in Santiago, Chile' (January 2010), 18.

[109] *Ibid.* [110] *Ibid.*

further impairs residents' ability to access services and employment.[111] Subsidy programmes in South Africa, Mexico and Brazil have also been criticised for replacing widespread informal housing with low-standard and stigmatised market-based housing typologies concentrating on low-income families.[112] The result is greater urban and social segregation, an increase in the disparity in access to urban services, a worsening of local living conditions, increased environmental damage and urban security problems.

The housing habitability aspect has also been neglected in these programmes. The homes that have been produced have often been not only poorly located, but also very small or of very poor quality and with restricted chances of upgrading.[113] Some countries have attempted to regulate the quality standards, but this has often resulted in a substantive increase in administrative costs owing to the institutional capacity required for monitoring, and an increased backlog in housing delivery.[114]

Originally designed to target the poorest and most disadvantaged, capital-grant programmes have had difficulties reaching low-income households, mainly owing to the inability of low-income families to assemble significant down payments or to meet the monthly payments of market-rate loans.[115] In some cases, the subsidy was set so low as to prevent, a priori, the possibility of purchasing a housing unit without additional

[111] *Ibid.* See also A. Rodríguez and A. Sugranyes, 'El problema de vivienda de los "con techo"' in A. Rodríguez and A. Sugranyes (eds.), *Los Con Techo: Un Desafío para la Política de Vivienda Social* (Santiago: Ediciones SUR, 2005), pp. 53–65, p. 61.

[112] See, e.g., M. d. A. B. Fix, 'Financeirização e transformações recentes do circuito imobiliário no Brasil' (Doctoral thesis presented at the Instituto de Economia da UNICAMP, Campinas, Brazil, 2011); UN-Habitat, *Housing Finance Mechanisms in Mexico* (Nairobi: UN-Habitat, 2011); F. Jiménez-Cavieres, 'Chilean Housing Policy: A Case of Social and Spatial Exclusion?' (Doctoral dissertation, Technical University of Berlin, 2006).

[113] For example, the basic state house in Santiago in 1990 was only 33–4 m^2 in size. While the average size rose during the 1990s, in 1998 each family had only 9.3 m^2 per occupant. In South Africa, the average floor space was initially only 25 m^2 and the houses had no partitions. A. G. Gilbert, 'Free Housing for the Poor: An effective way to address poverty?', *Habitat International*, 41 (2014), 253–261, 258.

[114] Reply by the Centre for Affordable Housing Finance in Africa to the questionnaire. Habitability, location and accessibility problems have led South Africa to alter its subsidy programme and increase government intervention. Under the Breaking New Ground subsidy implemented beginning in 2004, supply-side components were included in an attempt to mitigate the adverse impact on subsidy housing habitability and location that unfolded during the first stage; in 2005 the government announced that land would be funded outside the housing subsidy amount, and then in 2007 that services would also be additional, funded directly by municipalities. In addition, a savings component was added to the subsidy and the qualifying borrower was required to make a contribution or deposit.

[115] UN-Habitat, *Financing Urban Shelter*, p. 60.

substantial credit or savings.[116] Even when able to meet the credit or savings requirement, many of the new owners could not afford to maintain the accommodation or pay the charges for their water and electricity, and were forced to sell their homes.[117]

Capital grants can use means testing to determine eligibility; however, targeting mechanisms have proven very complex and costly, as they require accurate and updated information on income and household consumption, which is often in poor supply in developing countries owing to, inter alia, high levels of informal employment.[118] Some countries rely on proxy measures of income to determine eligibility and benefit levels, such as the ownership of a car or the volume of electricity consumed by a household.[119] However, even the best proxy systems can suffer from substantial exclusion and inclusion errors.[120]

Attempting to complement resources, some States have promoted the involvement of both private banks and non-governmental organisations (NGOs) in supplying low-income households with micro-credit, in addition to state subsidies. These programmes act as institutional and financial intermediaries between the poor and the State, enabling the poor to 'bridge the finance gap' in order to be eligible for the subsidy. However, research indicates that the combination of housing micro-finance and subsidies has not been successful. Problems emerge, particularly in instances where the same micro-finance institution manages both the need-based subsidy and the demand-driven loan, as the amount of the subsidy is inversely related to the amount of the credit.[121]

In some cases, administrative barriers or strict eligibility requirements prevent low-income households from benefitting from subsidies. Enrolment remains low when people find it difficult to travel to apply to the programme because of time constraints, transportation expenses or disabilities.[122] Having to produce expensive documentation of their eligibility for the programme, such as birth certificates or proof of residency, also increases their transaction costs, and thus restricts enrolment.[123]

[116] A mandatory savings component limited the reach of Ecuador's subsidy, which required a contribution of about 30 per cent, between savings and fees, from the household. UN-Habitat, *Affordable Land and Housing in Latin America and the Caribbean*, p. 55.

[117] Gilbert, 'Power, Ideology and the Washington Consensus', 321–2.

[118] Buckley and Kalarickal (eds.), *Thirty Years of World Bank Shelter Lending*, p. 55; Council of Europe, *Housing Policy and Vulnerable Social Groups*, p. 50.

[119] *Ibid.* [120] *Ibid.*

[121] For more on these points, see Chiquier and Lea (eds.), *Housing Finance Policy in Emerging Markets*, pp. 405–6; UN-Habitat, *Financing Urban Shelter*, p. 95.

[122] See Katsura and Romanik, 'Ensuring Access to Essential Service', 10.

[123] *Ibid.*

Inefficient land registration systems in many developing countries have sometimes created severe backlogs in title registration, circumventing the security of tenure of subsidy beneficiaries.[124]

Despite substantial government budgetary investment and specific targeting of low-income households, capital-grant subsidies have partially promoted only the affordability aspect of the right to adequate housing (by substantially reducing housing deficits in some developing countries), at the expense of the broader aspects of habitability, location, availability of services and infrastructure and non-discrimination, which have been largely ignored. As one commentator observed, the new stock of subsidised housing often created a greater housing problem: 'the problem of those "with roofs"'.[125]

C. *Housing micro-finance*

In 2005 over one-third (37 per cent) of the urban population in developing countries lived in slums, and UN-Habitat estimates that by 2020 the world slum population will reach almost 1 billion.[126] The majority of the urban poor live in unplanned and unserviced urban settlements and self-produce their habitat incrementally, mobilising their own material and financial resources.[127]

Until the 1980s, slum dwellers and the urban poor had not been a market for financial services.[128] As previously mentioned, the reasons for this were: the inability of low- and even middle-income households to afford housing finance debt; the incompatibility of formal finance loan requirements (such as complex collateral and extended repayment capabilities) with the characteristics of low-income households (low level and irregularity of income and lack of security of tenure); and the fact that financial institutions perceived few incentives to lend to the poor, who usually 'consume' small loan amounts and entail high transaction costs. As a result, low- and even middle-income households adopted 'informal'

124 See South Africa Financial and Fiscal Commission, 'Building an Inclusionary Housing Market', 7, 15, 23.

125 See A. Rodríguez and A. Sugranyes, 'Introducion', in A. Rodríguez and A. Sugranyes (eds.), *Los Con Techo: Un Desafio para la Política de Vivienda Social* (Santiago: Ediciones SUR, 2005), pp. 13–20, p. 15.

126 UN-Habitat, *State of the World's Cities 2010/2011: Cities for All: Bridging the Urban Divide* (Nairobi: UN-Habitat, 2010), p. xii.

127 S. A. Sheuya, 'Reconceptualizing Housing Finance in Informal Settlements: The Case of Dar es Salaam', *Environment and Urbanization*, 19 (2007), 441–56.

128 UN-Habitat, *Financing Urban Shelter*, p. xxiv.

housing finance strategies based on individual savings, family loans and remittances, or moneylenders or pawnbrokers.[129]

However, in the 1980s a new finance paradigm emerged, one that appeared to be able to address poverty through the expansion of small, informal-sector income-generating credit: micro-finance. Private financial investors became convinced of the profitability of micro-finance and came to regard the poor as 'bankable'.[130] The result has been a dramatic rise in the flow of private investment capital (supported by donors, multilateral banks and international organisations) into the micro-finance sector and, more recently, into housing finance services adapted to support incremental building processes.[131] The growing commercial presence of major Western banking groups in developing countries and their interest in micro-finance (including for housing) has been based on the idea that the 'bottom of the pyramid' represents a large untapped market.[132]

In the past 10 years,[133] a growing number of housing micro-finance programmes have been initiated, offering loans to homeowners ranging from $300 to $5,000, frequently with repeating lending opportunities and repayment terms of 1–15 years.[134] In comparison with enterprise micro-finance, housing micro-finance loans are generally larger and given for longer periods. Housing micro-finance loans are also much smaller than mortgage loans, typically granted for shorter terms, and their target population is that not served by formal private or public financial institutions.[135] Owing to their limited scope, housing micro-finance loans are used mainly to finance improvements to housing (e.g. building sanitary

129 UN-Habitat, *Housing for All: The Challenges of Affordability, Accessibility and Sustainability: The Experiences and Instruments from the Developing and Developed Worlds* (Nairobi: UN-Habitat, 2008), p. 11; UN-Habitat, *Financing Urban Shelter*, pp. 99–100.

130 D. Johnston and J. Morduch, 'The Unbanked: Evidence from Indonesia', *The World Bank Economic Review*, 22(3) (2008), 517–37.

131 See, e.g., the UN-Habitat Slum Upgrading Facility and the Shelter Finance for the Poor Initiative of Cities Alliance; B. Ferguson and P. Smets, 'Finance for Incremental Housing; Current Status and Prospects for Expansion', *Habitat International*, 34 (2010), 288–98, 288–9; Chiquier and Lea (eds.), *Housing Finance Policy in Emerging Markets*, p. 395.

132 C. K. Prahalad and S. L. Hart, 'The Fortune at the Bottom of the Pyramid', *Strategy and Business*, 26 (2002), 1–14.

133 Although micro-finance institutions such as Grameen Bank have had housing loan programmes since the 1980s, housing micro-finance only began to attract significant attention in the last 10 years.

134 Some housing micro-finance institutions offer loans up to $8,000. UN-Habitat, *Housing for All*, p. 18.

135 Center for Urban Development Studies, Harvard University Graduate School of Design, 'Housing Micro-finance Initiatives: Synthesis and Regional Summary: Asia, Latin America and Sub-Saharan Africa with Selected Case Studies' (May 2000).

amenities) and expansions to an existing dwelling, or for the incremental construction of a home.[136]

Housing micro-finance is offered by a wide variety of institutions including: micro-finance agencies, such as Grameen Bank and affiliates of the Accion organisation; banks and commercial institutions, such as HDFC Bank in India and the CEMEX company in Mexico (the Patrimonio Hoy programme); and intergovernmental organisations and NGOs specialising in shelter provision, such as the Rural Housing Loan Fund in South Africa and Habitat for Humanity.[137] A distinction can be made between financial institutions offering micro-enterprise loans and institutions whose main purpose is improving the shelter situation of the poor, which may or may not be financial institutions.[138]

As is the case with micro-finance agencies, most housing micro-finance initiatives originate in developing countries and emerging markets. Latin America has the largest housing micro-finance portfolio.[139] Housing micro-finance is also growing in Asia and, to a lesser extent, in Africa.[140] Examples of lenders include the Kuyasa Fund (South Africa), the Jamii Bora Trust (Kenya), KixiCasa (Angola), PRIDE (United Republic of Tanzania), BRI (Indonesia) and CARD (Philippines).[141] The size of some housing micro-finance programmes may be considerable; Grameen Bank, for example, has provided more than 650,000 housing loans.[142] However, housing micro-finance portfolios worldwide remain very small relative

[136] Chiquier and Lea (eds.), *Housing Finance Policy in Emerging Markets*, p. 399; B. Ferguson, 'Housing Micro-finance: A Key to Improving Habitat and the Sustainability of Micro-Finance Institutions', *Small Enterprise Development*, 14 (2003), 21–31.

[137] UN-Habitat, *Financing Urban Shelter*, pp. 106–12; D. Porteous, 'Housing Finance and Financial Inclusion' in D. Köhn and J. D. von Pischke (eds.), *Housing Finance in Emerging Markets: Connecting Low-Income Groups to Markets* (Berlin: Springer, 2011), pp. 7–48, pp. 33–5.

[138] UN-Habitat, *Housing for All*, pp. 12–13; UN-Habitat, *Financing Urban Shelter*, pp. 103–4.

[139] These include MiBanco in Peru, BancoSol in the Plurinational State of Bolivia, Banco Solidario in Ecuador, Banco Ademi in the Dominican Republic, Calpia in Honduras and Genesis Empresariál in Guatemala. UN-Habitat, *Housing for All*, p. 22; UN-Habitat, *Financing Urban Shelter*, p. 106.

[140] FinMark Trust, 'Scoping the Demand for Housing Micro-finance in Africa: Status, Opportunities and Challenges' (February 2010), 10.

[141] A. Nilsson, 'Overview of Financial Systems for Slum Upgrading and Housing', *Housing Finance International*, 23 (December 2008), 19–26, 20–1; S. Merill and N. Mesarina, 'Expanding Micro-finance for Housing', *Housing Finance International*, 21 (December 2006), 3–11, 3.

[142] See Grameen Bank, 'Past Five Years of Grameen Bank', www.grameen-info.org/index.php?option=com_content&task=view&id=1122&Itemid=973, last accessed 10 October 2013.

to GDP and the overall micro-finance activity.[143] Housing micro-finance is still heavily directed towards existing business loan clients of micro-finance institutions and, in typical micro-finance schemes, the housing portfolio share ranges between 4 per cent and 8 per cent.[144]

Housing micro-finance institutions employ diversified and more relaxed collateral strategies compared with traditional mortgage collateral, including co-signers, assignment of future income, payroll deduction, other financial assets such as life insurance, and 'social collateral' (borrowers' reputations, or the social networks to which they belong).[145] Some micro-finance agencies seek to minimise the need for collateral by using existing client history.[146] Many home micro-finance agencies, particularly in Asia and Africa, have savings requirements, which serve both as an assessment of the borrower's repayment capacity and as a means to acquire funds.[147]

Although micro-finance agencies' interest rates are typically lower than those of informal moneylenders, they are much higher than those charged by formal financial institutions and have much shorter maturities. In most cases, the interest rates range between 20 per cent and 50 per cent.[148] For example, MiBanco in Peru charges a 37 per cent annual rate[149] and Compartamosbanco in Mexico charges almost 70 per cent interest on its housing micro-finance programme.[150] The poorer the client, the more likely the housing micro-finance agency will attempt to manage default risk by reducing the time over which the client must repay the loan, increasing the interest rate and reducing the size of the loan.[151] In some cases, the

[143] Chiquier and Lea (eds.), *Housing Finance Policy in Emerging Markets*, p. 398.

[144] Bruce Ferguson, 'Housing Microfinance: Is the Glass Half Empty or Half Full?', *Global Urban Development Magazine* (November 2008), www.globalurban.org/GUDMag08Vol4Iss2/FergusonHousingMicrofinance.htm, last accessed 19 January 2014. A 2011 study of Latin America financial institutions found that portfolio allocations for housing micro-finance fall between 5 and 30 per cent of total institutional portfolios. Habitat for Humanity, 'Status Report: Housing Micro-finance in Latin America' (9 November 2011), www.habitat.org/lac_eng/pdf/Informe_Estado_MFV_en_AL_eng.pdf, last accessed 10 October 2013. See also Chiquier and Lea (eds.), *Housing Finance Policy in Emerging Markets*, p. 401.

[145] UN-Habitat, *Housing for All*, p. 20; S. R. Merrill, 'Micro-finance for Housing: Assisting the "Bottom Billion" and the "Missing Middle"' (Urban Institute Center on International Development and Governance IDG Working Paper No. 2009–05, June 2009), 4.

[146] UN-Habitat, *Enabling Shelter Strategies: Review of Experience from Two Decades of Implementation* (Nairobi: UN-Habitat, 2006), p. 91.

[147] UN-Habitat, *Financing Urban Shelter*, p. 114.

[148] UN-Habitat, *Housing for All*, p. 19.

[149] Chiquier and Lea (eds.), *Housing Finance Policy in Emerging Markets*, p. 410.

[150] See Gentera, www.compartamos.com, last accessed 10 October 2013.

[151] UN-Habitat, *Housing for All*, pp. 24–5.

small loan amount is not sufficient and needs to be supplemented by additional borrowing from external sources, which carry very high interest rates and expose the household to increased risk.[152] The use of floating rate interest also leads to increased interest over the repayment period, sometimes up to double the original rate.[153] High interest rates increase clients' indebtedness and reinforce a vicious cycle of poverty and the likelihood of default.[154] In some cases, long-held family assets (such as equipment or land) need to be sold or other income flows (remittances, pensions) to be diverted into repayment. These 'fall back' strategies account for the generally high repayment rates of housing micro-finance, but reduce household equity, economic resilience and housing affordability. As is often the case in sub-prime mortgage lending, housing micro-finance clients have been penalised for their 'low profitability' by being forced to pay higher prices for access to housing finance. Therefore, despite the fact that housing micro-finance loans are seemingly more accessible and affordable to the poor, they are, in effect, extremely discriminatory and remain highly unaffordable.

The small scale and the nature of most housing micro-finance programmes, in particular their focus on profitability, prevent them from addressing the issues of tenure security, location, infrastructure and availability of services. Whereas the provision of financial services for incremental housing construction or improvement constitutes a relatively straightforward, manageable undertaking, participation in the process of acquiring land and delivering infrastructure is legally, financially and politically complex, requiring extensive institutional and financial capacities and legal powers typically available only to national and local government agencies. The incremental approach may, in some cases, promote the habitability aspect of the right to adequate housing by assisting slum dwellers to improve existing homes, but it does little to promote other aspects of adequate housing. Housing micro-finance borrowers increase their housing expenditure substantially but, even after the improvements, their dwellings tend to remain segregated from public services and employment opportunities and, without secure tenure, they may eventually find themselves evicted (without compensation or resettlement) from their improved homes.

[152] P. K. Manoj, 'Prospects and Problems of Housing Micro-finance in India: Evidence from "Bhavanashree" Project in Kerala State', *European Journal of Economics, Finance and Administrative Sciences*, 19 (2010), 178–94, 190.

[153] *Ibid.*

[154] UN-Habitat, *Housing for All*, pp. 23–5.

It also appears that the housing micro-finance industry fails to reach the poorest. Many housing micro-finance programmes, being financially oriented, appear to target the higher-income urban poor (i.e. those with incomes above 50 per cent of the national poverty line) and near poor (a household income of up to 120 or 150 per cent of the national poverty line),[155] and the 'economically active poor'.[156] The ultra-poor, i.e. those who are below the 15th percentile in the income distribution (who are often dispersed in rural areas which are costly to serve with credit or physical infrastructure) are not addressed.[157] The requirement imposed by some micro-finance institutions for secure tenure may further define the client group as being the relatively 'better off' poor.

A more recent form of housing micro-finance, developed mainly in Africa and Asia, is community funds. These funds work with group loans and/or savings in order to assist communities to finance land regularisation and acquisition, infrastructure and service provision, and home improvements.[158] Community funds provide financial and technical support for the purchase of land parcels and communal infrastructure (roads, drainage, water distribution and connection, etc.). The process typically involves negotiations with other stakeholders such as the original owners of the land and governments.[159] Some organisations (e.g. the National Housing Cooperative in Kenya) provide both individual housing micro-finance loans and community group loans.[160] International umbrella organisations have been created to enable and assist the operations of local community-based organisations such as Slum Dwellers International and the Society for the Promotion of Area Resource Centres in India.[161]

Some community funds, such as *Baan Mankong* in Thailand and the Community Mortgage Programme in the Philippines, have demonstrated a great capacity to expand their coverage and to execute complex housing and infrastructure projects that involve national and local governments, landowners and several communities.[162] The *Baan Mankong* Programme,

[155] D. Porteous, 'Housing Finance and Financial Inclusion', p. 36–7.
[156] Those with formal employment and often those with diversified household livelihood strategies.
[157] Center for Urban Development Studies, Harvard University Graduate School of Design, 'Housing Micro-finance Initiatives', 24.
[158] UN-Habitat, *Financing Urban Shelter*, p. 120.
[159] Nilsson, 'Overview of Financial Systems for Slum Upgrading and Housing', 19.
[160] E. Sigvaldsen, *Key Issues in Housing Micro-finance* (Oslo: Nordic Consulting Group, 2010), pp. 16–7.
[161] UN-Habitat, *Financing Urban Shelter*, p. 99.
[162] See UN-Habitat, *Community Based Housing Finance Initiatives – The Case of Community Mortgage Programme in the Philippinnes* (Nairobi: UN-HABITAT, 2009).

introduced in 2003 by the Government of Thailand and implemented by an independent government agency (the Community Organizations Development Institute) aimed to improve living conditions for 300,000 families by 2008. Its strategy for delivering low-income housing was to channel funds to community-based organisations that plan and carry out the projects themselves.[163] The programme became an exemplar for community-supported slum upgrading, although it has been implemented on a smaller scale than originally envisaged.[164]

While such programmes developed in tandem with the evolution of housing micro-finance, they have a significantly different approach, emphasising community ownership and broader aspects of adequate housing such as location, access to infrastructure and services, and security of tenure.[165] Community funds are less finance-oriented – therefore, interest rates on loans are usually lower than housing micro-finance rates and loan periods are often longer, up to 25 years.[166] Community funds require government budgetary assistance and intense involvement by local and national governments in the planning and implementation stages, in order to achieve the necessary scale and sustainability.[167]

It is still too early to assess the impact of community funds on the access to adequate housing for the poor, and more systemic and long-term research is required. However, the financial sustainability of community funds has already emerged as a problem.[168] Owing to their large scale and reliance on multi-stakeholders, community funds depend heavily on donor financial and technical support, which can prove erratic, and research indicates that community funds suffer from low repayment rates and high arrears.[169] Additional concerns have been raised that the communal loans lead to internal conflicts and power imbalances within the borrower communities, owing to differences in repayment capabilities.[170]

[163] Ferguson and Smets, 'Finance for Incremental Housing', 293–4; UN-Habitat, *Housing for All*, pp. 88–9; S. Boonyabancha, 'Baan Mankong: Going to Scale with "Slum" and Squatter Upgrading in Thailand', *Environment and Urbanization*, 17 (2005), 21–46.

[164] As of January 2011, 1,546 communities and 90,000 households had been involved in *Baan Mankong* projects. UN-Habitat, *Affordable Land and Housing in Asia* (Nairobi: UN-Habitat, 2011), p. 50.

[165] UN-Habitat, *Financing Urban Shelter*, p. 120.

[166] In the case of the Community Mortgage Programme in the Philippines.

[167] See Nilsson, 'Overview of Financial Systems for Slum Upgrading and Housing'.

[168] UN-Habitat, *Financing Urban Shelter*, pp. 122–3, 126, 137.

[169] *Ibid.*, p. 128. [170] *Ibid.*, pp. xvii, 131–2, 135.

V. Summing up and setting out an alternative: a human rights-based approach to housing policies

During the past three decades housing policies have increasingly been reduced to housing finance systems in both developed and developing countries. The current predominant paradigm of housing policies holds that housing financial markets, if well designed and regulated, can provide access to adequate housing for all segments of society. At the same time, housing finance has become a central pillar of global financial markets, critical to the development of the financial sector at country and international levels. The focus on the financial aspects of housing has led to the conceptualisation of housing as a commodity and a financial asset distributed only by the market. The interconnection between global financial markets and national housing sectors appeared, until the 2008 crisis, to benefit almost all stakeholders – from the multinational banking system to the individual householder, who suddenly had access to finance.

The limited accessibility of housing finance systems to the poor was soon recognised by States and development agencies resulting in the design and promotion of three main housing financing mechanisms (sub-prime mortgage loans, demand-side subsidies and housing microfinance) to specifically facilitate the access of lower-income households to housing finance, promoting homeownership. These policies have been implemented in the context of a changing role of the State from supplier of affordable housing to enabler of housing and financial markets.

Are housing finance policies and programmes sufficient and efficient in promoting access to adequate housing for all segments of society, particularly the poorest and most marginalised? In other words, did releasing the housing finance 'genie'[171] benefit most households everywhere?

As our analysis illustrates, housing finance policies have largely failed to promote access to adequate housing for the poor. Evidence indicates that housing policies based exclusively on facilitating access to credit for homeownership are incompatible with the full realisation of the right to adequate housing of those living in poverty, failing to supply habitable, affordable and well-located housing solutions accessible to the poor, as well as increasing inequalities in housing distribution.

[171] Quoting 'The housing finance genie is out of the bottle' in Buckley and Kalarickal (eds.), *Thirty Years of World Bank Shelter Lending*, p. 39 ('Housing Finance: The Genie Is Out of the Bottle').

First, housing finance policies based on credit are inherently discriminatory against lower-income households, and, at their best, primarily increase housing affordability for upper- and middle-income groups. Even when specifically designed to meet the housing needs and characteristics of the poor, housing finance policies (whether mortgage based or housing micro-finance in nature) 'redline' the socio-economically disadvantaged, who are required to pay much higher prices for financial services, exposing them to financial risks intrinsic to global financial markets and indebtedness. Moreover, all three housing finance models examined in this chapter fail to reach the poorest of the poor.

At the same time, housing finance policies tend to focus solely on housing affordability while failing to address the broader aspects of the right to adequate housing: location; access to infrastructure and services; habitability; and security of tenure. However, even when gaining access to credit, low-income groups have no capacity to negotiate credit conditions or housing typologies and are forced to comply with the housing solutions allocated by the economic and profitability considerations of the housing market.

The housing market has not led to adequate housing solutions for the poor. In many cases, housing finance policies have resulted in increasing inequalities in access to housing, increased tenure insecurity, poor location and low habitability, social segregation and, sometimes, increased homelessness. As illustrated above, the sole focus on housing finance as the main housing policy, together with poor regulation, the loosening of credit requirements and the increased connection to global capital markets have led to an affordability crisis, defaults and foreclosures.

Our research further reveals the falsity of another of the main pillars of the 'enabling housing markets' paradigm. Demand-side housing finance policies have been promoted with the aim of reducing state expenditures and overcoming problems related to social housing programmes, such as urban segregation. However, it has become evident that – whether in the form of tax exemptions, 'bail-outs' for financial institutions following housing market busts such as that witnessed in 2008 or subsidies for low-income households – States still invest huge public resources in housing. In addition, these policies have often resulted in problematic outcomes, similar to those affecting social housing. Thus, while trying to limit their responsibility for housing provision and its costs, States have still found themselves deeply involved in housing markets, being obliged to regulate, fund and sometimes rectify devastating market failures. This has clear implications for the 'maximum resources' available to States to satisfy the right to adequate housing in accordance with their international human rights law obligations.

In the face of these problems, we suggest that a human rights-based approach can provide a relevant and practical framework for the design of alternative, more balanced and more sustainable housing policies. Housing finance can be an important component of a housing strategy and it is particularly effective in relation to middle- and high-income groups. However, it cannot be the Sole or the main policy and the full realisation of the right to adequate housing cannot be based exclusively on financial mechanisms. A human rights-based approach to housing policies therefore calls for broader state policies and interventions, including, inter alia, public investments in infrastructure and basic services, human settlements upgrading and rehabilitation, urban planning and land management policies, public financing, land and housing provision, as well as a plurality of tenure options, and related legal and institutional frameworks.

In terms of this approach, the design of housing policies should be based on an assessment of adequate housing needs. This entails taking into consideration the specific conditions in each country, in particular, demographic, geographic, economic and social conditions, and the characteristics and composition of the various disadvantaged groups (including low-income households), their housing conditions and forms of tenure. This contrasts sharply with the 'one size fits all' housing finance solution that has been implemented across the world over the past two decades.

Even when designed with the best intentions and with the participation of the relevant communities, housing policies and programmes may have less than desired outcomes. To this end, resources need to be allocated to facilitate effective monitoring at all stages of housing programmes. Human rights indicators can be an effective tool in identifying trends that signal progress, stagnation or retrogression in the realisation of the right to adequate housing.

However, monitoring the impacts of housing policies is not sufficient. The overarching human right obligation to ensure equality and non-discrimination requires that States develop housing policies that rectify existing inequalities in terms of access to adequate housing and target disadvantaged groups, including lower-income households. These policies and programmes cannot solely be based on finance mechanisms and should ensure access to affordable land and to the physical and social infrastructure that is needed to ensure adequate housing. Conversely,

States should refrain from focusing their housing policies on housing finance schemes with predominantly regressive effects, such as mortgage interest rate subsidies or mortgage interest tax exemptions.

Finally, the recent crises exemplify the importance of the promotion of a variety of housing policies, programmes and tenure systems. A mixture of tenure solutions is essential for the promotion of access to adequate housing for the various segments of society and in order to shield the housing sector from economic and financial shocks. States should therefore promote (through appropriate legal, financial and tax conditions) a mixture of tenure systems, including a public housing sector that is not tied to liberalised markets and limited-profit rental or regulated rent schemes, in order to prevent social exclusion and segregation.

This chapter critically examines the well-documented failure of the neoliberal approach to housing to provide stable and sustainable solutions for national housing systems and particularly for those segments of society located at the bottom of the economic pyramid. The call for a paradigm shift from the financialisation of housing to a rights-based approach to housing policies stems from States' international obligations, as well as from the recurring and cross-regional evidence indicating that the former simply does not work. As indicated throughout the chapter, there are several examples of national housing systems that have been shielded from the recent crises, thanks to a different and more balanced approach. While most countries opted for austerity measures as the main means to recover from the crises (without addressing the more systemic flaws of the housing markets), we believe that a closer look at some of these more balanced approaches may hold the key for preventing future turbulence in the housing sector and for promoting the progressive realisation of the right to adequate housing without discrimination.

3

The role of global governance in supporting human rights: the global food price crisis and the right to food

OLIVIER DE SCHUTTER

I. Introduction

The global food price crisis of 2008, and the financial and economic crises that followed, have led governments to reassess the complementarity between actions to be undertaken at the domestic level to protect and fulfil the right to food, and the measures to be adopted at the supranational level to create an international environment 'enabling' such efforts. In effect, the crisis has resulted in redefining food security as a 'global public good', requiring collective action on the part of States, as well as a reform of global governance to take into account the growing interdependence between States in the realisation of the right to adequate food. The crisis made States rediscover that national efforts are doomed to fail unless supported by measures at the international level. It has led them to realise that beggar-thy-neighbour policies pursued by governments may not only undermine other countries' efforts to realise human rights in the short term, but are also ultimately self-defeating in the long term. And, perhaps most importantly, it has made them aware that, contrary to the current trend of fragmentation of global governance and the multiplication of fora to deal with discrete issues, greater policy convergence is required in order to ensure that sectoral policies in the areas of trade, investment and food aid converge towards fulfilling the right to food.

This chapter documents the shift towards economic and social rights as global public goods in international legal discourse, a shift that

Much of what follows is based on the author's experience of interacting with governments and others stakeholders in the context of the reform of the Committee on World Food Security (CFS), first as a member of the 'Friends of the Chair' during the 2008–9 reform process, and then as a member of the Advisory Board of the Committee in 2009–14.

acknowledges the need to create mechanisms at the international level in support of domestic efforts to move towards the full realisation of these rights. Taking the right to food as an example, it assesses the significance of the reform of the Committee on World Food Security (CFS). Was this attempt to reshape the structures of global governance successful, if success is to be measured by its effective contribution to the right to food? And how do the principles of accountability and participation, that are central to human rights-based approaches at the domestic level, get taken into account at the international level? Did the inclusion in the CFS of non-state actors, particularly small-scale farmers' organisations and non-governmental organisations (NGOs), make a difference to how hunger is understood, and to the solutions it calls for?

Initially established as an intergovernmental committee within the United Nations Food and Agriculture Organization (FAO) in 1974 following the first World Food Summit, the CFS was reformed in 2009 to become 'the foremost inclusive international and intergovernmental platform for a broad range of committed stakeholders to work together in a coordinated manner and in support of country-led processes towards the elimination of hunger and ensuring food security and nutrition for all human beings'.[1] This redefinition constituted a strong recognition that governments will only manage to make true progress towards food security if they work in a bottom-up fashion. That is, by learning not only from one another's experiences but also from the experience of those who are on the front line of combating hunger – the international agencies and the NGOs – as well as from the victims themselves. The reform also acknowledged the need for governments to refrain from beggar-thy-neighbour policies and, instead, to justify their actions in the light of the impacts on others and on the smooth functioning of the global food system as a whole. Crucially, by its reference to the need to further improve coordination, the definition of the role of the CFS also reflected an awareness of the limitations of the current system of global governance that accepts (and to a certain extent encourages) the absence of convergence between different regimes or policy areas. This fragmentation of global governance replicates what international lawyers call the fragmentation of international law – i.e. the differentiation of international law into a number of self-contained regimes, each with their own norms

[1] Food and Agriculture Organization (FAO) Committee on World Food Security (CFA), 'Reform of the Committee on World Food Security' (October 2009) CFS:2009/2Rev. 2, para 4, ftp://ftp.fao.org/docrep/fao/meeting/018/k7197e.pdf, last accessed 5 September 2013.

and dispute-settlement mechanisms, and relatively autonomous both vis-à-vis each other and vis-à-vis general international law.[2] It results in the proliferation of fora for international cooperation that work in isolation from one another, thereby losing opportunities for synergies and at times undermining their respective efforts to address global problems.

The remainder of this chapter unfolds as follows. Section II recalls briefly the origins of the global food price crisis of 2008, and why it was seen by many as a 'wake-up call' showing the need for greater and better coordinated international action in order to achieve global food security. Section III then addresses the failure to overcome policy incoherence with regard to the realisation of the right to adequate food as a symptom, or an example of a broader problem, which I describe as the fragmentation of global governance. This fragmentation results in a misalignment between various international regimes and the requirements of internationally recognised human rights. Taking the global food price crisis as its departure point, the chapter argues that the realisation of social rights at the national level can only be achieved by reshaping the international economic environment. Section IV shows what such a reshaping could look like. It puts forward the elements of what I call the 'Rome Model', based on the recent experiment of the establishment of the Committee on World Food Security.

The experiment described here seeks to improve the global governance of food security, recognising that the right to adequate food for all constitutes a global public good for the delivery of which more international cooperation is required. But the experiment could be replicated in other fields, such as in relation to the right to health, basic labour rights or the right to social security. This would be a return to the original promise of the Universal Declaration of Human Rights, which contains the promise of 'a social and international order in which the rights and freedoms in this Declaration can be fully realised'.[3] It is this promise that we must now reclaim.

[2] International Law Commission, 'Fragmentation of International Law: Difficulties Arising from the Diversification and Expansion of International Law: Report of the Study Group of the International Law Commission' (18 July 2006) UN Doc. A/CN.4/L.702, para. 8; B. Simma, 'Self-Contained Regimes', *Netherlands Yearbook of International Law*, 16 (1985), 111–36.

[3] Universal Declaration of Human Rights (adopted 10 December 1948), UNGA Res. 217 A(III) (UDHR), art. 28.

II. The shock of 2008: a short history of the food price crisis

The realisation that food security was a global public good, requiring international cooperation and coordination to be achieved, came as a result not of theoretical reflection, but of a sudden shock that took many observers by surprise, sending waves across all regions. The 'shock' was, of course, the sudden surge of the prices of agricultural commodities on international markets that began in late 2007, reaching its peak in June 2008.[4] There were immediate causes of this crisis. Certain weather-related events in 2005 and 2006 led to worse-than-expected harvests in a number of major cereal-exporting countries.[5] The resulting price impacts were magnified by export restrictions put in place, in a matter of weeks, by a significant number of countries[6] suddenly panicking that the prices of staples could continue to increase and concerned that they needed to protect their population from future price spikes – just as other countries decided to resort to panic buying, further worsening the situation.

But these events would never have had such significant consequences if other factors had not contributed so as to create a context that increased the panic on the markets. First, agricultural production has grown over the years to become highly dependent on fossil energies in the major cereal-producing regions. Any increase in the price of oil therefore leads to

[4] These evolutions are reflected in the real value of the FAO's extended Food Price Index, which the FAO has updated since 1990 (base 100) based on the weighted average of a total of 55 commodity price quotations falling into five groups (meat, dairy, cereals, oils and fats, and sugar). Between 2000 and 2005, the Food Price Index increased moderately at a rate of 1.3 per cent per year. The rate of increase then reached 15 per cent in 2006, and continued to climb in 2007 and 2008, resulting in a peak in June 2008 (224); the average price level in 2008 was 200. For the latest food price indexes, see FAO, FAO Food Price Index, www.fao.org/worldfoodsituation/wfs-home/foodpricesindex/en/, last accessed 5 September 2013.

[5] See K. Baltzer, H. Hansen and K. M. Lind, 'A Note on the Causes and Consequences of the Rapidly Increasing International Food Prices' (May 2008), 2 (noting in 2008 that '[t]he current high wheat prices are mainly caused by three consecutive years (2005–2007) of weather-induced harvest shortfalls in some of the most important exporting regions, Australia, Europe, Former Soviet Union and North America, at a time where wheat stocks are historically low').

[6] According to one count, 29 countries resorted to export bans or restrictions in the spring of 2008, including in the form of export tariffs (T. Benson, N. Minot, J. Pender, M. Robles and J. von Braun, 'Global Food Crises: Monitoring and Assessing Impact to Inform Policy Responses' (International Food Policy Research Institute (IFPRI) Food Policy Report No. 19, September 2008). Another study estimates the number at 20 (World Bank, 'Global Economic Prospects. Commodities at the Crossroads' (2009), 123 (based on evidence available until 30 November 2008)).

a corresponding rise in the cost of producing food, making it difficult for producers to respond to sudden price increases of agricultural commodities by boosting production.[7] Second, combined with higher oil prices, the move towards renewable fuels for transport has, since the mid-2000s, led to a higher demand for agrofuel feedstock – particularly maize, soybean, rapeseed and palm oil. This has created a surge in the demand for grain and more competition for cropland between food, feed for livestock and fuel.[8] Third, the nervousness of the agricultural markets was magnified by financial speculation: increased investments by financial actors in 'derivatives' from agricultural commodities, in the form of futures contracts, options or swaps, significantly worsened volatility on the spot markets.[9]

These various factors combined to create a climate in which the market actors, States included, came to fear that the markets could not be trusted to ensure a steady supply of foodstuffs at affordable prices, because of the low level of stocks at global level and the inability of agricultural producers to respond swiftly to the rise in demand for agricultural commodities. However, we find yet more structural causes if we move up the causality chain and further back in time.

[7] Research from the World Bank indicates that a 10 per cent rise in crude oil prices translates into a 1.7 per cent increase in agricultural commodity prices. See John Baffes, 'Oil Spills on Other Commodities' (World Bank Policy Research Working Paper No. 4333, August 2007), 6.

[8] See, e.g., D. Mitchell, 'A Note on Rising Food Prices' (World Bank Policy Research Working Paper No. 4682, July 2008), 16. Mitchell notes:

> The increase in internationally traded food prices from January 2002 to June 2008 was caused by a confluence of factors, but the most important was the large increase in biofuels production from grains and oilseeds in the US and EU. Without these increases, global wheat and maize stocks would not have declined appreciably and price increases due to other factors would have been moderate. Land use changes in wheat exporting countries in response to increased plantings of oilseeds for biodiesel production limited expansion of wheat production that could have otherwise prevented the large declines in global wheat stocks and the resulting rise in wheat prices. (*Ibid.*)

Mitchell estimates that, because mandates and subsidies encouraging biofuels production and consumption in the United States and in the European Union have increased competition for land and water between energy and food (thereby encouraging speculation and export bans as stocks declined), up to 75 per cent of the food price rise of 2007–8 can in fact be traced back to these policies. *Ibid.* 17.

[9] See generally O. De Schutter, Special Rapporteur on the Right to Food, 'Food Commodities Speculation and Food Price Crises: Regulation to Reduce the Risks of Price Volatility' (Special Rapporteur on the Right to Food Briefing Note No. 2, September 2010), www.srfood.org/images/stories/pdf/otherdocuments/20102309_briefing_note_02_en_ok.pdf, last accessed 5 September 2013.

Indeed, what the crisis also brought to light were the imbalances brought about by the 'structural adjustment' programmes of the 1980s and 1990s devised by the World Bank and, as a component thereof, the trade liberalisation policies that many developing countries were forced to pursue. The aim of structural adjustment was to improve the macroeconomic conditions of heavily indebted developing countries, in order for them to continue to have access to international financial markets. But the impacts on the agricultural sector were often devastating.[10] As part of these reforms, the new orthodoxy had it that farmers henceforth should respond to the price signals from the market. Public interventions, like the establishment of commodity boards buying the crops at certain predefined prices, were seen as market distortions. Agriculture, it was said, should be freed from state interference; the private sector, it was hoped, would take over, investing where investments were needed, and encouraging the production of crops that markets wanted.[11] In fact, however, the removal of subsidies to agricultural producers and the dismantling of extension services were shocks with which many smaller farmers were unable to cope.[12]

[10] For assessments, see K. Mengisteab and B. I. Logan (eds.), *Beyond Economic Liberalization in Africa: Structural Adjustments and the Alternatives* (London: Zed Books, 1995); A. Adepoju (ed.), *The Impact of Structural Adjustment on the Population of Africa* (London: James Currey, 1989); S. Commander (ed.), *Structural Adjustment & Agriculture: Theory & Practice in Africa & Latin America* (London: Overseas Development Institute, 1989); J. Harrigan and P. Mosley, 'Evaluating the Impact of World Bank Structural Adjustment Lending: 1980–87', *Journal of Development Studies*, 27 (1991), 63–94.

[11] The price and market liberalisation followed prescriptions of the World Bank. See, e.g., World Bank, *Sub-Saharan Africa: From Crisis to Sustainable Growth* (Washington, DC: World Bank, 1989), pp. 91, 96 (noting that flexible prices will incentivise farmers to follow the signals of the market and switch to crops for which there is a demand and which will fetch higher prices, and advocating the removal of subsidies on inputs, which 'only encourages waste').

[12] See H. Stein, 'World Bank Agricultural Policies, Poverty and Income Inequality in Sub-Saharan Africa', *Cambridge Journal of Regions, Economy and Society*, 4 (2011), 79–90. Stein concludes that:

> The market approach to agriculture has exacerbated poverty in rural areas and likely contributed to worsening income equality ... Richer farmers have access to credit, storage, and transportation. In contrast, poor farmers were penalized in the new system due to the removal of fertilizer subsidy, a lack of infrastructural support and access to extension and few marketing and storage options. Poor farmers are also less able to bargain effectively with private traders or use transportation or storage capacities to improve the timing and location of their sales. (*Ibid.*, 87.)

In addition, although trade liberalisation was part of the package of reforms conducted in the name of structural adjustment, the lowering of import tariffs exposed the less competitive food producers of developing countries to competition from abroad. However, the 'competition' that resulted was particularly unfair: the governments of the least-developed countries (LDCs) were often unable to support their producers exposed to the dumping of agricultural products from Organisation for Economic Co-operation and Development (OECD) countries, which sold various products, at often highly subsidised prices, on the domestic markets of LDCs.[13] Small-scale farmers were especially hard hit. In contrast to middle-size or larger farmers, they could not switch to producing cash crops for export markets and thereby adapt to the new international division of labour that was being encouraged by trade liberalisation. They were also less competitive, since they were not in a position to achieve significant economies of scale. Finally, they were unable to overcome a range of barriers impeding access to the high-value markets of OECD countries, related both to the tariffs imposed by these countries and to non-tariff barriers, including both public and private standards.[14]

Not only were governments in LDCs unable to support their small-scale farmers. Official development assistance (ODA) also moved away from agriculture, which donors did not see as offering strong potential for development; in 2008, the World Bank reported that the share of ODA resources devoted to agriculture declined from 18 per cent in 1979 to 3.5 per cent in 2004, and that it declined in absolute terms from $8 billion (in 2004 dollars) in 1984 to $3.4 billion in 2004.[15] Although it was hoped that private investors would fill in the gaps, they did not. As a result of the huge

Other assessments have been more positive. See, e.g., L. H. Summers and L. H. Pritchett, 'The Structural-Adjustment Debate', *American Economic Review*, 83 (1993), 383–9, 385 (citing M. Schiff and A. Valdes, *The Plundering of Agriculture in Developing Countries* (Washington, DC: World Bank, 1992)). In this well-known paper, Summers and Pritchett summarise and debate the findings of the World Bank Review of Adjustment Lending. See World Bank Country Economics Department, *Adjustment Lending and Mobilization of Private and Public Resources for Growth* (Washington, DC: World Bank, 1992).

13 See FAO, 'The State of Agricultural Commodity Markets: 2009' (2009).

14 For a review of these obstacles and what would be required to overcome them, see A. F. McCalla and J. Nash (eds.), *Reforming Agricultural Trade for Developing Countries, Key Issues for a Pro-Development Outcome of the Doha Round* (Washington, DC: World Bank, 2007), vol. 1. See also O. De Schutter, 'Report of the Special Rapporteur on the Right to Food: Mission to the World Trade Organization' (4 February 2009) UN Doc. A/HRC/10/5/Add.2.

15 World Bank, *World Development Report 2008: Agriculture for Development* (Washington, DC: World Bank, 2007), p. 41.

subsidies provided to OECD producers by their governments,[16] overproduction was massive, and the prices of raw agricultural commodities on the international markets fell structurally since they had last peaked in 1973 and 1979.[17] The private sector was not interested in entering a sector that was perceived as being in decline.[18]

The net result of the policies of the 1980s was, therefore, a further increase in inequality and poverty in the rural areas.[19] Many small farmers were relegated to subsistence agriculture, with neither the incentives nor the possibility to produce beyond what was needed to feed their families.[20] Some took up work on large plantations. Many others migrated to cities, on a seasonal or more permanent basis, in search of better opportunities.[21] And the dependence of LDCs on food imports to feed themselves increased significantly, rendering them very vulnerable to price variations on international markets.[22]

It was this catalogue of failures that policymakers were suddenly faced with when they awoke to the global food price crisis in the spring of 2008.

[16] Government support to farmers in OECD countries was $258 billion in 2007, just before the crisis of 2008, representing 23 per cent of total farm receipts in these countries. Organisation for Economic Co-operation and Development (OECD), *Agricultural Policies in OECD Countries: At a Glance* (OECD, 2008), p. 9; K. Anderson, W. Martin and D. van der Mensbrugghe, 'Doha Merchandise Trade Reform: What is at Stake for Developing Countries?', *World Bank Economic Review*, 20 (2006), 169–95 (estimating that developed-country agricultural policies cost developing countries $17 billion per year, a cost equivalent to five times the recent levels of ODA to agriculture).

[17] See FAO, 'The State of Agricultural Commodity Markets', 12.

[18] As Hafez Ghanem notes: 'Because global production levels are technically sufficient and because world food prices have long been low and stable, investment in agriculture has been steadily declining since the 1970s. As a result, the rate of growth of agricultural capital stock (ACS) in the world fell from 1.1 percent in 1975–1990 to 0.50 percent in 1991–2007.' Hafez Ghanem, 'World Food Security and Investment in Agriculture', *International Economics Bulletin* (17 September 2009), www.carnegieendowment.org/publications/index.cfm?fa=view&id=23850, last accessed 5 September 2013.

[19] Comparing the data available for 19 sub-Saharan African countries for the period 1980–2000, Stein concludes that 'nearly 75% of all countries witnessed a worsening of income distribution with an overall mean decline for the total sample of 14% to around 50'. Stein, 'World Bank Agricultural Policies', 80. He notes that the increase in inequality particularly affected the rural poor – small-scale farmers who suffer structural disadvantages in the agricultural markets. *Ibid.*

[20] See *ibid.*

[21] The major study on rural-urban migration is K. Griffin, *The Political Economy of Agrarian Change: An Essay on the Green Revolution* (Cambridge, MA: Harvard University Press, 1974).

[22] United Nations Conference on Trade and Development (UNCTAD), *The Least Developed Countries Report 2010: Towards a New International Development Architecture for LDCs* (Geneva: UNCTAD, 2010), pp. iv, 8.

For the previous 30 years, neither investment and trade policies, nor development cooperation and food aid policies, nor the choices made concerning the type of farming to support had been geared towards achieving food security in the developing world. What these policies had created instead was a huge dependency trap; low-income, food-deficit countries that produced raw materials for the West and were addicted to buying heavily subsidised food on international markets in order to feed their growing populations – and worsening the situation of their own food producers as a result. But for this to change, much more policy convergence would have to be achieved between the various policy areas concerned; trade and development cooperation, as well as energy and climate change mitigation, would need to be realigned with the key objective of eradicating hunger and malnutrition in the developing world.

III. The diagnosis: the need for improved consistency across policy areas

The global food price crisis of 2008 could therefore be seen as a failure of global governance. Governments gradually came to be convinced that, in order for national right to food strategies to succeed, two conditions needed to be fulfilled. First, agricultural policies should achieve a balance between providing support for export-led agriculture and support for small-scale food producers producing for themselves, their families and communities. Supporting the local production of food crops is not only a way to reduce the dependence of a country on food imports, and thus the vulnerability of that country to price shocks on international markets. It is also a means to raise incomes in rural areas, where the vast majority of the extremely poor still often reside.[23] Second, jobs must be created in the industry and services sectors in order to absorb the excess workforce migrating from the rural areas. Thus, what is ideally required is a complementarity between these different sectors (agriculture, industry and services). In what Irma Adelman famously called 'agriculture-led industrialisation', a thriving small-scale, relatively labour-intensive agricultural sector, and the resulting reduction of rural poverty, should both ensure a market for the local producers or

[23] If we take into account not only its own growth performance but also its indirect impact on growth in other sectors, agriculture is 3.2 times more effective at reducing the number of very poor people (defined as those living below a USD one-per-day Purchasing Power Parity, or PPP, poverty line) in low-income and resource-rich countries than non-agriculture, at least in the absence of strong inequality. See L. Christiaensen, L. Demery and J. Kuhl, 'The (Evolving) Role of Agriculture in Poverty Reduction – An Empirical Perspective' (UNU-WIDER Working Paper No. 2010/36, April 2010).

manufactured goods and service-providers, and should allow the growth of a food processing industry and associated services, thus contributing to the strengthening of local food systems.[24]

If it comes too early and too fast, trade liberalisation imposed on poor agriculture-dominant countries leads to exactly the opposite of these outcomes. It encourages these countries to focus their efforts on cash crops for exports. But this type of agricultural production, which generally takes the form of large, relatively capital-intensive plantations,[25] is primarily for the benefit of large landowners, and has relatively small multiplier effects on local rural economies.[26] Moreover, such liberalisation increases the competition between export-led agriculture and the small-scale agricultural producers for land and water, for investment, and, of course, for political influence. And it discourages investments both in the production of agricultural inputs and machinery, and in food processing, since such 'infant industries' cannot be launched without some measure of protection from imported foodstuffs produced abroad.

[24] I. Adelman, 'Beyond Export-Led Growth', *World Development*, 12 (1984), 937–49.

[25] Coffee and cocoa can be exceptions, as fewer economies of scale can be achieved through mechanisation in these crops, making it easier for small-scale growers to be integrated in global supply chains.

[26] The question of linkages between agriculture and other sectors of the economy has been a classic theme of economic literature since the early 1960s. See B. F. Johnston and J. W. Mellor, 'The Role of Agriculture in Economic Development', *American Economic Review*, 51 (1961), 566–93. The argument that growth in agriculture can benefit other sectors is sometimes based on the view that it will lead to growth both upstream and downstream of the production process on the farm, by increasing demand for inputs and upping agro-processing activities. Since most agricultural inputs and machinery are imported, however, and since crops can be sold abroad as raw commodities, whether such a 'production' linkage occurs depends on the organisation of the commodity chain in the country concerned. A more significant linkage – one that recent research estimates to be typically four to five times more important than the production linkage – results from the fact that increased incomes in rural areas will raise demand for locally traded goods or services. Christiaensen, Demery and Kuhl, 'The (Evolving) Role of Agriculture in Poverty Reduction', 8–9. This 'consumption linkage' – in fact a Keynesian argument – is particularly likely where agricultural growth is widely spread across large segments of a very poor population. But it presupposes, of course, that the rural population will buy locally produced goods and locally provided services, and that supply can meet this increase in demand. See C. Delgado, J. Hopkins and V. A. Kelly, 'Agricultural Growth Linkages in Sub-Saharan Africa' (IFPRI Research Report 107, 1998), 107, www.ifpri.org/sites/default/files/pubs/pubs/abstract/107/rr107.pdf, last accessed 5 September 2013. The important implication is that diversification of the economy – the strengthening of the industrial and the services sectors – must precede the growth of a market for manufactured products and services by the increase of incomes in rural areas. One cannot accelerate a process that has not been launched.

Table 3.1. *Two versions of the responses to the global food price crisis, aimed at addressing a different set of causes*

	Causes of the 2007/8 global food price crisis	Two versions of the responses needed
Immediate causes	Weather-related events and export restrictions by food exporting countries	Focus on smoothening measures to facilitate movement of foodstuffs and market transparency
Intermediate causes	Dependence of food production on fossil energies, high prices of energy, competition for land resulting from a demand for agrofuels, financial speculation	Focus on reinvestment in agriculture in developing countries and on trade policies that incentivise small-scale food producers
Structural causes	Lack of investment in small-scale food producers in net food importing developing countries, due to an inequitable trading system and unfair competition	

This diagnosis, it should be immediately added, was not shared by all. Those focusing only on the most immediate causes of the food price crisis were quick to designate export restrictions by nations panicking about future supplies and increasing prices as the major culprit – and hence to argue that a further consolidation of the trade regime, to include prohibitions on export bans, was therefore the solution.[27] They also noted that more trade would be required as a result of climate change, as the most fragile regions will lose their ability to produce enough food to feed their

[27] This is the position that the Director-General of the World Trade Organization (WTO), Mr Pascal Lamy, took on various occasions in debates with this author. It is also a position some governments expressed in debates held at the Human Rights Council and at the Agriculture Committee of the WTO, where this author presented his report on the WTO and the right to food (Olivier De Schutter, 'Report on the Mission to the World Trade Organization').

population, and will have to import more in order to satisfy their needs. Free trade, these commentators insisted, should be seen as the 'ultimate climate change adaptation strategy', and should be encouraged.

Thus emerged a strong ideological battle between two very different views of how the food policies should evolve in order to improve the resilience of food systems to future shocks. While one faction insisted on the facilitation of trade and the improvement of market transparency, the other was intent on tackling the structural imbalances of the global food system and reshaping food policies in accordance with the needs of the small-scale agricultural producers in developing countries. Table 3.1 provides a stylised summary of this debate, between two sets of responses to the global food price crisis – one focused on the immediate causes, the other focused on the intermediate and structural causes.

Perhaps inevitably, these competing readings of the causes of – and solutions to – the global food price crisis led to contrasting views of how the crisis related to the organisation of global governance.[28] Some believed the food system was in deep trouble, and that significant reforms were required if future crises were to be avoided. These actors focused their attentions on the reform of the CFS, which was seen as an opportunity to improve the convergence of the various sectoral policies affecting food and agriculture, in order to ensure that they would contribute to food security. This group included NGOs and food producers' organisations. The most influential among them was the Via Campesina. A transnational network of small-scale farmers' organisations, the 'Via' was established in 1993 explicitly as a counterweight to the dominant pro-globalisation agricultural agenda. This agenda, they argued, was being pushed at the expense of the least competitive food producers, particularly from the global South.[29] Following the global food price crisis of 2008, that lay bare the imbalances in the food system, the Via and their allies convinced some governments of the need for a radical transformation in the food systems based on the alternative paradigm of food sovereignty. Most governments, however, were content with more modest changes, essentially

[28] For a mapping of these different positions, see T. A. Wise and S. Murphy, 'Resolving the Food Crisis: Assessing Global Policy Reforms Since 2007' (GDAE-IATP Policy Report, January 2012).

[29] See A. A. Desmarais, 'The Power of Peasants: Reflections on the Meanings of La Via Campesina', *Journal of Rural Studies*, 24 (2008), 138–49; J. Borras, M. Edelman and C. Kay (eds.), *Transnational Agrarian Movements Confronting Globalization* (Oxford: Wiley-Blackwell, 2008).

directed towards ensuring smoother market functioning and improved coordination between governments.

The governments belonging to this latter group could be convinced of the usefulness of a platform to improve coordination across countries and regions; that, after all, might ensure that States would not resort to beggar-thy-neighbour policies dictated by short-term considerations or panic in the face of spiralling prices. But the actors in this second group did not regard the current state of fragmentation of global governance as the major problem to be addressed. Nor did they consider the reshaping of international regimes in support of country-led efforts in order to realise the right to food as a priority in the current context. Instead they favoured each international agency pursuing its own objectives, within its own mandate, complementary to those of other agencies. For instance, eager to dissociate himself from the discredited 'Washington Consensus', Pascal Lamy, the Director General of the World Trade Organization (WTO), has been a vocal advocate for what he calls the 'Geneva Consensus'. The notion was inaugurated by a speech he delivered in Santiago de Chile, on 30 January 2006. There, he stated:

> We cannot ignore the costs of adjustment, particularly for the developing countries, and the problems that can arise with the opening up of markets. These adjustments must not be relegated to the future: they must be an integral part of the opening-up agenda. We must create a new 'Geneva Consensus': a new basis for the opening up of trade that takes into account the resultant cost of adjustment. Trade opening is necessary, but it is not sufficient in itself. It also implies assistance: to help the least-developed countries to build up their stocks and therefore adequate productive and logistical capacity; to increase their capacity to negotiate and to implement the commitments undertaken in the international trading system; and to deal with the imbalances created between winners and losers from trade opening – imbalances that are the more dangerous to the more fragile economies, societies or countries. Building the capacity they need to take advantage of open markets or helping developing countries to adjust is now part of our common global agenda.
>
> Part of this challenge falls under the WTO; but the WTO's core role is trade opening, we lack the institutional capacity to formulate and lead development strategies. The challenge to humanise globalization necessarily involves other actors in the international scene: IMF/WB and the United Nations family.[30]

[30] P. Lamy, 'Humanising Globalization', Speech at Santiago de Chile, Chile (30 January 2006), www.wto.org/english/news_e/sppl_e/sppl16_e.htm, last accessed 5 September 2013. See also P. Lamy, Speech at the Dies Academicus Ceremony of Award of a Doctor Honoris Causa – Geneva (5 June 2009), www.wto.org/english/news_e/sppl_e/sppl128_e.htm, last accessed 5 September 2013. The Geneva Consensus acknowledges that an increase in

The Geneva Consensus is an understanding of international governance in which a division of labour is encouraged between the various international agencies: while the WTO should focus on trade, the FAO should support agricultural policies, the International Labour Organization should promote international labour standards, the World Health Organization (WHO) is to strengthen initiatives in the area of public health, and the Office of the United Nations High Commissioner for Human Rights (OHCHR) and human rights bodies to push for compliance with human rights.

Rather than providing an impetus for change, this view offers an elegant justification for the *status quo*. This may explain its popularity with many governments and international agencies. But a number of questions arise. First, the idealised Geneva Consensus does not take into account the very different leverage that each of these various agencies can exercise on their Member States. It ignores the fact that such agencies differ widely in terms of their ability both to adopt rules and to enforce them. Second, the Geneva Consensus underestimates the risk of conflicts between international regulatory regimes, because of the strong overlaps that exist, in fact, between the different issues that are of international concern.

Indeed, this chapter will argue that what is needed in order to move towards resilient food systems that can ensure the full realisation of the right to food in the long term is greater consistency across policy areas that cannot be considered in isolation. In particular, the current regime of international trade has not worked for the benefit of smallholders in developing countries who form the majority of those who are hungry in the world today.[31] On the one hand, within their own domestic markets, agricultural producers from developing countries have often faced unfair competition from highly subsidised products exported by farmers from OECD countries.[32] On the other hand, producers from developing

trade opportunities creates winners and losers and may be disruptive. However, it places its bets on a functional differentiation between the WTO (in charge of setting trade rules to ensure that markets are open and rules-based) and other international agencies or fora (in charge of supporting countries and helping remedy any imbalances which may result between different groups of the population).

[31] In total, at least 1.5 billion individuals depend on small-scale farming for their livelihoods. They live mostly on subsistence agriculture on less than two hectares of land. World Bank, *World Development Report 2008*, p. 3. Among them, a significant proportion, most of whom are net buyers of food, are hungry. It is estimated that smallholders represent approximately half of the one billion hungry people in the world. See UN Millennium Project, *Halving Hunger: It Can be Done, Summary Version of the Report of the Task Force on Hunger* (London and Sterling, VA: Earthscan, 2005), p. 6.

[32] See text to n. 16.

countries have faced important obstacles when seeking access to the high-value markets of industrialised countries. They have failed to benefit even from preferential schemes such as the African Growth and Opportunity Act or the Caribbean Basin Initiative of the United States, the Everything But Arms initiative adopted by the European Union in favour of least-developed countries, or the Cotonou Agreement between countries of the European Commission and the African, Caribbean and Pacific Group of States (ACP).[33] This failure may be attributed to factors including the complexity of the rules involved (particularly the requirements resulting from rules of origin[34]), as well as the non-tariff barriers which potential exporters face, linked in particular to standards requirements.[35] Finally, many agricultural products are currently facing tariff peaks and tariff escalation (i.e. higher tariffs on processed products) which discourage diversification into higher value-added products, leading developing countries to have an excessive dependence on an often limited number of primary commodities.[36] These disadvantages explain why the domestic agricultural sector in developing countries has been unable to attract investment over the past 30 years, resulting in a vicious cycle in which unfair trade rules lead to further losses of competitiveness.

[33] For Africa, see UNCTAD, 'Economic Development in Africa 2008 – Export Performance Following Trade Liberalization: Some Patterns and Policy Perspectives' (2008) UN Sales No. E.08.II.D.22, ch. 2.

[34] 'Rules of origin' serve to prove that a particular good has been produced in a country that is granted preferential treatment in a trade agreement, allowing that good to be counted as originating from that country.

[35] See among many others, A. B. de Batisti, J. MacGregor and A. Graffham (eds.), *Standard Bearers. Horticultural Exports and Private Standards in Africa* (London: International Institute for the Environment and Development, 2009). For a less pessimistic view, see S. M. Jaffee and S. Henson, 'Agro-Food Exports from Developing Countries: The Challenges of Standards', in M. A. Aksoy and J. C. Beghin (eds.), *Global Agricultural Trade and Developing Countries* (Washington, DC: World Bank, 2005), ch. 6 (showing that in countries where the private sector is well organised and in which the public sector supports the efforts of exporters, producers have been able to enter markets such as those for seafood and fresh fruit and vegetables). In their study of the vegetable export chain in Senegal, Johan F. M. Swinnen and Miet Maertens conclude that exports grew despite tightening standards; such tightening, they conclude, led to a shift from smallholder contract farming to integrated estate production, leading poorest households to benefit through being employed on such estates rather than by producing themselves for the global markets (M. Maertens and J. F. M. Swinnen, 'Trade, Standards and Poverty: Evidence from Senegal', *World Development*, 37 (2009), 161–78).

[36] A. F. McCalla and J. Nash, *Reforming Agricultural Trade for Developing Countries. Key Issues for a Pro-Development Outcome of the Doha Round* (Washington, DC: World Bank, 2007), vol. I.

But to what extent is global governance to blame? The lowering of import tariffs by low-income countries is generally not required under the schedule of commitments of these countries under the Agreement on Agriculture – the WTO Agreement that deals specifically with agricultural products and that all WTO members must join as part of their 'single undertaking'. The failure to invest in domestic food production and the tendency towards greater dependence of poor countries on food imports are the result of trade policies that these countries have deliberately chosen to adopt (albeit following the advice of international financial institutions) in the interest of providing low-priced food to their population. This appears to be more of a failure of domestic policy rather than a shortcoming in the international governance framework.

At the same time, however, this failure is attributable to an international economic environment in which, instead of supporting poor countries to feed themselves and combating domestic rural poverty by investing in domestic food production, rich countries chose instead to feed them. In doing so, rich countries have actively contributed to the dependence for which the recipient countries now pay such a high price.

While the question of the compatibility of the WTO agreements with the requirements of the right to development and human rights generally remain debated,[37] it seems clear that trade policies, as encouraged by the existing trade regime, have not been supportive of food security strategies pursued at the domestic level. It was in part in order to improve the consistency across different policy areas in support of the progressive realisation of the right to food that the reform of global governance was seen as a priority in the months that followed the food price crisis of 2008. The result was an unprecedented attempt to support the realisation of the right to food at the domestic level by creating an 'enabling' international environment.

IV. The role of human rights in shaping international regimes: the Rome Model

The global food price crisis of 2008 therefore exposed the failure of the existing international arrangements to effectively support country-led

[37] See A. DiCaprio and K. P. Gallagher, 'The WTO and the Shrinking of Development Space. How Big Is the Bite?', *Journal of World Investment and Trade*, 7 (2006), 781–803. For a general assessment of the compatibility between WTO disciplines and human rights, see S. Joseph, *Blame It on the WTO? A Human Rights Critique* (Oxford University Press, 2011); J. Harrison, *The Human Rights Impact of the World Trade Organisation* (Oxford: Hart, 2007).

food security strategies. The problem was not limited to the lack of consistency across different policy areas. Another problem, also alluded to above, was the lack of coordination between countries. This lack of coordination led States to adopt beggar-thy-neighbour policies, such as export bans in a context of rising prices, leading to sub-optimal solutions for food security at the global level. In the absence of any forum where global food policy could be discussed, let alone decided, governments were also tempted to focus on the short-term objectives, namely, to ensure the supply of affordable food for their populations. They were not forced to think about food security in more strategic terms and to ask, for instance, whether the existing system was sustainable in a context of increasingly high and volatile prices. Finally, there was no possibility for the concerns of those most affected by food insecurity, especially poor farmers, to be heard. As a result, decisions were made without the benefit of the crucial information that such actors could provide.

The reform of the Committee on World Food Security was the response of the international community to these questions. This section provides an assessment of that reform.

A. *The reform of the Committee on World Food Security*

Following the food price crisis of 2008, a consensus soon emerged that a more consistent approach across policy areas for the realisation of the right to food required the establishment of a forum where different international actors – governments of course, but also international agencies and transnational networks of civil society organisations – could work together to ensure that their policies would converge, rather than undermining each others' efforts.

This shared conviction led to the reform of the Committee on World Food Security in 2009. As members of the CFS, governments are encouraged to participate at ministerial level, 'insofar as possible representing a common, inter-ministerial governmental position'.[38] Participants in the mechanism, who have the same rights as members except with respect to voting and decision-making, include the representatives of UN agencies and bodies with a specific mandate in the field of food security and nutrition, and representatives of other relevant UN System bodies whose overall work is related to attaining food security, nutrition and

[38] CFS, 'Reform of the Committee on World Food Security', para. 9.

the right to food (such as the Special Rapporteur on the Right to Food, OHCHR, WHO, the United Nations Children's Fund (UNICEF), the United Nations Development Programme (UNDP) and the Standing Committee on Nutrition (SCN)). Other participants include civil society and NGOs, international agricultural research systems, the World Bank, the International Monetary Fund, regional development banks, the WTO, the private sector and philanthropic foundations active in the area of food security.[39]

Civil society is not organised at the global level and the vast array of organisations forming transnational civil society are a highly diverse group, with largely varied forms of membership and representativity. Therefore, involving them in deliberative decision-making within the CFS poses a number of challenges. Governments, or the Secretariat of the CFS, might be tempted to choose whom to give a voice to, possibly circumventing the most dissenting or radical groups. In addition, within civil society itself, broad-based social movements coexist with international NGOs, and groups linked to the peasants' movements work side by side with development NGOs and human rights groups. How, under such conditions, could a dialogue effectively take place? The response was found in the principle of autonomy. In the Reform Document of the CFS, Member States recognised the right of civil society organisations (CSO) to 'autonomously establish a global mechanism for food security and nutrition which will function as a facilitating body for CSO/NGOs consultation and participation in the CFS'.[40] A year later, in October 2010, this led to the establishment of the 'International Food Security and Nutrition Civil Society Mechanism (CSM)'.[41] This umbrella group of hundreds of organisations working on food and nutrition issues either adopts common positions or identifies differences in approach which are then conveyed as such to the CFS, allowing the organisations to play a strong role in the deliberative processes of the CFS. The organising principles of the CSM emphasise that it is

> an inclusive space open to all civil society organisations, with priority given to the organisations and movements of the people most affected by food insecurity and malnutrition, i.e. smallholder producers, fisherfolk,

[39] *Ibid.*, para. 11. [40] *Ibid.*, para. 16.

[41] See CFS, 'Proposal for an International Food Security and Nutrition Civil Society Mechanism for Relations with CFS' (September 2010) CFS:2010/9; CFS. 'Report of the 36th Session of the Committee on World Food Security' (October 2010) CFS: 2010/ FINAL REPORT, para. 32.

> pastoralists, indigenous, urban poor, migrants, agricultural workers etc. The CSM is founded on the belief that the people most affected by food insecurity and malnutrition must be the agents of their own development, are best placed to represent their own interests and views and are not only victims but also bearers of solutions.[42]

The structuring of civil society at the global level is not unprecedented. This process built on the successful establishment of the Via Campesina[43] and, in 2002, of the International Planning Committee on Food Sovereignty (IPC), now a large platform of some 45 peoples' networks linked to at least 800 organisations in the world rallying behind the call for food sovereignty.[44] The ability of civil society to organise itself was a key success factor during the discussions that led to the reform of the CFS, and may also prove decisive during the implementation phase. Not only does such mobilisation strengthen civil society's ability to influence discussions within the CFS, it also ensures that commitments made within the CFS will be tracked, thanks to the monitoring by the organisations involved. It encourages national-level civil society organisations to hold their governments accountable in the shaping of agricultural policies at home. And it significantly enhances the legitimacy of the outcomes of the discussions held within the CFS.[45]

The CFS is expected to provide a platform for discussion and coordination to strengthen collaborative action among its members and participants; as defined in the Reform document of the CFS, its

[42] More details are to be found on the website of the CSM, CSM – International Food Security & Nutrition Civil Society Mechanism, www.csm4cfs.org, last accessed 5 September 2013.

[43] See A. Desmarais, 'The Power of Peasants'; S. Borras, M. Edelman and C. Kay (eds.), *Transnational Agrarian Movements Confronting Globalization* (West Sussex, UK: Wiley-Blackwell, 2008).

[44] On these developments, see N. McKeon, 'Strengthening Dialogue: UN Experience with Small Farmer Organisations and Indigenous Peoples' (United Nations NGO Liaison Service vol. 3, 2009); N. McKeon, M. Watts and W. Wolford, 'Peasant Associations in Theory and Practice' (United Nations Research Institute for Social Development Paper No. 8, May 2004). On the significance of food sovereignty as an alternative to the corporate-driven push for increased globalization of food systems, see S. Suppan, 'Food Sovereignty in an Era of Trade Liberalisation: Are Multilateral Means Towards Food Sovereignty Feasible?', *Global Security and Cooperation Quarterly*, 9 (Summer 2003).

[45] See J. Duncan and D. Barling, 'Renewal through Participation in Global Food Security Governance: Implementing the International Food Security and Nutrition Civil Society Mechanism to the Committee on World Food Security', *International Journal of Sociology of Agriculture and Food*, 19 (2012), 143–61, 144 ('By including civil society actors as official participants on the Committee, the CFS is championing a model of enhanced participation at the level of international policy-making, finding new ways to engage those civil

objective is to 'promote greater policy convergence and coordination, including through the development of international strategies and voluntary guidelines on food security and nutrition on the basis of best practices, lessons learned from local experience, inputs received from the national and regional levels, and expert advice and opinions from different stakeholders'.[46] It is also envisaged as providing support and advice to countries and regions.[47] The *Global Strategic Framework on Food Security and Nutrition* (GSF), adopted by the CFS in 2012, confirms these objectives:

> The persistence of widespread hunger, and in more recent years the economic crisis and excessive volatility of food prices, has exposed the fragility of global mechanisms for food security and nutrition. Coordination between actors at national, regional and global level has been inadequate. Overcoming the structural causes of hunger and malnutrition will require promoting coherence of all appropriate national and international policies with the right to food, convergent policies, strategies and programmes that give urgent priority to meeting both the long-term needs and emergency requests for food security and nutrition. Successful pursuit of these objectives requires cross-sectoral government support, political will and long-term coordinated actions. Interventions need to be properly financed and benefit from adequate capacities both to implement them and monitor their impact.[48]

The adoption of the GSF signals the launch of the second phase of the CFS' work.[49] The GSF is conceived as a flexible, 'rolling' document that can be regularly updated on the basis of new information and new priorities, 'in order to improve coordination and guide synchronised action by a wide range of stakeholders'.[50] It is seen as a contribution to improving accountability, on which the CFS has started focusing during this second phase. The added value of the GSF in this regard is to provide an overarching framework and a single reference document with practical guidance on core recommendations for food security and nutrition strategies, policies and actions validated by the wide ownership, participation and consultation afforded by the CFS.[51] The document is very detailed on the

society actors who have been located, previously, at the margins of official food security debates.').

[46] CFS, 'Reform of the Committee on World Food Security', para. 5.

[47] *Ibid.*

[48] FAO, 'Global Strategic Framework on Food Security and Nutrition – First Version' (September 2012) CFS 2012/39/5 Add.1, para. 70. The significance of the Global Strategic Framework (GSF) is discussed in greater detail below.

[49] *Ibid.* [50] *Ibid.*, para. 6. [51] *Ibid.*, para. 7.

implementation of the right to adequate food – and, specifically, on the steps countries must take towards implementing the *Voluntary Guidelines to Support the Progressive Realisation of the Right to Adequate Food in the Context of National Food Security*.[52] These guidelines were adopted in 2004 by the FAO Council following two years of intergovernmental negotiations within the CFS in its previous incarnation. Such implementation is listed among the core actions that countries should adopt in order to combat hunger.[53] Noting that 'those countries making the greatest progress on food security and nutrition are those that have demonstrated the greatest political will, with a strong political and financial commitment that is open and transparent to all stakeholders',[54] the GSF emphasises the importance of accountability for commitments. It lists five conditions that the monitoring and accountability systems to be set up should comply with:

> a) They should be human rights-based, with particular reference to the progressive realization of the right to adequate food; b) They should make it possible for decision-makers to be accountable; c) They should be participatory and include assessments that involve all stakeholders and beneficiaries, including the most vulnerable; d) They should be simple, yet comprehensive, accurate, timely and understandable to all, with indicators disaggregated by sex, age, region, etc., that capture impact, process and expected outcomes; e) They should not duplicate existing systems, but rather build upon and strengthen national statistical and analytical capacities.[55]

At the same time, given that past attempts to address hunger and malnutrition have failed, the GSF recognises the need for all parties to learn, rather than to rely on preconceived notions of the priority actions to be taken or on a narrow panoply of options: 'All stakeholders need to draw on lessons learned and glean insights that may be taken into account in devising more effective strategies for food security and nutrition'.[56]

Collective learning and monitoring for results are thus two key components of the work of the CFS.[57] Collective learning is to be promoted by the sharing of experiences across countries and regions, a process for

[52] FAO, 'Voluntary Guidelines to Support the Progressive Realisation of the Right to Adequate Food in the Context of National Food Security' (2005).

[53] See *ibid*., paras. 74–5.

[54] *Ibid*., para. 92. [55] *Ibid*., para. 93. [56] *Ibid*., para. 16.

[57] For initial proposals made in this regard during the reform process of the CFS, see Special Rapporteur on the Right to Food, 'Coordinating, Learning, Monitoring: A New Role for

which the CFS can serve as a platform. In addition, however, in order to ensure that it would make decisions based on the best scientific evidence available and in order to facilitate the move towards a consensus, the CFS established a High-Level Panel of Experts (HLPE). The role of the HLPE was modelled on that of the Intergovernmental Panel on Climate Change, which was established in 1988 at the initiative of the United Nations Environment Programme and the World Meteorological Organization 'to provide internationally coordinated scientific assessments of the magnitude, timing and potential environmental and socio-economic impact of climate change and realistic response strategies'.[58] Similarly, the role of the HLPE is not to produce new scientific evidence, but to assess the existing evidence available in order to guide policymakers. The reports of the HLPE should allow the members and participants of the CFS to shift their understanding of the causes of food insecurity and of the remedies it calls for. Gradually, the CFS should thus enter into what the organisational learning theories refer to as 'double loop learning' – not only improving policies in the light of whether existing policies succeed or fail, but also revising the objectives pursued, and the definition of success and failure itself, on the basis of the evidence provided and the alternative framings of the question of food security present within the Committee.[59] The various actors involved in the CFS each have their own views, shaped by diverse historical experiences and ideologies, about where hunger and malnutrition stem from, and what should be done about them. Only by agreeing to question these presuppositions, and by accepting that the framing of each of the questions to be addressed may not be the only framing possible, can true collective learning take place.

B. *The next steps*

Promising and innovative as it is, the reform of the CFS still falls short of providing a framework through which the true equivalent of country-

the Committee on World Food Security' (22 May 2009), www2.ohchr.org/english/issues/food/docs/CFS_reform_note22May09.pdf, last accessed 5 September 2013.

[58] UNGA Res. 43/53 (6 December 1988) UN Doc. A/RES/43/53.

[59] On 'double-loop learning', see esp. C. Argyris, 'Single-Loop and Double-Loop Models in Research on Decision Making', *Administrative Science Quarterly*, 21 (1976), 363–75; C. Argyris, *Reasoning, Learning and Action: Individual and Organisational* (San Francisco, CA: Jossey-Bass, 1982); C. Argyris, *Knowledge for Action: A Guide to Overcoming Barriers to Organizational Change* (San Francisco: Jossey Bass, 1993).

level national strategies for the right to food could emerge at the global level in the form of an action plan for the international community. For this to happen, the CFS should feel confident enough in its political weight to adopt a calendar of actions to be taken, to allocate responsibilities across actors and to define indicators so as to enable progress to be measured – thereby increasing accountability. While the *Global Strategic Framework on Food Security and Nutrition* constitutes a step in this direction, its current form is still a receptacle of key recommendations addressed to different actors. But it cannot be invoked against these actors to oblige them to implement the recommendations. In that sense, it is not actionable.

Yet, for the right to food to become a reality, what is needed is more than an ad hoc reaction to discrete violations resulting from the adoption of specific measures. We require a sustained effort towards a transition that can channel existing regimes towards a direction which is more conducive to the full realisation of human rights. Action plans are a way to overcome the gap between the 'what' and the 'how'; they are important not just for the end vision they propose, but for the identification of the pathways towards that vision. They bridge the gap between relatively small changes to the system that, in isolation, are unable to make a significant difference, and changes so broad that they seem at first impossible to achieve.

For such action plans to succeed, they should include appropriate indicators and benchmarks and a monitoring of the choices made by policymakers. This can constitute a powerful incentive to integrate long-term considerations into decision-making, and to effectively implement the roadmap that has been agreed upon. Such action plans should not be seen simply as a new form of rule-making, prescribing objectives and how to get there. They are also a learning device. They should be constantly revised in the light of the implementation problems faced by governments. In this iterative process, in which implementation feeds back into the formulation of guidelines set at the global level, the tools that are recommended should be gradually improved in order to achieve effective results. Thus, the definition of the objectives itself may have to be revisited and the paradigms under which actors operate will, in time, be challenged and revised. As such, learning and monitoring become indistinguishable in a process that is both top-down and bottom-up, and in which any recommendations addressed to States or other actors are provisional, formulated subject to the reservation that other ways of making progress towards agreed-upon objectives may in fact be more appropriate in certain settings, and that the objectives are amenable to change.[60]

The repeated crises which have affected food systems since 2008 reveal the need for the international community to adopt an action plan with clear commitments, and targets to be achieved within specific timeframes. They also highlight the need for policies pursued in other sectoral areas than food security per se to be aligned with the objective of eradicating hunger and malnutrition. An international environment should be shaped to facilitate the adoption of country-led plans to achieve this. Whether the CFS will succeed in effecting this shift remains an open question. A major challenge it will face, however, is that the international agenda concerning areas deeply affecting the effectiveness of food security strategies is increasingly being set outside the CFS. The G20, the group of the 20 most important economies, has been particularly active in such agenda-setting. When the G20 decided to put food security on its agenda at the initiative of the French presidency in 2011, this raised high hopes; governments at last, and the major agricultural powers in particular, would demonstrate leadership, and perhaps take the bold decisions that they, and only they, were in a position to take. But the reality is that on major issues, particularly agrofuels production and the fight against the causes of price volatility on agricultural markets, as well as on trade, the G20 has been preempting the debate, taking positions that were not only modest at best, but also might have had a chilling effect on the CFS, making it more difficult to tackle the structural causes of the food crisis.[61] Moreover, within the CFS itself, some governments, particularly from rich countries, appear to consider that particular issues may be 'off limits'

[60] There is an ample literature on learning in organisations on which this paragraph draws, and to which my contribution to the reform process of the CFS was heavily indebted. See in particular for a discussion of various learning-based theories of governance, O. De Schutter and J. Lenoble (eds.), *Reflexive Governance. Redefining the Public Interest in a Pluralistic World* (Oxford and Portland, OR: Hart Publishing, 2010). For an illustration of how such an approach can shed light on the approach of an international organisation, see C. F. Sabel and J. Zeitlin (eds.), *Experimentalist Governance in the European Union: Towards a New Architecture* (Oxford University Press, 2010). While learning can consist of one actor simply improving the instruments he uses to pursue certain objectives, double-loop learning consists, as already noted, of the objectives themselves being re-examined (see the preceding footnote). 'Triple-loop learning' would consist in an actor rethinking the core values by which he defines his identity and project. (On triple-loop learning, see J. Swieringa and A. F. M. Wierdsma, *Becoming a Learning Organization* (Reading, MA: Addison-Wesley, 1992)).

[61] See in particular Wise and Murphy, 'Resolving the Food Crisis'.

for the Committee, which, in the view of these actors, should refrain from discussing issues that are already dealt with in other fora. Yet this is a position that, if taken to its logical conclusion, would deprive the CFS of any ability at all to improve the coherence of global governance of food security.[62]

It is precisely this segmentation of global governance that must now be overcome. This means subjecting international regimes to a form of scrutiny that assesses their contribution to the realisation of the right to food in particular, and to human rights in general. It means re-establishing human rights as the reference through which we measure progress at both the national and international levels and relying on human rights indicators rather than, for instance, on macroeconomic indicators or development indicators alone. It means ensuring that the different regimes that have grown out of economic globalisation comply with the requirements of human rights.

Indeed, this is already a visible trend in international human rights law. International organisations are increasingly developing mechanisms to ensure their accountability towards human rights, and the special procedures of the Human Rights Council have occasionally contributed to ensuring that international organisations take human rights into account in their operations.[63] The responsibilities of transnational corporations towards human rights have also been clarified in recent years. Such actors are aware that they are now expected to respect human rights, and to ensure

[62] It is telling in this regard that, during the 39th session of the CFS held between 15 and 20 October 2012, the single most difficult discussion that the adoption of the Global Strategic Framework on Food Security and Nutrition led to revolved around the 'Issues That May Require Further Attention', under Chapter VI of the Framework. The chapter is introduced as such: 'As there is a diversity of views, some issues may require further attention by the international community where they are relevant to the international debate on food security and nutrition. The listing of issues here is not exhaustive and does not necessarily mean that they should be addressed by the CFS.' The chapter then lists a range of topics, including for instance 'the need for the international trade system and trade policies to better recognise food security concerns' or biotechnologies, that may be discussed in the future. But the resistance of some delegations to having these issues even listed as potential items for later discussion is indicative of their concern that the CFS might entertain issues covered in other fora.

[63] See, e.g., P. Hunt, 'Report of the Special Rapporteur on the Right of Everyone to the Enjoyment of the Highest Attainable Standard of Physical and Mental Health: Missions to the World Bank and the International Monetary Fund in Washington, D.C. (20 October 2006) and Uganda (4–7 February 2007)' (5 March 2009) UN Doc. A/HRC/7/11/Add.2; De Schutter, 'Report on Mission to the World Trade Organization'.

that they have a positive impact on their realisation.[64] Most recently, on 28 September 2011, a group of experts adopted the Maastricht Principles on Extraterritorial Obligations of States in the Area of Economic, Social and Cultural Rights. These Principles are the legal equivalent of the moral requirement of cosmopolitanism, i.e. the idea that, in an interdependent world, citizens in rich countries owe duties to those living in poor countries. The Maastricht Principles clarify the human rights obligations of States, both as they relate to state conduct that produces effects on the enjoyment of human rights outside of the States' territories and as they relate to 'obligations of a global character that are set out in the Charter of the United Nations and human rights instruments to take action, separately, and jointly through international cooperation, to realise human rights universally'.[65] It is also to this enterprise that the Guiding Principles on Human Rights Impact Assessments of Trade and Investment Agreements seek to contribute.[66] By providing methodological and procedural guidance to States as to how to go about preparing human rights impact assessments of the trade and investment agreements that they complete, the Guiding Principles seek to ensure that the trade and investment regimes that develop alongside the human rights system will be better aligned with the objectives of the latter, and support country-led efforts to realise human rights, rather than risking undermining them. In sum, the quest for an international economic order that supports the full realisation of human rights at the domestic level has been making significant progress in recent years.

V. Conclusion

It is in this regard that the reactions that followed the global food price crisis of 2008 may be seen as embodying a larger and more important

[64] See especially Guiding Principles on Business and Human Rights: Implementing the United Nations 'Protect, Respect and Remedy' Framework, in J. Ruggie, 'Report of the Special Representative of the Secretary-General on the Issue of Transnational Corporations and Other Business Enterprises and Human Rights (21 March 2011) UN Doc. A/HRC/17/31.

[65] See Maastricht Principles on Extraterritorial Obligations of States in the Area of Economic, Social and Cultural Rights (29 February 2012), www.fian.org/fileadmin/media/publications/2012.02.29_-_Maastricht_Principles_on_Extraterritorial_Obligations.pdf, last accessed 5 September 2013. For more on these Principles, see Balakrishnan and Heintz's contribution to this volume.

[66] O. De Schutter, 'Report of the Special Rapporteur on the Right to Food: Guiding Principles on Human Rights Impact Assessments of Trade and Investment Agreements' (19 December 2011) UN Doc. A/HRC/19/59/Add.5.

lesson. The bold attempt to reshape the global governance of food security to ensure that all sectoral policies would converge towards the realisation of the right to food is one that could serve as an inspiration for future attempts to create an international environment conducive to the realisation of other human rights such as the right to water or the right to health. The different crises that the international community has experienced in recent years – a food price crisis, a financial and an economic crisis, and a long-term, slowly unfolding but massive ecological crisis – are also opportunities for transformation and improvement. As transformative possibilities emerge, human rights can provide a signpost. They can gradually turn into what Buchanan and Keohane call a 'global public standard' to assess the normative legitimacy of global governance institutions – i.e. the 'right to rule' of these institutions, which cannot ensure compliance with their decisions unless they are perceived as legitimate by those, including States, to whom such decisions are addressed.[67]

Even apart from the preeminent position that they occupy in the original project of the United Nations, human rights possess three features that make them particularly suited to this goal. First, they are *relatively incomplete*. They are sufficiently precise to provide a focal point[68] for

[67] A. Buchanan and R. Keohane, 'The Legitimacy of Global Governance Institutions', *Ethics and International Affairs*, 20 (2006), 405–37. Buchanan and Keohane refer to human rights as one of the substantive criteria that are relevant in assessing the legitimacy of global institutions. Such institutions, they write, 'must not persist in committing serious injustices. If they do so, they are not entitled to our support. On our view, the primary instance of a serious injustice is the violation of human rights' (*ibid.*, 419). That refers to what they call the 'minimal moral acceptability' of global institutions. The position adopted here places the bar higher: it is that global governance institutions should be assessed primarily by the contribution they make to the realisation of human rights. Buchanan and Keohane presumably would not accept that position as overlapping with theirs, although they express some hesitation on this point. They write:

> For many global governance institutions, it is proper to expect that they should *respect* human rights, but not that they should play a major role in *promoting* human rights. Nonetheless, a theory of legitimacy cannot ignore the fact that in some cases the dispute over whether a global governance institution is legitimate is in large part a disagreement over whether it is worthy of support if it does not *actively promote* human rights. A proposal for a standard of legitimacy for global governance institutions must take into account the fact that some of these institutions play a more direct and substantial role in securing human rights than others. (*Ibid.*, 420, emphasis added)

[68] On the idea of a focal point that allows actors to negotiate based on certain baseline expectations, see T. C. Schelling, *The Strategy of Conflict* (Cambridge, MA: Harvard University Press, 1960), ch. 3.

deliberations as to how to build international regimes – for instance, as to how to regulate trade, how much to protect foreign investors, or how to allocate the responsibilities in combating climate change. Yet, they are vague enough not to preempt the result of these deliberations. They thus allow true ownership by the actors, primarily States, which contribute to the establishment of international regimes. As Buchanan and Keohane note, any standard of legitimacy should allow for a 'principled, informed deliberation about moral issues into the standard of legitimacy itself'.[69] That is precisely what human rights allow – at least as adequately as other potential candidates today such as 'sustainable development', 'green growth' or 'development goals'.

A second advantage of human rights is that they are both *legal rules*, binding upon States (and, in some respects, on non-state actors) and *ideals*. The legitimacy that human rights confer therefore includes the element of legality, without being reducible to that element. Human rights are violated or they are complied with. However, that simple dichotomy, which is the language of lawyers, does not exhaust their significance – for human rights can always be improved upon. Our quest for the full realisation of human rights is one in which we constantly learn and test the means we use against the ends that human rights are supposed to define.

A third advantage of human rights is that they effectively correspond to the requirements of moral cosmopolitanism. Human rights are the legal embodiment of the idea that, as Thomas Pogge writes, 'every human being has a global stature as the ultimate unit of moral concern'.[70] By their very definition, human rights are held by each individual, wherever he or she finds him- or herself to be, and all States are duty-bound to refrain from conduct that might lead to a violation of the rights of that individual. The reform of the CFS is, in many ways, characterised by a high level of ambition. In order to align trade and investment, development cooperation and food aid with the realisation of the right to adequate food, it seeks to bring together not only governments, but a wide range of international

[69] Buchanan and Keohane, 'The Legitimacy of Global Governance Institutions', 421. See also *ibid.*, 427: 'Because what constitutes appropriate accountability is itself subject to reasonable dispute, the legitimacy of global governance institutions depends in part upon whether they operate in such a way as to facilitate principled, factually informed deliberation about the terms of accountability.'

[70] T. Pogge, *World Poverty and Human Rights* (Cambridge: Polity Press, 2002), p. 169. The idea of moral cosmopolitanism is defined here using Pogge's characterisation, but the expression first appears in contemporary political philosophy with C. Beitz, *Political Theory and International Relations* (Princeton University Press, 1979).

agencies which should agree on a common agenda of action. The objective is, ultimately, to avoid repetition of the failures of the past, where a lack of convergence across these different policy areas frustrated the achievement of outcomes. In order to improve monitoring and accountability, the reform encourages a modest form of peer review, through the exchange of regional and country experiences, and by the adoption of global guidelines. In order to build legitimacy and improve the quality of the information upon which decisions are based, the reform involves civil society organisations. In turn, this also ensures that the positions adopted by governments shall be known, and their conduct judged. A new breed of international governance is emerging in which civil society, the private sector and international agencies are co-authors with governments of international law.

Yet for all its ambitions, the reform of the CFS is still most remarkable for its modesty. Its procedures make it an exploratory mechanism – seeking to learn from both successes and failures, and involving those most affected by food insecurity, in order to identify true solutions. While overcoming the current fragmentation of international law and global governance is a necessary condition for supporting the realisation of the right to food at domestic level, it will not be sufficient; improved coordination must be complemented by a constant search for experiments that work. If, by combining monitoring with learning, the CFS can become a tool for convergence of policies as well as a learning platform for governments, it shall have succeeded.

PART II

Teasing out obligations in a time of crisis

4

Two steps forward, no steps back? Evolving criteria on the prohibition of retrogression in economic and social rights

AOIFE NOLAN, NICHOLAS J. LUSIANI AND CHRISTIAN COURTIS

I. Introduction

This chapter provides an overview of an obligation that is of central importance to any consideration of the impact of financial and economic crises on economic and social rights (ESR): the prohibition of retrogressive measures. Despite the importance of the principle of non-retrogression, it has historically suffered from a lack of sufficient attention from the Committee on Economic, Social and Cultural Rights (Committee) and other supranational quasi-judicial and judicial human rights bodies. This is despite the fact that analogous legal rules have been applied by domestic courts addressing steps backwards in ESR enjoyment at the national level.

The relative neglect of the prohibition of retrogression has likewise been a feature of ESR-related academic scholarship. In recent times, however, the impacts of the global financial and economic crises – and, in particular, the proliferation of austerity measures (for example, deep public expenditure reductions, regressive tax increases, structural reforms to labour and pension protections) in response to them – have served to focus expert attention on this aspect of ESR law. However, much remains to be done in terms of providing conceptual clarification of the prohibition of retrogression, as well as delineating criteria for its practical application as a standard to evaluate state compliance with ESR and to guide the construction of policy alternatives. This chapter addresses these lacunae.

The chapter opens with an introduction to the prohibition of retrogression as derived from, and understood in terms of, Article 2(1) of the International Covenant on Economic, Social and Cultural Rights (ICESCR).[1] Having outlined some of the reasons for the relatively reticent approach of the

[1] International Covenant on Economic, Social and Cultural Rights, 993 UNTS 3 (ICESCR).

Committee to this state obligation, we proceed to consider the Committee's approach towards non-retrogression and the main conceptual issues posed by such. We then go on to consider the 'state of play' with regard to the specification of operative legal standards capable of assessing state conduct on this basis. In doing so, we engage with international and domestic judicial and quasi-judicial efforts to evaluate state compliance with the non-retrogression principle in the context of financial and economic crises.

II. The prohibition of retrogression under Article 2(1) of ICESCR: origins and key questions

Under Article 2(1) of ICESCR, States Parties undertake to take steps, to the maximum of their available resources, *with a view to achieving progressively the full realisation of the rights recognised in the Covenant* by all appropriate means.[2] Similar language can be found in other international and regional human rights instruments,[3] and also in national constitutional provisions.[4]

The Committee's analysis of progressive realisation can be understood to have two elements. According to the Committee, the fact that rights realisation is required of States over time and in line with resources should not be misinterpreted as depriving the obligation of all meaningful content. It is on the one hand a necessary contextualisation device, reflecting the constraints of the real world and the difficulties involved for any country in ensuring the full realisation of economic, social and cultural rights. On the other hand, the phrase must be read in the light of the overall objective of the Covenant which is to establish clear obligations for States Parties in respect of the full realisation of the rights in question. Article 2(1) thus imposes an obligation to move as expeditiously and effectively as possible towards that goal.[5] Therefore, progressive realisation does not simply offer States Parties some leeway in choosing the measures to be

2 Emphasis added.

3 See, e.g., Convention on the Rights of the Child, 1577 UNTS 3, art. 4; Convention on the Rights of Persons with Disabilities, 2515 UNTS 3, art. 4(2). In the regional context, see American Convention on Human Rights, OAS Treaty Series No. 36, art. 26. Progressive realisation is also common in the context of International Labour Organization (ILO) instruments. See, e.g., ILO Recommendation R202: Social Protection Floors Recommendation (Recommendation Concerning National Floors of Social Protection) (101st Conference Session Geneva 14 June 2012), art. 3 (g).

4 See, e.g., Constitution of the Republic of South Africa, arts. 26(2), 27(2); Constitution of Kenya, ss. 19(1), 21, 43.

5 UN Committee on Economic, Social and Cultural Rights (CESCR) 'General Comment No. 3' in 'Note by the Secretariat, Compilation of General Comments and General

adopted according to the context. Rather, it also has a second meaning, that of *improvement* or *advancement*, which entails the obligation to ensure a broader enjoyment and expand the coverage of the rights over time.[6]

It is the second, 'advancement-focused' meaning of progressive realisation that we will address first in our consideration of retrogression in the context of financial and economic crisis. The duty to provide for the improvement of economic, social and cultural rights entails at least a negative obligation: the prohibition of the adoption of measures reducing either the entitlements enjoyed by the right-holders when the particular State became a party to the Covenant, or the entitlements guaranteed as the result of each progressive improvement subsequent to the State ratifying ICESCR. As a State Party commits to expanding the coverage and protection of Covenant rights, it simultaneously assumes an obligation to refrain from annulling or reducing the existing level of protection of recognised rights other than in accordance with the limitations set out under the Covenant.[7] In sum, therefore, the natural corollary of the duty to make progress is the corresponding duty to not regress, lose ground or backslide, in the fulfilment of ESC rights.[8]

This prohibition of backwards steps in terms of the realisation of ESC rights involves two dimensions: normative and empirical. The first dimension of retrogression concerns steps backwards in terms of legal, de jure guarantees (i.e. the extent of the entitlements granted by a legal norm), while the second is concerned with de facto, empirical backsliding in the effective enjoyment of the rights.[9] Assessing empirical

Recommendations Adopted by Human Rights Treaty Bodies' (27 May 2008) UN Doc. HRI/GEN/1/Rev.9 (Vol. I), para. 9.

6 Reflecting this, the Committee has stressed that steps taken to achieve the full realisation of the rights 'should be deliberate, concrete and targeted as clearly as possible towards meeting the obligations recognized in the Covenant'. CESCR 'General Comment No. 3', para. 2.

7 This is evidenced by the fact that the CESCR introduced the prohibition of retrogressive measures as a corollary of the principle of progressive realisation in General Comment 3. *Ibid.*, para. 9. Similarly, the Committee has often identified as a violation of obligations to respect the formal repeal or suspension of legislation necessary for the enjoyment of a specific ESR. See, e.g., CESCR 'General Comment No. 12' in 'Compilation of General Comments', para. 19.

8 As early as 1987, the Limburg Principles on the Implementation of the International Covenant on Economic Social and Cultural Rights *Human Rights Quarterly* 9 (1987), 122–35 had already echoed, in paragraph 72, that a State Party violates the Covenant if 'it deliberately retards or halts the progressive realization of a right, unless it is acting within a limitation permitted by the Covenant or it does so due to a lack of available resources or force majeure'.

9 C. Courtis, *Ni un paso atrás: La prohibición de regresividad en material de derechos sociales* (Buenos Aires: Editores de Puerto s.r.l., 2006). These normative and empirical elements are recognised, implicitly at least, in the 1997 Maastricht Guidelines on Violations of

retrogression requires a comprehensive evaluation of state conduct (actions and omissions), including the generation and use of available resources. It will often require the use of quantitative indicators, as state conduct will manifest (or foreseeably will manifest) in objective socio-economic outcomes, such as unemployment (right to work) or the incidence of communicable disease (right to the highest attainable standard of physical and mental health).[10]

Returning to the work of the Committee, it is important to note that the contextual aspect of progressive realisation also plays a role with regard to understanding retrogression under ICESCR – primarily in tempering any notion of an absolute prohibition of such activity. The Committee has stated that 'any deliberately retrogressive measures in that regard would require the most careful consideration and would need to be fully justified by reference to the totality of the rights provided for in the Covenant and in the context of the full use of the maximum available resources'.[11] It is thus clear that the Committee considers Article 2(1) to encompass an understanding that progressive realisation may be limited by the 'realities' faced by States, such as a diminution of resources available to them. Hence – implicitly at least – Article 2(1) would appear to contemplate that retrogressive measures may be justifiable in some circumstances. That said, the Committee's statement creates a presumption that 'deliberately retrogressive measures' constitute a prima facie violation of the Covenant;

Economic, Social and Cultural Rights (22–26 January 1997). While the Guidelines state that violations include '[t]he adoption of any deliberately retrogressive measure that reduces the extent to which any such right is guaranteed' (Guideline 14(e)), they also highlight a range of different violations that would also appear to constitute retrogression, including: '[t]he formal removal or suspension of legislation necessary for the continued enjoyment of an economic, social and cultural right that is currently enjoyed' (Guideline 14(a)); '[t]he adoption of legislation or policies which are manifestly incompatible with pre-existing legal obligations relating to these rights, unless it is done with the purpose and effect of increasing equality and improving the realization of economic, social and cultural rights for the most vulnerable groups' (Guideline 14(d)); 'the calculated obstruction of, or halt to, the progressive realization of a right protected by the Covenant, unless the State is acting within a limitation permitted by the Covenant or it does so due to a lack of available resources or force majeure' (Guideline 14(f)); and '[t]he reduction or diversion of specific public expenditure, when such reduction or diversion results in the non-enjoyment of such rights and is not accompanied by adequate measures to ensure minimum subsistence rights for everyone' (Guideline 14(g)).

[10] See Center for Economic and Social Rights (CESR), 'OPERA: Assessing Compliance with the Obligation to Fulfill Economic, Social and Cultural Rights' (2012); Office of the United Nations High Commissioner for Human Rights (OHCHR), 'Human Rights Indicators: A Guide to Measurement and Implementation' (2012).

[11] CESCR 'General Comment No. 3', para. 9.

thus, where it can be demonstrated that a State has adopted such a measure, the burden of the proof shifts onto the State to justify it in terms of the Covenant.[12] A key question, which will be addressed below, is when and where such backsliding will be justifiable in terms of ICESCR compliance.

[12] The language employed by the Committee also suggests that a stringent standard will be used to assess the justification offered by the State Party – that is, the State must show the *strict necessity* of the measure. This will be discussed further below but see further: General Comment No. 13: '[i]f any deliberately retrogressive measures are taken, *the State Party has the burden of proving that they have been introduced after the most careful consideration of all alternatives and that they are fully justified* by reference to the totality of the rights provided for in the Covenant and in the context of the full use of the State Party's maximum available resources' (CESCR 'General Comment No. 13' in 'Compilation of General Comments', para. 45, emphasis added); General Comment No. 14: '[i]f any deliberately retrogressive measures are taken, the State Party *has the burden of proving that they have been introduced after the most careful consideration of all alternatives and that they are duly justified* by reference to the totality of the rights provided for in the Covenant in the context of the full use of the State Party's maximum available resources' (CESCR 'General Comment No. 14' in *ibid.* para. 32, emphasis added); General Comment No. 15: '[i]f any deliberately retrogressive measures are taken, *the State Party has the burden of proving that they have been introduced after the most careful consideration of all alternatives and that they are duly justified* by reference to the totality of the rights provided for in the Covenant in the context of the full use of the State Party's maximum available resources' (CESCR 'General Comment No. 15' in *ibid.* para. 19, emphasis added); General Comment No. 17: '[i]f any deliberately retrogressive measures are taken, *the State Party has the burden of proving that they have been introduced after careful consideration of all alternatives and that they are duly justified* in the light of the totality of the rights recognized in the Covenant' (CESCR 'General Comment No. 17' in *ibid.* para. 27, emphasis added); General Comment No. 18: '[i]f any deliberately retrogressive steps are taken, *States Parties have the burden of proving that they have been introduced after consideration of all alternatives and that they are duly justified* by reference to the totality of the rights provided for in the Covenant in the context of the full use of the States Parties' maximum available resources' (CESCR 'General Comment No. 18' in *ibid.* para. 21, emphasis added); General Comment No. 19: '[i]f any deliberately retrogressive measures are taken, *the State Party has the burden of proving that they have been introduced after the most careful consideration of all alternatives and that they are duly justified* by reference to the totality of the rights provided for in the Covenant, in the context of the full use of the maximum available resources of the State Party' (CESCR 'General Comment No. 19' in *ibid.* para 42, emphasis added); General Comment No. 21: '[a]ny deliberately retrogressive measures in relation to the right to take part in cultural life *would require the most careful consideration and need to be fully justified* by reference to the totality of the rights provided for in the Covenant and in the context of the full use of the maximum available resources' (CESCR 'General Comment No. 21' (16 March 2010) UN Doc. E/C.12/GC/21/Rev.1, para 65, emphasis added); CESCR Statement: 'in case of failure to take any steps or of the adoption of retrogressive steps, *the burden of proof rests with the State Party to show that such a course of action was based on the most careful consideration and can be justified* by reference to the totality of the rights provided for in the Covenant and by the fact that full use was made of available resources' (CESCR, 'An Evaluation of the Obligation to Take Steps to the "Maximum of Available Resources Under an Optional Protocol to the Covenant' (21 September 2007) UN Doc. E/C.12/2007/1, para 9., emphasis added).

III. Accounting for the Committee's reticence and the challenges posed by the crohibition of retrogression

As stated earlier, despite it being a cornerstone of international human rights law, the Committee on Economic, Social and Cultural Rights has, for the most part, been reticent about expressly relying on this prohibition to evaluate state compliance with the Covenant. This has included situations in which States have engaged in extensive cutbacks to their social and economic programmes in the context of financial or economic crisis.

During the various economic crises of the 1990s and early 2000s in the Czech Republic,[13] Hungary,[14] Mexico,[15] Thailand,[16] Indonesia,[17] South Korea,[18] Argentina[19] and Russia[20] for example, neither the Committee nor other relevant UN treaty-monitoring bodies deemed structural adjustment policies or public expenditure cuts to be in contravention of the Covenant or other international instruments affording protection to ESR.

[13] CESCR 'Concluding Observations on the Czech Republic' (5 June 2002) UN Doc. E/C.12/1/Add.76.

[14] CESCR 'Concluding Observations on Hungary' (1 October 1992) UN Doc. E/C.12/1992/2.

[15] CESCR 'Concluding Observations on Mexico' (8 December 1999) UN Doc. E/C.12/1/Add.41.

[16] Committee on the Elimination of Discrimination against Women (CEDAW) 'Concluding Observations on Thailand', in 'Report of the Committee on the Elimination of Discrimination against Women: Twentieth Session' (1999) UN Doc. A/54/38/Rev.1, para. 227 (noting that 'the recent financial crisis has been affecting the country's economic and social development and is an impediment to the implementation of the Convention').

[17] CEDAW 'Concluding Observations on Indonesia', in 'Report of the Committee on the Elimination of Discrimination against Women: Eighteenth and Nineteenth Sessions' (1998) UN Doc. A/53/38/Rev.1, paras. 262–311.

[18] CESCR 'Concluding Observations on Republic of Korea' (21 May 2001) UN Doc. E/C.12/1/Add.59; CEDAW 'Concluding Observations on Republic of Korea', in 'Report of the CEDAW: Eighteenth and Nineteenth Sessions', paras. 347–86.

[19] Committee on the Elimination of Racial Discrimination (CERD) 'Concluding Observations on Argentina' (27 April 2001) UN Doc. CERD/C/304/Add.112, para. 9 (noting that 'the poverty and unemployment indices among indigenous populations and other vulnerable groups have risen as a result of the economic crisis'); CEDAW 'Concluding Observations on Argentina', in 'Report of the Committee on the Elimination of Discrimination against Women: Twenty-Sixth and Twenty-Seventh Sessions and Exceptional Session' A/57/38 (2002), paras. 339–69; Committee on the Rights of the Child (CRC) 'Concluding Observations on Argentina' (9 October 2002) UN Doc. CRC/C/15/Add.187. For more on the Argentine experience of economic crisis, see Maurino and Nino's contribution to this volume.

[20] CRC 'Concluding Observations on the Russian Federation' (18 February 1993) UN Doc. CRC/C/15/Add.4, para. 8; CRC 'Concluding Observations on the Russian Federation' (10 November 1999) UN Doc. CRC/C/15/Add.110.

In the few situations where the Committee did analyse such measures, it confined itself to expressing general concern over their potential negative effects, rather than decrying these measures as impermissible under the Covenant.[21] This reticence is consistent with the Committee's historic, broader reluctance to link budgetary or economic policy decisions and their impacts with specific ESR obligations.[22]

Given the frequently severe impacts of economic crisis – and the decision by many governments to embark on austerity measures in response – upon ESR enjoyment, one is driven to ask: why has the Committee proven so averse to invoking the prohibition of non-retrogression in contexts of clear normative and/or empirical backsliding? In practice, we argue, a number of challenges are evident.

First among them are the *methodological* challenges.[23] Adjudging whether particular legislative provisions entail normative retrogression, or decreased legal protection of rights, can be relatively straightforward (certainly for judges and/or lawyers, who will generally find it relatively easy to compare prior and subsequent norms and to consider whether the latter broadens, reduces or eliminates rights or entitlements granted by the former). However, assessing the empirical aspect of retrogression is often much more challenging.

Unambiguously invoking the attribution of state responsibility requires an evidential link between particular state conduct (action or omission) on the one hand (e.g. legislative act, policy intervention, budget

[21] See M. Sepúlveda, *The Nature of the Obligations Under the International Covenant on Economic and Cultural Rights* (Antwerp: Intersentia, 2003) (citing, for instance, CESCR's Concluding Observations on Mauritius (1994), Nigeria (1998) and Germany (1999) concerning the introduction of tuition fees for education (Sepúlveda, *The Nature of the* Obligations, p. 325)). See also CESCR 'Concluding Observations on Canada' (10 June 1993) UN Doc. E/C.12/1993/5. See also CESCR 'Concluding Observations on Hungary', in 'Report of the Committee on Economic, Social and Cultural Rights: Seventh session' (1992) UN Doc. E/C.12/1992.2, para. 152 ('The Committee noted that the period of political and economic transition in which Hungary, currently found itself ... even forced it to take some retrogressive measures.') While the Committee is using the term retrogressive here, it does not necessarily equate that term with impermissibility.

[22] See, e.g., A. Nolan, 'Budget Analysis and Economic and Social Rights' in E. Riedel, G. Giacca and C. Golay (eds.), *Contemporary Issues in the Realisation of Economic, Social and Cultural Rights* (Oxford University Press, 2014), pp. 369–90, p. 369. For a discussion of the CESCR's reluctance to engage with macroeconomic policy issues more generally, see Dowell-Jones, *Contextualising the International Covenant on Economic, Social and Cultural Rights* (Leiden: Martinus Nijhoff Publishers, 2004).

[23] R. Uprimny Yepes and D. Guarnizo, '¿Es posible una dogmática adecuada sobre la prohibición de regresividad? Un enfoque desde la jurisprudencia constitucional colombiana' (Working Paper, 2006).

appropriation, tax measure, regulatory omission, etc.), and the factual outcome of decreased rights enjoyment on the other. Building this kind of empirical case is much less straightforward, requiring a careful monitoring of the degree of empirical retrogression over time – which itself can involve a complex computation of a wide range of sophisticated statistical and other information to assess the degree to which a particular policy intervention results in an adverse outcome for rights-holders. Until relatively recently, for example, empirical evidence on the human consequences of austerity policies stemming from the 2008 financial crisis were difficult to come by due to the lack of real-time and disaggregated data, not to mention the failure of governments to conduct *ex ante* impact assessments to discern the degree to which such policies would foreseeably undermine the equal enjoyment of rights.[24] Tying the crisis-induced impacts to particular government conduct has been equally challenging.

Further to the methodological challenges, assessing empirical retrogression will generally involve a comprehensive assessment of the allocation and generation of financial resources, and thus the role of government with regard to the economy. Different schools of economic thought have competing views on the proper role of the public sector, with different policy implications regarding, for example, counter- vs pro-cyclical fiscal policy and protection vs flexibility in labour markets. Judges and courts in this context often hesitate to enter into what are perceived to be polemical and irresolvable disputes about economic ideas with supposed empirical uncertainty.[25] From an instrumentalist perspective we could ask: is it reasonable to rescind certain labour protections, for instance, on the grounds that such restrictions might, according to neo-classical schools of thought, allow wages to fall, national firms to become more globally competitive and thus drive economic growth and more employment?[26] Or, from a neo-Keynesian

[24] See EU Agency for Fundamental Rights (FRA), 'Protecting Fundamental Rights During the Economic Crisis' (Working Paper, December 2010), http://fra.europa.eu/sites/default/files/fra_uploads/1423-FRA-Working-paper-FR-during-crisis-Dec10_EN.pdf, last accessed 4 October 2013. ('There is no evidence that EU Member States carry out systematic ex ante impact assessments of fiscal consolidation measures on different population groups.') See also CESCR, 'Concluding Observations on Spain' (6 June 2012) UN Doc. E/C.12/ESP/CO/5. See also *California Hospital Assn* v. *Douglas*, 848 F Supp 2d 1117 (C.D. Cal. 2011).

[25] Uprimny and Guarnizo, '¿Es posible una dogmática adecuada sobre la prohibición de regresividad?', 12.

[26] See, e.g., A. Aslund, 'Lessons from Reforms in Central and Eastern Europe in the Wake of the Global Financial Crisis' (Peterson Institute for International Economics Working Paper Series WP12–7, 2012).

perspective, is guaranteeing existing labour protections necessary in order to ensure workers' decent wages – which will in turn produce the necessary and stable aggregate demand to drive economic dynamism and decent job creation?[27] Similarly, are governments justified when arguing that prioritising deficit reduction now is necessary to lower the future borrowing costs and instil a sense of stability perceived as necessary to provide the fiscal grounds for progressive realisation of rights in the future? Or, by contrast, will large-scale contractions in public expenditure to address deep debt overhangs lead to an austerity trap, in which the anaemic demand resulting from these public spending cuts during a recession only leads to deeper unemployment, less government revenue, higher public deficits, increased interest rates on bonds, and thus increased need for future cutbacks? Established ideological predispositions on economic thought often lie at the heart of, and further accentuate, the long-standing resistance of adjudicative bodies to interfering in economic and social policy deemed to be the prerogative of the executive and the legislature. This continues to prove a formidable barrier to rights-based judicial scrutiny of economic policy, particularly of crisis-related measures.[28] Lacking the methodologies and empirical insights from the field of economics to approach such matters on solid ground, legal debates – including those of the Committee – have tended to focus more on the normative rather than empirical dimensions of retrogression, leaving adjudicators less-than-equipped to determine overall compliance in times of economic crisis.

Inquiries into retrogression are also stymied by the plurality of actors involved in the advancement (and decline) in ESR achievement. From intergovernmental supranational bodies to central government to subnational and private entities, many cases of empirical retrogression involve a wide range of potentially responsible actors. The difficulty in

[27] ILO, 'World of Work Report 2012: Better Jobs for a Better Economy' (26 April 2012); R. Freeman, 'Labor Market Institutions around the World' (National Bureau of Economic Research Working Paper No. 13242, July 2007); D. Howell, *Fighting Unemployment: The Limits of Free Market Orthodoxy* (Oxford University Press, 2004); M. Kumhof and R. Ranciere, 'Inequality, Leverage and Crises' (International Monetary Fund Working Paper WP10268, 2011).

[28] See J. Kissane, 'The Government's Approach to the Role of Economic and Social Rights in Relation to Austerity Measures' (presentation at seminar 'Economic and Social Rights in Times of Austerity', University of Oxford, 1 July 2011), www.esrinatimeofausterity.com/presentations.html, last accessed 4 October 2013. See also CESR, 'Fiscal Fallacies: 8 Myths about the "Age of Austerity" and Human Rights Responses' (Rights in Crisis Briefing Paper, July 2012), www.cesr.org/downloads/CESR-FiscalFallacies.pdf, last accessed 4 October 2013.

these circumstances of specifying the responsible agents and their correlative duties to bring about rights achievement is a second obstacle to assessing empirical retrogression in practice.[29] Rather than the simpler binary approach used to discern attribution in more straightforward circumstances of rights claims, such as a forced eviction, determining whether a government's conduct results in empirical backsliding often necessitates a *polycentric analysis* of responsible actors. This is especially the case in situations of economic crisis associated with increasing borrowing costs which are determined, for the most part, by private actors, especially credit-rating agencies and bondholders devoid of accountability to human rights or other social concerns. The proliferation of subnational, national, intergovernmental and super-national bodies involved in the economic crisis that has ravaged the Eurozone gives a case in point of the complexity of determining and delineating appropriate responsibility between national governments, the International Monetary Fund (IMF), the European Commission and the European Central Bank when considering human rights-infringing austerity measures.[30] Domestic judicial bodies, like UN human rights treaty-monitoring bodies, have frequently shown resistance to adjudicating these types of polycentric claims, especially those relating to resource allocation where responsibilities are to be considered more diffuse.[31]

Third, an overly strict interpretation of the prohibition of retrogression can have *unintended human rights consequences*. Petrifying public policy or the legal system by absolutely protecting against any adjustments can, in some circumstances, lead to inequitable or even discriminatory results,[32] perpetuating the privileges and power of acquisition

[29] A. Sen, 'Work and Rights', *International Labour Review*, 139 (2000), 119–28, 124.

[30] See, e.g., CESR, 'Mauled by the Celtic Tiger: Human Rights in Ireland's Economic Meltdown' (Rights in Crisis Briefing Paper, February 2012), www.cesr.org/downloads/cesr.ireland.briefing.12.02.2012.pdf, last accessed 4 October 2013.

[31] For a general discussion of the judicial treatment of polycentrism in jurisprudence, see L. Fuller, 'The Forms and Limits of Adjudication', *Harvard Law Review*, 92 (1978), 353–409; J. King, 'The Pervasiveness of Polycentricity,' *Public Law* (2008), 101–24, http://ssrn.com/abstract=1027625, last accessed 11 January 2014. For a discussion of polycentrism in the context of ESR jurisprudence specifically, see A. Nolan, *Children's Socio-economic Rights, Democracy and the Courts* (Oxford: Hart Publishing, 2011), pp. 200–204.

[32] One example of this is the case of pension reforms in Colombia. See Colombian Commission of Jurists, 'Report on the Prohibition against Regressivity in the Field of Economic, Social and Cultural Rights in Colombia' (2010); Uprimny and Guarnizo, '¿Es posible una dogmática adecuada sobre la prohibición de regresividad?', 18. For more on this issue, see Landau's contribution to this collection. For a discussion of this issue in the Inter-American context, see T. Melish, 'A Pyrrhic Victory for Peru's Pensioners: Pensions, Property, and the Perversion of Progressivity', *Revista CEJIL*, I (2005), 51–66.

of entrenched interests over more under-served and marginalised interests.[33] From a different perspective, taking adequate measures to fulfil economic and social rights in many circumstances requires investments in infrastructure, public institutions or regulatory bodies. The right mix and balance of support between different economic sectors, and decisions about what constitutes an effective investment, in order to respect, protect and fulfil human rights will differ from country to country and region to region. Properly regulated city beautification schemes in one country, for example, can support the right to decent work. In another, such schemes displace rights-holders from their homes and livelihoods. As noted above, ICESCR (and, indeed, other human rights treaties) allot a good degree of discretion to governments given the varying contexts and challenges faced by States Parties. Even while it is true that the need for trade-offs is very often exaggerated, not based on strong justifications, and a pretext to conserve an unequal status quo,[34] an unreasonably strict set of criteria on retrogressive measures would generate rigidity, and prohibit adjustments in social or economic policies necessary to protect ESR in a context of dynamic macroeconomic conditions.[35] An excessively stringent non-retrogression standard – if it sets out strict prohibitions to backsliding without clear conditions on the permissibility of adjustments – has also been argued to have the unintended effect of holding governments which have taken positive steps over previous years to a higher standard than those which have done nothing.[36]

The *emergency* nature of policy-making during times of crises generally poses a fourth obstacle to the working application of the prohibition of retrogression. Effectively applying the norm of non-retrogression almost inevitably involves questions of whether it is appropriate for adjudicative bodies to annul legislation speedily drawn up and passed in a context of crisis, especially regarding the economic implications of reversing policies and budgets for which resources have already been allocated. Recent

[33] For further discussion of this point, see, e.g., A. E. Yamin, 'Power, Suffering and Courts: Reflections on Promoting Health Rights through Judicialization', in A. E. Yamin and S. Gloppen (eds.), *Litigating Health Rights: Can Courts Bring More Justice to Health?* (Human Rights Program, Harvard Law School, 2011), pp. 333–72; U. Baxi, 'Taking Suffering Seriously: Social Action Litigation in the Supreme Court of India', *Third World Legal Studies*, 4 (1985), Article 6; O. Ferraz, 'Harming the Poor through Social Rights Litigation: Lessons from Brazil', 80 (2011), 1643–68.

[34] Sen, 'Work and Rights', 120–1.

[35] Sepúlveda, *The Nature of the Obligations*, p. 428.

[36] Dowell-Jones, *Contextualising the International Covenant on Economic, Social and Cultural Rights*, p. 52.

national jurisprudence illustrates that courts in several instances have found particular budget reductions unlawful, in some cases unconstitutional, but at the same time avoided substantively striking them down due to the perceived complications of retroactively re-writing budgets. The Portuguese Constitutional Court found in 2012 that certain austerity measures were unconstitutional, for example, yet the judges were clear in pointing out that the Court's ruling would not substantially alter the administration's austerity policy as designed, although it would have implications for future budgets.[37]

The perceived (at times exaggerated) urgency of responses required in times of crisis provides a considerable structural challenge to legal accountability. Theories of crisis governance suggest that the apparent exigencies of the moment coupled with psychological panic about the future tend to disrupt accepted legal and democratic constraints.[38] In such cases, checks and balances are often weakened and the executive is, by design or by default, allotted broader authority, regardless of whether an emergency is declared or not – or whether the moment can even be objectively described as such.[39]

Lastly, the reluctance of the Committee – as well as other supranational judicial and non-judicial bodies – to assess when state conduct amounts to non-retrogression in practical terms is both a cause and a consequence of the fact that we are in the early stages in the evolution of the *normative content* of non-retrogression. As such, we are still without a set of balanced and nuanced criteria necessary to adjudge the scope and the application of the standard. It is with this in mind that we turn to how the Committee has sought to develop its understanding of the prohibition of retrogression.

[37] Constitutional Court of Portugal, Judgment no. 353/2012 (5 July 2012).

[38] See, e.g., E. A. Posner and V. Adrian, 'Crisis Governance in the Administrative State: 9/11 and the Financial Meltdown of 2008' (University of Chicago Law & Economics, Olin Working Paper No. 442; University of Chicago Public Law Working Paper No. 248; Harvard Public Law Working Paper No. 08–50; Harvard Law School Program on Risk Regulation Research Paper No. 09–04, 13 November 2008), http://ssrn.com/abstract=1301164, last accessed 4 October 2013.

[39] For an example of a declaration of a state of economic, social and ecological emergency resulting in the Executive being accorded (or according itself) the power to bypass the legislature and issue decrees with force of law, see Landau's discussion of the Colombian experience in this collection. For a discussion of exercise of governmental powers in the context of economic emergencies in Argentina, see Maurino and Nino's contribution.

IV. Giving meaning to the prohibition of retrogression under ICESCR

Despite the challenges outlined in the previous section, the Committee has taken some steps to flesh out the approach that it will adopt in evaluating the acceptability of retrogressive measures.[40] In a statement on 'An Evaluation of the Obligation to Take Steps to the "Maximum of Available Resources" under an Optional Protocol to the Covenant', the Committee highlighted that, should a State Party use 'resource constraints' as an explanation for any retrogressive steps taken, the Committee would consider such information on a country-by-country basis in the light of 'objective criteria'.[41] Such criteria would include: the country's level of development; the severity of the alleged breach (in particular whether the situation concerned the enjoyment of the minimum core content of the Covenant); the country's current economic situation (in particular whether the country was undergoing a period of economic recession); the existence of other serious claims on the State Party's limited resources (for example, resulting from a recent natural disaster or from recent internal or international armed conflict); whether the State Party had sought to identify low-cost options; and whether the State Party had sought cooperation and assistance or rejected offers of resources from the international community for the purposes of implementing the provisions of the Covenant without sufficient reason.[42] The Committee did not, however, use this statement as an opportunity to define what a retrogressive measure actually is, apparently regarding the term as self-explanatory.

The conception of a retrogressive measure has thus remained murky. Amongst other things, the Committee has never addressed the difference between retrogressive measures that are 'deliberate' and those that are not, even if the distinction was introduced and reiterated by the same Committee.[43] Nor has the Committee consistently engaged with, or attempted to delineate, the circumstances in which such a measure might be permissible in terms of concrete examples. This is significant given that, as highlighted earlier, the prohibition of retrogressive

[40] This section is largely based on Nolan, 'Putting ESR-based Budget Analysis into Practice', pp. 47–52.

[41] CESCR, 'An Evaluation', para. 10. [42] *Ibid.*

[43] Sepúlveda has addressed this point, describing a deliberate retrogressive measure as backwards steps in the level of ESR enjoyment as 'a consequence of an *intentional* decision(s) by the state'. Sepúlveda, *The Nature of the Obligations*, p. 323 (emphasis added).

measures is not absolute, as evidenced by the Committee's statement that 'any deliberately retrogressive measures in that regard would require the most careful consideration and would need to be fully justified by reference to the totality of the rights provided for in the Covenant and in the context of the full use of the maximum available resources'.[44]

This language is echoed in a number of other General Comments,[45] some of which also set out the requirement to ensure 'there has been the most careful consideration of all alternatives'.[46] In practice, it would seem likely that the only way to prove that a reduction or elimination of rights that were already granted is justified against the totality of the rights provided for in the Covenant is by showing that such a measure will at least benefit the rights of some by having – to borrow the language of the Maastricht Guidelines on Violations of Economic, Social and Cultural Rights – 'the purpose and effect of increasing equality and improving the realisation of economic, social and cultural rights for the most vulnerable groups'.[47] As for the consideration of 'the context of the full use of the maximum available resources', this would seem to indicate that the State will only be able to show that retrogressive measures are justified when factors beyond its control have led to a decrease in the resources available to it. In any case, it seems that the State cannot justify retrogressive measures simply by referring to resource scarcity, fiscal discipline or savings: it needs to show why the measures in point were necessary for the protection of the totality of the rights provided for in the Covenant.

A number of other General Comments have further highlighted that the adoption of any retrogressive measures incompatible with the 'core obligations' under the Covenant would be impermissible.[48] Given that the notion of core obligations is considered a common element of all ESR, it can be understood that conceptually this condition is not limited to

[44] CESCR 'General Comment No. 3', para. 9.

[45] CESCR 'General Comment No. 21', para. 65; CESCR 'General Comment No. 19', para. 42; CESCR 'General Comment No. 18', para. 21; CESCR 'General Comment No. 17', para. 27; CESCR 'General Comment No. 15', para. 19; CESCR 'General Comment No. 14', para. 32; CESCR 'General Comment No. 13', para. 45.

[46] CESCR 'General Comment No. 19', para. 42; CESCR 'General Comment No. 18', para. 21; CESCR 'General Comment No. 17', para. 27; CESCR 'General Comment No. 15', para. 19; CESCR 'General Comment No. 14', para. 32; CESCR 'General Comment No. 13', para. 45.

[47] Maastricht Guidelines on Violations of Economic, Social and Cultural Rights, Guideline 14(d).

[48] See CESCR 'General Comment No. 19', para. 64; CESCR 'General Comment No. 17', para. 42; CESCR 'General Comment No. 15', para. 42; CESCR 'General Comment No. 14', para. 48.

the rights addressed in those General Comments.[49] In only one General Comment, however, has the Committee delineated detailed examples of retrogressive measures.[50] Furthermore, it was only in General Comment No. 19 in the context of the right to social security that the Committee proceeded to outline in detail some of the key factors it would employ in considering whether a retrogressive measure was justifiable in terms of the Covenant.[51]

[49] See CESCR 'General Comment No. 3', para. 10:

On the basis of the extensive experience gained by the Committee, as well as by the body that preceded it, over a period of more than a decade of examining States Parties' reports the Committee is of the view that a minimum core obligation to ensure the satisfaction of, at the very least, minimum essential levels of each of the rights is incumbent upon every State Party. Thus, for example, a State Party in which any significant number of individuals is deprived of essential foodstuffs, of essential primary health care, of basic shelter and housing, or of the most basic forms of education is, prima facie, failing to discharge its obligations under the Covenant. If the Covenant were to be read in such a way as not to establish such a minimum core obligation, it would be largely deprived of its *raison d'être*. By the same token, it must be noted that any assessment as to whether a State has discharged its minimum core obligation must also take account of resource constraints applying within the country concerned. Article 2(1) obligates each State Party to take the necessary steps 'to the maximum of its available resources'. In order for a State Party to be able to attribute its failure to meet at least its minimum core obligations to a lack of available resources it must demonstrate that every effort has been made to use all resources that are at its disposition in an effort to satisfy, as a matter of priority, those minimum obligations.

[50] See CESCR 'General Comment No. 18', para. 340:

As for all other rights in the Covenant, there is a strong presumption that retrogressive measures taken in relation to the right to work are not permissible. Such retrogressive measures include, inter alia, denial of access to employment to particular individuals or groups, whether such discrimination is based on legislation or practice, abrogation or suspension of the legislation necessary for the exercise of the right to work or the adoption of laws or policies that are manifestly incompatible with international legal obligations relating to the right to work. An example would be the institution of forced labour or the abrogation of legislation protecting the employee against unlawful dismissal. Such measures would constitute a violation of States Parties' obligation to respect the right to work.

[51] CESCR 'General Comment No. 19', para. 42. Here, the Committee stated that with regard to the justifiability of retrogressive measures in the area of social security, it would look carefully at whether:

(a) there was reasonable justification for the action; (b) alternatives were comprehensively examined; (c) there was genuine participation of affected groups in examining the proposed measures and alternatives; (d) the measures were directly or indirectly discriminatory; (e) the measures will have a sustained impact on the realization of the right to social security, an unreasonable impact on acquired social security rights or whether an individual or group is deprived of access to the minimum essential level of social security; and (f) whether there was an independent review of the measures at the national level.

The Committee has also not yet considered in detail the notion of limitations on Covenant rights under Article 4 of ICESCR.[52] According to that provision, States Parties may only subject the rights set out in that instrument to such limitations 'as are determined by law' and 'only in so far as this may be compatible with the nature of these rights and solely for the purpose of promoting the general welfare in a democratic society'. The question is, then, what is the connection between the prohibition of retrogression derived from Article 2(1) and the 'limitation' of rights' clause? Leckie, for instance, has argued that any deliberately retrogressive measure would limit the enjoyment of rights found in ICESCR and thus require justification with due regard for the limitations provisions of Article 4.[53] However, in the context of differentiating between Article 2(1) and Article 4 it has been suggested by other commentators that there is a distinction between formal limitations of rights on the one hand and 'a general level of attainment' of those rights on the other.[54] If one accepts that the latter is just a reflection of resource availability, then it seems probable that a resource-motivated reduction in the level of enjoyment/attainment of a particular right would not constitute a 'limitation' in terms of Article 4.[55]

Given the ongoing spending cuts and austerity measures impacting on ESR enjoyment globally, the Committee's early reluctance to delineate clearly the parameters of impermissible retrogressive measures or limitations in terms of ESR has proved problematic in the post-financial/economic crises era. In her 2011 annual report, the UN Independent Expert (now Special Rapporteur) on the Question of Human Rights and Extreme Poverty highlighted that a number of economic 'recovery measures' taken by States, such as cuts to social protection systems, may violate the prohibition of retrogressive measures.[56] It was not, however, until May 2012

[52] Some General Comments, though, do include mentions to article 4, even if they do not offer a full account of its scope. See, e.g., CESCR 'General Comment 13', para. 42.

[53] S. Leckie, 'Another Step Towards Indivisibility: Identifying the Key Features of Violations of Economic, Social and Cultural Rights', *Human Rights Quarterly*, 20 (1998), 81–124, 98.

[54] 'Draft International Covenants on Human Rights: annotation' (1 July 1955) UN Doc. A/2929 (cited in P. Alston and G. Quinn, 'The Nature and Scope of State Parties' Obligations under the International Covenant on Economic, Social and Cultural Rights', *Human Rights Quarterly*, 9 (1987), 156–229, 205).

[55] Alston and Quinn, 'The Nature and Scope of State Parties' Obligations'. For an argument that the CESCR does not regard retrogressive measures as limitations in terms of Art. 4, see A Müller, 'Limitations to and Derogations from Economic, Social and Cultural Rights', *Human Rights Law Review*, 9 (2009), 557–601.

[56] M. Sepúlveda, 'Report of the Independent Expert on the Question of Human Rights and Extreme Poverty: The Human Rights Based Approach to Recovery from the Global

that the Committee engaged extensively with the crises and their implications for Covenant rights. That month, the Chairperson addressed a letter to States Parties on behalf of the Committee 'in relation to the protection of Covenant rights in the context of the economic and financial crisis'.[57] In it, he stated that 'economic and financial crises, and a lack of growth, impede the progressive realisation of ESC rights and can lead to retrogression in the enjoyment of those rights'[58] and highlighted that the Covenant provides 'certain important guideposts which can help States Parties to adopt appropriate policies that deal with the economic downturn while respecting economic, social and cultural rights'.[59]

The most significant part of the letter centres on the requirements that 'any proposed policy change or adjustment' in response to the crises has to meet: first, the policy must be a *temporary* measure covering only the period of the crisis; second, the policy must be *necessary and proportionate*, in the sense that the adoption of any other policy, or a failure to act, would be more detrimental to economic, social and cultural rights; third, the policy must not be *discriminatory* and must comprise all possible measures, including tax measures, to support social transfers and mitigate inequalities that can grow in times of crisis and to ensure that the rights of disadvantaged and marginalised individuals and groups are not disproportionately affected; and, finally, the policy should identify the *minimum core content of rights*, or a social protection floor, as developed by the International Labour Organization (ILO), and ensure the protection of this core content at all times.[60] The letter also highlighted the obligations of States Parties vis-à-vis decision-making within international financial institutions (implicitly referring to the IMF and regional integration organisations, such as the European Commission and the European Central Bank), and expressed hope that governments would be guided by its Covenant obligations when developing international and regional programmes to overcome the crises.[61]

Economic and Financial Crises, with a Focus on Those Living in Poverty' (17 March 2011) UN Doc. A/HRC/17/34, paras. 44, 47. For more on the Special Rapporteur's report on this topic, see Sepúlveda's contribution to this volume.

[57] CESCR, Letter to States Parties dated 16 May 2012, Reference CESCR/48th/SP/MAB/SW.

[58] *Ibid.*, 1. [59] *Ibid.*, 2.

[60] For more on the concept of a 'social protection floor', see ILO and WHO, 'Social Protection Floor for a Fair and Inclusive Globalization' (2011); ILO Recommendation R202: Social Protection Floors Recommendation; M. Sepúlveda and C. Nyst, *The Human Rights Approach to Social Protection* (Finland Ministry for Foreign Affairs, 2012), 9–10, www.cdp-hrc.uottawa.ca/uploads/HumanRightsApproachToSocialProtection.pdf, last accessed 4 October 2013.

[61] CESCR, Letter to States Parties.

This letter undoubtedly represented progress on the part of the Committee in building a more operational doctrine on the prohibition of retrogression. However, it is notable that the words 'retrogressive measures' are not mentioned in it. Nor is there reference to the language of General Comment No. 3 with regard to the need for such measures to be 'fully justified by reference to the totality of the rights provided for in the Covenant and in the context of the full use of the maximum available resources'. Furthermore, while the letter is written on behalf of the Committee as a whole, it is not a General Comment. As such, it is unlikely that such a letter could be considered even soft law. As we will see below, however, the Committee's approach to the test in recent statements suggests that it may be well on its way to assuming such status.[62]

In its 2012 consideration of the Spanish periodic report,[63] for example, the Committee focused on a range of backward steps in terms of ESR enjoyment in that country, recommending that 'the State Party ensure that all the austerity measures adopted reflect the minimum core content of all the Covenant rights'[64] and drawing the State Party's attention to the Chairperson's letter.[65] The Committee also expressed concern about 'the constant rise in unemployment and long-term unemployment rates'[66] and recommended that 'the State Party avoid any step backwards in the field of employment, including with regard to the protection of workers' labour rights'.[67] The Committee recommended that the State Party review the reforms adopted in the context of the current economic and financial crisis to ensure that all the austerity measures introduced uphold the level of the protection already attained in the realm of economic, social and cultural rights and that, in all cases, such measures are temporary and proportionate and do not negatively impinge on such rights.[68] The Committee also urged the State Party to assess the impact of any proposed cuts on the access of the most disadvantaged and marginalised individuals and groups

[62] For a useful overview of the features and effects of 'soft law' in the area of international law, see D. Thürer, 'Soft Law' in R Wolfrum (ed.), *Max Planck Encyclopedia of Public International Law*, www.mpepil.com, last accessed 4 October 2013.

[63] For more on the Spanish periodic report process 2012, see CESR and Observatori DESC, 'List of Issues in Response to the 5th Periodic Report of Spain, Prepared for the Pre-Sessional Working Group of the Committee on Economic, Social and Cultural Rights, 46th Session (23–27 May 2011)', www.cesr.org/downloads/Spain%20Presessional%20Working%20Group%20Submission%20-%20CESCR%20Observatori%20DESC%20_%20CESR.pdf, last accessed 4 October 2013.

[64] CESCR 'Concluding Observations on Spain' (6 June 2012) UN Doc. E/C.12/ESP/CO/5, para. 8.

[65] *Ibid.* [66] *Ibid.*, para. 12. [67] *Ibid.* [68] *Ibid.*, para. 17.

to health services.[69] Even here, however, the Committee refrained from deeming the cutbacks impermissible under the Covenant.

A similar approach was adopted by the Committee in its Concluding Observations on the Icelandic periodic state report. In this instance, having expressed concern that 'despite measures taken by the State Party, the national financial and economic crisis has had a negative impact on the realisation of economic, social and cultural rights', the Committee proceeded to 'remind' the State of the requirements that any proposed policy change or adjustment by the State Party in reaction to the economic crisis must meet.[70] The Committee also criticised cuts made by Iceland to its budgets for public health care and the public education system and explicitly recommended that the budgets in these areas be increased.[71] In doing so, it reiterated the conditions highlighted in the Chairperson's letter,[72] but again, held back from assessing whether the government was acting in compliance with its treaty obligations.

In its review of New Zealand, the Committee similarly expressed its disquiet over the 'retrogressive nature and possible discriminatory impact of welfare reforms' and their impact on the rights to social security and to an adequate standard of living, especially of the most disadvantaged. The Committee called on the State to reconsider these measures, especially the work-test requirements, but again avoided determining whether New Zealand's conduct equated to impermissible retrogression.[73]

An important positive feature of the Concluding Observations on Spain, Iceland and New Zealand is that the Committee begins to apply the requirements outlined in the Chairperson's letters to specific country situations. Taking these together with the May 2012 letter, the Committee has advanced its application of the criteria on non-retrogression, thereby building the normative basis for jurists, advocates, legislators, national human rights institutions or others aiming to evaluate retrogression in specific circumstances.

V. Distilling criteria for determining impermissible retrogression

So where does this leave us in terms of legal argumentation and advocacy centred on retrogression in response to the crises? We have already

[69] *Ibid.*, para. 19.

[70] CESCR 'Concluding Observations on Iceland' (11 December 2012) UN Doc. E/C.12/ISL/CO/4, para. 6.

[71] *Ibid.*, paras. 17, 18. [72] *Ibid.*

[73] CESCR, 'Concluding Observations on New Zealand' (31 May 2012) UN Doc. E/C.12/NZL/CO/3, para. 17.

detailed the key standards set out by the Committee in terms of evaluating the permissibility of state action in this context. At this point, we are in a position to posit a set of general criteria to test retrogression for the purposes of Article 2(1) in practical terms.

In terms of the Committee's work, any measure which leads to backsliding in the realisation of ESC rights can only be deemed permissible when it meets the criteria that it: (i) should be temporary by nature and in effect and limited to the duration of the crisis;[74] (ii) should be necessary and proportionate[75] (and alternative measures comprehensively examined);[76] (iii) should be reasonable;[77] (iv) should not be directly or indirectly discriminatory;[78] (v) should accord particular attention to the rights of disadvantaged and marginalised individuals and groups and ensure that they are not disproportionately affected;[79] (vi) should identify the minimum core content of the right(s) in question and ensure the protection of this core content at all times;[80] (vii) should have involved genuine participation of affected groups in examining the proposed measures and alternatives;[81] and (viii) should be subject to meaningful review procedures at the national level.[82]

As stated in the introduction, post-crisis backward steps in terms of ESR realisation have not just been addressed by the Committee on Economic, Social and Cultural Rights. At the international level, the prohibition has been recognised in the jurisprudence of other UN treaty bodies,[83] with both

74 CESCR, Letter to States Parties. On this basis, substantive structural reforms to labour protections, which would have long-lasting effects on the enjoyment of rights at work, would not qualify as a temporary measure. Likewise, a temporary reduction in certain types of social spending will have enduring, sometimes permanent, effects. A short-term cut to budget support for essential medicines, for example, can have catastrophic, at times fatal, effects on poor people living with HIV/AIDS, no matter whether the government reinstates the previous funding line in its next annual budget.

75 *Ibid.* See also CESCR, 'An Evaluation', para. 8(d).

76 CESCR 'General Comment No. 19', para. 42.

77 *Ibid.*

78 *Ibid.*; CESCR, Letter to States Parties. See also CESCR, 'An Evaluation', para. 10(f).

79 CESCR, Letter to States Parties.

80 *Ibid.*; CESCR 'General Comment No. 19', para. 42. See also CESCR, 'An Evaluation', para. 10(b). See also *ibid.* para. 10(f).

81 CESCR 'General Comment No. 19', para. 42. See also CESCR, 'An Evaluation', para. 11.

82 CESCR 'General Comment No. 19', para. 42.

83 In more recent years, not only the CESCR, but also the CERD and the CRC have expressed grave concern in relation to the regression from previous levels of human rights protection as a result of austerity measures adopted in the context of the current financial and economic crisis. This is in accordance with a decision of the UN Human Rights Council, which in its 10th special session of 20 February 2009 invited 'the treaty bodies, within their respective mandates, to consider any of the impacts of the global economic and financial

the Committee on the Elimination of All Forms of Racial Discrimination[84] and the Committee on the Rights of the Child[85] restating it in the context of their post-2008 Concluding Observations on State Party reports. The prohibition of retrogression has also been elucidated in the work of the Special Procedures of the UN Human Rights Council[86] and the European Agency for Fundamental Rights (FRA).[87] While non-retrogression was not historically the subject of extensive attention of any of the regional judicial and quasi-judicial bodies with an ESR mandate, whether European,[88] African[89] or Inter-American,[90] this has changed in recent years. Indeed,

crises on the realization and effective enjoyment of all human rights, and to consider presenting recommendations thereon'. Human Rights Council, Resolution on the impact of the global financial and economic crises on the universal realization and effective enjoyment of human rights (23 February 2008) UN Doc. A/HRC/S-10/L.1.

84 See, e.g., CERD 'Concluding Observations on the United Kingdom of Great Britain and Northern Ireland' (23 August 2011) UN Doc. CERD/C/GBR/CO/18–20; CERD 'Concluding Observations on Portugal' (20 February 2012) UN Doc. CERD/C/PRT/CO/12–14; CERD, 'Concluding Observations on Lithuania' (2 March 2011) UN Doc. CERD/C/LTU/CO/4–5.

85 See, e.g., CRC 'Concluding Observations on Greece' (6 June 2012) UN Doc. CRC/C/GRC/CO/2–3; CRC 'Concluding Observations on Italy' (20 September 2011) UN Doc. CRC/C/ITA/CO/3–4; CRC 'Concluding Observations on Spain' (15 September 2010) UN Doc. RC/C/ESP/CO/3–4. See also 'Statement by the Chairperson of the Committee on the Rights of the Child at the 66th session of the UNGA in 12 October 2011'.

86 See C. Lumina, 'Report of the Independent Expert on the Effects of Foreign Debt and Other Related International Financial Obligations of States on the Full Enjoyment of All Human Rights, Particularly Economic, Social and Cultural Rights' (11 June 2012) UN Doc. A/HRC/20/23. See also Sepúlveda, 'Report of the Independent Expert on the Human Rights Based Approach to Recovery'.

87 In setting out its understanding of the acceptability of austere responses to the 2008 economic crisis, the European Union Agency for Fundamental Rights stated that austerity measures must be 'non-discriminatory, justified and continue to provide effective support to those at risk of discrimination'. FRA, 'Protecting Fundamental Rights during the Economic Crisis', 4.

88 The first reference made by the European Committee of Social Rights to the concept of retrogression in its decision-making occurred in May 2012. See European Committee of Social Rights (ECSR), *General Federation of Employees of the National Electric Power Corporation (GENOP-DEI) and Confederation of Greek Civil Servants' Trade Unions (ADEDY)* v. *Greece*, Complaint No. 66/2011 (23 May 2012) para. 47. While the European Court of Human Rights is mandated to consider violations of the right to education under article 2 of Protocal No. 1 to the Convention, the Convention is primarily a civil and political rights instrument and will not be considered here.

89 Thus far, despite reliance upon the statements of the CESCR in the context of much of its ESR jurisprudence, the prohibition of retrogression has not been explicitly addressed by either the African Commission on Human and People's Rights, the African Court of Human Rights or the African Committee of Experts on the Rights and Welfare of the Child in their jurisprudence.

90 In its discussions of 'progressive development' in terms of Article 26, the Inter-American Court of Human Rights has cited the CESCR's statements on progressive realisation in

the work of the European Committee of Social Rights has been particularly forthright in its engagement with the negative impact of the crisis and 'austerity measures' on ESR enjoyment in Europe post 2008.[91]

Constitutional doctrine has also been developing test criteria to elucidate the prohibition of retrogression,[92] and, in a number cases, domestic courts have reinforced the prohibition (or similar legal rules) to varying degrees.[93] What is notable is that the grounds employed

terms of Article 2(1) of ICESCR, and engaged with the notion of retrogressive measures. While it initially construed 'progressive development' (and, as a result, the permissible parameters of state retrogression) in a somewhat different way to that adopted by the CESCR, it has since followed the CESCR's approach to progressive realisation and retrogression more closely, citing the test set out in General Comment No. 3. (See *Case of the 'Five Pensioners'* v. *Peru*, Judgment of 28 February 2003, Inter-American Court of Human Rights Series C No. 98, paras 140–7; *Case of Acevedo Buendía et al. ('Discharged and Retired Employees of the Office of the Comptroller')* v. *Peru*, Judgment of 1 July 2009, Inter-American Court of Human Rights Series C No. 198, para. 103. The Inter-American Commission has considered allegations of impermissible retrogressive measures in some cases, particularly in *National Association of Ex-Employees of the Peruvian Social Institute et al.*, Inter-American Commission on Human Rights, Report No. 38/09, Case 12.670 (27 March 2009), paras 134–47. In that decision, the Inter-American Commission stated that in order to evaluate whether a retrogressive measure is justifiable in terms of American Convention on Human Rights, it is necessary to conduct 'a joint analysis of the individual affectation in relation to the collective implication of the measure'. *Ibid.* para. 140. For discussion of this point, see D. Gonzalez-Salzberg, 'Economic and Social Rights within the Inter-American Human Rights System: Thinking New Strategies for Obtaining Judicial Protection', *Int. Law: Rev. Colomb. Derecho Int.*, 18 (2011), 117–54, www.scielo.org.co/scielo.php?script=sci_arttext&pid=S1692-81562011000100005&lng=en&nrm=iso, last accessed 4 October 2013.

91 See, e.g., ECSR, *General Federation of Employees of the National Electric Power Corporation (GENOP-DEI) and Confederation of Greek Civil Servants' Trade Unions (ADEDY)* v. *Greece*; ECSR, *General Federation of Employees of the National Electric Power Corporation (GENOP-DEI) / Confederation of Greek Civil Servants' Trade Unions (ADEDY)* v. *Greece*, Complaint 65/2011 (23 May 2012); ECSR, *Federation of Employed Pensioners of Greece (IKA-ETAM)* v. *Greece*, Complaint 76/2011 (7 December 2012). See also ECSR, *Panhellenic Federation of Public Service Pensioners (POPS)* v. *Greece*, Complaint No. 77/2012 (7 December 2012); ECSR, *Pensioners' Union of the Athens-Piraeus Electric Railways (ISAP)* v. *Greece*, Complaint No. 78/2012 (7 December 2012); ECSR, *Panhellenic Federation of Pensioners of the Public Electricity Corporation (POS-DEI)* v. *Greece*, Complaint No. 79/2012 (7 December 2012); ECSR, *Pensioners' Union of the Agricultural Bank of Greece (ATE)* v. *Greece*, Complaint No. 80/2012 (7 December 2012). For more on the Committee's work in relation to the crisis, see O'Cinneide's contribution to this volume.

92 See, e.g., Uprimny and Guarnizo, '¿Es posible una dogmática adecuada sobre la prohibición de regresividad?'.

93 See C. Courtis, *Courts and the Legal Enforcement of Economic, Social and Cultural Rights: Comparative Experiences of Justiciability* (Geneva: International Commission of Jurists, 2008), pp. 29–33. See also the discussion of domestic case-law below. See also the other country-specific contributions in this volume.

by domestic courts in their review of retrogressive measures overlap extensively with those outlined by the Committee in its practice.[94] For instance, the Hungarian Constitutional Court found cuts to social benefits implemented in accordance with IMF strictures to be unconstitutionally disproportionate because, amongst other things, the relevant measure failed to protect vulnerable groups.[95] In Latvia, legislation providing for reductions in pensions that had been passed in an effort to reduce the State's budget deficit was found to be unconstitutional and in violation of the right to a pension because the State had not considered other less restrictive alternatives.[96] The Latvian Constitutional Court in that case also noted that minimum essential levels must be guaranteed irrespective of resources and vulnerable groups such as pensioners must be particularly protected. The Court's condemnation of the legislation for failing to include a plan for future compensation of the reduced pensions also chimes with the Committee's statements. The German Constitutional Court has held that changes to social protection systems (in the context of a pending demographic crisis that would ultimately have resulted in an economic crisis) must be consistent with the fundamental right to the guarantee of a subsistence minimum that is in line with human dignity – a concept similar to the minimum core.[97] The Court stated that its role was to ascertain whether the benefits were evidently insufficient and to examine the bases and the assessment method of the benefits to determine whether they do justice to the objective of the fundamental right. In doing so, the judges considered whether the legislature had chosen a fundamentally suitable method of calculation for assessing the subsistence minimum, had completely and correctly ascertained the necessary facts and had kept within the boundaries of what is justifiable within the chosen method and its structural principles in all stages of calculation, and with plausible figures. The Court thus considered the reasonableness of the legislature's decision-making process. In a final example, 2013 saw the Portuguese Constitutional Court strike down a range of proposed budget-related austerity measures, including cuts to public sector salaries and pensions, on the basis of constitutionally

[94] The analysis below is not intended to be an exhaustive account of national courts' consideration of retrogressive measures. Rather, it seeks to highlight key trends in terms of approach.

[95] Constitutional Court of Hungary, Decision 43/1995 (30 June 1995).

[96] Constitutional Court of Latvia, Case no. 2009–43–01 (21 December 2009).

[97] Constitutional Court of Germany, 'Hartz IV', 1 BvL 1/09, 1 BvL 3/09, 1 BvL 4/09 (9 February 2010).

impermissible differential treatment of the public and private sectors in the context of the right to a salary and the right to social security (including a pension).[98] The Court found that the imposition of contribution payable on unemployment and sickness benefits was unconstitutional for violating the principle of proportionality, on the grounds that the lack of a safeguard clause meant that it was not impossible for the cash amounts involved to be reduced to a point at which, in some cases, the benefit might fall below the minimum level already established in legislation and would affect the beneficiaries in the most vulnerable situations.

There is thus strong evidence of a growing body of international, regional and domestic jurisprudence, case-law and authoritative interpretations engaging with the challenge of providing a set of operational prerequisites and normative content for the prohibition of retrogression. The significant overlap between the standards identified and applied by the different bodies hints at common global concerns about post-crisis law and policy decision-making processes that impact on ESR. The financial and economic crises have thus put retrogression – and the delineation of criteria to evaluate its permissibility – firmly on the map of ESR legal practice and scholarship.

VI. Conclusion

This chapter has outlined the prohibition of retrogression under ICESCR. We have considered and sought to explain the historical neglect of this prohibition. Having outlined the framework set out by the Committee to assess state compliance with the principle, we highlighted how it has been addressed by international, regional and national judicial and quasi-judicial bodies in the context of the crises. In doing so, we have shed light on the substantive content of the prohibition and the appropriate standards for assessing state compliance with it. It is thus clear that the crisis and responses to it have played a key role in concretising the prohibition of retrogression.

That is not to suggest, however, that the methodological issues highlighted in Section III have fallen away. Nor is it to suggest that normative questions do not remain. For instance, when addressing cases of retrogression, is it preferable for the courts to primarily focus on the reasonableness or proportionality of state measures or should the emphasis

[98] Constitutional Court of Portugal, Judgment no. 187/2013 (5 April 2013).

rather be on the State's protection of the minimum core content of ESR?[99] Furthermore, while it seems that the financial and economic crises are serving to advance an evolving doctrine on the prohibition of retrogression, it is clear that much work remains to be done with regard to refining the criteria identified by the Committee and other international, regional and domestic bodies in evaluating the permissibility of retrogressive measures.

We have certainly seen progress (or a step forward) in terms of establishing the parameters of permissible state retrogression. However, further progress is required, both in terms of theory and practice, if a strong and coherent prohibition of retrogression is to be established under ESR law.

[99] For a discussion of these points, see, e.g., X. Contiades and A. Fotiadou, 'Social Rights in the Age of Proportionality: Global Economic Crisis and Constitutional Litigation,' *International Journal of Constitutional Law*, 20 (2012), 660–86; D. Bilchitz, 'Socio-economic Rights, Economic Crisis and Legal Doctrine', http://papers.ssrn.com/sol3/papers.cfm?abstract_id=2320432, last accessed 11 January 2014.

5

Extraterritorial obligations, financial globalisation and macroeconomic governance

RADHIKA BALAKRISHNAN AND JAMES HEINTZ

I. Introduction

The economies of the world have become increasingly interconnected. What happens in one country's economy spills over to other economies – a fact dramatically illustrated by the global financial crisis that unfolded in 2008. A meltdown that began in one part of the financial sector, the United States sub-prime mortgage market, sent shock waves to economies throughout much of the rest of the world. More generally, financial flows and productive resources are mobile across national boundaries and shift in response to changing economic conditions. Business entities operate in many countries simultaneously and move operations and activities across their affiliates. Production processes are frequently fragmented and organised into global supply chains, with different stages of production occurring across a range of countries. The growing integration of the world's economies means that actions taken by one government affect the economic environment elsewhere. Moreover, the liberalisation of financial flows between countries limits the policies that a government is able to adopt. These changes pose fundamental challenges to the ability of governments to fulfil their obligations for the realisation of human rights, both within and beyond their territorial borders.

In this chapter, we examine these relationships and their implications for the realisation of economic and social rights. Extraterritorial obligations refer to acts and omissions of a government that affect the enjoyment of rights outside of the State's own territory.[1] Given the current

Author names are listed alphabetically. Both authors have contributed to this article equally.

[1] Maastricht Principles on Extraterritorial Obligations of States in the Area of Economic, Social, and Cultural Rights (29 February 2012), Principle No. 8, www.fian.org/fileadmin/media/publications/2012.02.29_-_Maastricht_Principles_on_Extraterritorial_Obligations.pdf, last accessed 13 January 2014.

process of globalisation, the question of extraterritorial obligations has become increasingly central to understanding the barriers to realising human rights. Extraterritorial obligations are relevant for a range of economic issues – from the behaviour of transnational corporations to trade and investment policies. In this chapter, we focus on monetary and financial policies, areas in which the connections between a State's extraterritorial obligations and the realisation of rights are just beginning to be explored.

We begin by examining the definition and scope of extraterritorial obligations, with an emphasis on the interpretation of extraterritorial obligations developed in the Maastricht Principles, and consider how these concepts apply to global integration, monetary policy and the policy space available to governments. The chapter then turns to the issues of financial globalisation, economic crises, the need to regulate financial markets and the extraterritorial aspects of the obligation to protect. We argue that an effective policy response requires international coordination across countries and consider the implications for global institutions. We conclude that this may require rethinking existing institutions such as the World Bank, the International Monetary Fund (IMF) and the G20, and the creation of new institutions that would allow for greater international cooperation with regard to economic policy and would thereby support a more universal application of States' extraterritorial obligations.

II. Extraterritorial obligations, ICESCR and the Maastricht Principles

The International Covenant on Economic, Social, and Cultural Rights (ICESCR)[2] recognises that a country has obligations with regard to the realisation of economic and social rights beyond its borders.[3] Specifically, Article 2(1) of ICESCR states that States Parties should 'take steps, individually and through international assistance and cooperation, especially

[2] International Covenant on Economic, Social and Cultural Rights, 993 UNTS 3 (ICESCR).

[3] See, e.g., M. Sepúlveda, 'Obligations of "International Assistance and Cooperation" in an Optional Protocol to the International Covenant on Economic, Social, and Cultural Rights', *Netherlands Quarterly of Human Rights*, 24 (2006), 271–303; F. Coomans, 'The Extraterritorial Scope of the International Covenant on Economic, Social, and Cultural Rights in the Work of the United Nations Committee on Economic, Social, and Cultural Rights', *Human Rights Law Review*, 11 (2011), 1–35; F. Coomans and M. T. Kamminga (eds.), *Extraterritorial Application of Human Rights Treaties* (Antwerp: Intersentia, 2004).

economic and technical, to the maximum of its available resources, with a view to achieving progressively the full realization of the rights recognised in the present Covenant by all appropriate means'.[4]

Although ICESCR recognises the need for 'international assistance and cooperation' it does not provide a framework for interpreting the scope, application and nature of this obligation. Specifically, ICESCR does not provide sufficient guidance on critical aspects of international law, such as state sovereignty and jurisdiction.[5] Often, 'international assistance' is interpreted as an obligation of high-income countries to provide financial and other resources to poorer countries; for example, an obligation with regard to official development assistance (ODA).[6] International law implies a commitment to international cooperation, yet the nature and extent of this cooperation with regard to economic and social rights has not been clearly spelled out in international agreements.[7]

The potential scope of international cooperation and assistance has been explored for a variety of areas: international sanctions, ODA, international trade and corporate conduct. With regard to global institutions and governance, the obligations of States as members of influential international organisations that can shape the policies adopted by governments, such as the IMF and the World Bank, have received significant attention.[8] One issue that has received less attention is how the implementation of macroeconomic policy, including financial policies and regulations, by one country affects the policy choices available elsewhere in ways which have implications for the realisation of economic and social rights.[9] This is the focus of this chapter.

[4] International Covenant on Economic, Social and Cultural Rights, 993 UNTS 3 (ICESCR) art. 2(1).

[5] See S. Skogly and M. Gibney, 'Introduction', in M. Gibney and S. Skogly (eds.), *Universal Human Rights and Extraterritorial Obligations* (University of Pennsylvania Press, 2010), pp. 1–9, 2–4.

[6] See R. Künnemann, 'Extraterritorial Application of the International Covenant on Economic, Social, and Cultural Rights', in Coomans and Kamminga (eds.), *Extraterritorial Application*, pp. 201–31.

[7] See F. Coomans, 'Some Remarks on the Extraterritorial Application of the International Covenant on Economic, Social, and Cultural Rights', in Coomans and Kamminga (eds.), *Extraterritorial Application*, pp. 183–99, 185.

[8] See, e.g., M. Salomon, 'International Economic Governance and Human Rights Accountability', in M. E. Salomon, A. Tostensen and W. Vandenhole (eds.), *Casting the Net Wider: Human Rights, Development and New Duty-Bearers* (Antwerp: Intersentia, 2007), pp. 153–84; Coomans, 'Some Remarks on the Extraterritorial Application', p. 188.

[9] See, e.g., Salomon, 'International Economic Governance', p. 171.

The Committee on Economic, Social, and Cultural Rights has further interpreted aspects of the international obligations with regard to economic and social rights.[10] For instance, General Comment No. 12 of the Committee focuses on the right to food and explicitly emphasises international support, cooperation and obligations in the realisation of the right to food.[11] Similarly, in its General Comment on the right to health, the Committee recognises a collective responsibility to confront the health risks associated with diseases that can be transmitted across international borders, including the ability of low-income countries to meet these challenges.[12] Although this General Comment is focused on health, the need to confront issues of contagion through international cooperation has direct parallels with critical economic issues, such as the spread of financial crises from one country to another.

The ability to hold governments to account for their obligations with regard to international cooperation and assistance depends on the existence of institutional and governance mechanisms to facilitate this process. For instance, the Committee has put in place an Optional Protocol to ICESCR to provide a complaint mechanism.[13] In the deliberations leading up to the Optional Protocol, the question of how and whether international cooperation should be incorporated had been controversial.[14] Ultimately, Article 2 of the Optional Protocol provided that complaints can only be brought against a State Party by or on behalf of victims who are 'under the jurisdiction' of that State Party, significantly restricting the potential for using the individual complaints mechanism to address violations of extraterritorial obligations. The design of these kinds of institutional arrangements will have significant implications for the scope and interpretation of extraterritorial obligations to facilitate the realisation of economic and social rights. They also affect governance issues associated with the fundamental cross-cutting principles which underpin ICESCR, such as accountability, transparency and participation.[15] With regard to

[10] See Sepúlveda, 'Obligations of "International Assistance and Cooperation"', 276–9.

[11] See Künnemann, 'Extraterritorial Application', p. 210; Committee on Economic, Social and Cultural Rights (CESCR), 'General Comment No. 12' in 'Note by the Secretariat, Compilation of General Comments and General Recommendations Adopted by Human Rights Treaty Bodies' (27 May 2008) UN Doc. HRI/GEN/1/Rev.9 (Vol. I), para. 36.

[12] See Coomans, 'The Extraterritorial Scope', 21; CESCR, 'General Comment No. 14' in 'Compilation of General Comments', para. 40.

[13] Optional Protocol to the International Covenant on Economic, Social and Cultural Rights, UN Doc. A/63/435.

[14] See Sepúlveda, 'Obligations of "International Assistance and Cooperation"', 272.

[15] See *ibid.*, 292–4.

the specific topic of this chapter, global institutions are critical for the coordination of macroeconomic and financial policies which have cross-border effects, an issue we return to later.

As discussed, ICESCR lacked a detailed framework for defining the scope and nature of extraterritorial obligations. Given this gap, in 2011, a group of experts on international law and human rights convened in Maastricht in order to develop and elaborate a core set of principles on extraterritorial obligations in the area of economic, social and cultural rights. The result was the Maastricht Principles which explicitly recognised that the policies adopted by governments affect the realisation of rights beyond their own borders. The preamble to the Maastricht Principles states: 'The human rights of individuals, groups, and peoples are affected by and dependent on the extraterritorial acts and omissions of States. The advent of economic globalization in particular, has meant that States and other global actors exert considerable influence on the realization of economic, social, and cultural rights across the world.'[16] The Maastricht Principles reaffirm the existing framework for economic, social and cultural rights, as developed in the Universal Declaration of Human Rights, the International Covenant on Economic, Social and Cultural Rights and other international agreements. However, they further elaborated the concept of extraterritorial obligations with regard to jurisdiction, responsibilities and existing human rights obligations, including the obligations to respect, protect and fulfil.[17] Therefore, the Maastricht Principles have potentially far-reaching implications for the formulation and conduct of economic policies, the creation of an appropriate regulatory framework, the practices of international organisations and limits on the behaviour of transnational businesses.

A primary aim of the Principles is to shed light on and clarify the legal parameters within which obligations with respect to economic and social rights are discharged.[18] These Principles were signed on to by a group of experts and are based in existing international law. The Maastricht Principles have been further supported by expert commentary that identifies the existing treaties, agreements and covenants which provide a legal foundation for the Principles.[19] The Maastricht Principles document is

[16] Maastricht Principles on Extraterritorial Obligations, Preamble.

[17] With regard to the obligations to respect, protect and fulfil, see *ibid.*, Principles Nos. 19–35.

[18] See M. E. Salomon and I. Seiderman. 'Human Rights Norms for a Globalized World: The Maastricht Principles on Extraterritorial Obligations of States in the Area of Economic, Social, and Cultural Rights', *Global Policy*, 3 (2012), 458–62, 458.

[19] See O. De Schutter, A. Eide, A. Kalfan, M. Orellana, M. Salomon and I. Seiderman, 'Commentary to the Maastricht Principles on Extraterritorial Obligations of States in

not legally binding on governments but currently represents an authoritative interpretation of the extraterritorial human rights obligations of States.[20] In this regard, it constitutes an important step towards assessing the implications of global economic interdependencies for the realisation of economic and social rights. One of the central issues associated with extraterritorial obligations is the question of jurisdiction: whether human rights agreements extend to situations outside of the State's territory.[21] An essential contribution of the Maastricht Principles is to clarify when jurisdiction for human rights obligations extends beyond territorial borders.

Obligations with regard to economic and social rights are often discussed with regard to the threefold typology: the obligation to respect rights, the obligation to fulfil rights and the obligation to protect rights.[22] This same typology can be applied to international cooperation, and the Maastricht Principles provide guidelines for thinking about each of these obligations and how they apply to the question of extraterritorial obligations.[23] It is helpful to summarise these guidelines here.

With regard to the obligation to respect rights, the Maastricht Principles recognise two ways in which the State may interfere with the enjoyment of economic and social rights outside of the State's territory: direct interference and indirect interference.[24] Direct interference refers to conduct by the State itself that impairs the realisation of economic and social rights of people outside their territories. In contrast, indirect interference refers to actions by one State which undermine the ability of another State or international organisation to comply with economic and social rights obligations. This can happen, for instance, if the policy choices of one government determine the policy space available to another government in ways that undermine the realisation of rights. As we will see, indirect interference with the obligation to respect rights may represent a significant impediment to the enjoyment of economic and social rights.

The obligations to fulfil and protect economic and social rights are particularly important with regard to macroeconomic governance. The

the Area of Economic, Social, and Cultural Rights', *Human Rights Quarterly*, 34 (2012), 1084–169.

[20] These obligations are only legally binding on States that have ratified the legal instruments on which the Maastricht Principles are based.

[21] See Salomon and Seiderman, 'Human Rights Norms', 458; De Schutter *et al.*, 'Commentary to the Maastricht Principles', 1102; Skogly and Gibney, 'Introduction', p. 4.

[22] See Coomans, 'Some Remarks on the Extraterritorial Application', pp. 192–9; Sepúlveda, 'Obligations of "International Assistance and Cooperation"', 280–9.

[23] Maastricht Principles on Extraterritorial Obligations, Principles Nos. 19–35.

[24] *Ibid.*, Principles Nos. 20, 21.

extraterritorial dimensions of the obligation to fulfil rights, as spelled out in the Maastricht Principles, include the requirement that States should create an environment conducive to realising rights through their own policy choices and through international cooperation in a range of different areas: international trade, investment, finance, taxation, environmental protection and development cooperation.[25] Engaging in meaningful international coordination is central to the extraterritorial aspects of the obligation to fulfil. This includes actions within international organisations – such as the United Nations, UN agencies, the World Bank, the IMF and the World Trade Organization, among others – that contribute to the fulfilment of economic and social rights within and beyond each State's own territory.

The extraterritorial aspects of the obligation to protect are also enumerated within the Maastricht Principles, with significant implications for economic policy, financial governance and policing the actions of businesses operating across national boundaries.[26] The obligation to protect includes the obligation to establish a regulatory environment that prevents international organisations, transnational corporations and individuals from taking actions that undermine the realisation of rights beyond a State's borders.[27] These extraterritorial obligations include omissions by the State, such as one State's failure to adequately regulate the actions of third parties in ways that have negative consequences for rights elsewhere.[28] With regard to business activities that potentially threaten rights, the Maastricht Principles hold that States must enforce measures to protect economic and social rights beyond its borders when the company concerned is registered, has its main place of business or has its centre of activity in the country concerned.[29]

III. Monetary policy, capital flows and extraterritorial obligations

We begin with a consideration of monetary policy as a critical area of macroeconomic governance in which extraterritorial obligations are relevant. Actions by one country in the conduct of monetary policy, particularly a large influential economy, can affect the macroeconomic environment of other countries in ways that potentially undermine the

[25] *Ibid.*, Principle No. 29. [26] *Ibid.*, Principles Nos. 23–7.
[27] See De Schutter *et al.*, 'Commentary to Maastricht Principles', 1133–4.
[28] Maastricht Principles on Extraterritorial Obligations, Principle No. 24.
[29] *Ibid.*, Principle No. 25.

realisation of economic and social rights. As Mary Dowell-Jones points out: 'Problems that emerge in esoteric financial markets like credit derivatives can rapidly contaminate broader financial markets and the global economy, causing huge human costs.'[30] In addition, policy choices by one State can have an impact on interest rates, exchange rates and capital flows elsewhere. Moreover, these decisions affect the policy space of other countries, limiting the choices available to support economic and social rights.

To give a concrete example, suppose the central bank of a large influential country – e.g. the Federal Reserve in the US – decides to raise interest rates. It may raise rates because of a policy target to keep inflation at very low levels. Higher interest rates make credit more expensive and tend to lower spending on consumption and investment. Lower levels of spending reduce pressures on prices in the economy and, through this channel, can lower inflation. However, increases in interest rates in an influential economy can affect interest rates beyond its borders. Specifically, other countries will suddenly face pressures to also raise their interest rates. This occurs because investors tend to move financial resources out of low interest rate economies and into higher interest rate economies. To prevent these kinds of outflows, countries may have to take steps to raise rates in response to a policy move elsewhere. Raising interest rates potentially limits the level of borrowing in the country and can slow down the economy. Therefore an increase in interest rates in the US has the potential to decrease borrowing in another country that is trying to stop money from leaving the country. As will be explained in greater detail, higher interest rates and slower growth affect the realisation of economic and social rights through a number of channels. Slower growth limits the resources available to realise rights – including resources to support government spending. Higher interest rates make borrowing – both public and private – more expensive. As we discuss below, this limits government's ability to respond to a crisis by borrowing to support state expenditures during a downturn. Similarly, higher interest rates can also affect specific rights – such as the right to adequate housing – by affecting the costs of mortgage payments and the risk of default and foreclosure.

Comparable dynamics are involved with exchange rates. If an influential economy devalues its exchange rate – i.e. makes its currency less expensive relative to other currencies – the goods and services it exports

[30] See M. Dowell-Jones. 'International Finance and Human Rights: Scope for a Mutually Beneficial Relationship', *Global Policy*, 3 (2012), 467–70, 467.

will become relatively cheaper, while imports will become more expensive. Other countries may find that the volume of goods and services they are able to sell abroad drops off, and imported products become more attractive than those produced domestically. In order to counteract these trends, States may respond by lowering their exchange rates. Exchange rates can be managed through transactions in foreign exchange markets – i.e. buying and selling foreign currencies to decrease or increase the value of the domestic currency relative to other currencies. Once again, policy choices taken in one country affect key macroeconomic variables and the policy choices adopted elsewhere.

How do these macroeconomic dynamics affect the realisation of economic and social rights? As described earlier, higher interest rates reduce consumption and investment in ways that slow economic activity. The outcome may be a loss of employment opportunities and higher rates of unemployment or underemployment, with a direct bearing on the rights to work and an adequate standard of living. Studies have found that, in some countries, restrictive monetary policies affect women's employment more than men's, raising issues of non-discrimination and equality.[31] Interest rate policy probably contributed to the sub-prime mortgage crisis in the US. The Federal Reserve raised its policy interest rate prior to the crisis contributing to the upward pressures on the monthly payments for adjustable rate mortgages.[32] The foreclosures that resulted from the sub-prime crisis undermined the right to adequate housing.[33] These examples show how domestic interest rates affect the realisation of economic and social rights. Insofar as actions by other governments have an impact on domestic interest rates in other States, extraterritorial obligations come into play.

Similarly, shifts in exchange rates affect the realisation of rights. A devalued exchange rate raises the costs of imported products relative to exports. For some countries – e.g. those that rely on imported essentials – a devaluation could mean a higher price for food or other basic goods. This lowers living standards and threatens access to food, outcomes with important consequences for the realisation of economic and social rights. The relationship between these macroeconomic variables and human rights outcomes will vary across countries, but the more general point

[31] See E. Braunstein and J. Heintz, 'Gender Bias and Central Bank Policy: Employment and Inflation Reduction', *International Journal of Applied Economics*, 22 (2008), 173–86.

[32] See J. Heintz and R. Balakrishnan, 'Debt, Power, and Crisis: Social Stratification and the Inequitable Governance of Financial Markets', *American Quarterly*, 64 (2012), 387–409.

[33] For more on this point, see Rolnik and Rabinovich's contribution to this volume.

is that these dynamics have potentially important consequences for economic and social rights.

The interactions between interest rate and exchange rate policies in different countries are linked to a concept of an economic 'trilemma'.[34] The trilemma states that three conditions cannot hold simultaneously: (1) a fixed exchange rate; (2) independent monetary policy; and (3) free movement of capital (i.e. free financial flows between countries). If financial capital is free to move between economies, a country can use policies to influence exchange rates or interest rates, but not both. For instance, if a country lowers interest rates through monetary policy, financial outflows to the rest of the world will increase causing an exchange rate devaluation. On the other hand, if a country tried to prevent such a devaluation, it must raise interest rates (or cannot lower them) in order to reduce financial outflows. Higher interest rates or a devaluation of the currency affect the realisation of economic and social rights through the channels already discussed.

Policy choices and real outcomes in different countries are connected through similar dynamics involving inflows and outflows of financial capital. Empirical studies have uncovered evidence of these linkages. Foreign interest rates (i.e. rates set elsewhere) have been shown to have a negative impact on growth in high-income developed economies, with this relationship being sensitive to exchange rate policies.[35] In other words, interest rates in one country can affect real economic performance elsewhere, and, as discussed, this affects the realisation of economic and social rights. This raises important issues of extraterritorial obligations with respect to the conduct of monetary policy.

These issues are relevant to the extraterritorial dimensions of the obligation to fulfil, as described in the Maastricht Principles. The Principles stress the need to create an 'enabling environment' for the realisation of rights, both domestically and extraterritorially, as part of a State's obligation to fulfil economic and social rights.[36] Applied to monetary policy,

[34] The concept of a trilemma can be traced to papers by Robert Mundell and Marcus Fleming that form the basis of what is often called the 'Mundell-Fleming Model'. The trilemma is derived from this theoretical framework. R. Mundell, 'Capital Mobility and Stabilization Policy under Fixed and Flexible Exchange Rates', *Canadian Journal of Economic and Political Science*, 29 (1963), 475–85; J. M. Fleming, 'Domestic Financial Policies under Fixed and Floating Exchange Rates', *IMF Staff Papers*, 9 (1962), 369–79.

[35] See J. di Giovanni and J. Shambaugh, 'The Impact of Foreign Interest Rates on the Economy: The Role of the Exchange Rate Regime' (National Bureau of Economic Research (NBER) Working Paper No. 13467, 2007).

[36] Maastricht Principles on Extraterritorial Obligations, Principle No. 20.

this would suggest that those conducting interest rate and exchange rate policy in one country should consider the effects that it has on the macroeconomic environment elsewhere. Pushed further, ICESCR's language on international cooperation and the Maastricht Principles discussion of the obligation to fulfil would imply that policy choices should be coordinated across countries in ways that facilitate the enjoyment of economic and social rights. We will return to this issue of global cooperation and macroeconomic governance later in the chapter.

IV. Financial globalisation, contagion and crisis

The 2008 global financial crisis demonstrated how macroeconomic and financial dynamics affect the environment for realising economic and social rights on a global scale.[37] The crisis was associated with dramatic declines in production and trade, rapidly rising unemployment, plunging government revenues, foreclosures, growing indebtedness and a dramatic loss of wealth.[38] The crisis had devastating effects with regard to a range of economic and social rights: the right to work, the right to adequate housing, the right to food, the right to education and the right to an adequate standard of living, among others.[39] Moreover, the policy response in many countries – the adoption of austerity programmes to reduce indebtedness primarily through cuts in government spending – has created further challenges for the realisation of human rights obligations.[40] Because

[37] In this chapter, we date the beginning of the financial crisis to 2008, the year that, in US financial markets, Lehman Brothers went bankrupt and Bear Stearns, facing collapse, was absorbed by JP Morgan Chase through a government-assisted acquisition. In 2008, the true global extent of the crisis became evident. Some prefer 2007 as marking the beginning of the crisis, in part because this was the start of recession in the US economy. However, in 2007 the magnitude of the crisis with regard to the global economy still was not fully realised.

[38] See, e.g., P. Swagel, 'The Cost of the Economic Crisis: The Impact of the 2008 Economic Collapse' (Pew Financial Reform Project, Briefing Paper 18, 2009), www.pewtrusts.org/uploadedFiles/wwwpewtrustsorg/Reports/Economic_Mobility/Cost-of-the-Crisis-final.pdf?n=6727, last accessed 16 October 2013. See also European Commission, 'Economic Crisis in Europe: Causes, Consequences, and Responses' (European Economy No. 7, 2009). For an analytical overview of these and related issues in the context of economic and social rights, see Heintz and Balakrishnan, 'Debt, Power, and Crisis'.

[39] See, e.g., the contributions to this volume by Sepúlveda, Rolnik and Rabinovich and De Schutter. See also Swagel, 'The Cost of the Economic Crisis'; European Commission, 'Economic Crisis in Europe'. For an analytical overview of economic crises in the context of economic and social rights, see Heintz and Balakrishnan, 'Debt, Power, and Crisis'.

[40] For more on the challenges posed by state responses to human rights realisation, see Sepúlveda's contribution to this volume.

of the global nature of the crisis, and because the crisis was due – at least in part – to government policies and government omissions in terms of taking proactive steps to prevent the crisis, extraterritorial obligations are relevant to the issues of financial globalisation and economic fragility.[41]

For the purposes of this chapter, we define financial globalisation as referring to the greater integration of financial markets across international borders, the expansion of the operations of financial institutions into new markets in other economies, increases in international acquisitions of banks and other financial institutions, and the growing tendency of investors to acquire securities and financial products from a range of countries beyond the country in which they are based.[42] The 2008 financial crisis provides a compelling example of how financial globalisation creates pathways of contagion through which economic crises can be transmitted across borders. More generally, financial globalisation creates the conditions for the extraterritorial transmission of a variety of economic shocks, both real and monetary.[43]

For instance, research that examined the channels through which US gross domestic product shocks are transmitted across industrialised countries found that the macroeconomic variables with the largest spillover effects are financial in character – e.g. interest rates, bond yields and stock prices.[44] Similarly, financial channels appear to play an important role in transmitting shocks in the US economy to countries in Latin America.[45] Therefore, the process of financial globalisation makes the issue of extraterritorial obligations with respect to the conduct of economic policy more pressing. Actions or omissions by one country that negatively impact its own economy and financial markets can be quickly passed on to other economies, with financial pathways playing a prominent role in the economic epidemiology of crises and contagion.[46]

41 For in-depth analysis of how regulatory failures in the US contributed to the global economic crisis, see Financial Crisis Inquiry Commission, 'The Financial Crisis Inquiry Report' (January 2011).

42 See G. Epstein, 'Introduction: Financialization and the World Economy', in G. Epstein (ed.), *Financialization and the World Economy* (Northampton, MA: Edward Elgar, 2005), pp. 3–16, 3.

43 See L. S. Goldberg, 'Understanding Banking Sector Globalization', *IMF Staff Papers*, 56 (2009), 171–97, 172.

44 See T. Bayoumi and A. Swiston, 'Foreign Entanglements: Estimating the Source and Size of Spillovers across Industrial Countries' (IMF Working Paper WP/07/182, 2007), 14.

45 See F. Canova, 'The Transmission of US Shocks to Latin America', *Journal of Applied Econometrics*, 20 (2005), 229–51, 249.

46 See Dowell-Jones, 'International Finance and Human Rights', 467.

Financial globalisation also alters the effectiveness of monetary policy and the channels through which monetary policy operates. The lending channel is one of the ways in which contractionary monetary policy (for instance, raising interest rates or reducing credit supply) is assumed to affect economic activity and price levels – i.e. altering the cost and availability of credit through its impact on the ability of banks to access funds.[47] Therefore, the effectiveness of monetary policy would be weakened if banks have access to alternative sources of funds when the central bank pursues a contractionary policy.[48] Banks with global operations may respond to tighter monetary policy by drawing on overseas sources of liquidity within their internal networks.[49]

Economists working at the Federal Reserve Bank of New York present evidence that this is indeed the case for US banks – more globalised banks limit the effectiveness of domestic monetary policy.[50] Moreover, global banks tend to be larger institutions and restrictive monetary policy appears to have a larger impact on the credit extended by smaller, domestic banking institutions.[51] This suggests that the trend toward more consolidated, increasingly globalised banks in economies like the US has important implications for the conduct of monetary policy. The study also finds that contractionary monetary policy has an effect on the cost of credit of global banks operating offices in *other* countries – i.e. financial globalisation creates channels through which monetary policy affects credit conditions elsewhere, but limits its effectiveness domestically.[52] We have argued that the policy space available to governments to adopt their own discretionary monetary and financial sector policies has important implications for the obligations to fulfil and protect. Therefore, the dynamics of financial globalisation raise important questions regarding extraterritoriality and macroeconomic policy choices.

Recent economic crises also raise important concerns about the extraterritorial dimensions of the obligation to protect. Changes in regulatory regimes involving financial markets and financial flows have been linked

[47] Specifically, contractionary monetary policy makes it more difficult or more expensive for banks to access resources for reservable deposits. When banks find it more difficult to maintain the reserves needed to support their current level of lending, they may cut back on the amount of credit they extend.

[48] See N. Cetorelli and L. S. Goldberg, 'Banking Globalization, Monetary Transmission, and the Lending Channel' (NBER Working Paper 14101, 2008), 2.

[49] See *ibid.*, 2. [50] See *ibid.*, 23.

[51] *Ibid.*, 1. In this research study, 'global banks' are defined as US banks that report positive assets from offices operating in other countries.

[52] See Cetorelli and Goldberg, 'Banking Globalization'.

to economic crises. For instance, the liberalisation of the movement of finance capital between countries appears to have contributed to the global financial crisis that unfolded in 1997 and that had a large impact on East Asian economies.[53] Similarly, the rollback of regulatory controls on US banks and financial institutions has been identified as a structural change contributing to the 2008 meltdown in US financial markets and the subsequent global financial crisis.[54] Financial and economic crises in one country are often linked to policy changes occurring elsewhere.[55] In other words, economic crises are not episodes of misfortune that are unconnected with governments, their policy choices and any failure to maintain an adequate regulatory framework. The actions of third parties – e.g. financial corporations and global investors engaged in speculative activities – are the proximate causes of such crises. Therefore, the failure to regulate financial markets in ways that reduce or minimise the likelihood of economic crises represents a failure to give effect to the obligation to protect with significant extraterritorial dimensions.

An economic crisis is not the only way in which a failure to adequately regulate financial institutions can affect the realisation of economic and social rights. The LIBOR rate-fixing scandal provides an example of how this could happen. LIBOR stands for the London Inter-Bank Offered Rate and it is meant to be a measurement of the interest rates banks pay when they borrow in the inter-bank market.[56] The LIBOR is widely used as a baseline rate for setting other interest rates – including rates on mortgages, higher education loans and a range of financial products. The calculation of LIBOR was overseen by the British Bankers' Association using the self-reported interest rates provided by major banks. In 2012, it was revealed that banks, including Barclays Bank based in London, had deliberately misreported interest rates in order to manipulate returns on certain financial investments (i.e. investments in derivatives).[57] Since the

[53] See J. Stiglitz, 'Capital Market Liberalization, Economic Growth, and Instability', *World Development*, 28 (2000), 1075–86.

[54] See J. Stiglitz, 'Reversal of Fortune', *Vanity Fair* (October 2008).

[55] See G. A. Calvo, L. Leiderman and C. M. Reinhart, 'Capital Inflows and Real Exchange Rate Appreciation in Latin America: The Role of External Factors', *IMF Staff Papers*, 40 (1993), 108–51.

[56] For a description of the LIBOR, see the British Bankers' Association, www.bbalibor.com, last accessed 16 October 2013.

[57] See C. Alessi, 'Understanding the Libor Scandal' (6 February 2013), www.cfr.org/united-kingdom/understanding-libor-scandal/p28729, last accessed 16 October 2013. See also 'Libor Rigging Scandal – Timeline', *The Guardian* (16 August 2012), www.guardian.co.uk/business/2012/aug/16/libor-rigging-scandal-timeline, last accessed 16 October 2013.

LIBOR is used to set rates on loans for housing and education, its manipulation could potentially affect the realisation of rights in areas affected by changes in interest rates; for instance, the costs of higher education loans and mortgages influence the realisation of the rights to adequate housing and education in certain country contexts. More generally, we have discussed how interest rates potentially affect the realisation of a range of economic and social rights including the right to work and the right to an adequate standard of living. A failure to adequately regulate the actions of third parties that distort major prices in the economy and/or a failure to enforce existing regulation would constitute a failure of the obligation to protect, insofar as the realisation of rights is compromised. Since interest rates in a number of countries are affected by the LIBOR, these kinds of manipulations have extraterritorial ramifications.

The structure of international finance not only affects the dynamics leading to economic fragility and the channels through which crises are transmitted from one country to the next. It also impacts upon policy responses. Larger, more systemically influential economies have a wider range of policy options available when responding to economic shocks, compared to smaller, more dependent economies and those that occupy more peripheral positions in the global economy.[58] Some economies, such as the US and China, were able to respond to the 2008 crisis by implementing countercyclical stimulus policies in an effort to at least partially offset the negative consequences of the financial shock.[59] However, a similar economic shock may have different effects on less well-positioned economies, which may experience capital outflows as financial investors seek out safe havens.[60] Under these conditions, more vulnerable economies tend to implement pro-cyclical policies such as higher interest rates and cuts to government spending in an effort to stem financial outflows.[61] The result is unbalanced policy responses to a global crisis with distinct consequences for economic and social rights. Countries that are able to implement economic stimulus policies can take steps to mitigate any backsliding due to the crisis, but many other countries will adopt policy

[58] See J. A. Ocampo and R. Vos, 'Policy Space and the Changing Paradigm in Conducting Macroeconomic Policies in Developing Countries' (Bank for International Settlement Papers No. 36, 2008).

[59] See International Labor Organization, 'A Review of Global Stimulus' (EC-IILS Joint Discussion Paper Series No. 5, 2011).

[60] See J. A. Ocampo, 'Rethinking Global Economic and Social Governance', *Journal of Globalization and Development*, 1 (2010). Article 6, 10–11.

[61] See Ocampo and Vos, 'Policy Space and the Changing Paradigm', 29.

positions which could contribute to, rather than alleviate, retrogression with regard to economic and social rights – e.g. raising interest rates or cutting government social spending.[62]

These asymmetries in the policy responses to economic crises are not pre-ordained. Rather, they are a result of the structure of the global economy and the ways in which capital flows between countries are managed. A coordinated policy response – one that tries to preserve the policy space available to countries in more vulnerable positions – would create the possibility for alternatives to a pro-cyclical response in the wake of an economic crisis. Global macroeconomic governance is critical here. International institutions could play a coordinating role so that countries experiencing capital outflows are not disproportionately affected by a global shock. However, institutions such as the IMF typically impose conditionalities on their emergency lending that reinforce existing asymmetries in global macroeconomic governance.[63] If extraterritorial obligations, as outlined in the Maastricht Principles, are to be taken seriously, there is a real need to transform the existing system of global economic governance to allow more coordinated responses.

V. Extraterritorial obligations, global institutions and international cooperation

The economic interdependence of nations affects the formulation of macroeconomic and financial policies to support the enjoyment of economic and social rights. Under these conditions, a single country acting alone may not have sufficient latitude for formulating and implementing economic policies which foster an environment for the progressive realisation of these rights. In these circumstances, global cooperation is necessary for the effective management of these interdependencies. As discussed previously, Article 2(1) of ICESCR stresses the need for international cooperation for the realisation of economic and social rights. Moreover, Principle 30 of the Maastricht Principles says that 'States should coordinate with each other … in order to cooperate effectively in the universal fulfilment of economic, social and cultural rights. The lack

[62] For more on this point, see the contributions by Sepúlveda and Nolan *et al.* to this volume.

[63] For a discussion of conditionalities imposed by international financial institutions as they relate to global cooperation and economic and social rights, see Salomon, 'International Economic Governance'.

of such coordination does not exonerate a State from giving effect to its separate extraterritorial obligations.'[64]

Uncoordinated approaches to macroeconomic management not only restrict policy space, but also may result in the inefficient use of resources.[65] For instance, some countries have accumulated large stocks of foreign exchange reserves as an insurance policy against future economic crises. These resources cannot be pressed into service to support the realisation of rights and therefore represent a cost of uncoordinated policies. Furthermore, an uncoordinated approach to financial regulation will prove to be ineffective. Financial investors can avoid an oasis of regulation in a select number of countries, by circumventing these markets. Regulations in key financial centres may be more critical than regulations elsewhere. For instance, the most influential commodity futures markets are concentrated in a few locations, New York, Chicago and London. How these major markets are regulated has implications for commodity price dynamics globally. Therefore, a common approach to global financial governance, requiring effective global institutions – and contrasting with current ad hoc national approaches – is essential.

The need for such coordination is explicitly recognised in the Maastricht Principles.[66] Concerns over a failure of global economic governance reached new heights in the aftermath of the 2008 crisis. Since the 1980s, the trend has been towards liberalising markets, yet unrestricted financial markets engender financial fragility, heighten volatility and create the propensity for crises, as the experience of the past several decades has shown.[67] Influential international players recognised that the global institutions to support a coordinated approach to managing finance were insufficient and this was the rationale for elevating the role of the G20 in coordinating macroeconomic policy.[68] Despite its elevated role, the G20's effectiveness in implementing a coordinated approach to financial regulation remains inadequate.[69]

The Maastricht Principles assert that: 'A State that transfers competences to, or participates in, an international organization must take all

[64] Maastricht Principles on Extraterritorial Obligations, Principle No. 30.

[65] This relates to the principle of the use of maximum available resources, put forward in Article 2(1) of the International Covenant on Economic, Social and Cultural Rights.

[66] Maastricht Principles on Extraterritorial Obligations, Principle No. 30.

[67] See Stiglitz, 'Capital Market Liberalization', 1075.

[68] See J. Heintz, 'Missing Women: The G20, Gender Equality and Global Economic Governance' (March 2013), 4.

[69] See *ibid.*, 9.

reasonable steps to ensure that the relevant organization acts consistently with the international human rights obligations of that State.'[70] If rendered enforceable, the Principles would thus have implications for the ways in which institutions such as the IMF, the World Trade Organization and the World Bank could be held accountable to a set of human rights obligations. The implications of the call for international cooperation for the realisation of economic and social rights has been recognised in arguments developed in greater detail elsewhere.[71] In addition, as has already been discussed, the current system for managing international financial flows also reinforces existing inequities between countries. Developing countries often have access to global finance on unequal terms, since their integration into global markets is segmented by perceptions of risk and creditworthiness. This creates conditions under which financial volatility has larger impacts on the economies of developing nations compared to high-income countries.[72]

Financial stability, a strong regulatory environment and appropriate macroeconomic management for the realisation of rights have the character of a 'global public good'.[73] Global public goods refer to goods and services whose benefits transcend national borders.[74] Coordination to ensure that there is an adequate supply of global public goods represents a particularly critical challenge since the provision of such goods and services has traditionally been seen to be the role of national governments, yet nation states, acting independently, cannot guarantee that global public goods will be adequately supplied – since such regulations are costly to individual governments and the benefits spill over national borders. When public goods have a global character, there is often an absence of institutions capable of overcoming the coordination failures associated with the provision of public goods. Existing institutions are often hampered by coordination failures between States – i.e. when countries protect their national interest instead of pursuing a coordinated approach. The failure to date to reach a comprehensive agreement on reductions in

[70] Maastricht Principles on Extraterritorial Obligations, Principle No. 15.

[71] See Salomon, 'International Economic Governance'.

[72] See Ocampo, 'Rethinking Global Economic and Social Governance'.

[73] For further consideration of economic and social rights as global public goods, see De Schutter's contribution to this volume

[74] See I. Kaul, P. Conceição, K. l. Goulven and R. U. Mendoza (eds.), *Providing Global Public Goods: Managing Globalization* (New York: United Nations Development Program, 2003). Ocampo broadens the definition of global public goods to include all issues that belong in the public domain or are of public interest. See Ocampo, 'Rethinking Global Economic and Social Governance', 7.

greenhouse gas emissions endorsed by all countries provides an example of these dynamics – i.e. individual countries prefer to opt out of such agreements to avoid the costs of adjustment associated with reducing pollutants that are harmful at the global level.

There is a need to consider global institutions which are capable of creating a financial system which supports, not undermines, human rights. This raises important questions about whether the extraterritorial obligations, as laid out in the Maastricht Principles, are sufficient for achieving this kind of global cooperation. If all States adhere to the extraterritorial obligations imposed by economic and social rights as reflected in these Principles, taking into account the external effects of their actions on others, the result would be the kind of coordination necessary for supporting economic and social rights globally. However, in the absence of the universal application of these Principles, extraterritorial obligations will fall short of true multilateral global cooperation. One can imagine a situation in which one State supports its extraterritorial obligations while other governments choose to opt out. When reciprocity in honouring extraterritorial obligations across all States is imperfect and incomplete, the outcomes will fall short of what could be achieved under true international coordination.

The Maastricht Principles outline some mechanisms for ensuring compliance with a State's extraterritorial obligations, including the need for accountability, a requirement for States to provide effective remedies for the violation of rights and the need for inter-state complaint mechanisms.[75] With regard to international coordination, the inter-state complaint mechanisms are particularly important. However, the focus remains on existing human rights agreements, treaties, international institutions and institutions to ensure this kind of cooperation, often without a clear means of sanctioning States for non-compliance or providing the appropriate institutional support for global cooperation. Because of this, the question of what types of global institutions need to be put in place to support a more universal application of these extraterritorial obligations remains an open one.

VI. Conclusion

Although it has been long recognised that States have extraterritorial obligations that bear on the realisation of economic and social rights, the

[75] Maastricht Principles on Extraterritorial Obligations, Principles Nos. 36, 39.

nature of these obligations has not been fully developed or expounded upon in detail. The Maastricht Principles represent an important first step in providing a more detailed interpretation of these extraterritorial obligations. This chapter has taken the Maastricht Principles and applied them to policy areas that remain under-explored with regard to economic and social rights – macroeconomic and financial governance. Financial globalisation has affected the policy space available to governments operating independently in liberalised market economies. It has created channels through which actions and omissions of States affect the realisation of rights across international boundaries, with financial channels playing an increasingly dominant role. All of these developments carry with them critical implications for extraterritorial obligations relating to economic and social rights.

We have argued that international coordination is essential for supporting individual States' ability to meet the obligations to protect, respect and fulfil rights. This includes the international cooperation needed to avoid devastating crises, such as the 2008 global financial crisis which had a dramatic impact on economic and social rights. Such global cooperation could be achieved through the universal acceptance of extraterritorial obligations. In the absence of the universal application of these principles, important questions surface concerning the best way to conduct economic policies to realise economic and social rights in a context of global integration. The solution will lie with the creation of institutions to support policy coordination across countries. The current set of global institutions does not appear up to the task, which raises important issues of how to move forward in the future to create a global economy that supports, rather than undermines, core human rights.

PART III

Exploring responses to financial and economic crises

6

Austerity and the faded dream of a 'social Europe'

COLM O'CINNEIDE

I. Introduction

Social rights remain better protected in Europe than almost anywhere else in the world. Most European citizens enjoy access to decent levels of health care and social security, while labour rights are relatively well-protected by national legislation backed up by the influence of strong trade unions. The notion that the State is responsible for the economic and social well-being of its citizens is also deeply rooted in European legal and political culture. Governments across Europe like to emphasise their commitment to social rights, and enjoy comparing their well-established welfare states with the more minimalist systems of social protection that exist in other parts of the developed world. Furthermore, most constitutional systems in Europe are based upon the assumption that the State should play an active role in securing the economic and social well-being of its people, almost all European States have ratified the European Social Charter (ESC)[1] and the key United Nations (UN) and International Labour Organization (ILO) instruments relating to social rights, while the European Union (EU) is committed to the establishment of a 'social Europe', which is supposed to be characterised by the 'constant improvement of the living and working conditions' of the people of Europe taken as a whole.[2]

However, serious gaps have opened up in the safety net that European welfare states are supposed to provide for all members of society. The level of state support provided to vulnerable groups has declined. Social inequality has grown, and irregular migrants and other politically marginalised groups are increasingly denied access to all but the bare minimum of social protection. The beginnings of this slow decline can be traced back to the ideological shifts of the 1980s, when the high tide of the European commitment to social rights began to ebb. Subsequently,

[1] European Social Charter CETS No. 035.

[2] Case C-43/75, *Defrenne* v. *Sabena (No. 2)* [1976] ECR 455, para. 10.

social protection was gradually eroded throughout the 1990s and early 2000s by reforms designed to balance the books and enhance the ability of European States to compete in the market economy. Now, the fallout from the economic crisis of 2008–10 has greatly accelerated the disintegration of the much-vaunted Europe social model. At the time of writing, the impact of the austerity measures introduced by most European States, and the scale of the social crisis that has engulfed Greece and other heavily indebted Eurozone States in particular, has made it clear that a gulf currently exists between the rhetoric and the reality of 'social Europe'.

These developments have begun to generate tension across and between the multiple layers of European governance; the human rights provisions of national and European law are increasingly being used to challenge austerity measures, even as social security and employment law across Europe is being re-shaped to conform with the requirement of ordo-liberal and neoliberal policy prescriptions. This chapter explores these tensions, and critically examines the extent to which respect for social rights can be said to be constitutionally embedded within European society. It also calls into question whether European States are seriously committed to translating the idea of a 'social Europe' into reality, given the disconnect that increasingly exists between their formal embrace of social rights and the steady erosion of social protection that is taking place across the continent.

II. The establishment of the European social model

Economic and social rights are sometimes viewed as recent conceptual innovations, born out of the post-1945 expansion of international human rights law. However, in Europe, social rights have a much older history, which can be traced back to the French Revolution. As early as 1793, Robespierre proposed that the Convention adopt a Bill of Rights that treated the right to work and to receive social assistance as core individual rights.[3] The Portuguese Constitutional Charter of 1826 contained provisions that assured access to 'public aid' and guaranteed access to free primary education, while Article 8 of the French Constitution of 1848 recognised the existence of a right to free primary education and to receive social assistance, even though these were viewed as imposing a moral rather than a legal obligation on the State. These prototypical social rights

[3] M. Robespierre, *Textes Choisis* (Paris: Editions Sociales, 1973), vol. II (August 1792–July 1793), p. 138.

provisions were all set out in constitutional instruments that failed to take root in national law. However, as Katrougalos has argued, they gave initial expression to the then radical idea that individuals were entitled as of right to receive protection from the State against hunger, poverty and want.[4]

Subsequently, this particular understanding of the relationship between citizens and the State gained traction across the political spectrum and ultimately led to the establishment of the European welfare states, which were designed to protect citizens against the more extreme consequences of capitalist commodification and inequalities in the distribution of wealth.[5] The foundation of these welfare states was laid down in the 1870s, when Bismarck introduced social insurance for workers as part of his attempt to stunt the growth of support for trade unions and socialist ideas in the newly united Germany. Subsequently, most continental European States followed the Iron Chancellor's example and developed welfare states based upon state-regulated social insurance schemes funded by employers and employees. The Nordic States went down a different policy route, basing their systems on universal social provision funded directly by the State. The UK followed a similar path inspired by the Beveridge Report of 1944, whereby the State took responsibility for the provision of health care and social security to the population at large and social housing to the less well-off.[6]

These post-war welfare states were far from perfect. Inequalities based on wealth, ethnicity and social status persisted.[7] Women and children were often treated as adjuncts to the primary male bread-winner,[8] while persons with disabilities were provided with little opportunity to participate as equals in the life of their communities.[9] Public housing

[4] G. Katrougalos, 'The (Dim) Perspectives of the European Social Citizenship' (Jean Monnet Working Paper 05/07), 2, centers.law.nyu.edu/jeanmonnet/papers/07/070501.pdf, last accessed 15 November 2013.

[5] See in general U. Preuss, 'The Concept of Rights in the Welfare State' in G. Teubner (ed.), *Dilemmas of Law in the Welfare State* (Berlin: W. de Gruyter, 1986), pp. 151–72; J. Habermas, 'Law as Medium and Law as Institution' in *ibid.*, pp. 203–20; C. Offe, *Contradictions of the Welfare State* (London: Hutchinson, 1984); G. Esping-Andersen, *The Three Worlds of Welfare Capitalism* (Cambridge: Polity, 1990); K. Polanyi, *The Great Transformation* (New York: Octagon, 1980).

[6] For the classic analysis of these different modes of 'welfare capitalism', see Esping-Andersen, *The Three Worlds*.

[7] See generally P. Alcock *et al.*, *Welfare and Wellbeing: Richard Titmuss's Contribution to Social Policy* (Bristol: Policy Press, 2001).

[8] G. Pascall, *Gender Equality in the Welfare State?* (University of Chicago Press, 2012).

[9] See, e.g., the comprehensive analysis of the situation in the UK set out in C. Barnes, *Disabled People in Britain and Discrimination* (London: Hurst, 2001).

programmes often created ghettoes, while poorly designed social welfare systems created 'poverty traps'.[10] Nevertheless, in general, the European welfare states enjoyed a golden age of more or less continuous expansion during the *trente glorieuse* between 1945 and the oil shocks of 1973/4. During this period, social rights came to be protected to an unprecedented degree and the foundations of what subsequently become known as the 'European social model' were laid down, which aimed to combine economic growth achieved through the functioning of a regulated 'social market economy' with the provision of a high level of social protection via the welfare state.[11]

This European social model was based around the concept of 'social citizenship' as famously outlined by T. H. Marshall, whereby the State assumed responsibility for ensuring that its citizens enjoyed the 'right to a modicum of economic welfare and security' and 'to share to the full in the social heritage and to live the life of a civilized being according to the standards prevailing in the society [in question]'.[12] This central animating idea inspired the establishment of the European welfare states, and became deeply engrained in European political culture.[13]

To this day, Europe as a whole is often conceptualised as a 'social space' where the State takes an active role in ameliorating inequality and protecting individuals against the commodifying effects of the free market, in contrast to the more laissez-faire ethos of US social and economic policy, or the more utilitarian policies of emerging economies such as China.[14] Public opinion across Europe tends to view this tradition of respect for

[10] For a comprehensive overview of the social policy dilemmas generated by the European welfare states, see G. Esping-Andersen, 'After the Golden Age? Welfare State Dilemmas in a Global Economy', in G. Esping-Andersen (ed.), *Welfare States in Transition: National Adaptions in Global Economies* (London: SAGE, 1996), pp. 1–31.

[11] See generally T. Judt, *Postwar: A History of Europe Since 1945* (New York: Penguin, 2005), pp. 777 et seq. The Eastern European States followed a different trajectory due to the imposition of Communist rule from the late 1940s on. After 1989, their state-socialist systems of social provision were replaced by welfare states broadly similar in structure and design to their Western European counterparts. See D. Adascalitei, 'Welfare State Development in Central and Eastern Europe: A State of the Art Literature Review', *Studies of Transition States and Societies*, 4(2) (2012), 59–70.

[12] T. H. Marshall, *Citizenship and Social Class* (London: Pluto, 1992) (reprinted from his 1949 Cambridge Lectures), p. 8.

[13] For a description of the 'European social model', see Commission, 'European Social Policy – A Way Forward for the Union', COM (94) 333 final, 2–5.

[14] On its website, the European Trade Union Confederation describes the European social model as

> a vision of society that combines sustainable economic growth with ever-improving living and working conditions. This implies full employment, good quality jobs,

social rights with pride, while commentators frequently refer to it as a unique and praiseworthy achievement.[15]

The phrase 'social Europe' has become a shorthand way of denoting the common commitment of European States to preserving their unique social model. It features prominently in the rhetoric of the EU institutions, and is also invoked frequently at the national level.[16] As a political concept, it suggests the existence of shared pan-European social values, a view that is also reflected in the rhetorical framework of the EU Treaties. For example, the Preamble to the Treaty of European Union (TEU) confirms the attachment of the EU Member States to 'fundamental social rights as defined in the European Social Charter ... and the 1989 Community Charter of the Fundamental Social Rights of Workers', while Article 3(3) of the TEU proclaims that the EU shall work towards the establishment of a 'highly competitive social market economy ... aiming at full employment and social progress', and promote 'social justice and protection'.

III. The legal dimension of 'social Europe'

This idea that Europe is committed to a distinct social model has also influenced legal developments across the continent. As Katrougalos has suggested, a 'European legal concept of social rights' evolved in tandem with the construction of the welfare state, which viewed the protection of social rights and regulation of the free market as part of the core functions of the State.[17] This legal understanding of social rights manifested itself in different ways in different European legal systems. In the UK and the Nordic States, it gave rise to a principle of judicial non-intervention: the courts granted public authorities a very wide margin of discretion

> equal opportunities, social protection for all, social inclusion, and involving citizens in the decisions that affect them ... This is what distinguishes Europe, where post-war social progress has matched economic growth, from the US model, where small numbers of individuals have benefited at the expense of the majority. Europe must continue to sustain this social model as an example for other countries around the world.

See European Trade Union Confederation, 'What is the "European Social Model" or "Social Europe"?', www.etuc.org/a/111, last accessed 15 November 2013.

[15] See, e.g., the analysis presented in J. Rifkin, *The European Dream: How Europe's Vision of the Future Is Quietly Eclipsing the American Dream* (New York: Tarcher, 2005).

[16] The European Commission has even established a 'Social Europe' Facebook page: see Social Europe, www.facebook.com/socialeurope, last accessed 15 November 2013.

[17] Katrougalos, 'The (Dim) Perspectives', 4.

when it came to reviewing the activities of public authorities in the socio-economic field, and issues of resource allocation came to be viewed as essentially non-justiciable.[18] In other legal systems, a more positive legal conception of the social role of the State came into being. States came to be regarded as subject to a positive constitutional obligation to take steps to protect the social rights of their citizens. This became known as the 'social state' or the *Sozialstaat* principle (the German phrase is in common usage, reflecting the highly developed nature of this principle in German law and legal scholarship): States were expected as part of their constitutional obligations to establish and maintain an adequate welfare state framework, and a failure to give effect to this obligation could at least in theory violate the requirements of constitutional law.[19]

This concept of the 'social state' was first given tangible legal expression in the 1920s when extensive lists of social rights were included in a number of European constitutions, including those of Weimar Germany (1919),[20] Finland (1919)[21] and Poland (1921).[22] Initially, these rights were not generally viewed as giving rise to subjective individual entitlements which could be enforced by courts. However, after 1945, the concept of the 'social state' was developed further, in particular in German legal theory. The German Basic Law of 1948 in contrast to its Weimar predecessor did not contain an express list of social rights. Instead, Article 20 of the Basic Law proclaimed that Germany was a 'democratic, federal, social state'. In other words, Germany was to be a 'social state' (*Sozialstaat*) where the State would take responsibility for protecting social rights and ensuring that its citizens would be treated with dignity.[23] In Katrougalos' words, this 'normative, prescriptive principle' became viewed as a fundamental organising norm of the new State, on a par with the rule of law; the German State was required both to act in accordance with the requirements of this principle and to take measures to give it concrete expression.[24] Furthermore,

[18] See C. Harlow and R. Rawlings, *Law and Administration*, 3rd edn (Cambridge University Press, 2009), ch. 1; R. Hirschl, 'The Nordic Counter-narrative: Democracy, Human Development and Judicial Review' *International Journal of Constitutional Law*, 9(2) (2011), 449–69.

[19] See Katrougalos, 'The (Dim) Perspectives'; see also G. Katrougalos and P. O'Connell, 'Fundamental Social Rights' in M. Tushnet, T. Fleiner and C. Saunders (eds.), *Routledge Handbook of Constitutional Law* (London: Routledge, 2012), pp. 375–85.

[20] See, e.g., Article 161. [21] See, e.g., Sections 13 and 15. [22] See, e.g., Article 102.

[23] C. Bommarius, 'Germany's *Sozialstaat* Principle and the Founding Period', *German Law Journal*, 12 (2011), 1879–86; H. M. Heinig, 'The Political and the Basic Law's *Sozialstaat* Principle – Perspectives from Constitutional Law and Theory', *German Law Journal*, 12 (2011), 1887–900.

[24] Katrougalos, 'The (Dim) Perspectives', 9–15.

the courts were empowered to enforce compliance with these requirements: while the *Sozialstaat* principle did not necessarily give rise to subjective individual rights, it constituted an objective legal norm which the State was required to respect.[25]

Many European constitutional texts now contain express affirmations that they are 'social states',[26] and/or set out a list of protected social rights,[27] while national constitutional courts have usually read some variant of the *Sozialstaat* principle into domestic law.[28] It is unusual (but not unknown) for this principle to give rise to subjective individual entitlements which can be directly enforced against the State. However, legislation and other legal norms are regularly interpreted in line with the dictates of the *Sozialstaat* principle, while it is often invoked to justify State action which imposes constraints on the free market or private property rights and also exercises a 'radiating effect' in the context of horizontal relationships between private parties.[29] Furthermore, it is possible in some States for state action which is incompatible with its requirements to be reviewed and struck down by the courts. In particular, retrogressive measures which effectively hollow out or nullify existing social entitlements, or failures by the State to provide the minimum level of state support that is compatible with human dignity, may be held to be unconstitutional.[30]

Thus, for example, the German Constitutional Court in its 2010 *Hartz IV* judgment held that a new method of calculating the rate of state benefits that had been introduced as part of the federal government's 'Hartz IV' social security reform package was not compatible with the principle

[25] *Ibid.*

[26] See, e.g., Constitution of Spain, art. 1(1); Constitution of Portugal, art. 2; Constitution of Slovenia, art. 2.

[27] See, e.g., Constitution of Belgium, art. 23; Constitution of the Netherlands, arts. 19, 20, 22; Constitution of Greece, arts. 21, 22; Constitution of Portugal, arts. 56, 59, 63–72, 108–9, 167, 216.

[28] See in general C. Fabre, 'Social Rights in European Constitutions' in G. De Búrca and B. De Witte (eds.), *Social Rights in Europe* (Oxford University Press, 2005), pp. 15–28. For an overview of the jurisprudence of constitutional courts in central and Eastern Europe, see W. Sadurski, 'Constitutional Courts in the Process of Articulating Constitutional Rights in the Post-Communist States of Central and Eastern Europe Part 1: Social and Economic Rights' (European University Institute (EUI) Working Paper Law No. 2002/14).

[29] For a sample of the French jurisprudence on this point, see Constitutional Council decision n° 2010-617 DC, 9 November 2010, paras. 7–9. See also L. Pech, 'France: Rethinking "Droits-créances"' in M. Langford (ed.), *Socio-Economic Rights Jurisprudence – Emerging Trends in Comparative and International Law* (Cambridge University Press, 2008), pp. 267–75.

[30] Katrougalos, 'The (Dim) Perspectives', 14.

of human dignity set out in Article 1 of the Basic Law.[31] The Court ruled that this principle required that persons in need be provided with sufficient material support to enable them to maintain a dignified physical existence and to participate in the social, cultural and political life of their society. The legislative branch was responsible for determining what state benefits would be paid to individuals in need. However, the Court considered that the amount of such benefits had to be calculated in a manner that reflected the requirements of the principle of human dignity, and concluded that this obligation had not been fulfilled by the manner in which the rate of benefits was calculated under the Hartz IV reform package.[32] Subsequently, in its *Asylum Seekers Benefits* judgment, the Constitutional Court similarly ruled that the amount of cash benefit paid to asylum seekers awaiting processing of their claims was similarly not compatible with the requirement of the principle of human dignity.[33] Both judgments thus affirm that the State's role as a social provider is linked to its fundamental obligation to uphold and give effect to the principle of human dignity.[34]

Other national constitutional systems provide an even greater level of protection for social rights. The Portuguese Constitutional Court has historically been prepared to invalidate legislation which it deemed to violate the constitutionally protected rights to receive adequate health care and social insurance.[35] Similarly, Polish, Hungarian, Latvian, Bulgarian, Croatian and Romanian courts have required modifications to be made to aspects of state socio-economic policy in order to ensure respect for social rights, while the Italian and Greek courts have treated social principles set out in the text of their national constitutions as giving rise to substantive

[31] BVerfG, 1 BvL 1/09 (9 February 2010), 1BvL 3/09, 1BvL 4/09 (9 February 2010).

[32] The Constitutional Court left it to the legislative branch to determine what alterations needed to be made to the existing method of calculating benefits. However, its judgment provided a clear steer as to how the legislature should go about making this adjustment, and it made provision for supplementary benefits to be awarded in the interim to persons in need who would otherwise not be entitled to the necessary minimum level of social assistance.

[33] BVerfG, 1 BvL 10/10 (18 July 2012), 1BvL 3/09, 1BvL 4/09 (9 February 2010).

[34] See C. Bittner, 'Human Dignity as a Matter of Legislative Consistency in an Ideal World: The Fundamental Right to Guarantee a Subsistence Minimum in the German Federal Constitutional Court's Judgment of 9 February 2010', *German Law Journal*, 12 (2011), 1941–60; S. Egidy, 'The Fundamental Right to the Guarantee of a Subsistence Minimum in the *Hartz IV Case* of the German Federal Constitutional Court', *German Law Journal*, 12 (2011), 1961–82. See also the following German Federal Constitutional Court (*BVerfG*) and Federal Administrative Court (*BVerwG*) decisions: BVerfGE 1, 97 (104f); BVerwGE 1, 159 (161); BVerwGE 25, 23 (27); BVerfGE 40, 121 (133, 134); BVerfGE 45, 187 (229); BVerfGE 82, 60 (85) and BverfGE 99, 246 (259).

[35] Constitutional Court of Portugal, Judgments no. 39/84 (right to health); nos. 12/88, 43/88, 191/88 (right to social insurance).

legal obligations.[36] The scope of protection granted to social rights in many of these States is often uncertain, fluctuating and context-specific.[37] However, the *Sozialstaat* principle has put down firm roots in all of these constitutional systems, just as it has in Germany, France and a number of other countries, and it consequently limits to some degree the extent to which social provision can be diluted or eliminated in these States.

Not every European State has adopted the *Sozialstaat* principle. For example, no equivalent principle exists in either UK or Irish law, and scepticism remains strong in both countries about whether social rights can or should be made justiciable in any way.[38] However, the UK Supreme Court has confirmed that administrative decisions to grant or withhold social assistance which may have a serious impact on an individual's life will be subject to close and exacting judicial scrutiny,[39] while the Court of Appeal has accepted that it would be a breach of common law rights for the executive to drive asylum seekers into a state of destitution by denying them access to basic forms of social assistance.[40]

These UK judgments illustrate a wider trend in constitutional and administrative law across Europe. In general, administrative courts across Europe have shown a readiness to review public authority decision-making in the socio-economic field for compliance with core rule of law principles. As a result, government decisions to limit access to social protection which are irrational, unreasonable or disproportionate, or which fail to respect the principles of equal treatment, legal certainty and fair procedure, will often be vulnerable to judicial challenge – even if the *Sozialstaat* principle has not taken root in the legal system in question.[41] Courts across

[36] For an overview, see Sadurski, 'Constitutional Courts in the Process of Articulating Constitutional Rights'. See also Katrougalos, 'The (Dim) Perspectives', 14.

[37] See generally Sadurski, 'Constitutional Courts in the Process of Articulating Constitutional Rights'.

[38] For an overview of the UK debate, see J. King, *Judging Social Rights* (Oxford University Press, 2012); E. Palmer, *Judicial Review, Socio-Economic Rights and the Human Rights Act* (Oxford: Hart, 2007). For a 'taster' of the Irish debate, see G. Hogan, 'Directive Principles, Socio-Economic Rights and the Constitution', *Irish Jurist*, 36 (2001), 174–98; A. Nolan, 'Ireland: The Separation of Powers Doctrine vs Human Rights' in M. Langford (ed.), *Social Rights Jurisprudence: Emerging Trends in Comparative and International Law* (Cambridge University Press, 2008), pp. 295–319.

[39] See *R (KM)* v. *Cambridgeshire County Council* [2012] UKSC 23; *R (L)* v. *Leeds City Council* [2010] EWHC 3324 (Admin); *R (on the application of Rodgers)* v. *Swindon Primary Care Trust* [2006] EWCA Civ 392.

[40] *R* v. *Secretary of State for Social Security, ex parte Joint Council for the Welfare of Immigrants* [1997] 1 WLR 275.

[41] Constitutional courts in Hungary, Poland, Latvia and elsewhere have been prepared to rule that cuts to social security violated the principle of legal certainty and other elements

Europe have also been willing to interpret constitutional texts as imposing obligations on States to take positive steps to enforce civil and political rights, which can prevent them denying individuals access to basic forms of health care, shelter or welfare support.[42] As a result, even in legal systems where social rights are not directly enforceable or where the status of the *Sozialstaat* principle is uncertain, social rights tend to receive indirect protection through national constitutional and/or administrative law.[43]

A similar trend can be detected in the case-law of the European Court of Human Rights.[44] For example, the Court has interpreted Article 3 of the European Convention on Human Rights (ECHR) as precluding state action which has the effect of driving individuals into a state of destitution; thus, in *MSS* v. *Belgium and Greece*, the Court held that the Greek authorities had violated the right of asylum seekers not to be subject to inhuman and degrading treatment contrary to Article 3, by failing to take adequate steps to prevent them sinking into a state of extreme poverty which involved 'living in the street, with no resources or access to sanitary facilities, and without any means of providing for [their] essential needs'.[45] The Court's case-law in respect of Article 8, Article 14 and other provisions of the ECHR has also recognised that States may be required to take positive steps to provide social protection to their citizens as part of discharging their obligations under the Convention.[46] In other words, while the *Sozialstaat* principle has not fully taken root in every European legal system, the idea that legal rights can have a social dimension is generally accepted across the continent. It is even possible to describe social rights as having become 'partially constitutionalised', in the sense that state action

of the rule of law. See Sadurski, 'Constitutional Courts in the Process of Articulating Constitutional Rights'; W. Sadurski, *Rights Before Courts? A Study of Constitutional Courts in Postcommunist States of Central and Eastern Europe* (Dordrecht: Springer, 2005), pp. 171–94.

42 See, e.g., *R (Adam)* v. *Secretary of State for the Home Department* [2005] UKHL 66; *V* v. *Einwohrnergemeine X und Regierungsrat des Kanton Bern*, BGE/ATF 121 I 367 (Swiss Federal Court).

43 For further analysis with specific reference to the UK context, see C. O'Cinneide, 'Legal Accountability and Social Justice' in N. Bamforth and P. Leyland (eds.), *Accountability in the Contemporary Constitution* (Oxford University Press, 2013), pp. 389–409.

44 See C. O'Cinneide, 'A Modest Proposal: Destitution, State Responsibility and the European Convention on Human Rights', *European Human Rights Law Review*, 5 (2008), 583–605.

45 *MSS* v. *Belgium and Greece* App. No. 30696/09 (ECtHR, 21 January 2011), para. 263.

46 See generally I. Koch, *Human Rights as Indivisible Rights: The Protection of Socio-Economic Demands Under the European Convention on Human Rights* (Dordrecht: Martinus Nijhoff, 2009).

affecting enjoyment of these rights is increasingly subject to legal controls rooted in national constitutional law or the requirements of the ECHR. The evolution of the *Sozialstaat* principle and the development of the ECHR jurisprudence has opened up legal avenues through which courts can scrutinise how States give effect to social rights, even if these rights rarely give rise to a subjective individual entitlement as such (as noted above in the context of the discussion of the *Sozialstaat* principle). As in other parts of the world, national courts are often reluctant to interfere with decisions of the legislative and executive branches of the State in the socio-economic field, on the basis that disputes about resource allocation, social policy and economic regulation should generally be resolved by elected officials. However, the possibility of judicial intervention in this field still casts a shadow over the development of national law and policy in many European States, and strong expectations exist that public authorities will act in a manner that is compatible with the *Sozialstaat* principle.[47]

Furthermore, EU law has also acquired an analogous 'social dimension'. The Court of Justice of the EU (CJEU) has acknowledged that EU legislation needs to be interpreted and applied with reference to the 'social objectives' of the Union; as far back as *Defrenne* v. *Sabena (No. 2)* in 1976, the CJEU interpreted the equal pay provisions of Article 119 of the Treaty of Rome (now Article 157 of the Treaty on the Functioning of the European Union) by reference to the 'social objectives of the Community, which is not merely an economic union, but is at the same time intended, by common action, to ensure social progress and seek the constant improvement of the living and working conditions of their peoples'.[48] Now, the EU Charter of Fundamental Rights,[49] which since December 2009 has the same legal status as the EU treaties, contains a list of social rights such as the right to choose an occupation and engage in work (Article 15), the right to social security and social assistance (Article 34), the right to health care (Article 35) and a series of employment rights set out in Articles 27–32.

Some of the social rights set out in the EU Charter, such as the rights of the elderly recognised in Article 25, do not appear to create directly enforceable subjective rights. Instead, they set out objective norms which may be given effect through EU 'legislative or executive acts' but 'become significant for the [c]ourts only when such acts are interpreted or reviewed' and do not

[47] Katrougalos, 'The (Dim) Perspectives', 9–15.

[48] Case C-43/75, *Defrenne* v. *Sabena (No. 2)* [1976] ECR 455, para. 10.

[49] Charter of Fundamental Rights [2000] OJ C364/01.

'give rise to direct claims for positive action by the Union's institutions or Member States authorities'.[50] Furthermore, the scope of the Charter is confined to situations where EU law or national legislation implementing EU law is at issue.[51] However, these provisions nevertheless establish the possibility that acts of the EU institutions or Member States implementing EU law which fail to respect the social rights requirements of the Charter may be reviewed by the CJEU. Once again, it is possible to speak of the 'partial constitutionalisation' of social rights within the framework of EU law.[52]

The potency of the idea of 'social Europe' is also reflected in the commitments that the European States have entered into under international human rights law. Virtually all European States have ratified the International Covenant on Economic, Social and Cultural Rights (ICESCR)[53] and participated actively in the monitoring process conducted by the UN Committee on Economic, Social and Cultural Rights (CESCR). European States have also accepted numerous binding commitments within the framework of ILO conventions. Furthermore, the vast majority of Council of Europe Member States have also agreed to be bound by the 1961 European Social Charter (ESC) or its successor instrument, the revised Social Charter of 1996.[54] By virtue of the provisions of the ESC, the socio-economic 'sister' instrument of the ECHR, States undertake to respect a number of social principles set out in Part I of the Charter, and select a number of specific rights guarantees set out in Part II by which they agree to be legally bound. They also participate in the ESC monitoring process, whereby the European Committee of Social Rights (ECSR) determines whether States are in conformity with their obligations under the Charter, while a Governmental Committee composed of state representatives and ultimately the Committee of Ministers of the Council of Europe respond to the

[50] See Explanations Relating to the Charter of Fundamental Rights [2007] OJ C303/32 (prepared by the Praesidium of the drafting Convention). Article 52(7) of the Charter provides that 'due regard' should be given to the 'explanations drawn up as a way of providing guidance' on the appropriate interpretation of the Charter.

[51] See Charter of Fundamental Rights, art. 51(1).

[52] See the collected papers contained in EUI Social and Labour Law Working Group, 'The Fundamentalisation of Social Rights' (EUI Working Paper Law 2009/05), cadmus.eui.eu/handle/1814/11214, last accessed 15 November 2013. For an example of the CJEU interpreting EU legislation in line with the social rights requirements of the Charter (in this case, the right to paid leave set out in Article 31(2) of the Charter), see Case C-282/10, *Dominguez* v. *Centre Informatique du Centre Ouest Atlantique, Préfet de la région Centre* (ECJ, 24 January 2012).

[53] International Covenant on Economic, Social and Cultural Rights, 993 UNTS 3 (ICESCR).

[54] European Social Charter (revised) CETS No. 163.

conclusions of the ECSR and make recommendations for remedial action where required.

The concept of a 'social Europe' has thus been given legal expression and infused into the multiple layers of European constitutional governance. It has therefore acquired both a political and a legal dimension, and become a touchstone for assessing the legitimacy of state action in the fields of social policy and labour market regulation.

IV. The slow decay of the European welfare states

However, the rhetorical commitment of European governments to the idea of a 'social Europe', and the manner in which social rights have become 'partially constitutionalised' at national and pan-European levels over the last few decades, have not prevented a gap opening up between image and reality. Despite Europe's legal and political commitment to maintaining its prized social model in place, over time, these undertakings have begun to ring hollow as substantial gaps have begun to open up in national welfare states.

Beginning in the early 1970s, the European welfare states entered what Taylor-Gooby has described as a 'period of uncertainty and challenge'.[55] The oil shocks and stagflation crisis of the 1970s ended the post-war era of full employment. Subsequently, the rapid pace of globalisation from the 1980s on, combined with the shift of many European countries from an industrial to a post-industrial service-based economy, destabilised existing employment patterns, eroded the political power of trade unions and generated new wealth inequalities. The fragmentation of post-industrial society also helped to erode the social solidarity of the post-war years and fuelled the growth of a more individualistic and libertarian ethos, best exemplified by the political rhetoric associated with Thatcherism in the UK.[56] At the same time, the ageing of European societies put pressure on already stretched social security and health care budgets, while popular unease about migration and the growing diversity of European societies served to weaken social bonds and undermine group solidarity.[57] Furthermore, policy-making elites become increasingly sceptical of the capacity of the State to distribute resources in

[55] P. Taylor-Gooby, 'The New Welfare State Settlement in Europe', *European Societies*, 10 (2008), 3–24, 3.

[56] For a general overview, see P. Pierson, *Dismantling the Welfare State? Reagan, Thatcher, and the Politics of Retrenchment* (Cambridge University Press, 1994).

[57] *Ibid.*

a fair and efficient manner, choosing instead to place their faith in the free market.[58]

These social, political and economic trends have persisted since the 1970s, and over time have radically re-shaped the European 'social space'.[59] Governments have become more reluctant to redistribute income through high taxation, to extend employment rights or to otherwise intervene in the functioning of the free market, even as wages for middle and low income jobs have stagnated. Job security has deteriorated and wealth inequalities have grown. As a result, a process of retrenchment has taken place at the national level, whereby State expenditure on social programmes has been reined in, access to social security benefits has been cut back, labour markets have been deregulated and systems of social protection and wealth redistribution have been allowed to decay. Furthermore, macroeconomic stability, fiscal discipline and the establishment of a 'flexible' labour market have become the central animating goals of state policy, while the ambition to secure genuine social citizenship for all has largely been relegated to the margins.[60]

A similar logic has been at work at the EU level. The Lisbon and Europe 2020 employment and growth strategies, the Stability and Growth Pact and other EU governance methodologies have emphasised the importance of fiscal discipline, macroeconomic stability and labour market flexibility, while social protection has been allowed to slip down the policy agenda. Furthermore, the manner in which the development of EU law has focused upon protecting free movement rights and deepening the European single market has led to what Scharpf has famously characterised as a 'decoupling' of economic integration from the various welfare traditions of the Member States.[61] Taken together, these factors have ensured that the social dimension of EU law remains chronically underdeveloped. EU legislation relating to the fields of employment law, social security and social assistance is limited in scope, and primarily focuses on facilitating free movement and preventing

[58] This development reflects the influence of public choice theory and the post-1960s re-emergence of ordo- and neoliberal political thought. See D. Stedman Jones, *Masters of the Universe: Hayek, Friedman and the Birth of Neoliberal Politics* (Princeton University Press, 2012).

[59] See in general K. Armingeon and G. Bonoli (eds.), *The Politics of Post-Industrial Welfare States: Adopting Post-war Social Policies to New Social Risks* (Abingdon: Routledge, 2006).

[60] See generally T. Judt, *Ill Fares the Land: A Treatise on Our Present Discontents* (London: Allen Lane, 2010).

[61] F.W. Scharpf, 'The European Social Model: Coping with the Challenges of Diversity', *Journal of Common Market Studies*, 40 (2002), 645–70, 646.

discrimination rather than setting out minimum standards.[62] Furthermore, the social provisions of national law remain vulnerable to being disrupted by the overriding requirements of the EU rules on market integration.[63] As yet, the social rights provisions of the EU Charter have had little impact on this problematic dynamic, and the same can be said of the various 'soft law' initiatives that have been adopted with a view to recalibrating the balance between the economic and social dimensions of EU governance.[64]

Many of the core elements of most European welfare states have, until recently, remained intact during this period of change and transformation. However, the safety net that the welfare state has historically provided for disadvantaged groups has nevertheless begun to fray at the margins as a result of this decades-long process of slow decay. The scaling-back of public investment in social services has tended to impact disproportionately on vulnerable groups, such as persons with disabilities, women and ethnic minorities. In particular, as Pierson has noted, 'the contemporary climate remains a harsh one for efforts to improve social provision for the vulnerable or to address newly recognized risks'.[65] Furthermore, individuals and groups who cannot function so easily in the new climate of 'flexicurity' increasingly receive much lower levels of social support. 'Activation' measures designed to encourage the long-term unemployed back into the labour market now often have a punitive character.[66] Eligibility conditions for access to social security benefits and employment rights have been tightened, which can often have a severe impact on the increasing number of casual or part-time workers.[67] *Sans-papiers* and other categories of irregular

[62] See, e.g., Directive 79/7/EEC, which prohibits gender discrimination in relation to statutory social security schemes but does not prescribe the form and content of such schemes.

[63] C. Joerges and F. Rödl, 'On De-formalisation in European Politics and Formalism in European Jurisprudence in Response to the "Social Deficit" of the European Integration Project: Reflections after the Judgments of the ECJ in *Viking* and *Laval*', *European Law Review*, 15 (2009), 1–19.

[64] Alexander Somek has developed a powerful critique of the manner in which European integration has served to weaken social policy at national level. See, e.g., A. Somek, 'De-Commodification Revisited: On the Absence of Emancipation in Europe' (University of Iowa Legal Studies Research Paper 06–04, August 2006), http://ssrn.com/abstract=927967, last accessed 15 November 2013.

[65] P. Pierson, 'Coping with Permanent Austerity: Welfare State Restructuring in Affluent Democracies' in P. Pierson (ed.), *The New Politics of the Welfare State* (Oxford University Press, 2001), pp. 410–56, p. 456.

[66] See A. Serrano Pascual, 'Reshaping Welfare States: Activation Regimes in Europe' in A. Serrano Pascual and L. Magnusson (eds.), *Reshaping Welfare States and Activation Regimes in Europe* (Brussels: Peter Lang, 2007), pp. 11–34 (especially pp. 14–19).

[67] See generally S. Fredman, 'Women at Work: The Broken Promise of Flexicurity', *Industrial Law Journal*, 33 (2004), 299–319.

migrants are often excluded from all but the most basic forms of social assistance, with the result that many individuals and families are forced to live in conditions of near-absolute poverty at the margins of society.[68]

In other words, the post-1980s retrenchment of the welfare state has combined with the fragmented nature of post-industrial society and widening income inequality to create clear categories of 'winners' and 'losers' – the majority of European citizens continue to have access to good pensions, decent health care and a strong system of employment rights protection, while a more economically vulnerable minority subsist on increasingly meagre benefits and are forced to the margins of the labour market. Furthermore, the socio-economically disadvantaged are increasingly viewed as 'deserving' the reduced and even punitive levels of state support that they now receive, on the basis that it reflects a failure on their part to compete effectively in the labour market.

As a result, even as the legal protection of social rights in national and EU law has expanded and the concept of a 'social Europe' has come to occupy a prominent place in the official rhetoric of European institutions, the European welfare states have ceased to expand and instead have gone into reverse gear. Until recently, the impact of these changes has mainly been felt at the margins of society. However, the austerity measures that many European governments have introduced in response to the economic crisis of 2008 have changed the picture: the gradual erosion of the European welfare states has sharply picked up pace, and the extent to which the European social model is under threat has suddenly become far more visible.

V. The crisis of austerity and the hollowness of the political discourse of 'social Europe'

The post-2008 austerity measures that many European States have introduced in response to the economic crisis and its aftermath have involved sweeping cuts to social security benefits, the further watering down of employment rights and sharp cuts in social expenditure.[69] These measures

[68] See, e.g., S. Conlan, 'State Policy Drives Asylum Seekers into Real Poverty', *Irish Times* (24 January 2013); J. A. Sweeney, 'The Human Rights of Failed Asylum Seekers in the United Kingdom', *Public Law* (2008), 277–301.

[69] For a Europe-wide overview of the social effects of austerity, see Council of the European Union, '2010 Update of the Joint Assessment by the SPC and the European Commission of the Social Impact of the Economic Crisis and Policy Responses' (26 November 2010), http://register.consilium.europa.eu/pdf/en/10/st16/st16905.en10.pdf, last accessed

are different in scale and scope to the retrenchment measures that preceded them: they have affected a wider swathe of the population and a greater range of social services, and consequently have had a more dramatic socio-economic impact. Austerity has helped to bring about record rates of unemployment, widened income inequalities,[70] generated mass social insecurity and produced measureable negative effects on the health and well-being of national populations taken as a whole.[71]

As noted by Hemerijck, the impact of austerity has been heterogeneous and uneven.[72] Some European welfare states have proved to be relatively resilient in the face of the crisis, just as they have over the last few decades of retrenchment and reform. This is particularly true in the case of the Nordic and Benelux States, France and Germany, whose welfare states remain strong.[73] However, in other States, the situation is very different. In the UK, the cuts in social protection introduced by the coalition government that came to power in 2010, taken together with the cost-cutting and privatisation measures introduced by previous governments, have led various commentators to argue that the UK welfare state has been effectively replaced by a much more minimalist system of social protection.[74] In Greece, Spain and the other States which have been forced to introduce sweeping austerity measures in return for receiving financial support from the IMF and other European governments, the impact of these measures has been devastating: substantial damage has been caused to the socio-economic fabric of these States, and their systems of social protection have come under unprecedented pressure.[75]

15 November 2013. See also European Commission, Eurostat Data on Poverty and Social Exclusion 2011, http://epp.eurostat.ec.europa.eu/portal/page/portal/income_social_inclusion_living_conditions/introduction, last accessed 15 November 2013.

70 D. Vaughan-Whitehead (ed.), *Work Inequalities in the Crisis: Evidence from Europe* (Geneva: ILO, 2012).

71 See, e.g., A. Kentikelenis *et al.*, 'Health Effects of Financial Crisis: Omens of a Greek Tragedy', *The Lancet*, 378 (2011), 1457–8.

72 See generally A. Hemerijck, *Changing Welfare States* (Oxford University Press, 2013).

73 *Ibid.*

74 See, e.g., S. Weir, 'The Welfare State is Dead – What is Rising from its Grave?', *Open Democracy* (15 January 2013), www.opendemocracy.net/ourkingdom/stuart-weir/welfare-state-is-dead-%E2%80%93-what-is-rising-from-grave, last accessed 15 November 2013.

75 For detailed analysis, see A. Heise and H. Lierse, 'Budget Consolidation and the European Social Model: The Effects of European Austerity Programmes on Social Security Systems' (Friedrich Ebert Stiftung Study, March 2011).

This post-2008 wave of austerity is sometimes described as representing a radical break with the European tradition of respect for social rights.[76] However, austerity is perhaps better understood as involving the intensification of already existing policy trends, rather than as the beginning of something new. The manner in which austerity measures have been implemented post-2008 faithfully reflects the underlying policy trends that have eaten away at the foundations of the European welfare states over the last few decades.

For example, States cutting back on public expenditure have reached for the same policy levers they used before the crisis, namely labour market deregulation, cuts to social security expenditure and the reduction of support to vulnerable groups lying outside of the social mainstream or with special needs. Furthermore, austerity appears to have impacted hardest on the marginalised groups which have already borne the brunt of previous reforms.[77] Austerity has also given a new twist to the already well-developed narrative of 'winners and losers'. Poorer groups in society are increasingly stigmatised as 'shirkers' who drain off national resources in a time of economic crisis and make it necessary for more economically productive members of society to bear some of the brunt of the cutbacks to public expenditure.[78] This narrative has even acquired a new transnational dimension. The countries most enmeshed in the Eurozone debt crisis, namely Greece, Ireland, Portugal and Spain, have been widely portrayed as 'deserving' the radical re-structuring of their systems of social protection that they have been forced to implement, on the basis that they were the sole authors of their own misfortune.

Furthermore, the EU's response to the crisis faithfully reflects the manner in which the imperatives of economic integration and macroeconomic stability dominate its policy agenda. European regulatory instruments such as the Euro Plus Pact and the 'six pack' of regulations adopted in the

[76] See, e.g., the contents of the 'Manifesto' issued by labour and social lawyers from across Europe calling upon the EU to respect and promote fundamental social rights. Transnational Trade Union Rights Experts Network (January 2013), www.etui.org/Networks/The-Transnational-Trade-Union-Rights-Experts-Network-TTUR, last accessed 5 January 2014.

[77] See Heise and Lierse, 'Budget Consolidation'; Vaughan-Whitehead, *Work Inequalities in the Crisis*. For the impact on children, see Eurochild, 'How the Economic and Financial Crisis is Affecting Children & Young People in Europe' (January 2011). For more on this point, see Sepúlveda's contribution to this volume.

[78] See, e.g., the comments made by George Osborne MP, the UK Chancellor of the Exchequer, in justifying cuts to social security benefits on the basis it was necessary to be 'fair to the person who leaves home every morning to go out to work and sees their neighbour still asleep, living a life on benefits'. *HC Deb* 5 December 2012, vol. 554, col. 877.

autumn of 2011, have served as primary motors of the drive towards cost-cutting and labour market deregulation at the national level, while the memoranda of understanding agreed between countries receiving emergency financial 'bail-outs' and the 'troika' of creditor institutions (the IMF, the European Central Bank (ECB) and the European Commission) have required the debtor States to make sweeping adjustments to their systems of social provision and labour market regulation.[79] Furthermore the EU's social agenda has ground to a halt: little has emerged from the EU institutions since the crisis began that gives substantive effect to the Union's commitment under Article 3 of the TEU to 'combat social exclusion' and to provide 'social justice and protection'.[80]

Austerity is therefore the logical culmination of national and EU socio-economic policies over the last few decades, and of the dynamics of social change that have underpinned many of these policy developments. In general, social concerns have been subordinated to the demands of the market in most European States for an extended period of time, dating back to the 1980s if not beyond. Indeed, as far back as 1998, Pierson was using the term 'permanent austerity' to describe the climate of cost-cutting and perpetual retrenchment in which the European welfare states were functioning at that time.[81] The manner in which States implementing austerity policies have sacrificed social protection to demonstrate their commitment to macroeconomic stability simply affirms the underlying pro-market orientation of the European public policy.

In light of the above discussion, it is clear that a substantial disconnect exists between rhetoric and practice when it comes to translating the abstract concept of a 'social Europe' into the language of social policy. At both national and EU levels, political rhetoric about Europe's 'social dimension' has not served as an effective counterweight to the pressure to conform to economic orthodoxy. Instead, austerity has exposed that

[79] See generally C. Barnard, 'The Financial Crisis and the Euro Plus Pact: A Labour Lawyer's Perspective', *Industrial Law Journal*, 41 (2012), 98–114; C. Kilpatrick *et al.*, 'Social Rights in Crisis in the Eurozone: The Role of Fundamental Rights Challenges' (EUI Working Paper Law No. 2014/05).

[80] The European Commission's own website states that the European institutions have been 'working closely together to support growth and employment, ensure financial stability, and put in place a better governance system for the future'. It makes no reference to social protection or to combating social exclusion. See European Commission, EU response to the crisis, http://ec.europa.eu/economy_finance/focuson/crisis/index_en.htm, last accessed 15 November 2013. For a sustained critique of the EU's response to the post-2008 crisis, see J. Habermas, *The Crisis of the European Union: A Response* (C. Cronin tr., London: Polity, 2012).

[81] Pierson, 'Coping with Permanent Austerity'.

little consensus exists about what respect for the notion of a 'social Europe' should entail in practice. In the heyday of the European welfare states, an overlapping consensus existed to the effect that the State should protect its citizens against a wide range of economic harms and strive to minimise income- and status-based inequalities. Now that overlapping consensus has begun to crumble, exposing the reality that sharp normative disagreement exists within Europe as to the status, scope and substance of social rights, and that little, if any, meaningful consensus exists across Europe as to what form of 'universal social minimum' should be provided by national welfare states even in times of economic turmoil.[82] In general, the claim that Europe has a uniquely admirable social model, and that both national governments and the EU institutions are committed to maintaining 'social Europe' as a living reality, is looking increasingly hollow.

VI. The limits of European social rights law

The hollow nature of the political commitment to a 'social Europe' has focused attention on the legal commitments that European States have accepted that relate to social rights. As discussed above, social rights have been 'partially constitutionalised' at both national and pan-European levels of governance; European States remain committed to giving effect to these rights under both national law and the provisions of international human rights such as ICESCR and ESC, while the EU institutions are bound by the social rights provisions of the EU Charter. This means that the tension that exists between the policies of 'permanent austerity' and the ideal of a 'social Europe' is not just a political issue. It also has a legal dimension, as laws and policies which fail to respect social rights are potentially open to challenge before national courts, the CJEU or international human rights bodies.

Trade unions, political parties and civil society groups have begun to make use of these legal avenues to challenge the legality of austerity measures, while academics and activists increasingly draw on the jurisprudence of bodies such as the CESCR to critique the trajectory of European social and economic policies.[83] There has in other words been a 'turn to the law', in an attempt to use

[82] This point has been forcefully made by Habermas in his recent analysis of the European response to the economic crisis. See generally Habermas, *The Crisis of the European Union*.

[83] See, e.g., Center for Economic and Social Rights (CESR), 'Mauled by the Celtic Tiger' (CESR Rights in Crisis Briefing Paper, February 2012). See also the contributions of Sepúlveda, Rolnik and Rabinovich, Nolan *et al.* and Lusiani to this this volume.

the conceptual framework of human rights law to define what forms of social protection individuals and groups are owed as of right. As such, the legal discourse of social rights has been put to work to fill the normative void that lies at the heart of the political discourse of a 'social Europe'.

In particular, since the economic crisis began in 2008, a variety of legal challenges have been launched against austerity measures in a number of different European countries. This 'turn to the law' has generated some significant judgments, which have reined in some austerity measures and given legal substance to abstract provisions of national law relating to principles of equality, rule of law and the enjoyment of social rights. For example, in 2012 the Portuguese Constitutional Court ruled that the suspension of holiday bonuses paid to public employees and pensioners as part of an austerity budget was unconstitutional on the basis that it violated the right to equality, as only particular categories of person were affected by this measure and more equitable measures could have been adopted to achieve the same financial results.[84] Subsequently, in April 2013, the Court ruled that a range of budget measures, including public sector salary and the imposition of a flat-rate solidarity tax, were incompatible with the principles of equality and proportionality and a number of constitutionally protected social rights.[85] Similarly, the Latvian Constitutional Court in 2009 ruled that pension cuts introduced as part of a deficit reduction programme violated the social rights provisions of the Latvian Constitution, on the grounds inter alia that the cut in question was excessive and the government had failed to make provision for an adequate transition period.[86]

Other courts have also recently proved to be relatively responsive to arguments that cuts in social protection may infringe constitutional or administrative law principles. Thus, for example, the judgments of the German Constitutional Court in the *Hartz IV and Asylum Seeker* cases discussed previously have affirmed that the German State is required to provide individuals with a minimum level of state support that is compatible with human dignity (the *Existenzminimum* in German terminology). The European Court of Human Rights in judgments such as *McCann* v. *UK* has shown a readiness to review whether national law grants adequate procedural protection for individuals and families facing eviction from public housing,[87] while in the *MSS* case referred to above the Court confirmed that a State may violate Article 3 of the Convention by failing to take action

[84] Constitutional Court of Portugal, Judgment no. 353/2012 (5 July 2012).
[85] Constitutional Court of Portugal, Judgment no. 187/2013 (5 April 2013).
[86] Constitutional Court of Latvia, Case no. 2009-43-01 (21 December 2009).
[87] *McCann* v. *UK* (2008) 47 EHRR 913.

to prevent individuals slipping into a state of destitution. Even in the UK, where social rights are not directly justiciable and the judiciary have limited powers to review the actions of public authorities for compliance with constitutional and human rights principles, courts have been increasingly prepared to scrutinise closely whether decisions to deny or limit access to welfare benefits comply with the requirements of fair procedure, statutory obligations to promote equality of opportunity, and the right of non-discrimination in the enjoyment of ECHR rights set out in Article 14 of the Convention.[88] Litigants have even obtained results by invoking EU consumer protection law to prevent banks evicting Spanish families in arrears with their mortgage payments.[89] This readiness of many courts across Europe to accept that certain legal rights can have a social dimension has provided some relief for vulnerable groups attempting to secure continuing access to the increasingly rationed benefits on offer from the European welfare states. However, it is important that the extent of protection provided for social rights by national legal systems across Europe is not exaggerated or overestimated. Social rights may be partially constitutionalised in many European States, but the substantive protection they offer against the steady encroachment of austerity measures is highly limited.

To start with, it needs to be borne in mind that conventional legal doctrine in most European States still views the legislative branch as having the primary responsibility for giving effect to the *Sozialstaat* principle and/or to fundamental social rights. In contrast, the role of the courts is often conceptualised in much more limited terms: their job is to step in where egregious breaches of social rights take place, such as a failure to provide an adequate *Existenzminimum* to vulnerable groups, or to interpret primary and secondary legislation by reference to the *Sozialstaat* principle. Much depends upon the individual court, its constitutional status and the political situation in a given State. However, national governments tend to enjoy wide discretion in framing and giving effect to their socio-economic policies, and in most States courts will only intervene in situations where the legislature or the executive has clearly failed to discharge their constitutional responsibilities.[90]

[88] See, e.g., *R (KM)* v. *Cambridgeshire City Council*; *R (W)* v. *Birmingham City Council* [2011] EWHC 1147 (Admin); *Burnip* v. *Birmingham City Council* [2012] EWCA Civ 629.

[89] Case C-415/11, *Mohamed Aziz* v. *Caixa d'Estalvis de Catalunya, Tarragona i Manresa (Catalunyacaixa)*, Judgment of 14 March 2013.

[90] For more on these points, see C. O'Cinneide, 'The Problematic of Social Rights – Uniformity and Diversity in the Development of Social Rights Review' in L. Lazarus, C. McCrudden and N. Bowles (eds.), *Reasoning Rights: Comparative Judicial Engagement* (Oxford: Hart, 2014), pp. 297–315.

Thus, for example, Heinig notes that German legal scholarship 'has developed a canon on the principle of the [*Sozialstaat*], emphasizing in particular the limits of the constitutional principle'; the legislature is regarded as having wide discretion in determining what concrete content should be given to social rights and how forms of social provision should be financed, while the *Sozialstaat* principle itself is generally not viewed as giving rise to subjective individual rights or an entitlement to receive any particular form of social assistance.[91] The *Hartz IV* and *Asylum Seeker* judgments have shown that the principle has some substantive content when its scope intersects with that of the overriding principle of human dignity. However, beyond such *Existenzminimum* cases, it is not clear when the German courts will be prepared to review government socio-economic policies.

Furthermore, the scope of the *Sozialstaat* principle, or the content of social rights explicitly listed in a constitutional text, or the extent to which civil and political rights and rule of law principles will be deemed to have acquired a social dimension, often remains unclear. Social provisions in national constitutions are frequently worded in vague terms, while doubt often exists as to the extent to which rule of law concepts or civil and political rights can be 'stretched' to protect access to specific forms of special protection. Furthermore, other constitutional norms can come into tension with social rights principles, including in particular the doctrine of separation of powers, and the relationship between these different principles is often ill-defined.

Much often depends upon the willingness of courts to protect social rights, and the extent to which they are viewed as having the legitimacy to take such decisions within the context of their own national legal systems. In systems where courts are not recognised as having the power to monitor respect for social rights, as in the UK, then the reach of judicial protection can be very limited.[92] This tendency is clearly illustrated by the case-law of the European Court of Human Rights. The Strasbourg Court appears reluctant to extend its jurisprudence too far into the socio-economic field, where it grants States a very wide margin of appreciation, presumably on the basis that it has not been given a clear mandate in this context.[93] This reluctance has been evident in the Court's consideration of austerity measures in cases brought before it.[94]

[91] Heinig, 'The Political and the Basic Law's *Sozialstaat* Principle', 1888–90.

[92] See generally C. O'Cinneide, 'Legal Accountability and Social Justice'.

[93] See, e.g., *Hatton* v. *UK* (2003) 37 EHRR 611, paras. 96–104.

[94] See, e.g., *Koufaki and Adedy* v. *Greece*. App. Nos. 57665/12 and 57657/12, 7 May 2013.

In other words, the 'partial constitutionalisation' of social rights across Europe remains at best a half-formed project, illustrating again the tenuous nature of 'social Europe'. Little consensus exists as to the extent to which courts should protect social rights, or whether the core constituent elements of the European welfare states should be regarded as constitutionally embedded and beyond the reach of legislative or executive 'reform'.

A similar vagueness exists at the EU level. As previously discussed, social rights have been incorporated into the EU Charter of Fundamental Rights, while EU primary and secondary legislation and the provisions of the European treaties are often interpreted by reference to the social objectives of the Union. However, the status and substantive content of the social rights set out in the Charter remains uncertain. In particular, it remains to be seen which Charter rights will be classified as giving rise to subjective individual entitlements, and how the Court will interpret the vague language of the Charter's social provisions.[95] The relationship between the social rights contained in the Charter and the economic integration goals and free movement rights that dominate EU law also remains contested and ill-defined.[96] EU free movement rights have already come into conflict with national laws which aim to uphold social rights, as illustrated by the highly controversial judgments of the CJEU in the *Viking* and *Laval* cases where the rights of trade unions under Swedish law to engage in industrial action to seek improvements in working conditions were subordinated to the right of employers to 'post' workers across borders in line with EU freedom of labour rules.[97]

Furthermore, the scope of application of the Charter itself is also uncertain. Article 52 of the Charter provides that it only applies to EU law and measures taken by national authorities to implement and give effect to the requirements of EU law. Thus far, the CJEU has taken the view that salary cuts and other austerity measures introduced by national governments to give effect to their general obligations to ensure monetary stability under Article 104 EC Treaty and the Stability and Growth Pact as laid out in

95 See generally D. Ashiagbor, 'Economic and Social Rights in the European Charter of Fundamental Rights', *European Human Rights Law Review*, 9 (2004), 63–72.

96 See generally Joerges and Rödl, 'On De-formalisation in European Politics and Formalism in European Jurisprudence'.

97 See Case C-438/05, *International Transport Workers Federation, Finnish Seaman's Union* v. *Viking Line* [2007] ECR I-10779; Case C-341/05, *Laval un Partneri Ltd* v. *Svenska Byggnadsarbetareförbudet* [2007] ECR I-11767.

EU Regulations 1466/97 and 1467/97 'clearly' fall outside the scope of EU law.[98] This means that the social rights provisions of the EU Charter would appear not to apply to austerity measures introduced by national governments which are not directly mandated by EU law. Given that the CJEU has confirmed in the *Pringle* case that the European Stability Mechanism, the main vehicle that currently exists for providing indebted Eurozone States with financial assistance subject to strict budget conditionality, also falls outside the framework of EU law in a de facto sense,[99] it is difficult to see how the Charter's provisions can have much impact on Eurozone austerity requirements in general. It would appear that the social provisions of the Charter may only apply to EU and national law relating directly to the implementation of the already limited 'social agenda' of the EU – in other words, the reach of the EU Charter may be limited by the already stunted commitment of the EU as a transnational entity to translating the rhetoric of social Europe into substantive law and policy.

In general, the austerity crisis has made it clear that the project of European integration is haunted by the 'social question'.[100] There is no clearly defined set of legal norms in place that delineates how social rights should be protected within the framework of EU law, or when Member States can invoke their national welfare traditions as a justification for restricting free movement rights or for resiling from their commitments under the various EU economic stabilisation instruments.[101] Furthermore, at the national level, the constitutional protection of social rights remains partial, limited and uncertain, notwithstanding the manner in which the *Sozialstaat* principle has become part of the constitutional framework of many European States. As a result, the rhetorical commitment of European States to the concept of a 'social Europe' is not backed up by firm legal standards at either the national or the pan-European level. In

[98] The fate of Case C-128/12, *Sindicato dos Bancários do Norte and Others* v. *BPN – Banco Português de Negócios, SA*, illustrates this point well. On 4 May 2013, the Sixth Chamber of the CJEU ruled that the Court 'clearly lacks the jurisdiction' to deal with this preliminary reference from the Portuguese courts regarding the impact of austerity measures. Case C-128/12, *Sindicato dos Bancários do Norte and Others* v. *BPN – Banco Português de Negócios, SA* [2013] OJ C129/04. See also Case C-134/12, *Corpul Național al Polițiștilor – Biroul Executiv Central* [2012] OJ C303/18 (declared inadmissible).

[99] Case C-370/12, *Pringle* v. *Government of Ireland* (ECJ, 27 November 2012).

[100] A. Somek, 'The Social Question in a Transnational Context' (LSE 'Europe in Question' Discussion Paper Series No. 39/2011, June 2011), www2.lse.ac.uk/europeanInstitute/LEQS/LEQSPaper39.pdf, last accessed 15 November 2013.

[101] Joerges and Rödl argue that national welfare traditions should not be subordinated to supranational economic integration goals. See Joerges and Rödl, 'On De-formalisation in European Politics and Formalism in European Jurisprudence'.

general, the European welfare states lack the type of firm constitutional foundation that might protect them against the cold wind of neoliberal economic imperative or the demands of austerity logic.

VII. The limited impact of international human rights standards in the social sphere

Similar gaps have existed in the past within both national and EU law in relation to the protection of civil and political rights. These gaps have however largely been plugged by the incorporation of the ECHR into national and EU law, and the willingness of European States and the CJEU to respect their international law obligations under the Convention by giving effect to judgments of the European Court of Human Rights. European States have also agreed to be bound by an extensive series of social rights obligations under international law, in particular (as previously discussed) those established under the framework of ICESCR, ESC and the ILO. In theory, these commitments should provide a bulwark against some of the financial and economic pressures that have contributed to the erosion of the European welfare states, just as the civil and political rights provisions of the ECHR have acted as a bulwark against the erosion of civil liberties and democratic rights.

However, once again, the rhetorical commitments of European governments do not necessarily translate well into practice. European governments often engage politely with international social rights monitoring mechanisms, while ICESCR, ILO and ESC standards are occasionally referred to in political debates and legal judgments.[102] But the impact of these standards often tends to be limited in practice: they are not viewed by European governments as embedding rights protection in the same manner as the ECHR.

Part of the reason for this is that international human rights law in the field of social rights can at times be of limited utility in the European context. This is particularly true of the standards developed under the framework of ICESCR. The UN Committee on Economic, Social and Cultural Rights (CESCR) is charged with interpreting ICESCR in a manner that makes sense in a global context, which means that it inevitably has to

[102] See, e.g., Case C-438/05, *International Transport Workers Federation, Finnish Seaman's Union* v. *Viking Line* [2007] ECR I-10779, para. 43 (where the ESC and ILO Convention No. 87 concerning Freedom of Association and Protection of the Right to Organise were taken into account by the CJEU in determining the fundamental nature of the right to engage in collective action).

frame its analysis of the Covenant's (often quite broad) provisions in general terms. This can limit the extent to which the Committee's conceptual approach can usefully be applied in the specific context of Europe. For example, the CESCR has indicated that 'deliberatively retrogressive' measures can cover 'a general decline of living and housing conditions, directly attributable to policy and legislative decisions by States Parties', which is not accompanied by targeted 'compensatory measures'.[103] However, without further detail, these standards by themselves provide little guidance to European governments reallocating resources across complex social welfare systems in response to a combination of internal and external economic factors. Furthermore, while the Committee often expresses concern about retrogressive developments in its comments on state reports submitted by European countries, it will not always identify when such retrogression has actually breached a State's obligations under ICESCR.[104] As a result, the Committee's expressions of concern can at times add little to the hard-fought political debates that are being fought out within European States about austerity measures and the cutting back of the welfare state.

However, the Committee's jurisprudence nevertheless provides an invaluable normative framework for analysing the impact of state policy on the enjoyment of social rights, especially when the CESCR engages in detail with the specifics of a national situation as it did in its 2012 report on Spain.[105] Furthermore, this normative framework is also complemented by the extensive and detailed jurisprudence of the ECSR, which monitors how European States have complied with their obligations under the ESC, the sister instrument within the Council of Europe framework to the ECHR. The ECSR has been able to develop more detailed standards

[103] CESCR, 'General Comment No. 4' in 'Note by the Secretariat, Compilation of General Comments and General Recommendations Adopted by Human Rights Treaty Bodies' (27 May 2008) UN Doc. HRI/GEN/1/Rev. 9 (Vol. 1), para. 59. See also CESCR, 'General Comment No. 3', para. 12. For more on retrogressive measures, see Nolan *et al.*'s contribution to this volume.

[104] A. Chapman, 'A "Violations Approach" for Monitoring the International Covenant on Economic, Social and Cultural Rights', *Human Rights Quarterly*, 18 (1996), 23–66. When the Committee begins to hear individual complaints under the Optional Protocol to ICESCR, it will for the first time develop a concrete and detailed case-law as to what constitutes a violation of the Covenant. The Optional Protocol entered into force on 5 May 2013 – at the time of writing, four European States, namely Bosnia and Herzegovina, Portugal, Slovakia and Spain, have ratified the Protocol, out of a total of ten ratifying States.

[105] See CESCR, 'Concluding Observations on Spain' (6 June 2012) UN Doc. E/C.12/ESP/CO/5.

in the field of social rights than the CESCR has, as it is able to take greater account of the relatively developed and homogeneous nature of European economies in interpreting the scope and substantive content of ESC rights.[106] Its jurisprudence can therefore be viewed as a more context-specific expression of the CESCR standards, tailored specifically for the European context.

For example, the ECSR has interpreted the right to social assistance set out in Article 13 ESC as requiring that States ensure that all persons in need receive 'the resources needed to live a decent life and meet basic needs in an adequate manner'. Such resources should last for an adequate duration, be available as of right to a person in need, and be of sufficient quantity to satisfy basic needs, with the Committee assessing this latter criterion on the basis that the minimum level of assistance offered by a State to an individual should not be less than the 'risk-of-poverty threshold value', usually defined as 40 per cent of median equivalised income.[107] This is a precise standard, which is based upon benchmarks used in social science research to assess whether social assistance is adequate to prevent vulnerable groups slipping into poverty. It effectively sets out the 'minimum core' of social assistance that European States should provide to those in need. However, the Committee has also interpreted the text of Article 13 and other ESC rights as requiring States to go beyond this minimum core requirement: State Parties to the Charter are also expected to take proportionate steps to secure the social rights of vulnerable groups and to ensure that ESC rights are effectively enjoyed by the population at large, even though they also enjoy a margin of appreciation when it comes to allocating resources and choosing which socio-economic policies are best suited to achieve these ends.[108]

The Committee adopts a similar approach when adjudicating complaints brought under the 1995 Additional Protocol to the Charter, whereby 'international' non-governmental organisations (NGOs) registered with the Council of Europe, national employer and trade union federations, and 'representative' national unions can bring a complaint to the ECSR against States which have ratified the Protocol alleging the existence of a

[106] See generally J.-F. Akandij-Kombé, 'The Material Impact of the Jurisprudence of the European Committee of Social Rights' in De Búrca and De Witte (eds.), *Social Rights in Europe*, pp. 89–108.

[107] European Committee of Social Rights (ECSR), Conclusions XIII-4, Statement of Interpretation on Article 13§1, 54–7.

[108] H. Cullen, 'The Collective Complaints System of the European Social Charter: Interpretatitve Methods of the European Committee on Social Rights', *Human Rights Law Review*, 9 (2009), 61–93, 76–81.

'collective' failure to comply with the Charter, i.e. one which affects more than a few specific individuals.[109] As Cullen has noted, this 'collective complaints procedure' is the first quasi-judicial process in international human rights law which has been established specifically to deal with social rights claims.[110] It has allowed the Committee to develop wide-ranging case-law which has put flesh on the provisions of the ESC and helped to clarify when States are not acting in conformity with its requirements.[111]

The Committee has recently begun to identify situations where austerity measures or other cuts in state systems of social provision will constitute an impermissible dilution of social rights and therefore breach the provisions of the Charter. Thus, in Complaint No. 48/2008, *European Roma Rights Centre* v. *Bulgaria*, the Committee ruled that newly introduced Bulgarian legislation which barred individuals unemployed for more than six months from receiving unemployment relief was not in conformity with the requirements of the right to social assistance set out in Article 13§1.[112] In its decision, the Committee acknowledged that States enjoyed a wide margin of discretion when it came to the design and funding of their social welfare systems; however, state measures which reduced or suspended the payment of welfare benefits to persons in need would 'only be in conformity with the Charter if they do not deprive persons in need of their means of subsistence' or their entitlement to 'live in a manner compatible with their human dignity'.[113]

Two 2012 decisions of the Committee are of particular importance in this respect, as they concern the effects of the severe austerity measures imposed in Greece as part of the 'bail-out' package negotiated with the troika of the IMF, the ECB and the European Commission. In Complaint 66/2011, *General Federation of Employees of the National Electric Power Corporation (GENOP-DEI) and Confederation of Greek Civil Servants'*

[109] Additional Protocol to the European Social Charter Providing for a System of Collective Complaints, ETS No. 158. See R. Churchill and U. Khaliq, 'The Collective Complaints System of the European Social Charter: An Effective Mechanism for Ensuring Compliance with Economic and Social Rights?', *European Journal of International Law*, 15 (2004), 417–56.

[110] See Cullen, 'The Collective Complaints System of the European Social Charter', 61.

[111] See R. Brillat, 'The Supervisory Machinery of the European Social Charter: Recent Developments and Their Impact' in De Búrca and De Witte (eds.), *Social Rights in Europe*, pp. 31–44. At the time of writing, the ECSR has received 103 such complaints, and handed down 82 decisions of conformity or non-conformity.

[112] *European Roma Rights Centre (ERRC)* v. *Bulgaria*, Complaint No. 48/2008 (18 February 2009).

[113] *Ibid.*, para. 37.

Trade Unions (ADEDY) v. *Greece*[114], the Committee ruled inter alia that cuts to the minimum wage for younger workers breached the right to fair remuneration set out in Article 4§1 as it takes them below the national poverty line. In Complaint 76/2012, *Federation of Employed Pensioners of Greece (IKA-ETAM)* v. *Greece*,[115] the Committee ruled that sweeping social security cuts had breached the requirements of Article 12§3 of the Charter, which requires States to 'endeavour to raise progressively the system of social security to a higher level'. The Committee accepted that States could restrict or reduce access to social security benefits in times of economic turbulence where this was necessary to ensure the financial viability of the social security system as a whole. However, the manner in which these particular cuts had been carried out and their cumulative effect on vulnerable groups was 'bound to bring about a significant degradation of the standard of living and the living conditions of many of the pensioners concerned' and therefore was incompatible with the requirements of Article 12§3.[116]

These decisions are especially significant as they establish that austerity measures cannot remove the floor of social protection that States are obliged to provide under the provisions of the ESC, even in times of economic crisis. The Committee has clarified what will qualify as an unacceptably retrogressive measure under the ESC, and emphasised that 'governments are bound to take all necessary steps to ensure that the rights of the Charter are effectively guaranteed at a period of time when beneficiaries need protection the most'.[117] Furthermore, the Committee has concluded that cuts in social protection which breach ESC rights cannot be justified on the basis that they are required by virtue of an international agreement or under EU law; austerity measures negotiated between the Greek government and the 'troika' thus enjoy no special protection.[118]

The ECSR has thus developed a set of standards that define with reasonable precision what European States should provide by way of social

[114] ECSR, *General Federation of Employees of the National Electric Power Corporation (GENOP-DEI) and Confederation of Greek Civil Servants' Trade Unions (ADEDY)* v. *Greece*, Complaint No. 66/2011 (23 May 2012).

[115] ECSR, *Federation of Employed Pensioners of Greece (IKA-ETAM)* v. *Greece*, Complaint No. 76/2012 (7 December 2012). See also Complaints 77/2012, 78/2012, 79/2012 and 80/2012, decided on the same day.

[116] *Federation of Employed Pensioners of Greece (IKA-ETAM)*, para. 78.

[117] ECSR, General Introduction to Conclusions XIX-2, 2009, para. 15; see also ECSR, Complaint 65/2011, *General Federation of Employees of the National Electric Power Corporation (GENOP-DEI) / Confederation of Greek Civil Servants' Trade Unions (ADEDY)* v. *Greece*, Complaint 65/2011 (23 May 2012), para. 18.

[118] *Federation of Employed Pensioners of Greece (IKA-ETAM)*, paras. 50–2.

protection. These standards reflect the general thrust of the CESCR's jurisprudence, and also relevant aspects of the case-law of the ECHR.[119] They also take into account the standards relating to employment rights and social security that have been developed through the framework of the ILO. Indeed, the Committee regularly refers to ILO instruments and the findings of ILO expert groups in formulating its conclusions.[120]

The Committee's case-law, in tandem with the CESCR and ILO standards, thus serve as a template or point of reference for defining what a commitment to achieving a 'social Europe' should mean in practice. Furthermore, many of the social rights provisions of the EU Charter on Fundamental Rights are based on equivalent provisions set out in the text of the Social Charter. This suggests that the case-law of the ECSR should serve as a point of reference for the CJEU and other EU institutions when it comes to interpreting and giving effect to these provisions, which in turn may influence how national courts, parliaments and governments engage with the overlapping provisions of both Charters.[121]

However, for now, the Committee's jurisprudence, and indeed the Social Charter as a human rights instrument, remains marginalised within European political and legal discourse. The ESC has always been overshadowed by the success of the ECHR, and it remains primarily known as a labour rights instrument, with its wider social dimension often overlooked.[122] Furthermore, European governments at times show little inclination to engage closely with the ESC or the case-law of the ECSR. Most States Parties to the ESC have not ratified the Collective Complaints Protocol, and the Committee of Ministers of the Council of Europe is slow to recommend that States take action in response to a finding of non-conformity by the ECSR.[123]

[119] For more on the interrelationship between the Committee's case-law and that of the ECSR and the ECHR, see A. Nolan, '"Aggravated Violations", Roma Housing Rights and Forced Expulsions in Italy: Recent Developments under the European Social Charter Collective Complaints System', *Human Rights Law Review*, 11 (2011), 343–61, 355–9.

[120] See, e.g., ECSR, *General Federation of Employees of the National Electric Power Corporation (GENOP-DEI) and Confederation of Greek Civil Servants' Trade Unions (ADEDY)* v. *Greece*, Complaint No. 66/2011, para. 61.

[121] See in particular Charter of Fundamental Rights, arts. 25 (rights of the elderly), 26 (rights of disabled persons), 27–35 (dealing with 'solidarity').

[122] P. Alston, 'Assessing the Strengths and Weaknesses of the European Social Charter's Supervisory System', in De Búrca and De Witte (eds.), *Social Rights in Europe*, pp. 45–67.

[123] See, e.g., the mildness of Council of Europe, Committee of Ministers, Resolution CM/ResChS(2010)8 (21 October 2010) (adopted in response to the ECSR's strong findings against Italy in *Centre on Housing Rights and Evictions (COHRE)* v. *Italy*, Complaint No. 58/2009 (6 July 2010)).

In general, European States may formally endorse the elements of international human rights law that relate to social rights, but for the most part this theoretical commitment is not translated into genuine practical engagement. Once again, a gap exists between image and reality: European States endorse the idea of a 'social Europe' where international human rights standards are respected, but are very slow to translate this commitment into a serious engagement at the level of substantive law and policy with the standards laid down by binding treaty instruments such as ICESCR and ESC.

VIII. Conclusion

European States together with the EU as a transnational entity formally embraced the idea of a 'social Europe', founded on respect for the *Sozialstaat* principle and the social rights set out in instruments such as ICESCR and ESC. However, this formal embrace of the idea of 'social Europe' is not necessarily reflected in law and policy. The slow erosion of the European welfare states that has been underway for the last few decades has recently gained momentum with the 2008 economic crisis and the intensification of austerity measures across much of the continent. This has exposed the hollowness that lies at the heart of social Europe; the European commitment to social rights is essentially rhetorical in nature, and their partial constitutionalisation remains an incomplete project. As demonstrated above, in certain parts of Europe, and in particular in Germany, France and the Nordic and Benelux States, political and economic conditions still favour the preservation of the welfare state. However, experience from Greece and other countries at the heart of the Eurozone crisis has shown that the European social model is vulnerable to being diluted or even swept away in times of straitened budgets and economic turbulence.

As a result, with every passing year, the dream of a 'social Europe' looks increasingly faded. Indeed, in some parts of the continent, it has already begun to dissolve in the cold dawn of the new era of austerity. However, certain elements of European law and political practice point the way towards how the concept of a social Europe could be given new vitality. The welfare state remains alive and well in parts of Europe, and continues to attract broad popular support across the continent. The constitutional principle of the *Sozialstaat* gives legal expression to the concept of 'social citizenship' that originally underpinned the historical development of the European social model. Furthermore, courts across Europe have recently shown a readiness to give this principle substantive legal content. The EU Charter of Fundamental Rights contains social rights which have their origins in the text of the ESC. As a result, the possibility exists that international human rights law may yet influence the development of EU law in the social field, and, by extension, national law and policy.

Therefore, the picture is not all negative. However, it remains to be seen whether European States will be prepared to translate their formal commitment to respecting social rights into concrete legal and policy measures, or whether the current economic crisis marks the end of the attempt to establish a 'social Europe' and to embed social rights protection into the legal and political landscape of the continent.

7

Rationalising the right to health: is Spain's austere response to the economic crisis impermissible under international human rights law?

NICHOLAS J. LUSIANI

I. Introduction

In the fall of 2012, workers marching across Spain's most populous region, Andalucía, arrived in Seville chanting, 'We won't pay the debt with our health care!'[1] As the enduring effects of government austerity policies continue to unravel the social contract across the country with generational setbacks to the enjoyment of human rights, in particular the right to health, to what degree can international human rights law – especially the International Covenant on Economic, Social and Cultural Rights (ICESCR) – guide the Spanish government's responses to the economic crisis gripping the country?

Considering their long-lasting and discriminatory effects, the degree to which they threaten minimum core levels of socio-economic rights, and especially given the existence of human rights-centred fiscal alternatives to offset decreased revenue in times of recession, this chapter will examine the degree to which the government's austerity measures and structural reforms set out between 2010 and 2012 effectively violate the human right to the highest attainable standard of health as protected under international human rights law. Drawing on existing literature,[2] jurisprudence

This chapter was inspired by a collaboration between the Center for Economic and Social Rights (CESR) and 18 Spanish organisations to expose the human consequences of austerity in Spain and to propose human rights-centred alternatives. The article benefitted greatly from comments by Marta Mendiola and Ignacio Saiz, and research assistance from Emily Button-Aguilar. All errors are strictly the author's.

[1] R. Harding and M. Johnson, 'Lagarde endorses Spain economic reforms', *Financial Times* (1 August 2012), www.ft.com/cms/s/0/7f8326b2-dbf6-11e1-86f8-00144feab49a.html, last accessed 18 December 2013.

[2] See, e.g., S. Way, N. Lusiani and I. Saiz, 'Economic and Social Rights in the "Great Recession": Towards a Human Rights-Centered Economic Policy in Times of Crisis' in

and new methodologies[3] for monitoring the obligation to fulfil socio-economic rights through economic policy, the chapter will also explore how the case of Spain can inform ongoing debates about the nature of States' human rights obligations in times of economic crisis, in particular the emerging normative content of the prohibition of retrogression and the related requirement to maximise the availability of resources through fiscal and budgetary policy in line with the obligations set out in international human rights law.

Having opened with a discussion of Spain's international obligations related to the human right to health, the chapter details the socio-economic outcomes of the first and second waves of the current economic crisis on the enjoyment of the right to health in Spain. The next section follows by charting out Spain's obligations to respect, protect and fulfil the right to the highest attainable standard of health of different groups, analysed against Spain's austerity-driven policy responses to the economic crisis. The chapter concludes with a reflection on the opportunities and remaining challenges in using international human rights law to contest austerity policies, to protect economic and social rights guarantees under threat in times of deep economic recession, and to deliver meaningful and effective remedies for those whose rights have been breached.

II. Spain's legal obligations to realise the human right to the highest attainable standard of health

As a State Party to ICESCR, Spain is duty-bound to respect, protect and fulfil 'the right of everyone to the enjoyment of the highest attainable

E. Riedel, G. Giacca and C. Golay (eds.), *Economic, Social and Cultural Rights: Contemporary Issues and Challenges* (Oxford University Press, 2014), pp. 86–110; R. Balakrishnan and D. Elson, 'Auditing Economic Policy in the Light of Obligations on Economic and Social Rights', *Essex Human Rights Review*, 5 (2008); R. Balakrishnan and D. Elson (eds.), *Economic Policy and Human Rights: Holding Governments to Account* (London and New York: Zed Books, 2012).

3 Council of Europe Commissioner for Human Rights, 'Safeguarding Human Rights in Times of Economic Crisis' (Issue Paper, November 2013); Center for Economic and Social Rights (CESR), 'The OPERA Framework: Assessing Compliance with the Obligation to Fulfill Economic, Social and Cultural Rights' (2012); CESR, 'Assessing Fiscal Policies from a Human Rights Perspective: Methodological Case Study on the Use of Available Resources to Realize Economic, Social and Cultural Rights in Guatemala' (2012); R. Balakrishnan, D. Elson, J. Heintz and N. Lusiani, 'Maximum Available Resources & Human Rights: Analytical Report' (June 2011); A. Nolan, R. O'Connell and C. Harvey (eds.), *Human Rights and Public Finance: Budgets and the Promotion of Economic and Social Rights* (Oxford: Hart, 2013).

standard of physical and mental health'.[4] The Spanish Constitution, under Article 43, also guarantees the right to health, as does the European Social Charter and the European Union (EU) Fundamental Rights Charter, both of which Spain has also ratified.[5] The UN Committee on Economic, Social and Cultural Rights (CESCR) has interpreted the right to health as protecting access 'not only to timely and appropriate health care but also to the underlying determinants of health, such as access to safe and potable water and adequate sanitation, an adequate supply of safe food, nutrition and housing, healthy occupational and environmental conditions, and access to health-related education and information'.[6]

The Committee has further stressed the critical importance of transparency and 'participation of the population in all health-related decision-making at the community, national and international levels'.[7] While like other social rights, the fulfilment of the right to health must be achieved progressively over time,[8] Spain has an immediate obligation to prevent and end discrimination, in law and in practice.[9] Discrimination in access to health care and the socio-economic determinants of health on the basis of national or social origin, property or socio-economic status, for example, is expressly forbidden. The principle of equity, furthermore, 'demands that poorer households should not be disproportionately burdened with health expenses as compared to richer households', pointing to a legal requirement of a progressive health financing system.[10] Under its international obligations, Spain furthermore has an immediate duty 'to ensure the satisfaction of, at the very least, "minimum essential levels" of the [right to health] universally'.[11] The failure by the State to meet these minimum levels is assumed to be a prima facie violation unless the State can demonstrate that 'every effort has been made to use all resources that

[4] International Covenant on Economic, Social and Cultural Right, 993 UNTS 3 (ICESCR) art. 12.

[5] Spain also has right to health-related obligations under Article 24 of Convention on the Rights of the Child, 1577 UNTS 3 (CRC), Article 5(e)(iv) of the Convention on the Elimination of All Forms of Racial Discrimination, 660 UNTS 195 (CERD), Article 12 of the Convention on the Elimination of All Forms of Discrimination Against Women, 1249 UNTS 13 (CEDAW) and Article 25 of the Convention on the Rights of Persons with Disabilities, 2515 UNTS 3 (CRPD).

[6] UN Committee on Economic, Social and Cultural Rights (CESCR), 'General Comment No. 14' in 'Note by the Secretariat, Compilation of General Comments and General Recommendations Adopted by Human Rights Treaty Bodies' (27 May 2008) UN Doc. HRI/GEN/1/Rev.9 (Vol. I), para. 11.

[7] *Ibid.* [8] See ICESCR, art. 2(1). [9] See *ibid.* art. 2(2).

[10] CESCR, 'General Comment No. 14', para. 12(b)(iii).

[11] CESCR, 'General Comment No. 3' in 'Compilation of General Comments', para. 10.

are at its disposition in an effort to satisfy, as a matter of priority, those minimum obligations'.[12] Even in times of economic recession, deliberate and well-targeted measures must be taken to ensure – in revenue raising as well as in expenditures – that the most vulnerable sectors of the population can enjoy at least these minimum levels of rights enjoyment.[13]

Beyond those immediate obligations of non-discrimination and ensuring minimum essential levels of the right to health, Spain has the duty to move as expeditiously and effectively as possible in taking deliberate, concrete and targeted steps towards fully realising the right to the highest attainable standard of health.[14] The natural corollary of this duty to take steps progressively is the corresponding duty to not regress, or backslide, in the fulfilment of the right to health. This prohibition of retrogression involves two dimensions: both normative (that is, limitations in legal, de jure guarantees), as well as an empirical dimension, or de facto backsliding in the effective enjoyment of economic, social and cultural rights, including the right to health.[15] Any de facto retrogressive measures, such as budget cuts to the health care system or employment programmes, can only be justified under certain strict conditions as recently reaffirmed by the CESCR, following its review of Spain in May 2012.[16] Any government conduct (actions or omissions) which leads to empirical, de facto backsliding in the realisation of the right to health can only be deemed justifiable under the Covenant when such measures are temporary and limited to the period of economic contraction; are non-discriminatory, in law and in practice; protect the minimum essential levels of the right to health; and are proportionate and strictly necessary, having considered all alternatives, including options for re-allocating and/or mobilising additional resources.[17]

[12] *Ibid.*

[13] *Ibid.*, para. 12; CESCR, 'General Comment No. 12' in 'Compilation of General Comments', para. 28; CESCR, 'General Comment No. 14', para. 18; 'Statement on Allocation of Resources', E/C.12/2007/1 CESCR, 'An Evaluation of the Obligation to Take Steps to the Maximum of Available Resources under an Optional Protocol to the Covenant' (21 September 2007) UN Doc. E/C.12/2007/1, paras. 4 and 6.

[14] CESCR, 'General Comment No. 14', para. 30.

[15] C. Courtis (ed.), *Ni un paso atrás: la prohibición de regresividad en material de derechos sociales* (Buenos Aires: Editores de Puerto s.r.l., 2006). For more on this point, see Nolan *et al.*'s contribution to this volume.

[16] See, e.g., CESCR 'Concluding Observations on Spain' (6 June 2012) UN Doc. E/C.12/ESP/CO/5.

[17] CESCR, Letter to States Parties dated 16 May 2012, Reference CESCR/48th/SP/MAB/SW; CESCR, 'General Comment No. 3'.

Like other States, Spain is duty-bound to provide an effective remedy for human rights breaches, including, when necessary, judicial remedies.[18] This implies an obligation on governments to provide accessible mechanisms (via courts, political institutions, administrative bodies or other quasi- and non-judicial mechanisms) to allow rights-holders to seek corrective action. To be effective, remedies must lead to an end to any ongoing violations, be capable of leading to a prompt, thorough and impartial investigation, be open to appeal, and ensure adequate reparation, including, as necessary, restitution, compensation, satisfaction, rehabilitation and guarantees of non-repetition.[19] Violations of the right to health, more specifically, require 'adequate reparation, which may take the form of restitution, compensation, satisfaction or guarantees of non-repetition'.[20]

Having outlined Spain's key obligations with regard to the right to the highest attainable standard of health, we now turn to consider the impacts of the recent economic crisis on the enjoyment of that right.

III. The two waves of impacts of recession and austerity on the enjoyment of the human right to health in Spain

Like many countries facing the enduring fiscal, social and human consequences of the 2008 global financial and economic meltdown, two successive phases or waves of the economic crisis in Spain can be identified[21] – each with distinct consequences for both the social determinants of health, and health outcomes. The first wave of the economic crisis commenced in 2008, initially a largely exogenous economic

[18] See, e.g., CESCR, 'General Comment No. 14', para. 59.

[19] See ICCPR, arts. 2(3), 14. See also CESCR, 'General Comment No. 9' in 'Compilation of General Comments', paras. 2, 9; UN Basic Principles and Guidelines on the Right to a Remedy and Reparation for Victims of Gross Violations of International Human Rights Law and Serious Violations of International Humanitarian Law (2006), www.ohchr.org/EN/ProfessionalInterest/Pages/RemedyAndReparation.aspx, last accessed 18 December 2013 (stating in Parts I and II that the obligation pertains to all violations, not just gross violations). See also Universal Declaration of Human Rights (adopted 10 December 1948); UNGA Res. 217 A(III) (UDHR) art. 8; UN Convention on the Rights of the Child, 1577 UNTS 3 (CRC) art. 39; International Law Commission Draft Articles on Responsibility of States for Internationally Wrongful Acts, with Commentaries (2001), http://untreaty.un.org/ilc/texts/instruments/english/commentaries/9_6_2001.pdf, last accessed 18 December 2013.

[20] CESCR, 'General Comment No. 14', para. 59.

[21] I. Ortiz, J. Chai and M. Cummins, 'Austerity Measures Threaten Children and Poor Households: Recent Evidence in Public Expenditures from 128 Developing Countries' (UNICEF Social and Economic Policy Working Paper, September 2011), www.unicef.org/socialpolicy/index_59872.html, last accessed 18 December 2013.

shock stemming from financial market failures in the US. The knock-on effects of this financial crisis eventually destabilised Spain's already over-leveraged financial and housing sectors, leading to a series of bank rescues.[22] Unemployment (especially in the construction sector) skyrocketed, and government revenue shrank as a result.[23] What had been a public budget surplus in Spain – indeed, more solid than that of Germany[24] – quickly became a deficit due to the economic contraction and bank bail-outs.

Health outcomes suffered in several ways during this first wave of Spain's economic crisis, even before any concrete policy or structural reforms in the health system.[25] As households were forced by economic circumstances to move away from more expensive fresh produce to less-expensive processed foods, obesity is estimated to have increased,[26] while hunger became simultaneously more rampant.[27] According to public health experts, the incidence of mental health disorders rose in Spain, particularly affecting the unemployed and those facing mortgage payment difficulties.[28] This attests to comparative studies, which show strong correlations between recessions on the one hand, and mental health,

[22] V. Mallett and M. Johnson, 'The bank that broke Spain', *Financial Times* (21 June 2012), www.ft.com/cms/s/0/d8411cf6-bb89-11e1-90e4-00144feabdc0.html#ixzz2DXjLItl6, last accessed 18 December 2013.

[23] International Monetary Fund, World Economic Outlook Database, October 2013, www.imf.org/external/pubs/ft/weo/2013/02/weodata/index.aspx, last accessed 18 December 2013.

[24] 'A very short history of the crisis', *The Economist* (12 November 2011) www.economist.com/node/21536871, last accessed 18 December 2013.

[25] A. Ruckert and R. Labonte, 'The Global Financial Crisis and Health Equity: Toward a Conceptual Framework', *Critical Public Health*, 22 (2012), 267–79.

[26] Organisation for Economic Co-operation and Development (OECD), 'Obesity and the Economics of Prevention: Fit Not Fat – Spain Key Facts, Update' (2012).

[27] In the first half of 2008, for example, household consumption of pastries increased while consumption of fresh fruit and fresh fish decreased, according to estimates. According to non-governmental organisation and other reports, in recent years there have also been many requests for financial assistance for food. M. L. Oliveros, 'Analisis de impacto de la crisis en la sanidad. Deterioro de la calidad asistencial en servicios sanitarios', *Portales Medicos* (24 September 2012), www.portalesmedicos.com/publicaciones/articles/4611/1/Analisis-de-impacto-de-la-crisis-en-la-sanidad.-Deterioro-de-la-calidad-asistencial-en-servicios-sanitarios, last accessed 18 December 2013; M. R. Sahuquillo, 'Demanda récord en bancos de alimentos', *El País* (24 December 2012) http://sociedad.elpais.com/sociedad/2012/12/24/actualidad/1356370730_504380.html, last accessed 18 December 2013; C. Española, 'De la coyuntura a la estructura: Los efectos permanentes de la crisis. VII Informe del Observatorio de la Realidad Social Equipo de Estudios' (20 September 2012).

[28] See M. Gili, M. Roca, S. Basu, M. McKee and D. Stuckler, 'The Mental Health Risks of Economic Crisis in Spain: Evidence from Primary Care Centres, 2006 and 2010', *European Journal of Public Health*, 23 (2013), 103–8.

substance abuse and suicide on the other.[29] Evidence points to the existence of comprehensive social protection systems as perhaps the most critical variable in cushioning health outcomes (especially mortality) against recessionary shocks.[30]

Spain, like many countries facing economic downturns in this early period, embarked on a series of economic stimulus programmes through 2009 designed to prevent the worst fallouts of the crisis and stabilise employment. Investments in infrastructure, unemployment training and services, services for older persons, coupled with incentives to firms hiring unemployed workers during 2009, helped hundreds of thousands in this period to avoid the worst impacts of the crisis.[31] The government in early 2010 promised it would not cut expenditure in social security, education or international aid.[32]

Despite these initial responses, since 2010 both the Socialist government that was then in power and the post-2011 Partido Popular administration have presided over a second wave in Spain's economic crisis – namely, austerity. Facing pressure from international creditors, bond-holders and new European Union fiscal rules[33] to decrease its public deficit to 3 per cent by 2013, Spain initiated a set of extraordinary measures[34] between 2010 and 2012 to reduce public spending by historic margins, culminating in the May 2012 approval of €27.3 billion in public expenditure cutbacks,

29 See World Health Organization, 'Impact of Economic Crises on Mental Health' (2011) www.euro.who.int/__data/assets/pdf_file/0008/134999/e94837.pdf, last accessed 18 December 2013.

30 D. Stuckler, S. Basu and M McKee, 'Budget Crises, Health, and Social Welfare Programmes', *British Medical Journal*, 340: C3311 (24 June 2010), presenting a 25-year longitudinal study across the OECD showing that for each US$100 increase per person per year in social welfare spending was associated with a 1.19 per cent decrease in all-cause mortality.

31 For more, see European Union Agency for Fundamental Rights (FRA), 'Protecting Fundamental Rights During the Economic Crisis' (Working Paper, December 2010); European Commission Social Protection Committee, 'Second Joint Assessment of the Social Impact of the Economic Crisis and of Policy Responses', SOC 715/ECOFIN 808 (24 November 2009), 23.

32 FRA, 'Protecting Fundamental Rights During the Economic Crisis', 20.

33 See Treaty on Stability, Coordination and Governance, http://european-council.europa.eu/media/639235/st00tscg26_en12.pdf, last accessed 18 December 2013.

34 Royal Decree Law 8/2010, of 20 May, Adoption of extraordinary measures to reduce public deficit, BOE no 126, 24 May 2010; Programa de Estabilidad 2011–2014, http://ec.europa.eu/europe2020/pdf/nrp/sp_spain_es.pdf, last accessed 18 December 2013; Discurso de Mariano Rajoy en la sesión de investidura como presidente del Gobierno (19 December 2011), www.lamoncloa.gob.es/Presidente/Intervenciones/Sesionesparlamento/2011/191211DiscursoInvestidura.htm, last accessed 18 December 2013.

plus an additional €7 billion in additional cuts to health.[35] These budget enactments were complemented by structural reforms to the labour market and the health care sector during this period, which were designed to radically shrink public expenditures at the national and regional levels, boost confidence in the financial markets, and reduce wages and workers' bargaining power in the name of a more competitive economy.

Despite these drastic measures, the economy failed to rebound, especially as the government proceeded to take on increasingly more debt from failed financial institutions.[36] Debt almost tripled from 26.7 per cent of gross domestic product (GDP) in 2007 to almost 76 per cent in 2012.[37] Economic growth turned negative, unemployment continued to skyrocket and investor confidence remained shaky.[38] By mid-2013, the Spanish situation seemed to confirm what Nobel laureate in economics Amartya Sen called a 'spiralling catastrophe' when referring to the trappings of ever deeper recessions produced by austere contractions in public expenditures, thus leading to deeper unemployment, fewer tax revenues and even deeper structural deficits.[39]

While the severity of impacts and depth of the economic shocks of the first wave of economic crisis and recession depended to a large degree on exogenous factors and pre-existing social protection policies, Spain's austerity measures in this second period involved specific and deliberate state conduct, which the government justified as necessary to calm financial markets, to decrease the cost of financing public debt, and to uphold its international legal commitments to a balanced budget as set out in EU fiscal policy rules.[40] It is this round of austerity policies and structural reforms that forms the centre of the analysis below.

[35] Spanish Finance and Public Administration Ministry, 'Proyecto de Presupuestos Generales del Estado 2012', www.sepg.pap.minhap.gob.es/sitios/sepg/es-ES/Presupuestos/PresupuestosEjerciciosAnteriores/Paginas/Ejercicio2012.aspx, last accessed 18 December 2013.

[36] See McKinsey Global Institute, 'Debt and Deleveraging: Uneven Progress on the Path to Growth' (January 2012), 6, www.mckinsey.com/~/media/McKinsey/dotcom/Insights%20and%20pubs/MGI/Research/Financial%20Markets/Debt%20and%20Deleveraging%20-%20Uneven%20path%20to%20growth/MGI_Debt_and_deleveraging_Uneven_progress_to_growth_Report.ashx, last accessed 18 December 2013.

[37] See OECD, 'Sovereign Borrowing Outlook 2013' (2013) www.oecd-ilibrary.org/governance/oecd-sovereign-borrowing-outlook-2013_sov_b_outlk-2013-en, last accessed 15 July 2014.

[38] See 'Programa Nacional de Reformas' (2013), www.lamoncloa.gob.es/NR/rdonlyres/29B5272B-EC30-478C-80F2-B29D675CD4E7/0/PNREspa%C3%B1a2013.pdf, last accessed 18 December 2013.

[39] 'Nobel economist blasts Europe's austerity plans', *Financial Times* (14 December 2011), www.ft.com/intl/cms/s/0/00a8b866-265c-11e1-85fb-00144feabdc0.html#axzz1gRTBOGVh, last accessed 18 December 2013.

[40] See 'Programa Nacional de Reformas'.

A. *Austerity measures affect social determinants of health, especially decent work, housing and an adequate standard of living for all*

Several social determinants of health – integral factors for the equal enjoyment of the right to adequate health – have suffered under the austerity regime, despite specific recommendations from the Spanish Commission on the Reduction of Social Inequalities in Health on concrete ways to prevent these avoidable outcomes.[41] Decent work – itself a key economic human right and central social determinant of health equity[42] – has been severely affected as a result of a combination of overall fiscal contraction, the weakening of labour protections and specific cuts to jobs programmes.[43] Unemployment has been shown to be associated with a doubling of the risk of illness, and 60 per cent less likelihood of recovery.[44] Depression-level unemployment (Figure 7.1), especially amongst youth,[45] together with almost 44 per cent of the population facing wage precarity (the majority of those employed),[46] a minimum wage frozen well below regional standards,[47] wide gender disparities and by far the largest

[41] Commission on the Reduction of Social Inequalities in Health in Spain, 'Moving Forward Equity: A Proposal of Policies and Interventions to Reduce Social Inequalities in Health in Spain' (2010), www.instituteofhealthequity.org/projects/spanish-commission-to-reduce-inequalities-in-health, last accessed 18 December 2013.

[42] L. Artazcoz, J. Benach, C. Borrell and I. Cortes, 'Social Inequalities in the Impact of Flexible Employment on Different Domains of Psychosocial Health', *Journal Epidemiol Community Health*, 59 (2005), 761–7, www.ncbi.nlm.nih.gov/pmc/articles/PMC1733125/pdf/v059p00761.pdf, last accessed 18 December 2013.

[43] See, e.g., Royal Decree Law 20/2012, of 13 July, Measures to guarantee budget stability and promote competitiveness, BOE no 168, 13 July 2012.

[44] G. Kaplan, 'Economic Crises: Some Thoughts on Why, When and Where They (Might) Matter for Health – A Tale of Three Countries', *Social Science and Medicines*, 74 (2012), 643–6.

[45] Eurostat, 'European Union Labour Force Survey' (2012).

[46] Sindicato de Técnicos del Ministerio de Hacienda (Gestha), 'La crisis aumenta en dos millones el número de personas en situación de precariedad' (16 November 2012), www.gestha.es/index.php?seccion=actualidad&num=292, last accessed 18 December 2013. The report, compiled from official data from various state and regional agencies, reveals that the rate of precarity in Spain, which is defined as including both households with combined income at or below €12,000 gross per year and households receiving no income, increased to reach 43.7 per cent of the population, currently affecting a total of 20.6 million people. Employed households are the majority of this group, at 16 million, followed by adults with no income (2.9 million) and the other autonomous groups (almost 1.7 million).

[47] According to the Spanish Commission to Reduce Inequalities in Health Report, 'pension and minimum wage allocations [in 2010 were] particularly inadequate given the need of establishing and ensuring an adequate minimum wage or income to access the basic

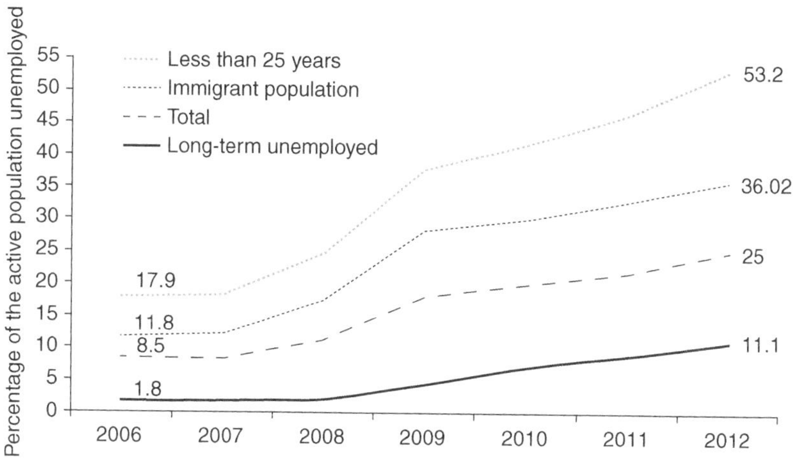

Figure 7.1 Unemployment rates in Spain annual averages (2006–12)
Source: Eurostat Labour Force Survey, 2012. Codes: tsdec460, tsiem110,tsisc070.

temporary workforce by percentage in Europe[48] are creating an environment ripe for increased ill-health and mortality.[49] High unemployment also tends to weaken workers' bargaining power, leading to higher worker vulnerability, according to the International Labour Organization (ILO), and lower economic growth rates.[50] Workers in vulnerable employment, especially women, are more prone to labour rights abuses and a further weakening of social protection and social security.[51]

requirements for a healthy life'. Commission on the Reduction of Social Inequalities in Health in Spain, 'Moving Forward Equity'. See also J. N. Morris, A. J. Donkin, D. Wonderling, P. Wilkinson and E. A. Dowler, 'A Minimum Income for Healthy Living', *J Epidemiol Community Health*, 54 (2000), 885–9; R. Bhatia and M. Katz, 'Estimation of Health Benefits from a Local Living Wage Ordinance', *Am J Public Health*, 91 (2001), 1398–402.

48 Eurostat, 'Labour Force Survey'; CESR, 'Visualizing Rights: Spain: Fact Sheet No. 12' (May 2012), www.cesr.org/article.php?id=1285, last accessed 18 December 2013.

49 P. T. Martikainen and T. Valkonen, 'Excess Mortality of Unemployed Men and Women During a Period of Rapidly Increasing Unemployment', *The Lancet*, 348 (1996), 909–12.

50 See, e.g., Ö. Onaran and G. Galanis, 'Is Aggregate Demand Wage-led or Profit-led? National and Global Effects, Conditions of Work and Employment Series No. 40' (International Labour Organization (ILO) Conditions of Work and Employment Series No. 40, 30 October 2012), www.ilo.org/travail/whatwedo/publications/WCMS_192121/lang--en/index.htm, last accessed 18 December 2013.

51 See ILO, 'Global Employment Trends 2012', www.ilo.org/wcmsp5/groups/public/---dgreports/---dcomm/documents/publication/wcms_212423.pdf, last accessed 18 December 2013.

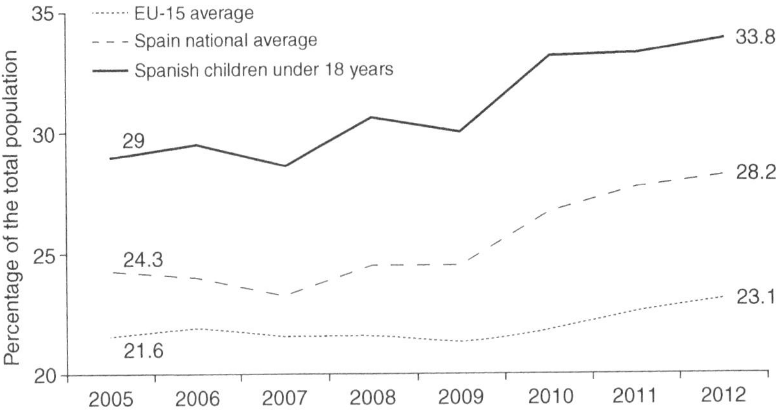

Figure 7.2 Population at risk of poverty or social exclusion (2005–12)
Source: Eurostat Survey on Income and Living Conditions, 2012. Code: ilc_peps01.

This backsliding in the enjoyment of decent work coupled with a morass in the mortgage market and a strict set of evictions laws have placed intense pressure on access to housing in the country, resulting in the foreclosure of over 400,000 properties between 2008 and 2012.[52] A recent independent report estimates that 83 per cent of those unable to pay their mortgages have no place to go in case of foreclosure and in 70 per cent of instances the reason for insolvency was the loss of their jobs.[53] The overall housing cost overburden rate, defined as percentage of the population living in households where the total housing costs represent more than 40 per cent of disposable income, has doubled between 2006 and 2012.[54] Among the poorest fifth of Spaniards, this figure grew from 16.6 per cent in 2005 to 51.9 per cent in 2012, a rise of almost 30 per cent.[55] Little surprise then

[52] Consejo General del Poder Judicial, 'Estimación del incremento de carga de los órganos judiciales atribuible a la crisis económica' (Boletín Información Estadística Nº 31 – Septiembre 2012).

[53] Preliminary results of an upcoming report by *Observatori DESC* and the Platform of People Affected by Foreclosures (Plataforma de Afectados por las Hipotecas) Observatori DESC, 'AVANCE: Nuevo informe sobre ejecuciones hipotecarias, desahucios y derecho a la vivienda con datos inéditos de la Plataforma de Afectados por la Hipoteca', www.observatoridesc.org/es/avance-nuevo-informe-ejecuciones-hipotecarias-desahucios-y-derecho-vivienda-con-datos-ineditos-plata, last accessed 18 December 2013.

[54] Eurostat, 'Housing Cost Overburden Rate by Age, Sex and Poverty Status' (2013), http://appsso.eurostat.ec.europa.eu/nui/show.do?dataset=ilc_lvho07a&lang=en, last accessed 20 December 2013.

[55] Eurostat, 'Housing Cost Overburden Rate by Income Quintile' (2013), http://appsso.eurostat.ec.europa.eu/nui/show.do?dataset=ilc_lvho07b&lang=en, last accessed 20 December 2013.

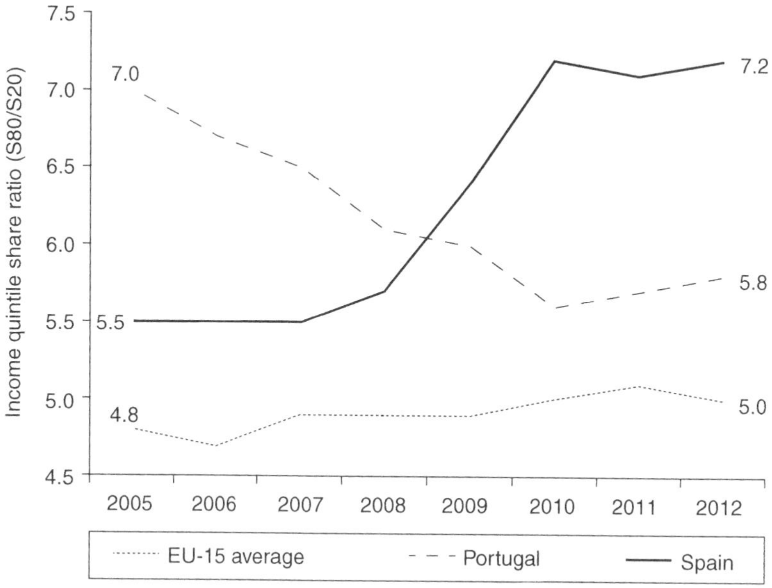

Figure 7.3 Inequality in Spain, Portugal and the European Union (2005–12)

to see a dramatic increase in homelessness.[56] Housing crises of these sorts very often lead to overcrowding and poor health outcomes.

A second set of social determinants of health – poverty and inequality – has also been affected during this period (see Figure 7.2). Poverty now affects over 28 per cent of all Spaniards, and since the crisis began, three million more people have found themselves at risk of poverty.[57] 80,000 more Spanish children entered the ranks of the poor between 2010 and 2011.[58]

Income inequality (Figure 7.3) for its part has skyrocketed in Spain since 2008, well above EU averages, rendering Spain the most unequal country in the EU-27 by far in 2012.[59]

[56] European Federation of National Organisations Working with the Homeless (FEANTSA), 'On the Way Home? FEANTSA Monitoring Report on Homelessness and Homeless Policies in Europe' (2012).

[57] Eurostat, 'People at Risk of Poverty or Social Exclusion by Age and Sex (2013), http://appsso.eurostat.ec.europa.eu/nui/show.do?dataset=ilc_peps01&lang=en, last accessed 18 December 2013.

[58] UNICEF Spain, 'La infancia en España: el impacto de la crisis en los niños' (May 2012).

[59] Measured using income quintile share ratio (S80/S20). Eurostat, Statistics on Income and Living Conditions Database, http://epp.eurostat.ec.europa.eu/tgm/table.do?tab=table&plugin=1&language=en&pcode=tessi180, last accessed 18 December 2013.

B. *Austerity measures threaten the universality, accessibility, affordability and quality of the Spanish health care system*

Until 2012, Spain's governing health legislation guaranteed both Spanish citizens and non-citizens, including irregular immigrants, the right to public health coverage.[60] Rather than being simply a delivery apparatus isolated from broader social justice prerogatives, the public health system was developed as a core institution of society with an explicit objective to ensure social participation and reduce health inequalities.[61] The public health care system has been amongst the most publically popular of social programmes in post-Franco Spain, resulting in, amongst other things, above-average life expectancy rates in the EU.[62] In the OECD, only Japan and Switzerland had a higher life expectancy than Spain in 2010.[63] Since 2002, most of the competencies of the Spanish public health system – including financing responsibilities – have been devolved to the 17 autonomous community governments in line with the move to decentralise many public services across the country. Even before the crisis, a degree of tension in the health sector was apparent between a vision of decentralised health policies driven (and funded) according to autonomous community prerogatives, and a need for national programmatic coherency to guarantee equal access to all, regardless of place of residence.[64]

Based on the governing priority of deficit reduction since 2009, however, a combination of budget, legislative, administrative and other structural measures were established to rationalise the public health care system.[65] Three main sets of concrete measures were instituted between 2010 and 2012 to transform the public health system in Spain, each with differentiated impacts on the universality, accessibility, affordability and quality of health care services in the country. First, a series of budget cuts in the public sector, including wage and hiring freezes, reportedly decreased the

[60] Spain's General Health Law 14/1986, 25 April, BOE no 102, 29 April 1986, and Law of Cohesion and Quality of the National Health Care System, Law 16/2003, 28 May, BOE no 128, 29 May 2003.

[61] *Ibid.*

[62] S. García-Armesto, M. B. Abadía-Taira, A. Durán, C. Hernández-Quevedo, E. Bernal-Delgado, 'Spain: Health System Review', *Health Systems in Transition*, 12(4) (2010), www.euro.who.int/__data/assets/pdf_file/0004/128830/e94549.pdf, last accessed 18 December 2013.

[63] OECD, 'OECD Health Data 2012, How Does Spain Compare' (2012), www.oecd.org/dataoecd/46/7/38980294.pdf, last accessed 20 December 2013.

[64] García-Armesto *et al.*, 'Spain: Health System Review'.

[65] Spanish Finance and Public Administration Ministry, 'Proyecto de Presupuestos Generales del Estado 2012'.

number of health professionals in public hospitals.[66] This drop in skilled personnel affected both the quality and quantity of public services essential for the right to health.[67] Hospital closures, reductions in the number of hospital beds and longer waiting lines have been reported in many autonomous communities.[68] The use of emergency services increased more in 2012 than it did in the previous ten years, as patients are increasingly turned away from other services due to the financial situation, waiting lists or lack of personnel.[69] The resultant backsliding in medical attention has, in certain cases, put the life of patients at risk.[70]

Second, the government instituted a new co-payment, or user fee, system aimed at simultaneously rationalising health care use, increasing revenue in the health system and deterring medically unnecessary use of goods and services, including pharmaceuticals. Overnight, this measure required increased out-of-pocket payments for pharmaceuticals, forcing employed people to pay on average 50 per cent more, including for life-saving essential medicines.[71] People earning less than €18,000 annually meanwhile will pay 40 per cent of the cost of medicines.[72] Pensioners on fixed incomes are for the first time forced to pay for their medicines, and are reported to

[66] Royal Decree Law 20/2011, of 30 December, Urgent fiscal tax and financial measures to correct public deficit, BOI no 315, 30 December 2011.

[67] See CESR *et al.* 'Joint Submission to the Committee on Economic, Social and Cultural Rights on the Occasion of the Review of Spain's 5th Periodic Report at the 48th Session' (May 2012), www.cesr.org/downloads/Joint%20Submission%20CESCR%2048%20Session%20Executive%20Summary%20English.pdf?preview=1, last accessed 18 December 2013; CESR, 'Visualizing Rights'.

[68] J. Gene-Badia, P. Gallo, C. Hernandez-Quevedo and S. Garcia-Armesto, 'Spanish Health Care Cuts: Penny Wise and Pound Foolish?', *Health Policy*, 106 (2012), 23–8; G. Rada, 'Wages Are Slashed and Waiting Lists Grow as Catalonia's Health Cuts Bite', *British Medical Journal*, 343 (7 October 2011).

[69] 'Los hospitales viven la mayor subida de ingresos por urgencias en 10 años', *El País* (26 December 2012), http://sociedad.elpais.com/sociedad/2012/12/26/actualidad/1356552420_772636.html, last accessed 18 December 2013.

[70] See, e.g., E. Valcárcel, 'Los recortes en la sanidad pública han puesto en peligro mi vida', *El País* (4 January 2012), http://elpais.com/diario/2012/01/04/catalunya/1325642842_850215.html, last accessed 18 December 2013; P. Ríos, 'La juez investiga el caso de la mujer fallecida por aneurisma tras recorrer cuatro hospitales', *El País* (18 November 2011), http://sociedad.elpais.com/sociedad/2011/11/18/actualidad/1321570802_850215.html, last accessed 18 December 2013.

[71] G. Casino, 'Spanish Health Cuts Could Create "Humanitarian Problem"', *The Lancet*, 379 (12 May 2012), 1777, http://download.thelancet.com/pdfs/journals/lancet/PIIS0140673612607454.pdf, last accessed 18 December 2013; J. S. del Pozo, 'Lo llaman eficiencia y no lo es (sobre los recortes sanitarios)' (4 May 2012), www.madrimasd.org/blogs/salud_publica/2012/05/04/133262, last accessed 18 December 2013.

[72] H. Legido-Quigley, L. Otero, D. la Parra, C. Alvarez-Dardet, J. M Martin-Moreno and M. McKee, 'Will Austerity Cuts Dismantle the Spanish Healthcare System?', *British Medical Journal*, 346 (13 June 2013).

be facing particular burdens as a result of the decreased affordability of medicines. As a result, a significant number of older persons on pensions have reportedly refrained from taking their medically prescribed medications.[73] Despite government arguments that such a system is needed to make the overall public health system more financially sustainable, evidence suggests that the introduction of co-payments is questionable from a fiscal, administrative and medical perspective. Co-payment systems are generally associated with high transaction costs, and do not promote good use of medicines as advertised, failing as they do to discriminate between medically necessary and unnecessary utilisation of certain medicines.[74] A recent study across Canada, the US and European countries found that in all circumstances, the introduction of health co-payment systems generally was associated with decreased use of health services, including those medically necessary. While the impact on health outcomes generally was somewhat ambiguous, both high-risk and low-income patients suffered worsening health outcomes due to the introduction of co-payment.[75]

The third significant austerity-driven measure in 2012 was reform of the health legislation which, with some important exceptions, effectively stripped immigrants with irregular status of their previously guaranteed right to access public health care in Spain. Until 2012, Spain's governing health legislation[76] guaranteed equal rights to access the public health system to everyone subject to Spanish domestic jurisdiction, including

[73] Federación de Asociaciones para la Defensa de la Sanidad Pública, 'Un 16,8 de los pensionistas de Madrid no retira sus recetas por el copago, según una encuesta', www.actasanitaria.com/noticias/actualidad/articulo-un-168-de-los-pensionistas-de-madrid-no-retira-sus-recetas-por-el-copago-segun-una-encuesta.html, last accessed 18 December 2013.

[74] D. P. Goldman, G. F. Joyce and Y. Zhen, 'Prescription Drug Cost Sharing: Associations with Medication and Medical Utilization and Spending and Health', *Journal of the American Medical Association*, 298 (2007), 61–9; R. H. Brook, J. E. Ware, W. H. Rogers *et al.*, 'Does Free Care Improve Adults' Health? Results from a Randomized Controlled Trial', *New England Journal Medicine*, 309 (1983), 1426–34; M. McKee, M. Karanikolos, P. Belcher and D. Stuckler, 'Austerity: A Failed Experiment on the People of Europe', *Clinical Medicine*, 12 (2012), 346–50; M. C. Gemmill, S. Thomson and E. Mossialos, 'What Impact Do Prescription Drug Charges Have on Efficiency and Equity? Evidence from High-Income Countries', *International Journal of Equity in Health*, 7 (2 May 2008).

[75] N. Mas, L. Cirera and G. Vinolas, 'Los sistemas de copago en Europa, Estados Unidos y Canada: Implicancias para el caso español' (IESE Business School, University of Navarra Documento de Investigación, DI-939, November 2011), www.iese.edu/research/pdfs/DI-0939.pdf, last accessed 18 December 2013.

[76] General Health Law, 14/1986 (Spain); Law of Cohesion and Quality of the National Health Care System, Law 16/2003; General Public Health Law 33/2011, of 4 October, BOE no 240, 5 October 2011 (art. 6 on equality), www.boe.es/boe/dias/2011/10/05/pdfs/BOE-A-2011-15623.pdf, last accessed 18 December 2013.

immigrants with irregular status. Despite intense pressures on its public finances stemming from the economic crisis, the government retained this policy of equal access through early 2012, on the grounds that, according to the former Prime Minister, it 'has been essential in order to protect people's basic human rights'.[77] Royal Decree 16/2012, entitled in the Orwellian language of Spanish crisis politics, 'Urgent Measures to Guarantee the Sustainability of the National Health System and to Improve the Quality and Security of Its Loans'[78] defied this promise. Besides three important exceptions for emergency treatment in cases of grave accidents or illnesses, pregnancy or if the patients are children, previously guaranteed access by irregular immigrants to health care was rescinded.[79] Approximately 570,000 people have reportedly lost their right to access health care as a direct result.[80] This number is likely growing by the day, as regular immigrants who lose their jobs also lose their residency status, and will then also lose access to public health goods and treatment, including for chronic illnesses.[81] A special payment scheme was initiated in July 2013 for people who lost their access to insurance and to the National Health System as a result of Royal Decree 16/2012.[82] Yet,

[77] A. Pinol and M. González, 'No admito que por un truco haya seres humanos sin sanidad o escuela. Zapatero avisa a los municipios que discriminan a los sin papeles', *El País* (21 January 2010), http://elpais.com/diario/2010/01/21/portada/1264028406_850215.html, last accessed 18 December 2013.

[78] Royal Decree Law 16/2012, of 20 April, Urgent measures to guarantee the sustainability of the National Health System and improve the quality of its services, BOE no 98, 24 April 2012, art. 1 (Spain).

[79] *Ibid.*

[80] Spanish National Statistics Institute (2012) (quoted in Iniciative Debate, 'Más de medio millón de inmigrantes se quedarán sin cobertura sanitaria' (2012), http://iniciativadebate.org/2012/04/24/mas-de-medio-millon-de-inmigrantes-se-quedaran-sin-cobertura-sanitaria/, last accessed 18 December 2013).

[81] Doctors of the World gives the example of Aisha, a woman who lost residency when she lost her job and as a result could no longer receive treatment for breast cancer. See Medicos Del Mundo, 'Amnistía Internacional, Médicos del Mundo y Red Acoge entregan más de 59.000 firmas en las Presidencias de las Comunidades Autónomas', www.medicosdelmundo.org/index.php/mod.conts/mem.detalle_cn/relmenu.111/id.2533, last accessed 18 December 2013. See also Amnesty International, 'Con la Reforma Sanitaria entra en vigor una nueva violación de derechos humanos' (31 August 2012), www.es.amnesty.org/noticias/noticias/articulo/con-la-reforma-sanitaria-entra-en-vigor-una-nueva-violacion-de-derechos-humanos/, last accessed 18 December 2013 (telling the story of Petru, a Romanian citizen who lives in Spain and has tuberculosis. Petru will not be able to continue treatment as a result of the new health care law and she will not be able to buy insulin for her diabetes, either).

[82] Royal Decree Law 576/2013, of 26 July, Special agreement to establish the basic requirements to provide healthcare to people without the condition of insured or beneficiaries of the National Health System, modifying the Royal Decree Law 1192/2012 regulating

the monthly rates of €60 for those under 65 and €157 for older persons make access unaffordable, and thus may still discriminate against those with limited resources who will remain unable to access medical attention and services.[83]

Concrete, far-reaching effects are already being felt since Law 16/2012 entered into force. The European Agency for Fundamental Rights has stressed that the exclusion of irregular immigrants from medical attention puts their lives and well-being in danger, increases the costs of future emergency treatment and poses potential health risks for the entire community.[84] Women with irregular status will be particularly affected. Not only will they be denied access to sexual and reproductive health, women with irregular status may well be exposed to higher levels of gender violence, as primary care attention is one of the main means of detection. A large proportion of female victims of trafficking will also lose access to free, public health care.[85] Organisations and medical professionals have expressed concern that spread of communicable diseases, such as tuberculosis and HIV, will increase since many people will now be unable to afford treatment.[86] The right to life of irregular immigrants with HIV/AIDS – whose lives literally depend on access to affordable life-saving essential medicines – has been put at risk by this law.

The deteriorations in the universality, accessibility, quality and affordability of health care resulting from these three measures in Spain, concomitant with a generalised economic recession and worsening living conditions, are already damaging health outcomes, according to public health experts. Spikes in communicable diseases are often associated with economic crises and radical changes in the health care system, especially affecting infants and older persons.[87] As highlighted above, mental health

the conditions to be insured or beneficiary of the National Health System BOE no 179, 27 July 2013, 55058–55056, www.boe.es/diario_boe/txt.php?id=BOE-A-2013-8190, last accessed 18 December 2013.

83 See Yo Sí Sanidad Universal, 'Un año de exclusión sanitaria, un año de desobediencia' (2013), 28, http://yosisanidaduniversal.net/media/blogs/materiales/DossierAniversarioRDL.pdf, last accessed 18 December 2013.

84 FRA, 'Migrants in an Irregular Situation: Access to Healthcare in 10 European Union Member States' (2011), http://fra.europa.eu/sites/default/files/fra_uploads/1771-FRA-2011-fundamental-rights-for-irregular-migrants-healthcare_EN.pdf, last accessed 18 December 2013.

85 Amnesty International, 'Con la Reforma Sanitaria entra en vigor'.

86 Asociación Salud y Familia and United Nations Association of Spain, 'Impacto de la reforma de La Asistencia Sanitaria en España Sobre la Cobertura Publica y Universal' (May 2012).

87 M. Suhrcke, D. Stuckler, J. E. Suk *et al.* 'The Impact of Economic Crises on Communicable Disease Transmission and Control: A Systematic Review of the Evidence', *PLoS One*,

problems and suicide rates are on the rise. While it is too early to tell from the lagging mortality, morbidity and life expectancy indicators, a number of concrete cases have been reported where delays in being attended, or outright rejections in treatment, put the patient's life at risk or resulted in death.[88] As a result of these measures and other 2012 cuts to health care (including cuts to HIV/AIDS prevention programmes[89]), it is estimated that between 1,800 and 3,220 people living with HIV/AIDS will go unattended. Not only is the resulting lack of attention and detection likely to increase the number of cases by 10–20 per cent – according to Spanish medical professionals, it would seem set to result in increased mortality rates not registered in this group since the 1990s, while at the same time increasing health costs.[90]

IV. Spain's austerity-driven responses to the economic crisis – impermissible under international law?

Stepping back from the breadth and severity of the repercussions of austerity measures for the right to health in Spain, we are compelled to assess the degree to which the Spanish government's justifications for this particular set of austerity measures hold weight against the State's existing right to health obligations, especially those related to the prohibition of retrogression under international human rights law. The Spanish government bases its rationale for these health reforms on the need to address escalating public deficits. 'To do nothing', according to the Ministry of Health, 'would have been irresponsible', and expose the Spanish national health care system to deeper cutbacks later on.[91] Does this justification alone hold weight against the country's existing international human rights obligations? And if not, to what degree has the Spanish State breached its legal

6 (10 June 2011), www.ncbi.nlm.nih.gov/pmc/articles/PMC3112201/, last accessed 18 December 2013.

88 See, e.g., Medicos del Mundo, 'La historia de Alpha Pam' (2013), www.medicosdelmundo.org/index.php/mod.conts/mem.detalle/id.3075/relcategoria.10961, last accessed 18 December 2013; Valcárcel, 'Los recortes en la sanidad pública'; Ríos, 'La juez investiga el caso de la mujer fallecida'.

89 CESR *et al.* 'Joint Submission'.

90 J. A. Pérez-Molina and F. P. Ortega, 'Evaluación del impacto del nuevo marco legal sanitario sobre los inmigrantes en situación irregular en España: el caso de la infección por el virus de la inmunodeficiencia humana', *Enfermedades Infecciosas y Microbiología Clínica*, 30(8) (2012), 472–8.

91 See generally Ministerio de Sanidad, Servicios Sociales e Igualdad, 'Reforma Sanitaria: Una Reforma de Futuro' (2012), www.msc.es/gabinetePrensa/reformaSanidad/home.htm, last accessed 27 October 2012.

obligations under the Covenant? On the basis of Spain's right to health duties, and particularly its obligation to avoid impermissible retrogressive measures, this section analyses the degree to which Spain's conduct can be considered impermissible under international law.

To begin, the principles of public participation and transparency require that States must actively involve all those affected by economic policy in meaningful channels of participation. As the UN Special Rapporteur on Extreme Poverty and Human Rights has stated: 'In formulating policies in response to the crises, such as reductions in public expenditure, increases in taxation or entering into conditional loans with donors or financial institutions, States must allow for the broadest possible national dialogue, with effective and meaningful participation of civil society, including those who will be directly affected by such policies.'[92] Real questions arise about the transparent and participatory nature of post-crisis legislative and budgetary enactments in Spain. Spain remains the only EU country without a freedom of information law,[93] and its executive branch is especially prone to opacity.[94] Spanish civil society organisations monitoring the impacts of the austerity measures reported a lack of effective mechanisms for meaningful consultation on these measures,[95] nor did the government conduct any ex ante impact assessment to determine any foreseeable adverse consequences for human rights.[96] The mid-2012 set of austerity measures in particular were rushed through Congress, with very little chance for a proper review to allow for the government to provide comprehensive justifications for economic and social rights backsliding at the national or regional level. Royal Decree 16/2012, for example, was never subject to parliamentary approval unlike other legislation of national importance. The CESCR's review of Spain in May 2012 was probably the highest profile inquiry into austerity measures in the country. The degree to which this review has provided an effective and meaningful

92 See M. Sepúlveda, 'Report of the Independent Expert on the Question of Human Rights and Extreme Poverty on the Human Rights Based Approach to Recovery from the Global Economic and Financial Crises, with a Focus on Those Living in Poverty' (17 March 2011) UN Doc. A/HRC/17/34, para. 26.

93 Coalición Pro Acceso, 'Propuestas de la Coalición Pro Acceso para mejorar la Ley de Transparencia, Acceso a la Información y Buen Gobierno' (2012), www.proacceso.org/wp-content/uploads/Propuestas-de-la-Coalicion-Pro-Acceso.pdf, last accessed 18 December 2013.

94 Transparency International, 'Spain's Institutional Integrity Framework: Current Situation and Recommendations (El Marco de Integridad Institucional en España: Situación Actual y Recomendaciones)', 4 (2012), www.transparency.org/whatwedo/pub/national_integrity_system_spain, last accessed 18 December 2013.

95 CESR *et al.* 'Joint Submission'.

96 FRA, 'Protecting Fundamental Rights During the Economic Crisis', 20.

'trigger for policy learning'[97] at the national level, however, is questionable, given indications that the requisite political will to implement the Committee's recommendations has been lacking.[98]

Second, any austerity measures to be considered permissible must avoid discriminatory effects, both in law and in practice. Notwithstanding the difficulty of assessing discrimination in Spain due to its failure to systematically collect disaggregated data on all pertinent social groups, reports demonstrate that women, children, immigrants, people with disabilities,[99] the lesbian, gay, bisexual transgender and intersex (LGBTI) community and older persons on pensions have all suffered disproportionately from government decisions to rationalise health care.[100]

The CESCR, for its part, deemed Spain's measures to mitigate the negative impacts of the crisis on the most vulnerable as inadequate.[101] The extent to which international human rights law imposes, or even implies through the prohibition of discrimination, a duty to fulfil the economic, social and cultural rights of non-citizens is far from settled, though an increasing degree of authoritative interpretation of human rights law supports it.[102] The CESCR, for example, has established that nationality cannot bar access to Covenant rights: 'The Covenant rights apply to everyone including non-nationals … regardless of legal status and documentation.'[103] The Committee's General Comment No. 14, furthermore, states that: 'States are under the obligation to respect the right to health by, inter alia, refraining from denying or limiting equal access for all persons, including prisoners or detainees, minorities, asylum seekers and illegal immigrants, to preventive, curative and palliative health services.'[104] Indeed, the Committee told Spain in its May 2012 review of

97 A. Lang, 'Rethinking Human Rights and Trade', *Tulane Journal of International and Comparative Law*, 15 (2007), 335–414, 401.

98 Universidad de Zaragoza, 'Laboratorio sobre la Implementación y Eficacia de los Derechos Sociales, Seguimiento del Informe sobre España del Comité DESC', http://derechosociales.unizar.es/exigibilidad.php, last accessed 18 December 2013.

99 H. Hauben, M. Coucheir, J. Spooren *et al.*, 'Assessing the Impact of European Governments' Austerity Plans on the Rights of People with Disabilities' (October 2012), www.efc.be/programmes_services/resources/Documents/Austerity%20European%20Report_FINAL.pdf, last accessed 18 December 2013.

100 CESR *et al.* 'Joint Submission'.

101 CESCR, 'Concluding Observations on Spain'.

102 H. Lewis and R. E. Rosenbloom, 'The Boston Principles: An Introduction', *Notre Dame Journal of International, Comparative and Human Rights Law*, 1 (2011), 145–56, http://ssrn.com/abstract=1975816, last accessed 18 December 2013.

103 CESCR, 'General Comment No. 20' (2 July 2009) UN Doc. E/C.12/GC/20, para. 30.

104 CESCR, 'General Comment No. 14'; Committee on the Elimination of Racial Discrimination (CERD), 'General Recommendation No. 30' in 'Note by the Secretariat,

the country that the health care reform should not limit access to health care for people that live in Spain, regardless of their legal situation.[105] The Committee on the Elimination of Racial Discrimination, meanwhile, interprets its treaty as obliging governments 'to respect the right of non-citizens to an adequate standard of physical and mental health by, inter alia, refraining from denying or limiting their access to preventive, curative and palliative health services'.[106]

A wide spectrum of public health and medical professionals domestically have likewise rejected the restriction of access to public health care by irregular immigrants, considering the situation to amount to 'medical apartheid' and affirming their 'right to cure,' no matter the residency status of the patient.[107] Andalusia, the Basque Country, Catalonia, Asturias and the Canary Islands – together making up 45 per cent of the population in the country – have adamantly opposed applying the new legislation, and promised to continue treating all people in their territory, regardless of whether they have documentation, as a matter of public policy.[108] The Spanish Bar Association meanwhile has declared that denying universality of a fundamental right such as health care is unconstitutional.[109] A recent Constitutional judicial order, while still provisional and so far only applicable in one autonomous community, permitted the Basque Country to continue providing access to irregular migrants against the central government's express dictates. The Tribunal's holding found that, given the grave health risks to individuals and the entire society posed by a denial of care to irregular migrants, the 'rights to health and physical

Compilation of General Comments and General Recommendations Adopted by Human Rights Treaty Bodies' (27 May 2008) UN Doc. HRI/GEN/1/Rev.9 (Vol. II).

105 CESCR, 'Concluding Observations on Spain', para. 19.

106 CERD, 'General Recommendation No. 30', para. 36.

107 Medicos del Mundo *et al.*, 'Objeción SEMFYC', www.medicosdelmundo.org/derechoacurar/objecion-semfyc/, last accessed 18 December 2013; M. Mir, 'Spain: Austerity cuts are promoting medical "apartheid"' (17 September 2012), www.globalpost.com/dispatch/news/regions/europe/spain/120913/Spain-doctors-austerity-euro-crisis, last accessed 18 December 2013.

108 Medicos del Mundo, 'Las Comunidades Autonomas, Ante la Exclusion de las Personas Migrantes Sin Permiso de Residencia de la Atención Sanitaria' (2012), www.derechoacurar.implicate.org/las-comunidades-autonomas-ante-la-exclusion-de-las-personas-migrantes-sin-permiso-de-residencia-de-la-atencion-sanitaria/, last accessed 20 December 2013.

109 María Sahuquillo, 'Los abogados ven inconstitucional negar la asistencia al inmigrante', *El País* (30 April 2012), http://sociedad.elpais.com/sociedad/2012/04/30/actualidad/1335783380_361892.html, last accessed 18 December 2013.

integrity ... cannot be invalidated by the mere consideration of a possible economic saving which has not been concretely established'.[110]

Third, the health-related core obligations delineated by the CESCR require *inter alia* the provision of essential drugs, the equitable distribution of health facilities, goods and services, and the guarantee of reproductive, maternal (pre-natal as well as post-natal) and child health care.[111] These core obligations, according to the UN Special Rapporteur on the Right to Health, 'establish a funding baseline below which States would be considered in violation of their obligations under the right to health'.[112] While the Spanish government has taken some important steps to maintain access to essential health care by children and mothers, many low-income and fixed-income people have suffered from financial inaccessibility of essential pharmaceuticals as a result of the new co-payment system. The reforms barring more than half a million irregular immigrants from previously guaranteed access to the public health system have deterred many of them from seeking essential care, thus also eroding the minimum essential levels of health care amongst this group. Many of the poorest irregular migrants will simply be unable to afford access to life-saving medicines and treatment as a direct result of these measures, putting their very lives at risk despite the minimum essential level of protection guaranteed to all under the Covenant. This is not a complex case of a diffusion of responsibilities or long chain of causality. If these patients receive their treatment, they will have chronic diseases. If they are stripped of access, they will die – all in the name of deficit reduction and a short-term obsession with austerity.

Austerity measures which affect the enjoyment of the right to health and other ESR, fourthly, must be temporary in nature,[113] rather than a long-term

[110] Constitutional Tribunal of Spain, 'Conflicto positivo de competencia n.º 4540–2012, contra el Decreto 114/2012, de 26 de junio, sobre régimen de las prestaciones sanitarias del sistema Nacional de Salud en el ámbito de la Comunidad Autónoma de Euskadi y, concretamente, contra los artículos 1; 2, apartados 2 y 3; 3; 4; 5; 6, apartados 1 y 2; 7, apartados 2 y 3; 8, apartados 1 y 2, y disposición final primera' (3 December 2012), www.intermigra.info/extranjeria/archivos/jurisprudencia/ATCAsistSan.pdf, last accessed 18 December 2013 (translation solely the author's).

[111] The Committee has adopted a General Comment, which defines the minimum core of the Covenant's right to health – CESCR, 'General Comment No. 14'. For more on the different interpretations of the content of minimum core obligations, see K. G. Young, 'The Minimum Core of Economic and Social Rights: A Concept in Search of Content', *Yale Journal of International Law*, 33 (2008), 113–75.

[112] 'Interim Report of the Special Rapporteur on the Right of Everyone to the Enjoyment of the Highest Attainable Standard of Physical and Mental Health' (13 August 2012) UN Doc. A/67/302, para. 9.

[113] CESCR, Letter to States Parties dated 16 May 2012.

or permanent retraction of basic guarantees necessary to progressively improve economic and social rights enjoyment. Whether the deep contractions in public expenditure will become a permanent fixture in the Spanish public health and financing system will depend on a number of factors, some of which are too early to gauge. It is telling that the previous government – with overwhelming consensus from both major political parties and in line with EU dictates – chose to adopt a constitutional amendment in 2011 to permanently fix a ceiling on public deficits starting in 2020, with exceptions for only the most extreme of circumstances and no exception clause for human rights.[114] While aimed at decreasing its borrowing costs by assuring skittish private financial markets, this intentionally permanent decision to place deficit caps at the highest order of the legal system – indeed legally superior than many other legislative and administrative economic and social rights protections – may well restrict future governments from instituting countercyclical fiscal measures necessary to mitigate the worst effects of economic recessions, and to invest in sectors such as health, education, infrastructure and employment, that are essential to sustainably fulfilling health rights.[115]

Many health professionals fear further that the measures described above are only the beginning of a concerted and politically irrevocable effort to transform a universal health care system into an employment-based one, relying on social security contributions and increased private sector involvement.[116] Indeed, the fact that the government chose to enact legislative and structural reforms, rather than more temporary budget enactments or policy changes, points to an intention to entrench those measures over the long term. Whether or not the budget cuts and weakening of human rights protections remain a permanent fixture, there is no question that the human consequences of these chosen austerity measures will be not be temporary or short term. Sustained youth unemployment, largely a consequence of the dampening effects of austerity on the economy,[117] has been shown to result in dilapidated skills, increased

[114] Kingdom of Spain, 'Stability Programme Update 2012–2015', http://marcaespana.es/upload/subhomes/documentos/programa%20de%20estabilidad%202012-2015%5B1%5D.ingles.pdf, last accessed 18 December 2013.

[115] CESR, 'Fiscal Fallacies: 8 Myths about the "Age of Austerity" and Human Rights Responses' (July 2012), http://cesr.org/downloads/CESR-FiscalFallacies.pdf, last accessed 18 December 2013.

[116] G. Rada, 'New Legislation Transforms Spain's Health System from Universal Access to one Based on Employment', *British Medical Journal*, 344 (9 May 2012).

[117] According to the government's own estimates, Spain's 2012 public budget slashing reduced GDP in the country by 2.6 per cent, with negative effects on employment levels,

difficulties in later entering the workforce and other long-lasting effects on young people's wage and economic opportunities.[118]

Finally, as stated in Section II, the Spanish government – to justify any austerity-driven backsliding – must prove that the steps taken are necessary and proportionate in the sense that the adoption of any other policy, or a failure to act, would be more detrimental to ESR.[119] Necessity is then our last criterion for determining whether health-related austerity policies in Spain are in fact in violation of international human rights law. In determining necessity, government has the onus to prove that the maximum resources have been made available and all other financing options have been thoroughly considered.[120] So, after having analysed the health outcomes of austerity measures, and the concrete legal and policy efforts taken in response to the crisis, we now triangulate this with an analysis of the resources available for realising the right to health.[121] For the full picture of resources potentially available for realising economic and social rights, five main areas are of interest: deficit financing; monetary policy; development assistance; government expenditure; and government revenue.[122]

Augmenting resources via further deficit financing in Spain, to begin, is constrained by existing legal requirements under the EU Fiscal Pact described above. Significant debt restructuring is not completely beyond the realm of the possible. A national debt audit, for example, could help determine the legitimacy of existing debt, and according to the UN Guiding Principles on Foreign Debt and Human Rights,[123] delineate the co-responsibilities of Spain on the one hand, and the extraterritorial

as quoted in M. Weisbrot, 'Spain's Government and European Authorities Bent on Dismantling Welfare State' (30 May 2012), *The Guardian*, www.cepr.net/index.php/op-eds-&-columns/op-eds-&-columns/spains-government-and-european-authorities-bent-on-dismantling-welfare-state, last accessed 18 December 2013.

118 ILO, 'Global Employment Trends for Youth 2012', www.ilo.org/wcmsp5/groups/public/---dgreports/---dcomm/documents/publication/wcms_180976.pdf, last accessed 18 December 2013.

119 CESCR, Letter to States Parties dated 16 May 2012.

120 See ICESCR, art. 2(1).

121 For more on triangulating outcomes, policy efforts and resources as a methodology to monitor the fulfilment of social rights, see CESR, 'The OPERA Framework'.

122 R. Balakrishnan *et al.*, 'Maximum Available Resources & Human Rights'. See also I. Ortiz, J. Chai and M. Cummins, 'Identifying Fiscal Space: Options for Social and Economic Development for Children and Poor Households in 184 Countries' (UNICEF Social and Economic Policy Working Paper, 2011), www.unicef.org/socialpolicy/files/Fiscal_Space_-_REVISED_Dec_2011.pdf, last accessed 18 December 2013.

123 C. Lumina, 'Report of the Independent Expert on the Effects of Foreign Debt and Other Related International Financial Obligations of States on the Full Enjoyment of All

obligations and responsibilities[124] of private and public creditors for the debt accrued during the financial crisis. This would include a sober assessment of the conduct of financial institutions based in other EU States, such as Germany, which engaged in reckless lending without a proper risk management and accountability system. Without such a full debt analysis, and given existing credit conditions, however, the government is constrained from increased deficit financing. Annual deficits are at a high in Spain, and even though the country's full debt load is lower than Germany and well below the European Union average,[125] international financial markets – to a large degree private bond-holders and credit rating agencies – determine the cost of government borrowing, which is thus largely outside the control of the government.

Moving on, monetary policy, including exchange rate policy, is out of the hands of the Spanish government as well, determined by the European Central Bank at the regional level. Development assistance, likewise, which Spain received much of from the European Union over the past decade for specific projects, is not likely to contribute significant, if any, sustainable source government revenue in the near future.

This leaves us with government expenditure and government revenue as the two central bases for determining the necessity of Spanish austerity policies, and by extension what financing alternatives to austerity are available and actionable. While these two areas of government policy are often considered in isolation from one another,[126] they are essentially the

Human Rights, Particularly Economic, Social and Cultural Rights: Guiding Principles on Foreign Debt and Human Rights' (10 April 2011) UN Doc. A/HRC/20/23.

124 By extraterritorial obligations, I refer to conduct of a State with effects on the enjoyment of human rights in another territory, or obligations of a global character under UN Charter and other treaties. See 'Maastricht Principles on Extraterritorial Obligations of States in the Area of Economic, Social and Cultural Rights, with Commentary' (September 2011), www.etoconsortium.org/en/library/maastricht principles/, last accessed 14 July 2014; O. De Schutter, A. Eide, A. Khalfan, M. Orellana, M. Salomon and I. Seiderman, 'Commentary to the Maastricht Principles on Extraterritorial Obligations of States in the Area of Economic, Social and Cultural Rights', *Human Rights Quarterly*, 34 (2012), 1084–169. For more on extraterritorial obligations, see Heintz and Balakrishnan's contribution to this volume.

125 D. H. Lojsch, M. Rodriguez-Vives and M. Slavik, 'The Size and Composition of Government Debt in the Euro Area' (European Central Bank Occasional Paper Series No. 132 (Oct. 2011), 44, www.ecb.europa.eu/pub/pdf/scpops/ecbocp132.pdf, last accessed 18 December 2013; V. Mallet, 'Alarm sounds over Spain's rising public debt', *Financial Times* (8 March 2012), www.ft.com/cms/s/0/2c02be0c-6870-11e1-b803-00144feabdc0.html#ixzz2DXmOLajb, last accessed 18 December 2013.

126 See, e.g., R. W. Bahl and R. M. Bird, 'Tax Policy in Developing Countries: Looking Back – and Forward', *National Tax Journal*, 62 (2008), 279–301, 288.

two flip sides of fiscal policy – how resources are raised in society, and how they are spent.

A brief exploration of changes in health care expenditures in Spain can help to assess whether funds and resources are allocated within the Spanish health systems in such a way as to ensure realisation of the right to health to the greatest possible extent. After a decade of increases in health expenditure averaging 4.1 per cent annually, Spain's total investment in health care dropped by almost 1 per cent in real terms between 2009 and 2010.[127] This was followed by €7 billion in cuts in mid-2012, ultimately resulting in a rapid 8 per cent contraction in health expenditure.[128] Some cost-saving measures, such as a mandated price reduction plan for generics in 2011,[129] can be justified on grounds of both efficiency and equity. In contrast, the financial benefits of failing to resource preventative and periodic care for migrants are unclear, and likely to be more than outweighed by the additional costs incurred to the emergency care system, as concluded by many health economists in Spain who question to what degree the government has done proper economic, let alone social, impact assessments.[130] This is not only bad social policy, in other words, it is bad fiscal policy, especially when considering recent evidence in Europe that migrants have actually mitigated some of the worst effects of the economic crisis as they tend to work for lower wages, receive fewer benefits and rely relatively little on public services.[131] Thus, the degree and abruptness of the 2012 cuts, combined with the disproportionate impacts on health described above, make government justifications questionable on human rights grounds.

127 OECD, 'Health at a Glance: Europe 2012', http://dx.doi.org/10.1787/888932705444, last accessed 18 December 2013; 'Spain and EU Health Exp/Capita in 2010', http://dx.doi.org/10.1787/888932705425, last accessed 18 December 2013. See also OECD, 'OECD Health Data 2012'.

128 'Programa Nacional de Reformas', 23.

129 Royal Decree Law 9/2011; C. Cochetti, 'Spanish Austerity Measures: Impact on Healthcare and Pharma', *IHS Healthcare and Pharma Blog* (19 October 2012), http://healthcare.blogs.ihs.com/2012/10/19/spanish-austerity-measures-impact-on-health-care-and-pharma/, last accessed 18 December 2013.

130 Grupo de Estudio del Sida (GESIDA) de la Sociedad Española de Enfermedades Infecciosas y Microbiología Clínica (SEIMC), summarised in 'Noticias: GESIDA recomienda a Sanidad que evite la exclusión de los inmigrantes ilegales afectados por VIH de la atención pública sanitaria', http://historico.medicosypacientes.com/sociedades/2012/07/12_07_24_gesida, last accessed 18 December 2013.

131 See generally I. Sirkeci, J. H. Cohen and D. Ratha (eds.), *Migration and Remittances during the Global Financial Crisis and Beyond* (Washington, DC: World Bank, 2012). In Spain, for example, inward migration offered a net fiscal benefit of 0.5 per cent of GDP,

This is especially the case given a plethora of revenue-raising alternatives, the most central through tax policy.[132] It has been said that '[t]axes formalize our obligations to each other. They define the inequalities we accept and those that we collectively seek to redress. They signify who is a member of our political community, how wide we draw the circle of "we". They set the boundaries of what our governments can do'.[133] As the Special Rapporteur on the Right to Health posits in the health context: 'Taxation provides States access to a variety of sources from which to fund health care, ... allows States to pool funds and spread financial risks associated with health care across the entire population, ... [and] is thus an instrument with which States may ensure adequate funds are available for health through progressive financing, as required under the right to health.'[134] Since 1999, taxation in Spain (regional and national – totally or partially shared) provides the lion's share of health financing – 94 per cent in 2010.[135] The link between tax policy and Spain's obligations to ensure adequate, equitable and sustainable domestic funding for health is thus of primary importance. It is unsurprising then that one of the 2010 'maximum priority' recommendations of the Spanish Commission on the Reduction of Social Inequalities in Health has urged the Spanish government to 'reduce income inequalities through progressive taxation, increased social spending and the strengthening of the mechanisms to prevent tax evasion and underground economy'.[136]

While a comprehensive analysis of tax policy in Spain is outside the scope of this chapter, a brief analysis does point to the availability of alternative, revenue-raising measures to offset the need for budget contractions, safeguarding equity without significantly compromising the other important tenet of tax policy, namely economic efficiency.[137] Spain is

or €4.5 million in 2005 alone. OECD, 'International Migration Outlook' (2013), www.oecd-ilibrary.org/social-issues-migration-health/international-migration-outlook-2013_migr_outlook-2013-en, last accessed 18 December 2013.

132 A. Christians, 'Fair Taxation as a Basic Human Right', *International Review of Constitutionalism*, 9 (2009), 211, http://papers.ssrn.com/sol3/papers.cfm?abstract_id=1272446, last accessed 18 December 2013.

133 I. W. Martin, A. K. Mehotra and M. Prasad (eds.), *The New Fiscal Sociology: Taxation in Comparative and Historical Perspective* (Cambridge University Press, 2009), 1.

134 'Interim Report of the Special Rapporteur on the Right of Everyone to the Enjoyment of the Highest Attainable Standard of Physical and Mental Health' (13 August 2012) UN Doc. A/67/302, para. 15.

135 García-Armesto *et al.*, 'Spain: Health System Review', 94.

136 Commission on the Reduction of Social Inequalities in Health in Spain, 'Moving Forward Equity', 37.

137 A. Infanti, 'Tax Equity', *Buffalo Law Review*, 55 (2008), 1191–260; D. J. Ventry Jr, 'Equity versus Efficiency and the U.S. Tax System in Historical Perspective' in J. J. Thorndike

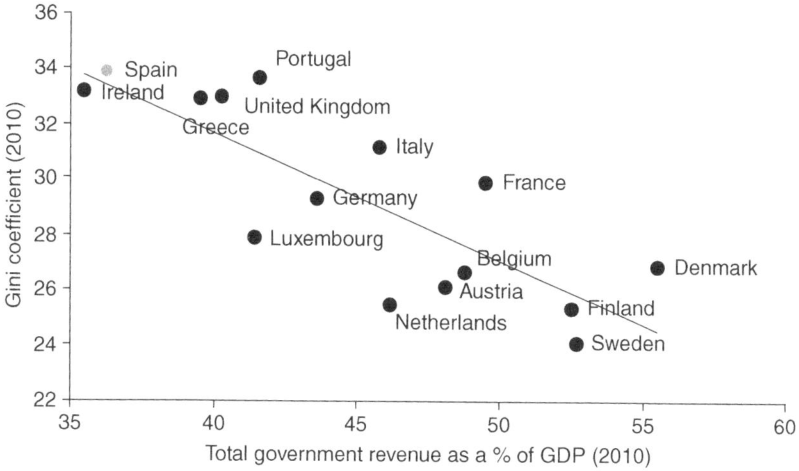

Figure 7.4 Government revenue and inequality in Europe (2010)
Source: Eurostat 2011. Codes: tec0021, tessi190.

among the EU countries with the lowest levels of government revenue as a percentage of GDP, indicating that it could raise revenue overall without jeopardising other economic priorities.[138] As Figure 7.4 shows, there is a strong correlation (correlation coefficient of −0.81 in 2010) between levels of government revenue and income inequality in Europe.

Among the various options for making available revenue in an equitable and efficient manner, personal income tax rates of top-income earners in Spain stand out as one option deserving attention. They are one of the lowest in the EU-15 (Figure 7.5), having actually dropped from 56 per cent in 1995 to 45 per cent in 2011.[139]

An extraordinary amount of revenue is also lost in Spain due to tax evasion. Spain is ranked one of the top ten absolute losers to tax evasion worldwide, resulting in a tax loss of €88 billion in 2010 (Figure 7.6).[140] It is

and D. J. Ventry, Jr (eds.), *Tax Justice: The Ongoing Debate* (Washington, DC: Urban Institute Press, 2002), pp. 25–70.

138 CESR, 'Visualizing Rights'.

139 Eurostat, 'Top Statutory Tax Rate on Personal Income, Taxation Trends in the European Union 2011: Data for the EU Member States, Iceland and Norway' (2011), 30, http://ec.europa.eu/taxation_customs/resources/documents/taxation/gen_info/economic_analysis/tax_structures/2011/report_2011_en.pdf, last accessed 18 December 2013.

140 Tax Justice Network 'The Cost of Tax Abuse: A Briefing Paper on the Cost of Tax Evasion Worldwide' (2011), www.tackletaxhavens.com/Cost_of_Tax_Abuse_TJN_Research_23rd_Nov_2011.pdf, last accessed 18 December 2013.

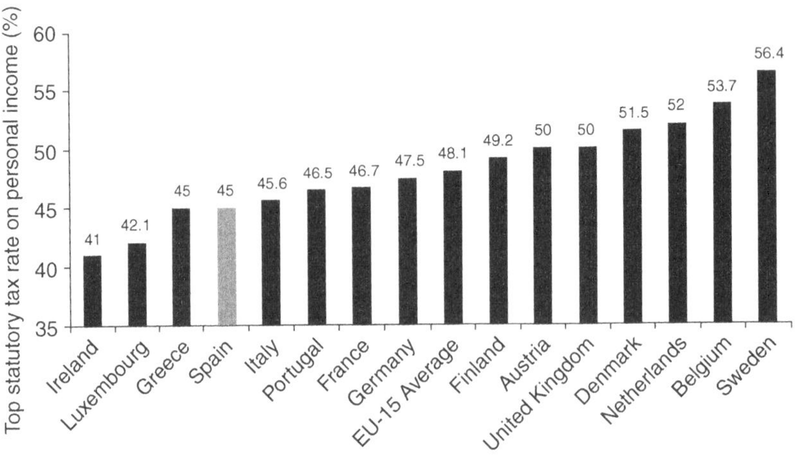

Figure 7.5 Top personal income tax rates in the EU-15 (2011)
Source: Eurostat, Taxation Trends in the European Union 2011.

estimated that 72 per cent of tax fraud is committed by large companies and wealthy individuals.[141]

Disputing the necessity of budget cutbacks on alternative financing grounds, the Spanish Union of Tax Inspectors (GESTHA) proposed measures to increase public revenue by €63.8 billion in 2012. If enacted, this revenue-raising proposal would have prevented the need for deep cutbacks while still meeting EU fiscal directives, avoiding altogether the disproportionate burden experienced by low-income families, not to mention the austerity-spurred economic distress felt by all. Three concerted, eminently actionable measures alone – reducing the elevated rates of the shadow economy to median rates in the EU-15, reforming the corporate tax rate and imposing a financial transaction tax – could raise €57.5 billion of additional revenue each year, alleviating the need for any budget cuts whatsoever and sending a resounding signal to financial markets on the solidity of Spanish public finances. Each of these measures could be taken unilaterally, but cooperation amongst OECD countries on the automatic exchange of information would likely bolster efforts on all sides to tackle the significant loss of revenue resulting from illegal tax evasion and the abuse of tax havens. Strengthening the efficiency and investigative power of public tax inspectors over cases of tax fraud and evasion

[141] CESR *et al.*, 'Joint Submission'.

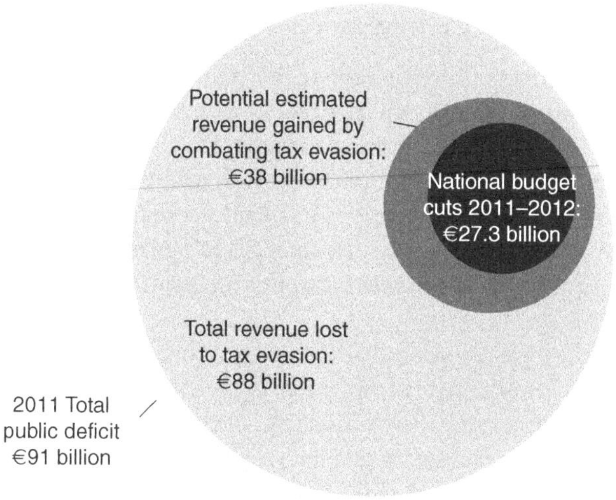

Figure 7.6 Budget cuts vs tax evasion in Spain (2012)
Source: Ministry of Finance and Public Administrations of Spain, 2012, and Gestha, 2011.

is estimated to result in over €6 billion of immediate revenue.[142] While Spain has taken laudable steps to introduce a financial transaction tax in cooperation with EU partners, its efforts to address the shadow economy through a tax amnesty programme have been less than fruitful.[143]

Given these human rights-centred fiscal alternatives to offset decreased revenue in times of recession, the long-lasting impacts of Spain's austerity policies, their opaqueness to public (even parliamentary) scrutiny, their discriminatory effects and the degree to which they threaten minimum essential levels of socio-economic rights in certain circumstances, a compelling picture emerges of a failure on the part of Spain to comply with its obligation under international human rights law to progressively realise economic and social rights, including the right to health, without discrimination.

142 GESTHA, 'Sí hay alternativas: Gestha propone medidas para ingresar 63.800 millones anuales' (26 July 2012), www.gestha.es/index.php?seccion=actualidad&num=280, last accessed 18 December 2013.

143 GESTHA, 'GESTHA dice que las declaraciones presentadas fuera de plazo han caido un 19,3% por amnistía fiscal' (26 October 2012), www.gestha.es/index.php?seccion=actualidad&num=290, last accessed 18 December 2013.

V. Conclusion: remedying retrogression in the right to health

Given the long-lasting effects of Spain's austerity policies from 2010 to 2012, their discriminatory effects, the degree to which they threaten minimum essential levels of socio-economic rights in certain circumstances, their opaqueness from public participation and the existence of human rights-centred fiscal alternatives to offset decreased revenue in times of recession, a compelling picture emerges of Spanish governmental failure to comply with its obligations under international human rights law.

Looking forward, the case of rationalising the right to health in Spain affords broader lessons for effectively implementing human rights guarantees in times of economic crisis. The protection of the human right to health during an economic crisis relies to a large extent on the degree to which other human rights – in particular the rights to information, to public participation, to social protection and to decent work (all key social determinants of health) – are enshrined, effectively institutionalised and shielded from the inevitable ups and downs of financial and economic cycles. The effective enjoyment of the right to health is a cross-cutting endeavour, which requires, amongst other things, concerted inter-sectoral alliances and inter-disciplinary monitoring methodologies conducted amongst the human rights community on the one hand, and fiscal and monetary economists on the other who are better placed to properly assess alternatives to austerity. Indeed, such methodologies have served as a key basis for the human rights-centred analysis in this chapter. Only together can these different communities of practice transform what some consider abstract human rights precepts into actionable, justiciable standards with weight and effect in legal processes and policy-making.

A further lesson relates to normative dissonance with the European Union. The fragmentation of international law, in this case the conflict between EU fiscal and economic rules on the one hand, and human rights treaties of EU Member States on the other, limits the ability to practically subject economic and fiscal policy to human rights and broader social justice concerns of a democratic polity. A full assessment of compliance in these contexts – especially in the European Union – must stretch beyond the limited confines of the national context, and involve a polycentric and extraterritorial analysis to better understand the roles and concrete responsibilities of the various relevant European Union institutions, the European Central Bank, other influential governments, as well as private financial actors such as credit-rating agencies which condition the fiscal space within which national governments can conduct fiscal and economic policy.

Lastly, the definition of what constitutes effective remedies for avoidable, austerity-driven breaches in human rights legal requirements is still only being very gingerly developed by national and international jurisprudence. Remedying retrogression in the right to health in Spain might arguably include revoking those national legislative measures, budget enactments and decrees in breach of international law, and perhaps even constitutional amendments to guarantee non-repetition of violations by enshrining rights not already protected in the Constitution. Yet, defining reparation for both the individual and systemic injustices of austerity – with the responsible parties being both supranational and domestic, public and private – is not straightforward. Even less is it within the politically possible in the absence of a concerted, enduring and effectively region-wide social movement to turn the tide on austerity as an idea and as a governing philosophy.

8

Tough times and weak review: the 2008 economic meltdown and enforcement of socio-economic rights in US state courts

HELEN HERSHKOFF AND STEPHEN LOFFREDO

I. Introduction

This chapter examines the effect of the 2008 meltdown on judicial willingness to enforce socio-economic rights in the United States. We present three short case studies examining court-based efforts to secure quality public schooling for children, to provide health care to immigrants and to protect homeowners from mortgage foreclosure. Consistent with structural features of US law, we take a localist perspective – the state courts of the US – and so fill a gap in a literature that tends to look at socio-economic rights from a nationalist and internationalist focus.[1] The cases surveyed do not comprise a scientific 'sample' and they yielded uneven results, highlighting the vulnerability of socio-economic rights during an economic downturn. Nevertheless, a number of the decisions reflect

The authors thank Amelia Frenkel, Brian Leary, Richard Sawyer and Melissa Siegel for research assistance; Robert Anselmi for administrative support; and Gretchen Feltes and Linda Ramsingh for library assistance. They also express appreciation to Sarah Dunne of the ACLU of Washington for helpful discussions, and to Janet Calvo, Sujit Choudhry, Sylvia Law, Alan White and Robert Williams for careful readings of earlier drafts.

[1] See generally J. L. Marshfield, 'Book Review: Dimensions of Constitutional Change', *Rutgers Law Review*, 43 (2013), 593–616, 593 ('Although comparative constitutional law has grown wildly as a field of study in recent decades, attention is almost always placed on national constitutional law with little mention of subnational issues.') (internal citations omitted); see, e.g., M. Langford (ed.), *Social Rights Jurisprudence: Emerging Trends in International and Comparative Law* (Cambridge University Press, 2008) (discussing national trends in South Africa, India, South Asia, Colombia, Argentina, Brazil, Venezuela, Canada, the United States, Hungary, France, the United Kingdom and Ireland; multi-national ('regional') procedures such as the Inter-American Commission on Human Rights; and international human rights procedures); S. Liebenberg, *Socio-Economic Rights: Adjudication under a Transformative Constitution* (Claremont, South Africa: Juta & Company Ltd., 2010) (South Africa).

surprisingly robust efforts to operationalise abstract rights using techniques of dialogue and coercion, and without triggering popular backlash or legislative resistance, notwithstanding the push toward austerity that accompanied the economic crisis.[2]

We draw four lessons. Overall, the case studies interrogate the emerging dichotomy between 'weak' and 'strong' judicial review and suggest instead a complementarity that has theoretical significance for assessing judicial legitimacy, for informing public discourse about taxing and spending, and for encouraging governmental implementation of socio-economic programmes. The case studies underscore the interdependence between socio-economic rights and classical liberal rights to equal protection and due process, as well as the importance of statutory and common-law baselines in judicial attitudes toward socio-economic claims. Finally, the case studies call attention to the countercyclical role of courts with respect to socio-economic rights. It frequently is said that courts play a countermajoritarian role in enforcing classical liberal rights against recalcitrant legislatures.[3] In a similar move, we might say that US state courts have played a countercyclical role with respect to socio-economic rights by preventing legislators from reneging on social-welfare commitments during times of fiscal crisis and economic distress.

II. The 2008 meltdown and US states

The 2008 meltdown highlighted the profound inequality that has been developing in the United States since at least the Reagan presidency. It also underscored the historic failure of states and localities to develop meaningful programmes to provide economic security for the poor and the middle class. In 2009, nearly 4 million foreclosure filings were reported on 2.8 million properties.[4] By the same year, requests for government-

[2] P. Krugman, 'How the Case for Austerity Has Crumbled', *The New York Review of Books*, 60 (6 June 2013), 67–73.

[3] The canonical work is A. M. Bickel, *The Least Dangerous Branch: The Supreme Court at the Bar of Politics* (New York: The Bobbs-Merrill Company, 1962), pp. 16–23.

[4] See 'A Record 2.8 Million Properties Receive Foreclosure Notices in 2009', RealtyTrac (13 January 2010), www.realtytrac.com/landing/2009-year-end-foreclosure-report.html, last accessed 9 June 2014. The number of families without shelter surged to more than 600,000 on any given night. See National Alliance to End Homelessness, 'Frequently Asked Questions', www.endhomelessness.org/section/about_homelessness/faqs, last accessed 5 August 2013.

funded food assistance and medical care had skyrocketed,[5] and median income and household wealth had declined in many states.[6] These adverse effects were uneven across economic and ethnic groups. Joblessness was highest among those without college degrees;[7] in both relative and absolute numbers, African Americans experienced longer-term diminished income, declining wealth and impeded economic mobility;[8] and corporate profits, along with the incomes of the top quintile of Americans, steadily increased.[9]

Prior to the meltdown, US states showed little willingness to reform systems of taxation or take other steps to ensure reliable revenue for public services.[10] On the contrary, spurred in part by the strong economy of the early 2000s and by ideological sentiment against 'big government', 43 states enacted permanent tax cuts that exacerbated later difficulties.[11] These political moves left states and localities fiscally weakened. When the 2008 downturn hit, even police departments had their budgets slashed and other basic services were outsourced to corporate actors.[12] Many states eliminated their programmes of 'general assistance', the cash programme of last resort for impoverished adults, or reduced benefits to below-subsistence levels.[13] Funding for state judiciaries dropped so low that one former

[5] Enrolment in the federal Supplemental Nutritional Assistance Program jumped 76 per cent between 2007 and 2012 to a record high of 46 million, approximately one-sixth of the population. S. Zedlewski, E. Waxman and C. Gundersen, 'SNAP's Role in the Great Recession and Beyond', Urban Institute (July 2012), www.urban.org/url.cfm?ID=412613, last accessed 5 August 2013. See E. McNichol, P. Oliff and N. Johnson, 'States Continue to Feel Recession's Impact', Center on Budget and Policy Priorities (27 June 2012), www.cbpp.org/cms/index.cfm?fa=view&id=711, last accessed 5 August 2013 (reporting requests for medical assistance).

[6] See 'Feeling the Effects of Recession', *Capitol Ideas* 54 (January/February 2011), 10–11.

[7] See D. Peck, 'Can the Middle Class Be Saved?', *The Atlantic*, 308(2) (September 2011), 60–78, 62.

[8] See The Pew Charitable Trusts Economic Mobility Project, 'Pursuing the American Dream: Economic Mobility across Generations' (July 2012), 3.

[9] See S. Tavernise, 'U.S. Income Gap Rose, Sign of Uneven Recovery', *The New York Times* (13 September 2012), A21.

[10] See D. Gamage, 'Preventing State Budget Crises: Managing the Fiscal Volatility Problem', *California Law Review*, 98 (2010), 749–810.

[11] See D. J. Hall, R. W. Tobin and K. G. Pankey, Jr, 'Balancing Judicial Independence and Fiscal Accountability in Times of Economic Crisis', *Judges' Journal*, 43 (Summer 2004), 5–10, 5–6.

[12] See M. J. Parlow, 'The Great Recession and Its Implications for Community Policing', *Georgia State University Law Review*, 28 (2012), 1193–238, 1206–8 (police budgets). See also R. J. Shiller, '"Framing" Prevents Needed Stimulus', *The New York Times* (2 September 2012), BU4.

[13] See L. Schott and C. Cho, 'General Assistance Programs: Safety Net Weakening Despite Increased Need' (Center on Budget and Policy Priorities, December 2011).

state chief justice said the entire court system was 'at the tipping point of dysfunction'.[14] Calls for austerity measures accelerated as the meltdown caused a record decline in state revenues.[15] With budget shortfalls exceeding $400 billion overall,[16] many US states announced that they were financially unable to meet the increased need for social services.[17] Some localities had locked their budgets into complex financial deals involving interest-rate swaps that made it difficult if not impossible to reduce fiscal burdens by calling in bonds, and states showed no political willingness to impose or raise taxes to close the budget gap.[18] At the same time, 'budget hawks' in Congress blocked a stimulus programme that would have created an estimated 1.3 million jobs by 2012, in part by extending federal financial resources to states.[19] Although the situation seemed grim, some commentators questioned whether deficits justified the cuts that many states declared essential,[20] suggesting instead that the states faced 'a political problem more than a constitutional or economic problem'.[21]

III. Subnational US judicial enforcement of socio-economic rights

Against this background, some advocates sought relief in US state courts in efforts to improve crumbling public schools, secure important social services and halt mortgage foreclosures. This localist strategy is

[14] G. A. Tarr, 'No Exit: The Financial Crisis Facing State Courts', *Kentucky Law Journal*, 100 (2012), 785–805, 785 n.3 (quoting former Chief Justice Margaret Marshall of Massachusetts). See also R. L. Marcus, 'Procedure in a Time of Austerity', *International Journal of Procedural Law*, 3 (2013), 133–58.

[15] See McNichol *et al.*, 'States Continue'. For a state-by-state table on budget gaps for fiscal years 2012–13, see Tables 1, 2.

[16] See J. E. Peterson, 'The Effect of Federal Budget Cuts on States and Localities', *Governing* (January 2011), www.governing.com/columns/public-finance/effect-federal-budget-cuts-states-localities.html, last accessed 8 August 2013.

[17] See State Budget Crisis Task Force, 'Report of the State Budget Crisis Task Force: New York Report' (July 2012).

[18] See W. J. Quirk, 'Too Big to Fail and Too Risky to Exist', *The American Scholar*, 81 (Autumn 2012), 31–43, 36–7.

[19] P. Krugman, 'Obstruct and Exploit', *The New York Times* (10 September 2012), A25.

[20] E.g., R. C. Schragger, 'Democracy and Debt', *Yale Law Journal*, 121 (2012), 860–86, 862; P. Krugman and R. Wells, 'Getting Away with It', *The New York Review of Books*, 59(12) (12 July 2012), 6–9, 9 (stating that 'conservatives have found deficit hysteria a useful way to attack social programs').

[21] I. Rodriguez-Tejedo and J. J. Wallis, 'Fiscal Institutions and Fiscal Crises', in P. Conti-Brown and D. A. Skeel, Jr (eds.), *When States Go Broke: The Origins, Context, and Solutions for the American States in Fiscal Crisis* (Cambridge University Press, 2012), pp. 9–39, 10. See also R. H. Frank, 'The Big Myth of Painful Choices', *The New York Times* (23 September 2012), BU8.

consistent with general and specific patterns of litigation in the United States. Estimates put over 90 per cent of all litigation in the United States in the courts of the 50 states.[22] Moreover, advocates concerned with socio-economic rights have tended to retreat from US federal courts given the pronounced resistance of the Supreme Court of the United States to 'public interest' litigation and its narrowing conceptions of equality and due process with regard to individual rights.[23] By contrast, at least pre-meltdown, state courts were active even if underutilised venues for litigation involving claims to public services such as education, housing and income support.[24] At least three structural features of US law explain this subnational engagement with socio-economic issues.

First, each state in the United States has its own court system and constitution, and a state's enforcement of its state laws generally is a matter of state authority, subject to review by the Supreme Court of the United States only when a question of federal law is presented.[25] US state constitutions include textual support for some socio-economic rights, and many state courts treat such rights as justiciable and have developed ways to review and enforce them.[26] In some states, courts even take these constitutional provisions into account when they decide common-law disputes between private actors.[27] By contrast, the federal Constitution protects rights to property and contract, but has yet to be interpreted as including socio-economic rights that figure in post-World War II constitutions.[28] Moreover, although state constitutions are easily amended

22 M. H. Marshall, Mass. Chief Justice, 'Remarks to the American Bar Association House of Delegates' (16 February 2009), www.abanow.org/wordpress/wp-content/files_flutter/1248455089_20_1_1_7_Upload_File.pdf, last accessed 5 August 2013. State-federal case comparisons are difficult given the variety of courts in the different systems. In 2010, 103 million civil and criminal cases were filed in the state courts. See R. LaFountain, R. Schauffler, S. Strickland and K. Holt, 'Examining the Work of State Courts: An Analysis of 2010 State Court Caseloads' (National Center for State Courts, 2012), 7. On the federal side, that year 367,692 civil and criminal cases were filed. See Administrative Office of the United States Courts, '2011 Annual Report of the Director: Judicial Business of the United States Courts' (2012), 10.

23 E.g., D. Black, 'Unlocking the Power of State Constitutions with Equal Protection: The First Step toward Education as a Federally Protected Right', *William and Mary Law Review*, 51 (2010), 1343–416, 1348 (stating that 'advocates have abandoned federal litigation as a strategy for improving educational quality and equity').

24 See H. Hershkoff and S. Loffredo, 'State Courts and Constitutional Socio-Economic Rights: Exploring the Underutilization Thesis', *Penn State Law Review*, 115 (2011), 923–82.

25 See, e.g., *Michigan* v. *Long*, 463 US 1032 (1983).

26 See Hershkoff and Loffredo, 'State Courts', 941.

27 See H. Hershkoff, 'Lecture – The Private Life of Public Rights: State Constitutions and the Common Law', *New York University Law Review Online*, 88 (2013), 1–23.

28 E.g., *Dandridge* v. *Williams*, 397 US 471 (1970) (finding no right to public assistance under the Fourteenth Amendment to the US Constitution); *San Antonio Indep. Sch. Dist.*

(again, by contrast to the federal Constitution), socio-economic provisions have proven to be remarkably durable, with education rights, for example, dating back to colonial charters.[29]

Second, socio-economic commitments in US subnational constitutions go hand-in-hand with a tradition of localism in the United States in which responsibility for provision of public education and other social services is assumed by states, cities and towns. Historically some states have taken the initiative in developing social-welfare programmes that have influenced Congress and other states to enter the field.[30] In the New Deal and post-World War II period, the national government took on a greater role in the provision and administration of need-based socio-economic programmes, but states in the United States retained shared, and in some cases primary, responsibility for particular aspects of social welfare.[31]

Finally, federalism in the United States often is associated with a strong central government that has federation-wide fiscal and deficit-spending authority, in contrast, say, to the European Union. It thus is theorised as having capacity to maintain countercyclical social welfare programmes when individual states are unable or unwilling to provide services.[32] Three of the largest social-welfare programmes in the United States, namely Medicare (health insurance for the elderly), Social Security (income support for retired and disabled workers) and the Supplemental Nutrition Assistance Program (food-assistance payments for needy families and individuals), are funded entirely by the federal government and in essence provide a federal fiscal backstop for states that may be unable to meet such expenses in an economic slump.[33] However, US federalism does

v. *Rodriguez*, 411 US 1, 35 (1973) (rejecting education as a fundamental right under the Fourteenth Amendment to the US Constitution); *Harris* v. *McRae*, 448 US 297, 318 & n. 20 (1980) (finding no right to government support to exercise reproductive choice).

[29] See H. Hershkoff, 'Positive Rights and State Constitutions: The Limits of Federal Rationality Review', *Harvard Law Review*, 112 (1999), 1131–96.

[30] See, e.g., D. Nelson, 'The Origins of Unemployment Insurance in Wisconsin', *Wisconsin Magazine of History*, 51 (Winter 1967–8), 109–12.

[31] See M. Katz, *In the Shadow of the Poorhouse: A Social History of Welfare in the United States* (New York: Basic Books, 1986), pp. 251–91.

[32] On the cyclical nature of state finances, see G. A. Tarr, 'The Recession: A View from the American States', Prepared for delivery at the annual conference of the International Association of Centers for Federal Studies, 16–18 September 2010, www.camden.rutgers.edu/federalism/assets/Tarr.pdf, last accessed 5 August 2013.

[33] US Office of Management and Budget, Historical Table 8.5, 'Outlays for Mandatory and Related Programs', www.whitehouse.gov/omb/budget/Historicals, last accessed 5 August 2013. But see S. Abramsky, 'Creating a Countercyclical Welfare System', *The American Prospect* (July-August 2012), 62–4 (arguing that national programmes have 'increasingly shed ... this key obligation' of generating countercyclical action).

not assign the centralised authority any duty to assist when subnational units fail to carry out responsibilities that devolution assigns to them.[34] If states claim to be unable to provide social services to their residents, the consequences may be dire for individuals lacking support from any other meaningful safety net.

IV. Modes of judicial review and socio-economic rights

Whether state courts would assume a countercyclical role by enforcing socio-economic rights was a serious but open question after the 2008 meltdown. The federal courts were unlikely to undertake the task.[35] Federal-judicial resistance to enforcing or even recognising constitutionalised socio-economic rights is a complex phenomenon.[36] One important factor involves the form of review used by the Supreme Court of the United States – characterised as final and supreme, and so perceived as raising concerns of institutional competence and democratic legitimacy when claims are asserted to government services that touch on budget and policy issues.[37] Outside the United States, some national constitutions, like state constitutions in the United States, explicitly provide for socio-economic rights;[38] moreover, they presume that the legislature and judiciary share interpretive authority over constitutional meaning.[39] National courts abroad have mitigated some of the concerns associated with federal judicial review of socio-economic claims in the US by devising alternative modes of review that reflect different constitutional and statutory frameworks.[40] Illustrative comparative examples that figure prominently

34 D. A. Super, 'Rethinking Fiscal Federalism', *Harvard Law Review*, 118 (2005), 2544–52.

35 See T. L. Banks, 'A Few Random Thoughts About Socio-Economic Rights in the United States in Light of the 2008 Financial Meltdown', *Maryland Journal of International Law*, 24 (2009), 169–81.

36 See S. Loffredo, 'Poverty, Inequality, and Class in the Structural Constitutional Law Course', *Fordham Urban Law Journal*, 34 (2007), 1239–67. See also A. M. Siegel, 'From Bad to Worse?: Some Early Speculation about the Roberts Court and the Constitutional Fate of the Poor', *South Carolina Law Review*, 59 (2008), 851–63.

37 See F. I. Michelman, 'Socio-economic Rights in Constitutional Law: Explaining America Away', *International Journal of Constitutional Law*, 6 (2008), 663–86.

38 See C. R. Sunstein, 'Why Does the American Constitution Lack Social and Economic Guarantees?' in M. Ignatieff (ed.), *American Exceptionalism and Human Rights* (Princeton University Press, 2005), pp. 90–110, pp. 91–2.

39 See, e.g., R. Dixon, 'Creating Dialogue About Socioeconomic Rights: Strong-form versus Weak-form Judicial Review Revisited', *International Journal of Constitutional Law*, 5 (2007), 391–418.

40 See generally M. Tushnet, *Weak Courts, Strong Rights* (Princeton University Press, 2008), pp. 18–42.

in the literature include the 'limitation clause' and 'override clause' of the Canadian Charter of Rights and Freedoms;[41] the '[s]o far as it is possible to do so' clause of the United Kingdom's Human Rights Act of 1998;[42] and forms of judicial review identified with the South African court in the *Grootboom* case and later decisions.[43] These practices – variously called 'Commonwealth',[44] 'polycentric',[45] 'reasonableness',[46] 'minimum core',[47] or, most typically, 'weak-form' review[48] – are cast in opposition to strong-form review by the Supreme Court of the United States. In application they can include a declaration interpreting a constitutional provision based upon an assumption of the coordinate interpretive authority of the legislature;[49] a declaration interpreting a constitutional provision based upon an assumption of judicial interpretive supremacy, yet according strong degrees of deference to the legislature's decisions on how to implement the right;[50] and other variants.[51]

41 Canadian Charter of Rights and Freedoms, Part 1 of the Constitution Act, 1982, being Schedule B to the Canada Act 1982 (UK), 1982, c. 11.

42 Human Rights Act 1998 (UK), c. 42 [Human Rights Act].

43 *Government of the Republic of South Africa* v. *Grootboom* 2000 (11) BCLR 1169 (CC); *Minister of Health* v. *Treatment Action Campaign (No. 2)* 2002 (10) BCLR 1033 (CC).

44 See S. Gardbaum, 'The New Commonwealth Model of Constitutionalism', *American Journal of Comparative Law*, 49 (2001), 707–59.

45 B. Ray, 'Policentrism, Political Mobilization, and the Promise of Socioeconomic Rights', *Stanford Journal of International Law*, 45 (2009), 151–201.

46 See S. Jackman and B. Porter, 'Rights-Based Strategies to Address Homelessness and Poverty in Canada: the Constitutional Framework' (University of Ottawa Working Paper Series No. 10, 2013), 5.

47 See, e.g., I. R. Masanque, 'Progressive Realization without the ICESCR: The Viability of South Africa's Socioeconomic Rights Framework, and Its Success in the Right to Access Health Care', *California Western International Law Journal*, 43 (2013), 461–87, 479.

48 M. Tushnet, 'Alternative Forms of Judicial Review', *Michigan Law Review*, 101 (2003), 2781–802.

49 See, e.g., *Treatment Action Campaign* v. *Minister of Health*, Constitutional Court of South Africa, Case CCT 8/02, 5 July 2002 (excerpts reprinted in P. Alston and R. Goodman (eds.), *International Human Rights: The Successor to International Human Rights in Context: Law, Politics and Morals* (Oxford University Press, 2013), pp. 363–9.

50 See, e.g., L. A. Williams, 'The Role of Courts in the Quantitative-Implementation of Social and Economic Rights: A Comparative Study', *Constitutional Court Review*, 3 (2010), 141–99, in which the author compares the German Federal Constitutional Court's opinion in BVerfG, 1 BVL 1/09, BVL 3/09, 1 BVL 4/09 (9 February 2010) (*Hartz* IV), with that of the South African Constitutional Court in *Mazibuko* v. *City of Johannesburg*, BCLR 569 (CC), 8 October 2009 (excerpts reprinted in Alston and Goodman, *International Human Rights*, pp. 376–8).

51 An overall review of judicial approaches to socio-economic rights is beyond the scope of this brief chapter. For a discussion of key national comparators, see K. G. Young,

Like many courts abroad, US state courts traditionally have not been bound to the strong-form paradigm followed by the Supreme Court of the United States.[52] As common-law courts, state courts share with the legislature power to develop policy along a broad range of socio-economic concerns; as the doctrines of contract, tort and property illustrate, state-court decisions are policy laden, conditional and open to legislative revision.[53] As constitutional courts, state courts assert interpretive supremacy but share policy-making with the other branches, and their constitutional decisions may be altered through constitutional amendment processes that are less arduous than under the Federal Constitution.[54] Transported into the realm of socio-economic rights, for at least the last 40 years many US state courts have embraced social-welfare claims as justiciable, and their decisions have reflected both weak and strong elements, ranging from declarations of rights without coercive orders to injunctions that compel the legislature to act within constitutional boundaries and even mandate that appropriations be raised.[55] Within the affected states and to interested outsiders, these decisions largely have been accepted as democratically legitimate and as falling within the judiciary's traditional competence, even while recognised to be politically contentious.[56] Moreover, despite some backlash, states overall have not rushed to remove socio-economic provisions from their constitutions or to punish electorally accountable state judges through removal from office.[57] Indeed, in some cases, judicial decrees have offered political 'cover' for legislatures otherwise reluctant to raise taxes.[58]

Constituting Economic and Social Rights (Oxford University Press, 2012); Langford (ed.), *Social Rights Jurisprudence*.

[52] See H. Hershkoff, 'State Courts and the "Passive Virtues": Rethinking the Judicial Function', *Harvard Law Review*, 114 (2001), 1842–941, 1836.

[53] See *ibid.*, 1889–90. [54] See *ibid.*, 1894–5.

[55] See Hershkoff and Loffredo, 'State Courts', 941–62.

[56] See, e.g., M. A. Rebell, 'The Right to Comprehensive Educational Opportunity', *Harvard Civil Rights – Civil Liberties Law Review*, 47 (2012), 47–117.

[57] See, e.g., M. S. Mandell, 'Preserving Judicial Independence', *Trial*, 35 (January 1999), 9 (discussing a judge who lost retention election because of her ruling in a death penalty case); S. J. Goodman and L. A. Marks, 'Lessons from an Unusual Retention Election', *Court Review: The Journal of the American Judges Association*, 2 (Fall–Winter 2006), 6 (reporting that a judge lost an uncontested retention election that became a referendum 'on the role of the courts in our system of governance ... especially as that relates to ... the use of public funds'). See generally J. Dinan, 'State Constitutional Amendments and Individual Rights in the Twenty-first Century', *Albany Law Review*, 76 (2012–13), 2105–40; K. P. Miller, 'Defining Rights in the States: Judicial Activism and Popular Response', *Albany Law Review*, 76 (2012–13), 2061–103.

[58] J. Dayton and R. Wood, 'School Funding Litigation: Scanning the Event Horizon', *Education Law Reporter*, 224 (2007), 1–19, 15.

In theory, courts may show less resistance to declaring rights to material benefits when a political safety valve exists should state resources be insufficient to meet constitutional requirements.[59] From this angle, weaker forms of judicial review that defer to legislative prerogative could serve to catalyse legislative activity even during tough economic times. However, deference may come at the price of ineffective enforcement, a significant concern when needs are urgent and legislative majorities may easily claim to be strapped for revenue. Litigation is never a cost-free venture, and some might argue that advocates should use different strategies if judicial review is not likely to produce effective relief.[60] Although aspirational orders that refrain from issuing mandates may produce long-term benefits by influencing political culture and energising political mobilisation, they are of cold comfort to a family that has lost its home or cannot secure needed medical treatment.[61] As the adverse effects of the 2008 meltdown began to be felt in the US states, it was not clear how far state courts would go in demanding the political branches' compliance with the socio-economic rights and commitments embedded in their constitutions.

V. Post-meltdown US state judicial enforcement of socio-economic rights

This section presents three short case studies of efforts to enforce socio-economic rights in US state courts in the post-meltdown period. We selected the cases based on two criteria. First, we looked to the salience of the issue relative to the consequences of the 2008 economic meltdown; our focus is on education, health care and housing. Second, we sought litigation that illustrated both the range of doctrinal pathways and the forms of remedies that are available to US litigants. The case studies include claims based on state and federal constitutions, statutes and common law, and remedies that include dialogic and/or coercive elements and that run against public and/or private actors.

59 For one account of this theory, see M. Tushnet, 'Social Welfare Rights and the Forms of Judicial Review', *Texas Law Review*, 82 (2004), 1895–919, 1904–6 (discussing *Grootboom* as an example of a weak socio-economic right enforced in light of available resources).

60 H. Hershkoff, 'Public Law Litigation: Lessons and Questions', *Human Rights Review*, 10 (2009), 157–81.

61 See, e.g., O. Ferraz, 'Harming the Poor Through Social Rights Litigation: Lessons from Brazil', *Texas Law Review*, 89 (2011), 1643–68; D. M. Davis, 'Socioeconomic Rights: Do They Deliver the Goods?', *International Journal of Constitutional Law*, 6 (2008), 687–711.

A. *Fostering legislative improvement of public schools*

We first examine the efficacy of a state-constitutional right to education in securing quality public schooling in the post-meltdown period. The 2008 crisis precipitated serious negative effects on public-school budgets. One report estimates that since 2008, 50 per cent of US states have cut their education funding by more than 10 per cent despite rising costs.[62] These cuts came notwithstanding the fact that every state constitution includes a right to education and a consensus, although not unanimity, that such a right is justiciable.[63] Moreover, because of local control over public schooling, budget cuts were likely to vary across a state given regional differences in taxable wealth that often mapped onto patterns of racial segregation. Prior to the meltdown, state-constitutional litigation had attempted to improve and equalise educational opportunity by shifting fiscal and legal responsibility for sufficient funding and programmatic quality from the locality to the state.[64] By 2005, courts in half of the states had ruled in plaintiffs' favour; between 1989 and 2006, plaintiffs had won 20 out of 27 lawsuits.[65] Judicial orders in some winning states included coercive mandates that the legislature carry out budget and programmatic reforms. As the Supreme Court of Ohio stated in 2002, in ordering 'a complete systematic overhaul' of the state's school funding system, '[w]e are not unmindful of the difficulties facing the state, but those difficulties do not trump the Constitution … The Constitution protects us whether the state is flush or destitute.'[66]

The meltdown, however, seemed to signal the end of litigation success.[67] In 2008 and 2009, courts dismissed lawsuits as moot,[68] found no

[62] See M. A. Rebell, 'Safeguarding the Right to a Sound Basic Education in Times of Fiscal Constraint', *Albany Law Review*, 75 (2011–12), 1855–976, 1859.

[63] See P. Trachtenberg, 'Education' in G. A. Tarr and F. Williams (eds.), *State Constitutions for the Twenty-first Century: The Agenda of State Constitutional Reform* (Albany: State University of New York Press, 2006), vol. III, pp. 241–306, 245 (constitutional provisions); S. A. Solow and B. Friedman, 'How to Talk about the Constitution', *Yale Journal of Law and Humanities*, 25 (2013), 69–100, 86 n.95, 87 (judicial enforcement).

[64] See R. A. Briffault, 'Our Localism: Part I – The Structure of Local Government Law', *Columbia Law Review*, 90 (1990), 1–115; R. A. Briffault, 'Our Localism: Part II – Localism and Legal Theory', *Columbia Law Review*, 90 (1990), 346–454.

[65] Black, 'Unlocking the Power', 1365.

[66] *DeRolph* v. *State*, 780 NE 2d 529 (Ohio 2002).

[67] See D. W. Black, 'Education's Elusive Future, Storied Past, and the Fundamental Inequities Between', *Georgia Law Review*, 46 (2012), 557–607, 559 (stating that school-finance litigation 'now shows signs of faltering').

[68] *Londonderry Sch. Dist. SAU # 12* v. *State*, 958 A 2d 930 (NH 2008).

constitutional right to a quality education,[69] held that existing school programmes met constitutional standards[70] and accorded 'substantial deference' to legislative prerogative.[71] Whether the economic downturn was the main driver cannot be said with certainty.[72] One study found a correlation between earlier litigation victories and the level of the Consumer Sentiment Index.[73] The influx of money to state judicial campaigns could be an explanatory factor;[74] so, too, could the increasing number of private educational options that may have reduced support for public education.[75]

Despite this trend, in 2012, the Washington Supreme Court issued *McCleary* v. *State*, holding that the state had violated its constitutional 'duty to make ample provision for "basic education"'.[76] The court ordered the legislature to formulate and implement measures to meet the constitutional mandate and retained jurisdiction to monitor compliance, explaining that this approach had the 'benefit of fostering dialogue and

[69] *Bonnor ex rel. Bonnor* v. *Daniels*, 907 NE 2d 516 (Ind 2009).

[70] *Abbott* v. *Burke*, 971 A 2d 989 (NJ 2009).

[71] *Lobato* v. *State*, 218 P 3d 358, 363 (Colo. 2009). The Colorado high court in 2013 upheld the constitutionality of the state's public school financing system. See *Lobato* v. *State*, 304 P 3d 1132 (Colo. 2013).

[72] J. Dayton, A. P. Dupre and E. Houck, 'Brother, Can You Spare a Dime?: Contemplating the Future of School Funding Litigation in Tough Economic Times', *Education Law Reporter*, 258 (2010), 937–54, 939 (predicting an 'inevitable collision of funding reform litigation efforts and state fiscal realities').

[73] See J. Dayton and A. Dupre 'School Funding Litigation: Who's Winning the War?', *Vanderbilt Law Review*, 57 (2004), 2351–2413, 2403 & n.287. The Consumer Sentiment Index is a monthly national survey that measures US consumer attitudes on economic outlook, business climate, personal finance and spending. See Thompson Reuters/University of Michigan, 'Surveys of Consumers', www.sca.isr.umich.edu/fetchdoc.php?docid=24770, last accessed 5 August 2013.

[74] J. Sample, A. Skaggs, J. Blitzer and L. Casey, 'The New Politics of Judicial Elections 2000–2009: Decade of Change' (August 2010), www.justiceatstake.org/media/cms/JASNPJEDecadeONLINE_8E7FD3FEB83E3.pdf, last accessed 5 August 2013. Participation in judicial elections by business interests that consistently press for reduced state taxes and public expenditures has ballooned over the past decade and recent empirical studies confirm 'a significant relationship' between those business group contributions and pro-business rulings by the state judges whose election campaigns benefit from corporate contributions. See J. Shepherd, 'Justice at Risk: An Empirical Analysis of Campaign Contributions and Judicial Decisions' (American Constitution Society, June 2013).

[75] See D. Ravitch, 'Do Our Public Schools Threaten National Security?', *The New York Review of Books*, 59 (10) (7 June 2012), 45–7.

[76] *McCleary* v. *State*, 269 P 3d 227, 257 (Wash 2012). The Washington Constitution provides: 'It is the paramount duty of the state to make ample provision for the education of all children residing within its borders, without distinction or preference on account of race, color, caste, or sex.' Wash. Const. Art. IX, § 1.

cooperation between coordinate branches of state government in facilitating the constitutionally required reforms'.[77] 'While we recognise that the issue is complex and no option may prove wholly satisfactory', the court stated, 'this is not a reason for the judiciary to throw up its hands and offer no remedy at all. Ultimately, it is our responsibility to hold the State accountable to meet its constitutional duty'.[78] In a later order, the court required the state to prepare and submit reports over a five-year period to 'demonstrate steady progress according to the schedule anticipated by the enactment of the program of reforms'.[79]

McCleary built on the state court's 1978 decision in *Seattle School District No. 1 of King County* v. *State of Washington (Seattle)*,[80] which had struck down the state's system of school financing. *Seattle* resolved a number of fundamental issues: that the state constitution 'imposes a judicially enforceable affirmative duty on the state'; that this duty 'gives rise to a corresponding [judicially enforceable] right of school children' to 'ample' state educational funding; and that the courts bear 'primary responsibility for interpreting [the right to education] to give it meaning and legal effect'.[81] Acknowledging the legislature's coordinate power to 'defin[e] and giv[e] substantive meaning' to the term education, *Seattle* articulated 'broad guidelines' as to the '*minimum* of the education that is constitutionally required' with the goal of channelling legislative power toward the establishment of instructional programmes and accompanying funding mechanisms.[82] '[B]eing confident', the court explained, that the legislature would comply with its constitutional duty, *Seattle* did not retain jurisdiction over the lawsuit to monitor enforcement.[83] In response, the legislature adopted the Basic Education Act devising programmes to carry out the court's guidelines.[84] In the ensuing years, the legislature heeded the court's directive to 'provide specific substantive content' to the constitutional mandate, and it periodically revised programmes, but nevertheless failed to authorise corresponding funding.[85]

77 *McCleary*, 269 P 3d at 261. 78 *Ibid.*

79 *McCleary* v. *State*, Sup Ct No. 84362-7, at 1 (Wash 18 July 2012) (order with dissent).

80 *Seattle Sch. Dist. No. 1 of King Cty.* v. *State*, 585 P 2d 71 (Wash 1978). Prior to *Seattle*, the Washington Supreme Court had held that the method of school financing then employed was constitutional. See *Northshore Sch. Dist. No. 417* v. *Kinnear*, 530 P 2d 178 (Wash 1975).

81 *McCleary*, 269 P 3d at 231–2, 246–7. 82 *Seattle*, 585 P 2d at 95–6.

83 *Ibid.* at 77.

84 The Basic Education Act initially was codified as the Revised Code of Washington (1977).

85 See *McCleary*, 269 P 3d at 236.

McCleary expanded on the court's analytic approach in two ways. First, *McCleary* articulated a theory of separation of powers that justified scrutiny of whether the legislature had carried out its coordinate constitutional duty. Accordingly, the court retained jurisdiction to ensure that the legislature discharged its duty going forward. *McCleary* distinguished positive rights from classical negative rights, but not in the ordinary judicial pattern of elevating the latter above the former. To the contrary, the court characterised the right to education as a '"true right", created by a "positive constitutional grant"' and not subject to 'invasion' or 'impairment', unlike negative rights 'such as freedom of religion or freedom of speech, which the state may impair "upon showing a compelling state interest"'.[86] The judiciary's role in enforcing positive rights, the court explained, is not 'to police the outer limits of government power', but rather to ensure that 'the state action achieves or is reasonably likely to achieve "the constitutionally prescribed end"'.[87]

Second, in putting this approach into action, the court recognised that the legislature was a collaborative partner in defining the education right, but that its interpretive role differed from that of the judiciary. The court's role was to interpret the education right by articulating guiding principles; the legislature's role was to give content to these principles by designing and establishing instructional programmes and funding mechanisms. The court saw the education right not as fixed or static; rather, the right changed in light of the 'specific substantive content' that the legislature developed to carry out the court's constitutional guidelines.[88] The legislature's pedagogically grounded laws, established in response to *Seattle* and enacted and revised in later statutes and programmes, thus informed constitutional meaning and could not be eliminated other than for constitutionally permissible reasons related to education. 'We agree with the State that this court has the final say on the meaning of the constitution', the court countered. 'But we disagree that the legislature, as a coordinate branch of government, does not supply substance to the constitutionally required "education"'.[89] The court thus insisted that the legislature, having given programmatic content to the term 'education' in response to the *Seattle* court's guidelines, could not dilute the education right 'for reasons unrelated to educational policy, such as fiscal crisis or mere expediency'.[90]

86 *McCleary*, 269 P 3d at 248.

87 *Ibid.* at 248 (quoting Hershkoff, 'Positive Rights', 1137).

88 *McCleary*, 269 P 3d at 247. 89 *Ibid.* at 250. 90 *Ibid.* at 252.

Applying this standard, the court found that the state had failed to make 'ample' provision for education; in particular, the state's funding formulas 'did not correlate to the real cost of amply providing students with the constitutionally required "education"'.[91] Citing evidence of 'massive underfunding', the court held that state-education appropriations had 'consistently fallen short of the actual cost of implementing the basic education program' and therefore the legislature had breached its constitutional 'duty to make ample provision for "basic education"'.[92] As part of its analysis, the court emphasised that the constitution's description of education as a '*paramount duty*' accorded education the 'first and highest priority before any other State programs or operations'.[93] Although the legislature's authority to interpret the education clause is broad, it does not include discretion, the court emphasised, to deviate from the constitutional mandate in order to meet competing budget demands.[94]

Turning to remedy, the Washington Supreme Court credited the legislature's ongoing reform efforts and reversed the trial court's order that the state undertake a cost and funding study. The trial court's order, the higher court explained, crossed the line 'from ensuring compliance ... into dictating the precise means by which the State must discharge its duty'.[95] Nevertheless, the Washington Supreme Court said it would be 'unacceptable' simply to 'await the legislature's implementation schedule'.[96] Although the court refused to impose a one-year implementation deadline as plaintiffs requested, it retained jurisdiction, explaining that carrying out the constitutional right would require not only legislative action, but also 'continued vigilance on the part of courts'.[97] Going forward, the court explained that it planned to review the legislature's status reports and would focus on whether 'the actions taken by the legislature show real and measurable progress toward achieving full compliance', underscoring that '[w]hile it is not realistic to measure the steps taken in each legislative session ... the State must demonstrate steady progress

[91] *Ibid.* at 253. [92] *Ibid.* at 255–6. [93] *Ibid.* at 248–9 (emphasis in original).

[94] *Ibid.* at 253–7. The American Civil Liberties Union of Washington, appearing as amicus curiae, submitted a brief to the Washington Supreme Court on the history of the state's education clause, showing that it was enacted shortly after Seattle's 'Great Fire' in 1889, 'by which the greater part of the business portion of Seattle was destroyed'. Amicus Curiae Brief of the American Civil Liberties Union of Washington, at 4, *McCleary* v. *State*, 269 P 3d 227 (No. 84367-7), 2011 WL 2456697 (quoting W. L. Hill, 'Washington, a Constitution Adapted to the Coming State: Suggestions' (1889), p. 11).

[95] *McLeary*, 269 P 3d at 259. [96] *Ibid.* at 259–60.

[97] *Ibid.* at 262, quoting J. E. Ryan, 'Standards, Testing, and School Finance Litigation', *Texas Law Review*, 86 (2008), 1223–62, 1260.

according to the schedule anticipated by the enactment of the program of reforms'.[98] The court left open whether future orders would include requests for additional information, further fact-finding, the appointment of a special master, or other steps.[99]

McCleary's approach to socio-economic rights enforcement reflects a variant of weak-form review associated with the South African court in the celebrated *Grootboom* decision.[100] In both, the court asserted judicial supremacy but deferred to legislative judgments about complex policy and budget matters. Under this approach, the court's role is to ensure that the legislature acts in ways likely to meet constitutional commitments. In *McCleary*, this inter-branch collaboration did not seek to fix the content of the education right for all time, but rather acknowledged that the right has a dynamic nature that embraces developments drawn from legislative expertise. As such, *McCleary* interrogates an often expressed critique of court-based strategies for socio-economic reform: that judicial approaches are lawyer-focused, politically draining and substantively empty – indeed, that they narrow and confine social expectations in ways that are disempowering and counterproductive and do not improve conditions for marginalised groups.[101] To the contrary, the decision reveals significant value-added from the court's approach: inter-branch dialogue coupled with judicial enforcement served to protect and enhance programmatic content that the legislature had devised. Some scholars have argued that long-standing statutory commitments to social provision may become assimilated into a 'constitutional regime' and acquire a sturdier status than ordinary legislation.[102] Possibly, a variant of this process was at work in Washington, reflected in the court's insistence that programmes established in response to the *Seattle* court's

[98] *McCleary* v. *State*, No. 84362-7, at 1 (order with dissent).

[99] *Ibid.*

[100] *Government of the Republic of South Africa* v. *Grootboom*. See Liebenberg, *Socio-Economic Rights*, pp. 399–409; A. Klein, 'Judging as Nudging: New Governance Approaches for the Enforcement of Constitutional Social and Economic Rights', *Columbia Human Rights Law Review*, 39 (2008), 351–423, 375–86; M. Wesson, '*Grootboom* and Beyond: Reassessing the Socio-Economic Jurisprudence of the South African Constitutional Court', *South African Journal of Human Rights*, 20 (2004), 284–308. For more on this decision, see Pillay and Wesson's contribution to this volume.

[101] The literature on this subject is large. E.g., R. Hirschl, *Towards Juristocracy: The Origins and Consequences of the New Constitutionalism* (Cambridge, MA: Harvard University Press, 2007); G. N. Rosenberg, *The Hollow Hope: Can Courts Bring About Social Change?* (University of Chicago Press, 1991).

[102] See, e.g., J. M. Balkin, 'The Roots of the Living Constitution', *Boston University Law Review*, 92 (2012), 1129–60, 1135.

guidelines could not be eliminated absent a constitutionally permissible reason to do so.

Whether *McCleary* will improve public schools on the ground remains to be seen: certainly the litigation galvanised political action during a period of economic crisis. The state House Ways and Means Committee held hearings to develop the reform bill that had been under consideration at the time of the *McCleary* appeal. The legislation passed with 72 per cent of the vote and was signed by the Governor in May 2012.[103] The statute created a joint task force to develop and to recommend 'a permanent funding mechanism' for public schooling.[104] In related litigation, the court struck down a voter-approved initiative requiring a supermajority for the raising of taxes as violative of the state constitution.[105] Advocates had argued that the supermajority rule would hamper implementation of the right to education recognised in *McCleary* by making it more difficult to raise the revenue needed to provide constitutionally adequate educational services.[106] The lawsuit also has enhanced public discourse. For example, the legislature's 2012 Citizen's Guide explicitly refers to the state's 'paramount duty' under the constitution to support public schooling, and emphasises the fact that '[n]either fiscal crisis nor financial burden change the legislature's constitutional duty'.[107] The democratic conversation, once dominated by the goal of short-term fiscal efficiency, was broadened after *McCleary* to include explicit consideration of socio-economic rights as constitutional commitments.

B. *Using equality norms to protect health care for immigrants*

We next examine the role of the equality doctrine in securing socio-economic rights after the meltdown, focusing on challenges to decisions

[103] For a discussion of the legislative hearings, see TVW Video, House Ways and Means Committee, 4 April 2012, www.tvw.org/index.php?option=com_tvwplayer&eventID=2012040047, last accessed 5 August 2013.

[104] See HB 2824, 62d Legislature, 1st Special Session (Wash 2012), http://apps.leg.wa.gov/documents/billdocs/2011-12/Pdf/Bills/House%20Passed%20Legislature/2824.PL.pdf, last accessed 5 August 2013.

[105] See *League of Education Voters* v. *State*, 295 P 3d 743 (Wash 2013) (en banc).

[106] See K. Johnson, 'Washington State's Top Court Strikes Down Law on Taxes', *The New York Times* (1 March 2013), A14 (quoting president of the Washington Education Association).

[107] Senate Ways and Means Committee, 'A Citizen's Guide to Washington State K–12 Finance' (2012), 4, www.leg.wa.gov/Senate/Committees/WM/Documents/K12%20Guide%202012%20FINAL5.pdf, last accessed 5 August 2013.

by various states to deny state-funded health benefits to lawful immigrants. Public provision of health care in the US reflects the complex pattern of localism and federalism previously mentioned. In 1965, Congress established 'Medicaid', a state-federal cooperative programme that provides health insurance to specified categories of needy people, including minor children and their parents, disabled adults and the elderly.[108] Under the law, the federal government provides matching funds to any state that agrees to administer a Medicaid programme in accordance with federal guidelines. States are not required to participate in Medicaid, but by the 1980s, every state had elected to do so, in large part because the federal funding formula reimburses between 50 and 83 per cent of a state's programme costs.[109] Congress structured Medicaid as an 'entitlement program', in the dual sense that individuals meeting statutory eligibility criteria have a judicially enforceable right to the benefit, and that the federal government and participating states are legally required to make whatever appropriations may be necessary to provide benefits to all eligible individuals.[110] As a result, Medicaid functions in a countercyclical manner: during economic downturns, programme enrolment and governmental expenditures expand, cushioning the human impact and offsetting demand-weakness elsewhere in the economy. The national government typically has covered increased costs through deficit spending, but state laws generally forbid deficit financing, so states instead must increase revenues and/or adjust other budget priorities.[111]

In 1996, Congress enacted the Personal Responsibility and Work Opportunities Reconciliation Act ('PRA'), a controversial, far-reaching statute best known for 'ending welfare as we know it' and terminating Aid to Families with Dependent Children as an entitlement programme.[112] The PRA also disqualified millions of legal immigrants from federal

[108] For a comprehensive description of Medicaid and its history see S. Rosenbaum, 'Medicaid at Forty: Revisiting Structure and Meaning in a Post-Deficit Reduction Act Era', *Journal of Health Care Law & Policy*, 9 (2006), 5–47.

[109] See 42 USC § 1396d(b). [110] 42 USC § 1396a.

[111] See, e.g., Super, 'Rethinking Fiscal Federalism', 2591–3.

[112] Personal Responsibility and Work Opportunities Reconciliation Act of 1996, Pub L No. 104–193, 110 Stat 2105 (1996). See W. J. Clinton, 'The New Covenant: Responsibility and Rebuilding the American Community', Remarks to Students at Georgetown University, Democratic Leadership Council (23 October 1991), www.dlc.org/ndol_ci4c81.html?kaid=127subid=1738&contentid=2783, last accessed 5 August 2013 (setting out the presidential campaign promise 'to put an end to welfare as we have come to know it').

social welfare programmes.[113] But the Act allowed individual states to choose whether or not to furnish Medicaid to these non-citizens, on condition that any benefits provided be paid for with state or local funds.[114] In response, most states dropped significant segments of their lawful non-citizen populations from Medicaid.[115] Additional states took this step after the economic downturn of the early 2000s, and the trend continued after 2008. These cuts overall sparked ten constitutional challenges in state and federal courts, each raising arguments under the federal Equal Protection Clause and/or an analogous state constitutional provision.[116]

Prior to 2008, all three state courts to address the issue held that the state's exclusion of immigrants violated state and/or federal constitutional equality rights, and mandatory injunctions were issued in each case.[117] After 2008, only one of the three state court challenges succeeded.[118] While the data set is small, we attempt in this section to draw insights from a pair of cases that reached directly contrary results on nearly identical facts: the

113 Personal Responsibility and Work Opportunities Reconciliation Act of 1996, Title IV. The Act, with certain exceptions, disqualifies legal immigrants from federally funded assistance during the first five years of residence in the US.

114 8 USC §§ 1621, 1622, 1624. The PRA is quite complex in its treatment of legal immigrants. The Act categorically bars federal reimbursement of Medicaid benefits for lawful immigrants residing in the United States for less than five years. However, the PRA continues federal reimbursement for lawful immigrants residing in the United States for more than five years. In addition, the PRA gives states the option to exclude one or both categories of immigrants from their Medicaid programmes.

115 See R. Wasem, 'State Medicaid and SCHIP Coverage of Noncitizens' (Congressional Research Service Report R40144, 12 February 2009).

116 Plaintiffs prevailed in three of the four pre-2008 cases but only two of the six post-2008 cases. See *Korab* v. *Fink*, 748 F 3d 875 (9th Cir 2014) (Hawai'i) (court rejected plaintiffs' federal equal protection claim); *Bruns* v. *Mayhew*, 931 F Supp 2d 260 (D Maine 2013) (court found no likelihood of success on plaintiffs' federal equal protection claim); *Finch* v. *Commonwealth Health Insurance Connector Authority*, 959 NE 2d 970 (Mass 2012) (plaintiffs prevailed on Massachusetts equal protection claim interpreted in lockstep with federal claim); *Unthaksinkun* v. *Porter*, No. C11–0588JLR, 2011 WL 4502050 (WD Wash 28 September 2011), appeal pending (plaintiffs prevailed on federal equal protection claim); *Hong Pham* v. *Starkowski*, 16 A 3d 635 (Conn 2011) (court rejected federal and state equal protection claims); *Guaman* v. *Velez*, 23 A 3d 451 (NJ Super A D 2011) (court rejected federal equal protection claim); *Ehrlich* v. *Perez*, 908 A 2d 1220 (Md 2006) (plaintiffs prevailed on Maryland constitutional claim); *Kurti* v. *Maricopa County*, 33 P 3d 499 (Ariz Ct App 2001) (plaintiffs prevailed on federal equal protection claim); *Aliessa ex rel. Fayad* v. *Novello*, 754 NE 2d 1085 (NY 2001) (plaintiffs prevailed on New York Constitution's welfare clause and on state and federal equal protection claims); *Soskin* v. *Reinertson*, 353 F 3d 1242 (10th Cir 2004) (Colorado) (court rejected federal equal protection claim).

117 *Ibid.* (*Ehrlich* v. *Perez*; *Kurti* v. *Maricopa Co.*; *Aliessa* v. *Novello*).

118 *Ibid.* (*Finch* v. *Commonwealth Health Connector Authority*).

Connecticut Supreme Court's decision in *Hong Pham* v. *Starkowski* ('*Hong Pham*'),[119] finding no equal protection violation in the state's withdrawal of assistance, and the Massachusetts Supreme Judicial Court's decision in *Finch* v. *Commonwealth Health Insurance Connector Authority* ('*Finch II*'),[120] invalidating the state's withdrawal of assistance as a violation of equal protection.

Following the 1996 federal Medicaid cutbacks, Connecticut and Massachusetts initially elected to provide state-funded medical assistance to legal immigrants.[121] But when faced with multi-billion dollar budget gaps as the recession took hold, both states curtailed health care benefits to some or all of this population. In 2009, Connecticut outright terminated 'State Medical Assistance for Noncitizens', the state-funded programme it had established to maintain health benefits for federally ineligible immigrants.[122] That same year, Massachusetts disqualified nearly 30,000 federally ineligible immigrants from 'Commonwealth Care', a means-tested health insurance programme operated in lieu of the standard Medicaid programme as part of the state's plan to achieve universal health care coverage.[123] Massachusetts eventually offered an inferior, bare-bones health plan to the immigrants it had expelled from Commonwealth Care as a compromise between the Legislature and the Governor who, while acknowledging fiscal concerns, emphasised support for the state's universal health care initiatives and criticised the exclusion of immigrants as 'a major step backwards'.[124]

Equal protection challenges were filed in each state's court, raising claims under the federal and/or respective state constitutions. In both states, the courts generally interpret their state equality provisions in lockstep with the federal.[125] State courts have concurrent authority with the federal courts to enforce the federal constitution.[126] However, state courts

[119] *Hong Pham* v. *Starkowski*, 16 A 3d 635 (Conn 2011).

[120] *Finch* v. *Commonwealth Health Insurance Connector Authority*, 959 NE 2d 970 (Mass 2012).

[121] *Hong Pham*, 16 A 3d at 638; *Finch* v. *Commonwealth Health Insurance Connector Authority*, 946 NE 2d 1262, 1267–8 (Mass 2011) ('Finch I').

[122] *Hong Pham*, 16 A 3d at 638–9.

[123] *Finch I*, 946 NE 2d at 1267–8. See An Act Providing Access to Affordable, Quality and Accountable Healthcare, 2006 Mass Acts 111–202, codified at Mass Gen Laws ch. 11M, §§ 1–5 (2006).

[124] *Finch I*, 946 NE 2d *Ibid.* at 1267–8.

[125] See *Finch II*, 959 NE 2d at 975; *City Recycling, Inc.* v. *State*, 778 A 2d 77, 86–7 (Conn 2001).

[126] United States Constitution, Art. VI, § 2.

must follow US Supreme Court precedent – one aspect of which establishes judicial supremacy in federal constitutional interpretation – and so they lack discretion to invite inter-branch dialogue as to the meaning of federal Equal Protection Clause. And as the courts of Connecticut and Massachusetts have chosen to follow the federal standard in state constitutional equality cases, they likewise apply strong review in adjudicating state constitutional challenges.[127] Thus, beyond recognising the legislature's discretion to achieve equality by eliminating benefits rather than extending them to an excluded group, existing doctrine gave the state courts little room for sharing interpretive or enforcement authority with the other branches of government.

From a doctrinal perspective, the federal Equal Protection Clause provides clear support for overturning the states' denial of state-funded benefits to lawful immigrants while providing such benefits to US citizens. The Supreme Court of the United States has held repeatedly that the Equal Protection Clause of the Fourteenth Amendment prohibits *state* discrimination against lawful immigrants absent extraordinary justification,[128] and this rigorous standard of 'strict scrutiny' applies even when social welfare benefits are implicated.[129] Most notably, in *Graham* v. *Richardson*, the Court held that state laws imposing special restrictions on immigrants' eligibility for public assistance violate the Fourteenth Amendment and may not be justified either by 'a State's desire to preserve limited welfare benefits for its own citizens' or by the entirely legitimate goal of 'saving welfare cost', or preserving the state's 'fiscal integrity'.[130] By contrast,

[127] Cf. J. R. Long, 'State Constitutional Prohibitions on Special Laws', *Cleveland State Law Review*, 60 (2012), 719–67, 732–3 (discussing interpretive congruence between state and federal constitutional equal protection doctrine).

[128] See, e.g., *Nyquist* v. *Mauclet*, 432 US 1 (1977); *Application of Grifiths*, 413 US 717 (1973); *Graham* v. *Richardson*, 403 US 365 (1971).

[129] In the argot of equal protection doctrine, actions by states that classify on the basis of alienage or national origin are 'inherently suspect' and presumed unconstitutional unless the state demonstrates that its discrimination is 'narrowly tailored' to achieve a 'compelling state interest'. Equal protection doctrine mandates special judicial protection for lawful immigrants in part because the courts consider them to be 'discrete and insular minorities' or 'politically powerless minorities' – historically disadvantaged and vulnerable groups unable to protect themselves through ordinary political processes. See *Takahashi* v. *Fish & Game Commission*, 334 US 410 (1948). By contrast, the Supreme Court of the United States has declined to require meaningful justification for state actions that are harmful to the poor, and instead requires only a showing of minimum rationality. See S. Loffredo, 'Poverty, Democracy and Constitutional Law', *University of Pennsylvania Law Review*, 141 (1992–3), 1277–389.

[130] *Graham* v. *Richardson*, 403 US at 374–5.

the Court has applied a more deferential standard to *federal* laws that classify on the basis of immigration status; these statutes are presumed constitutional and must be upheld unless they are shown to be 'wholly irrational'.[131] The Court accords Congress this deference because of the national government's exclusive constitutional authority over immigration, the multitude of federal statutes that necessarily distinguish between citizens and immigrants, and the intricate connection between immigration, foreign policy and international relations, areas long entrusted to the near unreviewable discretion of Congress and the President.[132] Thus, although Congress may exclude immigrants from federal social welfare programmes,[133] and may, perhaps, create a uniform national rule barring states from extending state benefits to immigrants, it may not authorise states to choose for themselves whether to disqualify immigrants.[134]

In *Hong Pham*, the Connecticut court dismissed the plaintiffs' equal protection claim on the theory that the state's termination of the Medical Assistance for Noncitizens programme did not constitute discrimination against immigrants. The Court reasoned that Connecticut's decision to eliminate its state-financed health programme for immigrants, while continuing to provide assistance to US citizens through the federal-state Medicaid programme, discriminated only on the basis of plaintiffs' ineligibility for federal Medicaid funding, not on the basis of their citizenship status.[135] The Court's argument might have been plausible except that Connecticut was continuing to provide state-financed health insurance to federally ineligible *US citizens* even as it terminated health insurance to federally ineligible *immigrants*.[136] The state's disparate treatment of these otherwise identically situated groups demonstrated that Connecticut had indeed withheld medical benefits on the constitutionally prohibited ground of citizen status. Having rejected plaintiffs' claim of discrimination, the court held that there was no reason to apply 'strict scrutiny' to Connecticut's selective termination of their medical assistance. Indeed, the court insisted that the plaintiffs' challenge did not sound in equal protection at all, but rather presented

[131] *Mathews* v. *Diaz*, 426 US 67 (1976) (upholding federal Medicare statute prescribing more restrictive eligibility criteria for immigrants than for citizens, even while acknowledging that the Constitution prohibits *states* from drawing such lines).

[132] *Ibid.* at 79–82.

[133] See *City of Chicago* v. *Shalala*, 189 F 3d 598 (7th Cir 1999) (upholding against equal protection challenge to PRA's exclusion of non-citizens from the federal Food Stamp programme and federal Supplemental Security Income programme).

[134] *Graham* v. *Richardson*, 403 US at 381; *Shapiro* v. *Thompson*, 394 US 618, 638–41 (1969); *Saenz* v. *Roe*, 526 US 489, 508–10 (1999).

[135] *Hong Pham*, 16 A 3d at 646–7. [136] *Ibid.* at 642–3.

a due process claim, 'that once the state has provided assistance to a certain class, it is forever barred from eliminating or diminishing that assistance' – an argument that the Connecticut high court had earlier rejected in a suit challenging the state's elimination of a different form of public assistance.[137] Emphasising that the state had no duty to 'remediate … the void in coverage' created by the federal government's withdrawal of Medicaid benefits for immigrants, the court justified dismissing plaintiffs' equality claims on the additional ground that it furthered Congressional intent to promote self-sufficiency among immigrants.[138]

Finch II, decided by the Supreme Judicial Court of Massachusetts, stands in marked contrast. The lower court determined that the state's reduction in appropriations for immigrant health care discriminated on the basis of alienage, but the Attorney General insisted that the appropriation did not violate equal protection because it advanced a compelling interest: 'the furthering of national immigration policies expressed by Congress', namely, achieving immigrant self-sufficiency.[139] The Supreme Judicial Court rejected the state's argument for two reasons. First, the record showed that the state legislature's sole purpose in enacting the exclusion was fiscal, and the Supreme Court of the United States in *Graham* had made clear that '[f]iscal considerations alone cannot justify a State's invidious discrimination against aliens'.[140] Second, the state failed to show, as required under federal constitutional doctrine, that it had undertaken an independent inquiry as to whether withholding benefits was a narrowly tailored approach to achieving the federal goal of immigrant self-sufficiency, and instead had relied on federal policy without investigating 'whether its own invidious discrimination is truly necessary'.[141] In addition, although the Supreme Judicial Court acknowledged that strict scrutiny of the state's action would not be warranted if Massachusetts were following a congressional rule that was general and uniform, it found that Massachusetts was not compelled by federal law or policy to discriminate against immigrants. To the contrary, the state had made a voluntary decision to do so in order to save money.[142]

[137] *Hong Pham*, 16 A 3d at 648–9 n. 23 (citing *Moore* v. *Ganim*, 660 A 2d 742 (1995)).

[138] *Ibid.* at 649 n. 23, 661 n. 34. For a discussion of the PRA's self-sufficiency goals, see E. G. Patterson, 'Mission Dissonance in the TANF Program: Of Work Self-Sufficiency, Reciprocity, and the Work Participation Rate', *Harvard Law and Policy Review*, 6 (2012), 369–405.

[139] *Finch II*, 959 NE 2d at 973. [140] *Ibid.* at 976.

[141] *Ibid.* at 981. [142] *Ibid.* at 975–81.

Both the trial and appeals courts in *Finch* acknowledged the state's fiscal crisis and the 'significant financial burden' that invalidating the immigrant exclusion would impose on the state. Nevertheless, the Supreme Judicial Court underscored that principles of equal protection prohibited the state from closing its budget deficit by eliminating health insurance for legal immigrants.[143] The court stated:

> We recognize that our decision will impose a significant financial burden on the [state]. Nonetheless, the fiscal consequence of any judgment on the merits cannot be permitted to intrude on consideration of the case before us. Minorities rely on the independence of the courts to secure their constitutional rights against incursions of the majority, operating through the political branches of government. If plaintiffs' right to equal protection of the laws has been violated ... then it is our duty to say so.[144]

What accounts for the starkly divergent results from these two state courts, and what role, if any, was played by the nature of asserted rights and the available judicial methodologies? Constitutional equality guarantees occupy a grey area between positive and negative rights. The constitutional command of equal protection – although typically associated with classical first-generation rights – may acquire positive-right characteristics in the social welfare context because it imposes affirmative duties that demand more than non-interference with liberty or property rights: enforcement of equality guarantees in this setting typically requires the state to extend economic benefits to groups it had excluded from public programmes or legal protections. On the other hand, equality guarantees fall short of affirmative rights in that they do not obligate government to make social provision in the first place. Nevertheless, calling the court's role 'interstitial'[145] should not obscure the practical significance of the court's jump-starting a process that results in extending benefits to individuals otherwise excluded from an ongoing programme or that improves the quality of services within an existing programme.

Judicial enforcement of equality norms in the social welfare setting also defies easy categorisation as 'weak' or ' strong' review. Review is strong in the interpretative dimension, because the judicially determined meaning of constitutional equality is 'conclusive on other political actors',[146] and

[143] *Ibid.* at 973.

[144] *Ibid.* at 984 (internal citations, quotations and ellipses omitted).

[145] G. Liu, 'Rethinking Constitutional Welfare Rights', *Stanford Law Review*, 61 (2008), 203–69, 245.

[146] M. Tushnet, 'State Action, Social Welfare Rights, and the Judicial Role: Some Comparative Observations', *Chicago Journal of International Law*, 3 (2002), 435–53, 447.

rarely have such judgments been regarded as open to 'inter-branch dialogue' or legislative second-guessing.[147] But in the remedial dimension, judicial enforcement of equality norms leaves space for legislative discretion. Relief customarily consists of a mandatory injunction ordering the state to extend the disputed benefit to the wrongfully excluded group, presumably on an assumption that legislatures would prefer 'equalising up' in these circumstances.[148] The legislature, however, remains free to recalibrate policy and to satisfy equality norms by 'equalising down', either by scaling back the benefits provided to the judicially enlarged beneficiary population or by eliminating the programme altogether.[149] The ultimate authority to manage fiscal priorities remains with the political branches, subject to judicial limits that bar particular means of achieving state fiscal goals (e.g. cost-cutting through discrimination against a constitutionally protected group).

In the wake of the fiscal crisis, the Connecticut court declined even to acknowledge the role of the constitutional equality norms in protecting against the denial of socio-economic benefits, despite controlling federal precedent to the contrary and the state court's own contrary pre-crash precedent.[150] This willingness to evade enforcement of established equality rights suggests that the 'weak' aspect of Equal Protection remediation (the legislature's option to 'equalise down'), if recognised at all, did not overcome the court's disinclination to oversee political judgements on budget priorities during a fiscal crisis. The Connecticut decision also may reflect a jurisprudential strand that does not fully accept the legitimacy of enforceable socio-economic rights, even those bound to constitutional equality guarantees.[151] By contrast, the Massachusetts court applied strong review to the equality claim and in the process extended health care coverage to an additional 34,000 lawful immigrants.[152]

Although it is impossible to say with certainty why the courts reached divergent results, certain factors seem salient. First, different political

[147] Compare *Katzenbach* v. *Morgan*, 384 US 641 (1966) (arguably permitting Congress to define constitutional equality rights more expansively than courts), with *City of Boerne* v. *Flores*, 521 US 507 (1977) (denying any such role for Congress).

[148] See *Califano* v. *Westcott*, 443 US 76, 89 (1979).

[149] *Ibid.*

[150] *Barannikova* v. *Greenwich*, 643 A 2d 251 (1994).

[151] See Hershkoff and Loffredo, 'State Courts', 937.

[152] J. Yang and S. Chroback, 'Commonwealth Care FY 2013 Procurement Results', presented at Commonwealth Health Insurance Connector Authority Board of Directors meeting 12 April 2012, http://archives.lib.state.ma.us/bitstream/handle/2452/119155/ocn793126395.pdf?sequence+1, last accessed 5 August 2013.

cultures and contexts might have influenced the courts' receptivity to social welfare claims. Although the Massachusetts Constitution does not contain a right to health care, the state is the first in the United States to have adopted near universal health care for its residents.[153] Indeed, the Massachusetts programme provided a model for the national Patient Protection and Affordable Care Act ('Obamacare') adopted during the Obama Administration.[154] Moreover, the Massachusetts legislature did not view the budgetary effects of universal health care in zero-sum terms, but rather attempted to expand the available budgetary pie through market-based cost-controls aimed at securing quality care within manageable spending limits.[155] In addition, the Massachusetts court had an ally in the executive branch; the Governor earlier had signalled his opposition to withholding benefits from immigrants and his support for universal health care.[156] Whether or not one views *Finch* as an instance of inter-branch collaboration, the decision offered 'cover' to elected officials who supported the principle of universal health care but feared using scarce state funds for a disfavoured minority. It also bears noting that in both the Connecticut and Massachusetts cases, the states' claims of fiscal over-burden might have been overstated or at least seen as a transitional problem: the federal Patient Protection and Affordable Care Act, while not restoring federal Medicaid reimbursement for legal immigrants, makes many of them eligible for federal subsidies to purchase health insurance beginning in 2014, and so alleviates some of the states' fiscal burden.[157] In any event, even in the face of fiscal crisis, the Massachusetts state court used strong-form review to strike down legislative cutbacks and so protected immigrant rights to health care.

As in *McCleary*, the Washington education case, baseline expectations may have influenced the state courts' interpretation and administration of classical equality rights in a socio-economic setting. Massachusetts had

[153] P. Belluck and K. Zezima, 'Massachusetts Legislation on Insurance Becomes Law', *The New York Times* (13 April 2006), A1.

[154] See E. W. Leonard, 'State Constitutionalism and the Right to Health Care', *University of Pennsylvania Journal of Constitutional Law*, 12 (2010), 1325–406, 1388–91.

[155] After *Finch* was decided, the Governor signed a cost-control plan into law that the federal government is now considering as a model for national regulation. See R. Alonso-Zaldivar, 'Health Cost Controls Follow Mass. Lead', Telegram.com (3 September 2012), www.telegram.com/article/20120903/NEWS/109039973/1116, last accessed 5 August 2013.

[156] See *Finch II*, 959 NE 2d at 977–9.

[157] See A. Siskin, 'Treatment of Noncitizens Under the Patient Protection and Affordable Care Act' (Congressional Research Service Report R41714, 22 March 2011).

made a sustained, highly visible public commitment to universal health coverage, creating a background norm that, while not sufficiently robust to support an affirmative constitutional claim to health care, nevertheless was adequate to inoculate equal protection rights against dilution even during hard times. The theoretical claim finds indirect support in the landmark 2012 health care decision of the Supreme Court of the United States, barring the national government from conditioning continued federal funding of state Medicaid programmes on state agreement to adopt expanded federal eligibility rules.[158] The Supreme Court implicitly regarded the long-standing federal commitment to Medicaid as embedding baseline expectations about social welfare funding that Congress could not casually abandon.[159] As yet, no US court has blocked a state or the national government from eliminating a social welfare programme on this basis.[160] Perhaps a theory of this sort is nascent in the Massachusetts court's unwillingness to validate the state's exclusion of immigrants from an otherwise universal system of health care.

C. *Offering common-law protection against contractual foreclosure*

Finally, we focus on the role of common law in protecting the family home from an unwarranted mortgage foreclosure. A major contributing factor to the 2008 economic crisis was the rampant and largely unregulated marketing of sub-prime mortgages to borrowers whose mortgages were pooled with others, securitised and sold to investors, in a process that generated tremendous profits for the financial services industry.[161] From 2002 to 2006, sub-prime mortgages expanded from 9 per cent of all new mortgages to 47 per cent of new mortgages,[162] and they were

158 *National Federation of Independent Business* v. *Sebelius*, 132 S Ct 2566 (2012).

159 *Ibid.* at 2601–7.

160 Cf. E. Rubin, 'The Affordable Care Act, the Constitutional Meaning of Statutes and the Emerging Doctrine of Positive Constitutional Rights', *William & Mary Law Review*, 53 (2012), 1639–715 (arguing optimistically that passage of the national health care act 'suggests that the U.S. Constitution guarantees so-called positive rights, such as ... basic health care ... [and] encourages the Supreme Court to declare [such rights] part of the Constitution').

161 See K. Eggert, 'The Great Collapse: How Securitization Caused the Subprime Meltdown', *Connecticut Law Review*, 41 (2009), 1257–312.

162 See D. Cavell, 'Ghetto Loans: Discrimination against African American Borrowers in Mortgage Markets and the Impact of the *Ibanez* Decision', *Georgetown Journal of Legal Ethics*, 25 (2012), 449–68, 455 (citing C. J. Mayer and K. Peace, 'Subprime Mortgages: What, Where, and to Whom?' (National Bureau of Economic Research, Working Paper No. 14083, 2008).

disproportionately marketed to African American households.[163] By March 2008, one in six sub-prime borrowers had fallen behind on mortgage payments.[164] Within a year, 2.8 million foreclosure cases had been filed in state and federal courts.[165] The lawsuits brought to light a range of illegal practices by companies that process mortgage paperwork, including 'robo-signing' of documents,[166] fraud[167] and lack of legal capacity to bring the foreclosure action in the first place.[168] Legally defective foreclosure proceedings caused thousands of distressed borrowers to lose their homes, to face credit impairment and to be burdened by impermissible service fees. The social effects of these foreclosures spilled over to communities that face blight, reduced housing prices and increased crime.[169]

In this section, we discuss a decision of the Massachusetts Supreme Judicial Court, *US Bank National Association* v. *Ibanez*,[170] involving contractual 'power of sale' clauses that allow a private entity to foreclose on and reclaim title to a mortgaged property without going to court – so-called non-judicial foreclosure, which is the prevalent mode of foreclosure in 30 US states and the pervasive method of foreclosure in the states with the highest rates of post-meltdown foreclosure.[171] *Ibanez* held that 'power of sale' foreclosure is limited to the mortgagee and may not be enforced

163 See R. H. Brescia, 'The Cost of Inequality: Social Distance, Predatory Conduct, and the Financial Crisis', *NYU Annual Survey of American Law*, 66 (2011), 641–725, 687–8 (collecting data).

164 D. R. Greenberg, 'Comment: Neglected Formalities in the Mortgage Assignment Process and the Resulting Effects on Residential Foreclosures', *Temple Law Review*, 83 (2010), 253–93, 256.

165 T. A. Froehle, 'Note – Standing in the Wake of the Foreclosure Process: Why Procedural Requirements Are Necessary to Prevent Further Loss to Homeowners', *Iowa Law Review*, 96 (2011), 1719–44, 1721.

166 See D. E. Woolley and L. D. Herzog, 'MERS: The Unreported Effects of Lost Chain of Title on Real Property Owners', *Hastings Business Law Journal*, 8 (2012), 365–403, 372–8.

167 A. M. White, 'Losing the Paper – Mortgage Assignments, Note Transfers and Consumer Protection', *Loyola Consumer Law Review*, 24 (2012), 468–503; R. H. Brescia, 'Leverage: State Enforcement Actions in the Wake of the Robo-Sign Scandal', *Maine Law Review*, 64 (2011), 17–44, 19.

168 Greenberg, 'Neglected Formalities', 253–93 (discussing foreclosing entity's lack of standing when assignment not shown or made).

169 See P. Cox, 'Foreclosure Reform Amid Mortgage Lending Turmoil: A Public Purpose Approach', *Houston Law Review*, 45 (2008), 683–745, 693–8.

170 *US Bank National Association* v. *Ibanez*, 941 NE 2d 40 (Mass 2011).

171 A. P. Williams, 'Foreclosing Foreclosure: Escaping the Yawning Abyss of the Deep Mortgage and Housing Crisis', *Northwestern Journal of Law and Social Policy*, 7 (2012), 455–509, 466.

by a mortgage servicer that does not hold the mortgage.[172] In so ruling, the court potentially affected foreclosure proceedings in any title-theory state in the United States where debtors face loss of their homes by entities that have no right to bring the action because – as in *Ibanez* – they service but do not hold the mortgage.[173] *Ibanez* did not give distressed households new socio-economic entitlements and is not a right-to-housing case in the conventional sense. Rather, it protected existing property rights against misappropriation by private actors who otherwise could seize and sell defaulted properties despite a lack of authorisation and in violation of statutory and common-law restrictions. The decision illustrates the ways in which a classical right to procedural regularity can protect social-welfare interests when judicially enforced.

Ibanez consolidated two related quiet-title actions brought in the Massachusetts Land Court. In both, the mortgage servicer had foreclosed on a home before having been assigned the mortgage – it held only the note underlying the mortgage.[174] The borrowers' situation was typical of post-meltdown mortgage relations. As one commentary explains:

> The *Ibanez* mortgage followed a typical path of modern securitization and foreclosure. On December 1, 2005, Antonio Ibanez purchased a $103,000 mortgage from Rose Mortgage, Inc., on a property in Springfield, Massachusetts. A few days later, Rose assigned this mortgage 'in blank', not specifying the name of the buyer. Over the next year, the mortgage was assigned five times: from Rose to Option One Mortgage Corporation, then (also 'in blank') to Lehman Brothers Bank, then to Lehman Brothers Holdings, then to Structured Asset Securities Corporation, and finally to U.S. Bank, where it was pooled as [a mortgage backed security]. U.S. Bank filed a complaint to foreclose on April 17, 2007, and on July 5 purchased the property in a foreclosure sale. On September 2, 2008, 'more than one year after the sale, and more than five months after recording of the sale', U.S. Bank finally received a written assignment of the mortgage from Option One Mortgage's 'successor-in-interest'.[175]

Because Massachusetts is a power-of-sale foreclosure state, no court authorisation was required prior to the foreclosure sale.[176] As typically transpires in such proceedings, the foreclosed-upon homeowners did not initially appear to contest the action, and the servicer purchased

[172] *Ibanez*, 941 NE 2d at 55.

[173] M. R. Goodman, 'The Buck Stops Here: Toxic Titles and Title Insurance', *Real Estate Law Journal*, 42 (2013), 5–51, 36–41.

[174] *Ibanez*, 941 NE 2d at 44.

[175] Cavell, 'Ghetto Loans', 465–6.

[176] See *Ibanez*, 941 NE 2d at 49.

the property at the foreclosure sale. Unable to secure title insurance, the servicer then filed suit to clear title thereby triggering judicial involvement. The Land Court, however, refused to clear title and entered judgment against the servicer on the ground that state law limited the self-help remedy of non-judicial foreclosure to the mortgagee. Since the mortgage had not been assigned to the servicer prior to its commencing the foreclosure proceeding, it lacked authority to foreclose under the power-of-sale clause. The court explained: 'To accept the plaintiffs' arguments is to allow them to take someone's home without any demonstrable right to do so, based upon the assumption that they ultimately will be able to show that they have that right'.[177]

The Supreme Judicial Court in *Ibanez* affirmed the Land Court's judgment, and declined to make its decision prospective, meaning that each and every foreclosure conducted by a servicer who lacked title to the mortgage became vulnerable to judicial challenge.[178]

In so holding, the Supreme Judicial Court emphasised that the statutory mechanism of non-judicial foreclosure delegates 'substantial power ... to a mortgage holder to foreclose without immediate judicial oversight'; exercise of that authority, however, is subject to 'the familiar rule that "one who sells under a power [of sale] must follow strictly its terms"'.[179] This rule was rooted, the court explained, in the state's common law, which draws a distinction between the assignment of the mortgage and the associated note[180] – a distinction that was 'well established' in Massachusetts law[181] (a point confirmed by scholars[182]) and which the legislature had incorporated into the 1912 law establishing the statutory power of sale.[183] None of the common-law principles applied by the *Ibanez* court were novel or unconventional; as a concurring justice in *Ibanez* stated, 'what is surprising about these cases is not the statement of principles articulated by the court regarding title law and the law of foreclosure in Massachusetts, but rather the utter carelessness with which the plaintiff banks documented the titles to their assets'.[184]

177 *US Bank National Association* v. *Ibanez*, Nos. 08 MISC 384283(KCL), 08 MISC 386755(KCL), 2009 WL 3297551, at *12 (Mass Land Ct. 14 October 2009).

178 *Ibanez*, 941 NE 2d at 54–5.

179 *Ibid.* at 50 (quoting *Moore* v. *Dick*, 72 NE 967 (Mass 1905)).

180 *Ibanez*, 941 NE 2d at 53–4 (relying on *Young* v. *Miller*, 72 Mass 152, 152 (1856) and *Barnes* v. *Boardman*, 21 NE 308 (Mass 1889)).

181 *Ibanez*, 941 NE 2d at 55.

182 E. Renuart, 'Property Title Trouble in Non-Judicial Foreclosure States: the *Ibanez* Time Bomb?', *William and Mary Business Law Review*, 4 (2013), 111–80.

183 *Ibanez*, 941 NE 2d at 54.

184 *Ibid.* at 55 (J. Cordy, concurring).

Significantly, the Supreme Judicial Court did not constitutionalise the rules pertaining to non-judicial foreclosure; it maintained a statutory and common-law approach in which interpretative authority is shared with the legislature and indeed legislative prerogative takes precedence. In this sense 'review' was weak. But by limiting non-judicial foreclosure to the mortgagee, the decision used strong review to enforce procedural protections and, by so doing, made substantive opportunities available to the debtor – most notably, the chance to modify a loan in lieu of sale and the raising of defences to recover property even after a sale.[185] Decisions subsequent to *Ibanez* enforced other procedural protections that likewise bolstered the household's socio-economic position: that a quitclaim deed following a defective foreclosure sale does not convey title;[186] that a mortgage separated from a note does not convey power to foreclose to the mortgagee;[187] and that the Housing Court has jurisdiction to determine whether the purchaser at a foreclosure sale can bring a summary eviction proceeding against a defaulting homeowner who raises as an affirmative defence a defect in the purchaser's title.[188] By insisting upon procedural regularity, the Supreme Judicial Court – without invoking a constitutional right to housing or even to due process – protected those households that had not yet been dispossessed. The decisions do not control, but may influence, courts in other states that follow a title theory and likewise provide for non-judicial foreclosure.[189] Indeed, even in states that follow a different common-law rule, *Ibanez* offers guidance on the problems that may develop if courts allow foreclosing entities to cut procedural corners.[190]

Ibanez illustrates how common-law decisions may provide a pathway for extending public norms to private actors in circumstances when constitutional regulation is not available or desired. In a mixed economy, a great deal of material well-being is left to market transactions. How best

[185] See M. Johnson and L. A. Johnson, 'Defending Foreclosure Actions', *Real Estate Law Journal*, 40 (Spring 2012), 439–68.

[186] *Bevilacqua* v. *Rodriguez*, 955 NE 2d 884 (Mass 2011).

[187] *Eaton* v. *Federal National Mortgage Association*, 969 NE 2d 1118 (Mass 2012).

[188] *Bank of NY* v. *Bailey*, 951 NE 2d 331 (Mass 2011).

[189] See E. Renuart, 'Property Title Trouble'. See also *Bain* v. *Metropolitan Mortg. Group, Inc.*, 285 P 3d 34 (Wash 2012) (permitting fraud action to be brought under Consumer Protection Act against electronic registration system that as beneficiary of deed of trust brought non-judicial foreclosure action).

[190] See H. J. Brackey, 'Foreclosure Errors a Result of Swamped System', *Pittsburgh Post-Gazette* (29 March 2012), www.post-gazette.com/stories/sectionfront/life/foreclosure-errors-a-result-of-swamped-system-267498/, last accessed 5 August 2013.

to regulate corporate behaviour is an ongoing and contentious problem. As a governance theory of property teaches, a contractual-foreclosure remedy serves a dual purpose: it protects private-property interests, and it carries out a public function that is judicial in nature.[191] Massachusetts' delegation of this power to a private entity carried conditions, limiting use of the remedy to a category of property holder under specified circumstances. By insisting upon strict compliance with the statute, the court made explicit a norm of procedural regularity as applied to a private actor that it housed in the common law and which the legislature is free to operationalise.

The *Ibanez* approach resembles that of weak-form review by national courts outside the United States, in the sense of offering a conditional approach that the legislature has prerogative to endorse or revise; but the decision produced strong effects in terms of catalysing legislative reform and extending procedural norms into a private realm that is outside direct constitutional regulation. Indeed, *Ibanez* jump-started a legislative process to reform financial practices that until then had been impervious to control.[192] In 2011, the Massachusetts legislature began considering codifying *Ibanez* and the next year adopted legislation requiring the foreclosing entity to show that it holds the mortgage prior to undertaking foreclosure proceedings; in some circumstances lenders also must offer to modify borrowers' loans rather than foreclosing.[193] Although the *Ibanez* judgment ran only against private actors and issued no coercive mandate against the legislature, it generated a political dialogue that has had important positive effects in securing material well-being during a time of financial distress.

VI. Conclusion: US state courts and socio-economic rights

By highlighting the experience of US state courts, our goal has been to contribute to an ongoing global discussion about the enforcement of

[191] See L. Katz, 'Governing through Owners: How and Why Formal Private Property Rights Enhance State Power', *University of Pennsylvania Law Review*, 160 (2012), 2029–59; B. H. Mattingly, 'The Shift from Power to Process: A Functional Approach to Foreclosure Law', *Marquette Law Review*, 80 (1996), 77–133, 92.

[192] See J. Ruby and A. Kuehnhoff, 'The Massachusetts Supreme Judicial Court's Foreclosure Jurisprudence: A Review of 2011 and a Preview of 2012 and Beyond', *Boston Bar Journal*, 56 (Winter 2012), 29–35, 35 (discussing pending bills regarding foreclosures).

[193] An Act Preventing Unlawful and Unnecessary Foreclosures, Massachusetts Session Laws, St. 2012, c.194.

socio-economic rights. The cases surveyed in this chapter show uneven but nevertheless important positive effects of enlisting the judiciary in this effort. The 2008 meltdown coincided with economic and policy trends that had caused deepening inequality and declining income for significant segments of the American population. During economically flush times, states and localities failed to invest in necessary infrastructure or to devise sound systems of public financing. As the recession fuelled a burgeoning need for public services, states and localities sounded the alarm that they were unable financially to provide important public goods and were unwilling politically to raise the revenues required to do so. At such a moment, judicial enforcement of socio-economic rights not only secures the broad countercyclical benefits of such rights, but also ensures that political and policy discourse, which otherwise might focus exclusively on austerity, takes account of fundamental democratic values and preservation of human dignity. The US state court experience reflects an essential, yet fragile and contingent, judicial commitment to this critical endeavour.

9

The promise of a minimum core approach: the Colombian model for judicial review of austerity measures

DAVID LANDAU

I. Introduction

The Colombian Constitutional Court has been one of the most activist and creative in the world in enforcing socio-economic rights. It has developed a rich jurisprudence on rights such as the rights to health, social security, life and housing. There is little doubt that many of its decisions in the area of socio-economic rights – such as those reorganising the housing financing system in 1999 and 2000, and that declaring a state of unconstitutional conditions for the country's three to four million internally displaced persons in 2004 – have had dramatic effects on public policy and on the national budget. The Court's relatively long history of rich and creative enforcement of socio-economic rights, including against a backdrop of economic crisis, makes it an ideal institution from which to draw lessons for courts around the world currently confronting the effects of governmental austerity.

Among those courts in Europe and elsewhere considering their role in light of sweeping austerity measures, the following questions are among the key ones: do courts have the incentives and capacity necessary to protect the poor during economic crises? Are there ways doctrinally for courts to meaningfully review austerity measures without overstepping the bounds of the judicial role or causing macroeconomic havoc? In other words, can courts give their review of these measures' 'teeth' in a sustainable way? The Colombian experience suggests a cautious optimism on these questions.

This chapter considers the response of the Colombian Constitutional Court to two different economic crises – the very deep financial crisis of 1999–2000 and a shallower, but still harmful, crisis following the

I owe thanks to Carlos Bernal-Pulido and an anonymous peer reviewer for helpful comments on this chapter.

worldwide problems in 2008. In particular, I argue that the Court's jurisprudence demonstrates the viability and attractiveness of a judicial review model that emphasises the minimum core of socio-economic rights within the broader framework of the principle of a social state of law. Both are core principles of the Colombian constitutional order.

Section II of this chapter lays out the conceptual framework for the protection of socio-economic rights under the 1991 Colombian Constitution, placing particular emphasis on both the right to a vital minimum ('minimo vital') and the social state of law principle. Section III considers the initial response of the Colombian Constitutional Court to the deep financial crisis of 1999–2000. At first, the Court responded with sweeping interventions in the housing and public sector salary sectors; these interventions were spectacular in scope but, as I discuss, may ultimately have benefitted relatively affluent groups and provoked substantial political backlash because of their significant budgetary and macroeconomic effects.

After a turnover in terms of the Court's personnel in 2000, new justices shifted to a more targeted approach, as demonstrated in Sections IV and V. While maintaining a robust review of austerity measures on socio-economic grounds, this new Court focused especially on preventing harm to the poorest through a renewed focus on the vital minimum. Proportionality review of austerity measures, in other words, was carried out in light of the imperatives of the vital minimum, and proportionality and the vital minimum were seen as compatible instruments carrying out separate functions. Section VI concludes by suggesting that the Colombian model of review may be an attractive one for courts elsewhere considering how to carry out effective but sustainable review of governmental austerity.

II. The Colombian constitutional framework: the vital minimum and the social state of law

The 1991 Constitution was written in the midst of a social and political crisis – traditional political forces had lost much of their legitimacy amidst sharply escalating violence associated with drug cartels, guerrilla groups and paramilitary organisations.[1] A group of outsider political movements,

[1] M. J. Cepeda, 'Judicial Activism in a Violent Context: The Background, Role, and Impact of the Colombian Constitutional Court', *Washington University Global Studies Law Review*, 3 (2004), 529–700, 542–52.

including demobilised guerrilla groups, won a significant share of the votes in the Constituent Assembly and cooperated with members of the traditional parties to write a new Constitution that was supposed to create space for a political renewal.[2] New institutions like the Constitutional Court were established to ensure that this transformation occurred. The Assembly created a Constitution that was rich in rights provisions, and a strong Constitutional Court to ensure that these rights were enforced.[3]

The Colombian constitutional system is unusually easy to access. Any citizen is allowed to file a petition, on abstract review, to challenge any law at any time. This 'public action', which has no standing requirements, has been one of the defining features of Colombian constitutional law since the beginning of the twentieth century.[4] Further, the Colombian constitutional complaint created in the 1991 Constitution, called the *tutela*, is a very attractive mechanism for petitioners. Unlike similar actions in other Latin American systems which are often encrusted with formalities and are thus difficult, costly and time-consuming to navigate, the Colombian *tutela* is both easy to file and very fast.[5] Petitions may generally be filed in any court and are highly informal – petitions need not be drafted by lawyers. Further, decisions are made quickly, in stark contrast to the long delays in the normal Colombian system: under the constitution petitions must be decided within ten days.[6] Because of these features, the *tutela* has reached a kind of mythic status within Colombia – it is a key part of popular discourse and is seen as perhaps the best-functioning part of the judicial system.[7]

Unlike the prior Constitution of 1886, which included relatively few rights of any kind and no real socio-economic rights, the 1991 Constitution

[2] F. C. Ulloa, 'Colombia: The Governability Crisis' in J. I. Dominguez and M. Shifter (eds.), *Constructing Democratic Governance in Latin America* (Baltimore, MD: Johns Hopkins University Press, 2003), pp. 193–219, p. 197.

[3] D. Landau, 'Political Institutions and Judicial Role in Comparative Constitutional Law', *Harvard International Law Journal*, 51 (2010), 319–77, 338–9.

[4] Cepeda, 'Judicial Activism in a Violent Context', 555–6.

[5] *Ibid.*, 552–4. See also A. R. Brewer-Carias, *Constitutional Protection of Human Rights in Latin America: A Comparative Study of Amparo Proceedings* (New York: Cambridge University Press, 2009), pp. 147–51 (describing the *tutela* within the framework of a general study of *amparo* and individual complaint mechanisms in Latin America).

[6] Constitution of Colombia, art. 86 ('In no case may more than 10 days elapse between the filing of the writ of protection and its resolution').

[7] R. U. Yepes, 'Las Tranformaciones de la administracion de justicia en Colombia' in B. d. S. Santos and M. G. Villegas (eds.), *El caleidoscopio de las justicias en Colombia* (Bogota: Siglo de Hombres, 2001), pp. 261–315, pp. 300–2 (noting the importance of the *tutela* in the 'symbolic function' of the Constitution).

has an extensive list of rights provisions including socio-economic rights.[8] These include rights to health care, housing, education and social security, among others.[9] The members of the Assembly were uncertain about whether and how these rights should be made enforceable. Some argued that such rights should essentially be treated like directive principles, and the final constitutional text left it ambiguous whether or not these rights could be enforced using the *tutela*.[10] Yet, from early on, the Colombian Constitutional Court developed a role conception that revolved largely around the enforcement of these rights.

The Court elaborated on two key concepts early in its existence. The first is the right to a vital minimum, which is not enumerated in the Constitution but which was also inferred by the first Constitutional Court in 1992 based on principles such as human dignity and the social state of law, as well as the explicit socio-economic rights provisions and the right to life found in the text.[11] The right to a vital minimum gave citizens a right to have at least the minimum level of satisfaction of social needs to be able to live a dignified existence. As the Court has noted, it implied a right 'to the guarantee of the most elemental material conditions without which a person is at risk of perishing and remaining converted into a being that succumbs before the impossibility of autonomously ensuring her own subsistence'.[12]

The vital minimum doctrine is important first because it gave the Court a clear path allowing enforcement of socio-economic rights in some circumstances via *tutela*, despite the ambiguity in the Constitutional

[8] For a comparison between the rights provisions of the Constitution of 1886 and the Constitution of 1991, see M. J. Cepeda, *Los Derechos Fundamentales en la Constitucion de 1991* (Bogota: Temis, 1992).

[9] Constitution of Colombia, arts. 44 (listing socio-economic rights for children); 48 (social security); 49 (health); 51 (housing); 53 (rights connected to work); 67 (education).

[10] The article defining the *tutela* states that the instrument may only be used to protect 'fundamental rights', and the Assembly's codification committee placed most of the first-generation rights in a chapter labelled 'fundamental rights', while socio-economic rights were placed in a separate chapter labelled 'economic, social, and cultural rights'. But it is unclear what weight should be given to this labelling. Moreover, article 85 of the Constitution lists certain rights as being of 'immediate application'; this list does not include the socio-economic rights. See Constitution of Colombia, art. 85. But it is unclear how the concept of 'immediate application' interacts with the concept of a right being 'fundamental'.

[11] T-426 of 1992, §§ 4–5 (deducing such a right as 'a direct consequence of the principles of human dignity and the social state of law').

[12] T-458 of 1997, § 23. See also C-776 of 2003, § 4.5.3.3.2 (noting that the 'right protects the person ... against any form of degradation that compromises not only his physical subsistence but above all his intrinsic worth').

Convention's original formulation. Under the Court's connectivity doctrine, socio-economic rights could be fundamental rights enforceable by *tutela* whenever they were connected to other rights like the right to life and human dignity.[13] The vital minimum doctrine thus gave the Court an opening for making socio-economic rights judicially enforceable.

Second, the vital minimum doctrine has performed a prioritisation function not unlike the one played by the minimum core concept in international law. The minimum core approach, as articulated by the Committee on Economic, Social and Cultural Rights in charge of interpreting the International Covenant on Economic, Social and Cultural Rights,[14] asserts that all actors are entitled to receive a minimum package of economic and social rights (ESR)-related goods and services so that they can live a dignified life.[15] Advocates of the minimum core approach assert that it is possible to define a set of minimum entitlements to basic rights that must be afforded by the State to all citizens, regardless of resources.[16] The vital minimum and connectivity doctrines suggest that a similar obligation to that of the minimum core exists under Colombian constitutional law.[17] By making socio-economic rights directly enforceable by the courts whenever citizens fall below a threshold necessary for dignified survival, jurisprudence would aim primarily at reducing extreme poverty. The vital minimum principle has since become a core

[13] M. F. Q. Ramirez, *Derecho constitucional colombiano: de la carta de 1991 y sus reformas* 300 (Bogota: Editorial Universidad del Rosario, 2009) (noting that the court began with a connectivity doctrine but has since held that some socio-economic rights are fundamental in their own right).

[14] International Covenant on Economic, Social and Cultural Rights, 993 UNTS 3 (ICESCR).

[15] UN Committee on Economic, Social and Cultural Rights (CESCR), 'General Comment No. 3' in 'Note by the Secretariat, Compilation of General Comments and General Recommendations Adopted by Human Rights Treaty Bodies' (27 May 2008) UN Doc. HRI/GEN/1/Rev.9 (Vol. I), para. 9. Some courts and commentators have rejected the concept as being too vague. For example, the South African Court has repeatedly refused to define a minimum core obligation in the context of rights like the right to housing and water. For more on this point, see Section V (discussing critiques).

[16] See, e.g., D. Bilchitz, *Poverty and Fundamental Rights: The Justification and Importance of Socio-Economic Rights* (New York: Oxford University Press, 2007), pp. 183–97.

[17] The vital minimum and the minimum core are not identical concepts. In particular, the vital minimum doctrine is a freestanding right to a minimum level of subsistence, while the minimum core is an interpretive approach used to interpret rights like the rights to housing and health care. Nonetheless, the Court often uses the vital minimum as either a justiciable core of the socio-economic rights found in the Constitution or as an especially prioritised socio-economic right, placed above other such rights. Either usage is quite similar to the minimum core doctrine in international law.

part of the Court's sense of mission: it is referred to in almost all of its socio-economic rights jurisprudence, and operates as a kind of orienting principle for the Court's work.

The second key concept delineated by the Court in its early jurisprudence is the constitutional principle of a social state of law, which is mentioned in article 1 of the 1991 Constitution as a feature of the Colombian State.[18] In 1992, the first Court held that the social state of law is a basic principle of the Colombian Constitution and requires that the Colombian government take action to protect social welfare.[19] The social state of law is not a directly enforceable constitutional right. Rather, as a principle it informs the interpretation of the various constitutional rights found in the Colombian Constitution. It is one of the most cited concepts in Colombian constitutional law. As the Court has defined it, the social state of law goes beyond the historic conception of the 'rule of law' to require,

> in addition, the legal linkage of the authorities to principles tending to ensure the effectiveness of the rights and duties of everyone, especially through the provision of a vital minimum, the promotion of participation by individuals in political, economic, and cultural life, the special protection of excluded groups and persons, and intervention in the economy with a view towards using redistributive measures to correct the situations of grave inequality and inequity existing in society.[20]

Among other things, the social state of law replaces the formal equality of a classical rule of law, which was the traditional conception in Colombian constitutional law before 1991, with a requirement that the State promote material equality.[21] It is perhaps best understood as a complex principle of institutional design; among other ends, the social state of law requires that the Colombian State progressively improve its social welfare system,

[18] The article reads: 'Colombia is a social state of law, organised in the form of a unitary and decentralised republic, decentralised and with autonomy for its territorial entities, democratic, participatory and pluralistic, founded on respect for human dignity, work and the solidarity of the people that integrate it and in the prevalence of the general interest.' Constitution of Colombia, art. 1.

[19] See T-406 of 1992, § I (noting that the social state of law principle 'has an importance without precedent in the context of Colombian constitutionalism').

[20] C-1064 of 2001, § 3.2.3.

[21] C-044 of 2004, § VI.4 ('One of the bases of the social state of law is the consecration of the principle of material equality, that is, real or effective equality, as an expression of the design of the public power to eliminate or reduce the conditions of inequity and marginalisation of persons or social groups and achieve living conditions that accord with the dignity of human beings and a just political, economic, and social order').

and that this system prioritise the needs of the poorest, along the lines suggested by the right to a vital minimum.[22]

In 2012, the Court issued an important decision on the relationship between these two concepts and budgetary constraints. The relationship between socio-economic rights and financial limitations is of course particularly relevant during times of austerity. The Court reviewed a constitutional amendment which established, among other things, that 'fiscal sustainability must act as an instrument to achieve in a progressive way the objective of the Social State of Law' and that '[f]iscal sustainability must orient the branches and organs of the public power, inside their competencies, in a framework of harmonious collaboration'.[23] This amendment stemmed, in part, from political concerns that the Court's decisions were having excessive effects on the national budget.[24] The petitioners argued that the amendment was unconstitutional because it subordinated basic constitutional values like the vital minimum and the social state of law to fiscal considerations, or at least created a new principle of fiscal sustainability that was placed on the same level as the social state of law principle and had to be balanced against it. They argued that the norm in question thus constituted a 'substitution' of the existing constitutional order, rather than a mere amendment of the existing constitution.[25]

The Court upheld the amendment only after concluding that it did not in fact create a new constitutional principle of fiscal sustainability. Instead,

[22] See C-288 of 2012, § VI.24-VI.25 (defining the principle and noting that it 'imposes concrete goals' on the State to 'overcome existing social inequalities and to offer everyone the necessary opportunities to develop their aptitudes and to overcome material pressures').

[23] *Ibid.*, § II (reproducing the text of the relevant constitutional amendment). The amendment also created a special appeal mechanism by which state officials could request a 'procedural decision regarding the fiscal impacts', asking high courts to reconsider their rulings in light of their budgetary effects. The Court upheld this provision as well, noting that it did not force the Constitutional Court or other high courts to rule in any particular way and merely gave them discretion to modify the effects of their orders in particular cases. See *ibid.* § VI.74.3.

[24] See *ibid.*, § VI.54 (reproducing parts of the congressional debates that discussed the executive's fears that Constitutional Court decisions were having an excessive impact on the budget).

[25] *Ibid.*, § III. The substitution of the constitution doctrine, like the Indian basic structure doctrine, holds that some proposed constitutional amendments are unconstitutional because they subvert core principles of the existing constitutional order. These changes can only be carried out by a Constituent Assembly tasked with replacing the existing constitution, rather than by the Congress under the guise of constitutional amendment. See C. Bernal-Pulido, 'Unconstitutional Constitutional Amendments in the Case Study of Colombia: An Analysis of the Justification and Meaning of the Constitutional Replacement Doctrine', *International Journal of Constitutional Law*, 11 (2013), 339–57.

it established 'fiscal sustainability' as a mere 'instrument' in service of the larger goals of a social state of law.[26] In other words, the concept of 'fiscal sustainability' is 'subordinate' to the social state of law, rather than constituting a new principle that somehow should be balanced against it or overcome it.[27] The Court also held that, properly understood, the amendment merely codified its own jurisprudence and international legal standards on the 'progressive' nature of socio-economic rights. That is, it recognised that full enforcement would occur over time, but did not act as 'an instrument to deny the effective protection of constitutional rights'.[28] Instead, it meant that 'States cannot remain immobile before the satisfaction of these rights, [and] must move towards increases in coverage and in their guarantees'.[29]

The decision is important in establishing a hierarchical relationship between the vital minimum doctrine and the social state of law principle on the one hand, and fiscal and budgetary considerations on the other. The Court suggests that within a social state of law, fiscal considerations are relevant to constitutional enforcement but must always be subordinated to the effective realisation of constitutional rights, including socio-economic rights. The State may not use alleged resource constraints or even economic crisis as an excuse for ignoring the progressive realisation of socio-economic rights, and it must always prioritise the unsatisfied needs of the poorest. Austerity, in other words, is not an all-purpose excuse for reducing existing benefits or failing to construct or improve new social safety nets for the vulnerable, and socio-economic rights do not disappear in times of economic crisis. With these concepts established as a starting point, I turn now to consider the Court's evolving responses to economic crisis.

III. Initial response to crisis: large-scale interventions, middle-class beneficiaries and political pushback

In the late 1990s, Colombia faced a severe economic crisis. As shown in Figure 9.1, the economy contracted very sharply during this period – shrinking by 4 per cent in 1999 alone.[30] Unemployment spiked and peaked

The doctrine was used most famously in 2010, when the Court struck down a proposed referendum that would have allowed then-President Alvaro Uribe to run for a third consecutive term. See C-141 of 2010.

26 *Ibid.*, § VI.64.4 ('There is no normative conflict ... between fiscal sustainability and the social and democratic state of law, because they are on markedly different hierarchical planes').

27 *Ibid.*, § VI.71. 28 *Ibid.*, § VI.66. 29 *Ibid.*

30 The World Bank, 'GDP Growth (annual %)', http://data.worldbank.org/indicator/NY.GDP.MKTP.KO.ZG, last accessed 14 July 2014.

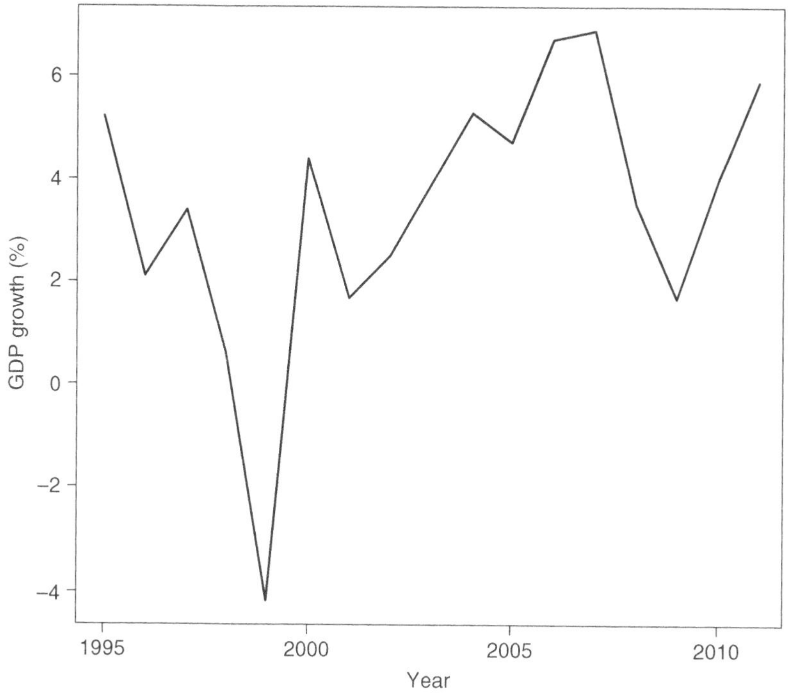

Figure 9.1 GDP growth in Colombia (1995–2011)

at over 20 per cent in 2000, while the deficit ballooned to over 5 per cent of gross domestic product (GDP).[31] The crisis placed pressure on rights like those to housing and health care. For example, the crisis caused interest rates in the housing sector to spike, which placed around 200,000 mortgagors at risk of losing their homes and led to significant increases in the payments for about 800,000 mortgagors.[32] It also affected the health care system: the number of people covered by the system, which had been on a steady increase since the early 1990s, dropped slightly between 1997 and

[31] A. F. Arias, 'The Colombian Banking Crisis: Macroeconomic Consequences and What to Expect' (Banco de la Republica de Colombia, Borradores de Economia No. 157, 2000), 2, www.banrep.gov.co/docum/ftp/borra157.pdf, last accessed 28 September 2013.

[32] R. Uprimny Yepes, 'The Enforcement of Social Rights by the Colombian Constitutional Court' in R. Gargarella, P. Domingo and T. Roux (eds.), *Courts and Social Transformation in New Democracies: An Institutional Voice for the Poor* (Burlington, VT: Ashgate, 2006), pp. 127–51, p. 136.

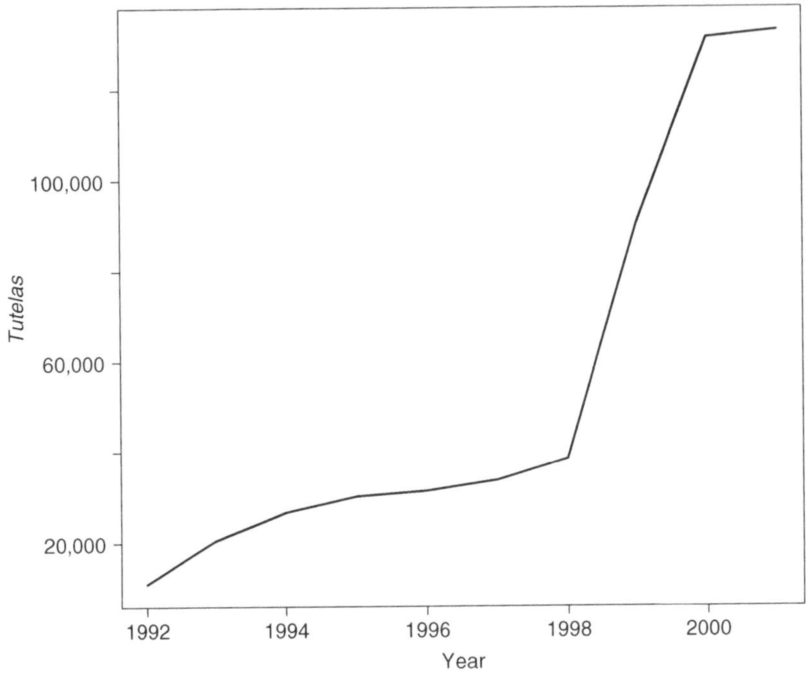

Figure 9.2 Total number of *tutelas* filed (1992–2001)

2000, and total health care spending as a percentage of GDP fell sharply from 9.6 per cent in 1997 to 7.7 per cent in 2000.[33]

Rights-bearers responded by turning to the *tutela*. Figure 9.2 demonstrates that there was a sharp spike in overall *tutela* claims in the late 1990s.[34] Many of these claims dealt with socio-economic rights like the rights to health, pensions and housing. Systematic data on the right to health is available beginning in 1999, and the data show that the right to health was invoked in 25 per cent of cases in that year.[35] Many of these new claimants were from middle-class groups experiencing pressure in the face

[33] C.A. Agudelo, J. C. Botero, J. O. Bolanos and R. R. Martinez, 'Sistema de salud en Colombia: 20 anos de logros y problemas', *Ciencia y saude colectiva*, 16 (2011), 2817–28, 2819 tbl.1, 2820 fig.1.

[34] See Defensoria del Pueblo, 'La Tutela y El Derecho a la Salud 2011: 20 anos del uso efectivo de la tutela, 1992–2011' (2011), 91, tbl. 2, www.defensoria.org.co/red/anexos/publicaciones/tutelaDerechosSalud2011a.pdf, last accessed 28 September 2013.

[35] The right was invoked in 21,301 *tutelas* in 1999, 24,843 in 2000 and 34,319 in 2001. *Ibid.*, 102, tbl. 7.

of the financial meltdown, and the courts began protecting these rights on a massive scale in individual cases.[36]

As Rueda has documented in detail, the vital minimum doctrine underwent an important evolution during this period. The Court's initial case-law on this principle was highly specific and focused on plaintiffs who were structurally marginalised from the market for various reasons.[37] For example, in the Court's first decision defining this right, T-426 of 1992, the Court protected an elderly and ill petitioner's right to a pension.[38] In protecting the social right at issue, the Court explained concretely how the deprivation was connected to fundamental rights like the right to life and human dignity.[39] Because the petitioner was impoverished, sick, elderly and unemployed and had been evicted from his house, the failure to provide the pension would gravely impact his right to a minimum level of subsistence.[40] In other words, pension rights were not always protectable by *tutela*, but rather only in particular circumstances where the failure to pay the pension gravely affected the minimum level of subsistence enjoyed by a petitioner.[41]

The meaning of this principle shifted during the crisis, as the Court began protecting the rights to pension and health care on a large scale. In the process, the Court ceased asking the same kinds of questions about the individual status of the petitioner.[42] Plaintiffs tended to win health cases, for example, regardless of their individual circumstances.[43] Indeed, an attempt by the founder of the vital minimum doctrine, Justice

36 P. Rueda, 'Legal Language and Social Change during Colombia's Economic Crisis' in J. Couso, A. Huneeus and R. Sieder (eds.), *Cultures of Legality: Judicialization and Political Activism in Latin America* (New York: Cambridge University Press, 2010), pp. 25–50, pp. 42–4.

37 *Ibid.*, pp. 36–40.

38 The right to social security is protected in Article 48 of the Constitution. However, in rendering the right justiciable, the Court emphasised the link to the right to a vital minimum.

39 T-426 of 1992, §10. 40 *Ibid.*, § 8.

41 For an overview of relevant case-law on the idea that pension rights were only protected if a link to the vital minimum were shown, see A. C. Parra, 'Procedibilidad de la accion de tutela en material pensional. Sistematizacion y analisis de la jurisprudencia de la Corte Constitucional' in M. J. Cepeda, E. Montealegre and A. Julio (eds.), *Teoria constitucional y politicas publicas: Bases Criticas para una discussion* (Bogota: Universidad Externado de Colombia, 2007), pp. 293–369.

42 Rueda, 'Legal Language and Social Change', pp. 44–5.

43 See Defensoría del Pueblo, 'La Tutela y el Derecho a la Salud, Periodo 2006–2008' (2009), 91 (showing that complainants won 86 per cent of health *tutelas* between 2006 and 2008). There is no data available for the period of the economic crisis.

Cifuentes, to scale back the doctrine towards its original foundations failed.[44]

But the Court went further than just altering its *tutela* jurisprudence. It also began undertaking larger-scale interventions in ways that would aid the struggling middle class. One of its prime targets was the housing sector, where adjustments to the system used to calculate interest rates threatened about 200,000 citizens with foreclosure. The nominal interest rate used to calculate mortgage payments spiked to over 33 per cent, far higher than the rate of inflation.[45] The Court began to receive *tutelas* on the issue, but the Congress and the President took no steps to ameliorate the problems.[46]

The Court thus stepped in with a series of decisions protecting the rights of the debtors; for example, by banning prepayment penalties and the capitalisation of interest.[47] In the key case, the Court first held a legislative-style hearing with input from a variety of civil society groups and economists, and then struck down the entire system of financing (known as UPAC) as unconstitutional.[48] However, the Court issued a modulated decision that maintained the system in effect for a set period while the legislature prepared a replacement; the failure to construct such a system would obviously be disastrous because it would leave the country with no system for housing finance once the prescribed period had expired.[49]

The grounds for decision ostensibly dealt with the procedure by which the system had been enacted, rather than the substance of the system. The remedy cleverly left the political branches with an unacceptable status quo – if they did not reconstruct the entire housing finance system within a set period of time, then they would be left with no system at all. In effect, it impelled those branches to act where they had previously been

[44] SU-111 of 1997, § 15 (noting that courts are unable to 'protect all of those who are in the same position as the petitioner' and are unable to determine 'its final cost', and thus proposing that judicial relief not be granted under the vital minimum doctrine unless the failure to provide a given health care treatment constituted a 'grave attack against the human dignity of persons pertaining to vulnerable sectors of the population and the State ... has failed to provide the minimum material assistance without which the defenseless person will succumb before his own impotence'). This standard did not provide a limitation in subsequent jurisprudence, and the Court's *tutela* docket continued to grow. See D. L. Medina, '"Sistema de salud" y "derecho a la salud": Historia de su interrelacion en la jurisprudencia constitucional' (unpublished manuscript, 24 April 2008), 38.

[45] Uprimny Yepes, 'The Enforcement of Social Rights', p. 136.

[46] For background on this case, see *ibid.* pp. 135–7.

[47] C-747 of 1999. [48] C-700 of 1999.

[49] *Ibid.*, § 5 (noting that it was necessary to 'consider an adequate transition between the two systems, without traumatizing the economy').

silent. The President responded by sending the Congress a new financing system, which was conditionally upheld by the Court only after certain provisions were reworked in a way that was more favourable to the debtors.[50] For example, interest rates under the new system were capped by the Court at the 'lowest levels' existing in the Colombian economy.[51]

A second major intervention occurred in the area of public sector salaries. The State, under significant budgetary pressure, proposed in the national budget nominal salary increases of 9 per cent for government workers making less than twice the minimum wage (which ran just about at the rate of inflation), and no increases for workers making more than twice the minimum wage. The Court struck down this budget as unconstitutional, holding that all government workers had a right to raises that at least kept up with the rate of inflation.[52] Since poorer government workers were already being offered raises that kept pace with the rate of inflation, the major beneficiaries of this decision were middle-class civil servants. Nonetheless, the Court cited the vital minimum doctrine as a core support for its decision, which is consistent with the general evolution in the concept during the beginning of the economic crisis.[53]

Both of the Court's major decisions were heavily criticised, especially by state officials and by economists.[54] The crux of the attack was that the housing and salary decisions had substantial macroeconomic and budgetary effects by essentially forcing expenditures in certain directions. Furthermore, the critics alleged that the Court had overstepped its proper role and meddled in areas of technical policy-making where it lacked the necessary expertise and democratic legitimacy. Finally, many critics pointed out that these decisions benefitted the middle class and not the poor.[55]

The author of the key housing decision, Justice Jose Gregorio Hernandez, gave interviews to the press where he responded to criticism of the court as follows: '[I]f you are talking about the criticisms, there is no need for the Court to discuss them because they have already been defeated, and in what a fashion, by public opinion … [T]he work of the Constitutional Court has been well received by the people. Because the people are much

[50] C-955 of 2000. [51] *Ibid.*, § V.B.4.

[52] C-1433 of 2000. [53] *Ibid.*, § 2.6.

[54] See S. Kalmanovitz, 'Los efectos economicos de la Corte Constitucional', http://economia.uniandes.edu.co/content/download/46688/392272/file/K-EfectosCorte.pdf, last accessed 15 January 2014 (critiquing the UPAC decisions); S. Clavijo, *Fallos y fallas de las altas cortes: El caso de Colombia 1991–2000* (2000), pp. 21–38 (analysing the economic and political effects of the UPAC and salary decisions).

[55] Clavijo, *Fallos y fallas*, p. 25 (arguing that the UPAC bail-outs gave substantial benefits to wealthier debtors).

more intelligent ... than their leaders'.[56] Hernandez, who subsequently became known in the press as the 'housing justice' and gained notoriety due to the decision, left the Court in 2000 and became the vice-presidential candidate on the Liberal party ticket.[57]

In short, the Court's jurisprudence during the early part of the economic crisis of the late 1990s had a somewhat populist element, in that it had both the effect and, arguably, the aim of garnering favour from the middle class. At the same time, the housing and salary decisions had significant budgetary and macroeconomic effects, which caused pushback against the Court.

In comparative terms, these decisions – and especially the salary decision – can perhaps best be grouped with others in Latin America and around the world in which a court makes it difficult for governments in crisis to take austerity measures that cut existing social benefits. In Hungary, for example, the Constitutional Court held in 1995 that a series of sweeping cuts to social welfare programmes were unconstitutional because citizens had property-like protections in existing benefits.[58] Some cuts could not be undertaken at all, while others required longer periods of transition. Scholars have debated the legal correctness and democratic legitimacy of decisions of this nature.[59] But for our purposes, what is important is that they tend to have substantial effects on the macroeconomy and may be politically contentious. Moreover, these decisions may raise substantial equity concerns in contexts where they protect pensions and other assets owned by the relatively affluent rather than the poor.

At any rate, the Court's jurisprudence in the housing and salary decisions became an issue in the selection process to pick a new Court in 2000, and some candidates expressed reservations about the Court's decisions.[60]

[56] 'Entrevista: Jose Gregorio Hernandez', *La Republica* (12 November 2000) (quoted in Clavijo, *Fallos y fallas*, p. 3).

[57] 'El Efecto "Vice"', *Semana* (8 April 2002), www.semana.com/noticias-nacion/efecto-vice/20354.aspx, last accessed 28 September 2013.

[58] Andras Sajo, 'Social Rights as Middle-Class Entitlements in Hungary: The Role of the Constitutional Court', in Gargarella *et al.* (eds.), *Courts and Social Transformation*, pp. 83–105, pp. 88–9.

[59] See, e.g., *ibid.*, pp. 88–9 (attacking the Hungarian ruling because it benefitted middle-class groups and prevented the enactment of needed reforms); K. L. Scheppele, 'A Realpolitik Defense of Social Rights', *Texas Law Review*, 82 (2004), 1921–61 (arguing that the decision helped to soften the adverse impact of austerity measures imposed by international financial institutions by giving domestic actors cover to resist some of those institutions' demands).

[60] '¿Aqui Quien Manda?', *Semana* (27 November 2000), www.semana.com/nacion/articulo/aqui-quien-manda/44166-3, last accessed 28 September 2013.

In that sense, the political system helped to push the Court towards a somewhat different approach, as I will explain in the next section.

IV. Proportionality and the vital minimum: targeted review of austerity measures

The new Court altered the prevailing jurisprudential approach in important ways. It maintained scrutiny over austerity measures in the context of continued economic struggles. However, it adopted a more targeted approach which focused on whether the measures were adequately justified and on whether they harmed the poorest and most vulnerable members of the population. In so doing, the Court relied on a renewed focus on the meaning of the right to a vital minimum, and applied the proportionality test in light of that right. The advantage of such an approach is that the Court could allow the State more flexibility to respond to the economic crisis while requiring it to prioritise the poor.

This shift was evident almost immediately, when the Court revisited its jurisprudence on public sector salaries in light of the next year's budget. The administration challenged the Court's earlier ruling by passing a budget that held salary increases for higher-income employees below the rate of inflation.[61] The Court this time upheld the budget, altering its jurisprudence to hold that salaries only needed to maintain their real value for those workers making less than twice the minimum wage.[62]

The Court's reasoning emphasised two points: the proportionality of the budgetary measures at issue, and the fact that the vital minimum doctrine gave the most protection to the poor. The Court held that the right of a salary to maintain its real value was not 'absolute'.[63] Applying proportionality analysis, the Court accepted the argument of the authorities that the reduction in the real value of salaries of high-earning public employees was necessary to maintain social spending at acceptable levels, which itself was a constitutionally prioritised end.[64] Indeed, the Court noted

[61] Cepeda, 'Judicial Activism in a Violent Context', 646.

[62] C-1064 of 2001. [63] *Ibid.*, § 4.2.2.2.

[64] Proportionality analysis, as generally articulated, requires (1) that the end pursued by the measure be sufficiently important; (2) that the means involving the restriction on the right are rationally related to the achievement of the end and do not restrict its enjoyment more than necessary; and (3) that the social benefit in terms of the achievement of the end outweighs the harm done by the restriction of the right. See L. E. Weinrib, 'The Postwar Paradigm and American Exceptionalism' in Sujit Choudhry (ed.), *The Migration of Constitutional Ideas* (Cambridge University Press, 2007), pp. 84–111, pp. 95–7. The Court found that the end of maintaining social spending was of great importance given

that textually, social spending was given priority over any other spending during times of resource shortages.[65] The Court also emphasised the genuine difficulties in the macroeconomic environment and the heavy cost of salaries within the budget.[66]

Moreover, the Court emphasised the right to a 'vital minimum', which it held provided 'reinforced' protection for lower-income workers because they needed their income in order to access basic goods and services.[67] In contrast, limiting salary increases for higher-income workers did not affect their right to a vital minimum.[68] In short, the Court conducted its proportionality analysis in light of the priority given to spending on the poor both through salary increases and social spending.

The Court followed a similar approach in a 2003 decision striking down part of a reform to the Value Added Tax (VAT).[69] An element of this sweeping reform broadened the tax base by taxing basic necessities that had previously been excluded from the tax. In striking down the expansion of the VAT base, the Court again emphasised the (ir)rationality of the Congress' actions in light of the priority given to the poor in Colombian constitutional law.[70] The Court extensively reviewed the context and legislative history of the provision. It emphasised that the Congress had a 'broad margin of discretion' on tax measures and that the reform as a whole had been extensively reviewed and debated in Congress.[71] However, the particular provision widening the base to include necessities was 'the result of an indiscriminate decision to tax a great quantity of completely diverse goods and services that was not accompanied by a minimum of public deliberation'.[72] The Court found that the provision was added as

its textual articulation in the Constitution and the definition of Colombia as a social state of law, that the real salary cuts appeared necessary to achieve that end given the great weight of salaries in the Colombian budget, and that the gain to poorer Colombians from maintaining social spending constant outweighed the harm to higher-income workers. C-1064 of 2001, § 5.2.3.

[65] Constitution of Colombia, art. 366 ('The general welfare and the improvement of the quality of life of the population are social ends of the State. A fundamental objective of its activity will be the solution of basic unsatisfied needs in health, education, environmental quality, and drinking water. For those effects, in the plans and budgets of the nation and the territorial entities, social public spending will have priority over all other spending').

[66] This was particularly relevant to the 'necessity' stage of the proportionality inquiry, with the Court noting that 'given the critical economic situation and the great demands imposed by the social spending ordered by the Constitution, on the one hand, and that spending on personnel is some of the most substantial spending sources, on the other, the Court considers that the means chosen by the Congress are necessary'. C-1064 of 2001, § 5.2.2.3.1.

[67] *Ibid.*, § 5.2.2.1. [68] *Ibid.*, § 5.2.4. [69] C-776 of 2003.
[70] *Ibid.*, § 4.5.6.1. [71] *Ibid.*, § 4.5.3.1. [72] *Ibid.*, § 4.5.6.1.

a last-minute compromise, hammered out by a Conference Committee, which was not a product of reasoned deliberation but was instead merely a way to fill unanticipated revenue needs quickly.[73]

In conducting proportionality analysis, the Court noted that collections from VAT (which was often regarded as a regressive tax) had risen as a percentage of GDP when compared to collections from the income tax (which tended to have a progressive incidence and mostly hit the middle and upper classes). Further, collections from income tax, particularly from the wealthy, were further reduced as a consequence of widespread evasion, exemptions and corruption within the system. Finally, the Court noted that the additional funds would be spent on security rather than social spending, and that the poverty and indigence rates had risen sharply in Colombia in recent years.[74] The Court also noted that the Colombian context was quite different from the European one, where '[VAT] tax had been generalised in the context of a very developed social welfare net'.[75] These factors were all relevant to the proportionality analysis because they showed that the taxation of primary necessities was not a necessary way of reaching the government's goal of increasing revenue, and was a particularly burdensome route for the poor.[76]

As in the second salary case, the proportionality analysis in the VAT case was carried out in light of the constitutional principle of a social state of law and the right to a vital minimum. The Court held that the State has an obligation to take action to 'provide a dignified life for the entire population' and the 'public spending plays a clearly redistributive role' in that process.[77] Specifically in the tax realm, the principle of a social state of law underpinned constitutional obligations to create an 'efficient, equitable, and progressive' tax code.[78] The Court emphasised that the taxation of

[73] *Ibid.*, (noting that the provision was not in the original proposal but was instead introduced by the executive in order to attend to unanticipated fiscal needs at the last minute, and was not the subject of deliberation by Congress).

[74] *Ibid.*, §§ 4.5.5.1–4.5.5.5 (reviewing basic characteristics of the socio-economic context and the taxation system).

[75] *Ibid.*, § 4.5.6.1.

[76] *Ibid.*, ('The Court finds that the decision to tax all goods and services of primary necessity, without weighing considerations about the concrete implications of the imposition of the respective tax in light of the principles of the tax system, was indiscriminate and lacked the minimum public deliberation to allow the extension of the VAT base against the arguments previously explained … in order to promote real and effective equality').

[77] *Ibid.*, § 4.5.3.3.1.

[78] Constitution of Colombia, art. 363 ('The taxation system is founded on the principles of equity, efficiency, and progressiveness. Taxation laws may not be applied retroactively').

primary necessities would 'put persons with few resources at grave risk' by, for the first time, placing a tax on items that the poor would need to consume, such as food, housing and transportation. It thus taxed 'goods and services that are necessary to conserve a dignified life and which cannot be avoided without depriving [people] of them or substituting other goods taxed at an equal or higher rate'.[79]

These decisions show the Court using a targeted approach that viewed proportionality analysis in light of the right to a vital minimum and the constitutional principle of a social state of law.[80] The vital minimum in particular gave substance to the proportionality analysis by forcing the State to satisfy a particularly heavy burden of proof when harming the poor through spending cuts or increased taxes. In essence, the vital minimum doctrine acted as the substantive principle underlying the proportionality analysis by telling the Court that austerity measures primarily impacting the poor were particularly problematic.

Proportionality review and the minimum core did not appear to be viewed by the Court as antagonistic concepts. Instead, they were seen as complementary and as playing distinct roles; the minimum core was critical in interpreting the socio-economic rights at issue, giving them clearer content by requiring prioritisation of the interests of the poor. Proportionality was then used at a subsequent stage in order to compare the infringement on the socio-economic rights with the government's justification.

These decisions also avoided the political pushback caused by the housing and first salary decision. They had smaller effects on the budget and gave the authorities more flexibility for action, while protecting the most vulnerable.[81] Further, rhetorically the Court captured solid ground that

[79] C-776 of 2003, § 4.5.6.1.

[80] As noted by Uprimny and Guarnizo, the Court has at times utilised other approaches to reviewing austerity measures and programme cuts. For example, in some cases involving cuts to pensions and other programmes it has either rendered these rights untouchable or held that they were 'mere expectations' that received no protection. See R. Uprimny and D. Guarnizo, 'Es posible una dogmatica adecuada sobre la prohibicion de regresividad? Un enfoque desde la jurisprudencia constitucional colombiana' (unpublished Working Paper, June 2006), www.dejusticia.org/index.php?modo=interna&tema=derechos_sociales&publicacion=180, last accessed 28 September 2013. They argue convincingly that these approaches require courts to undertake difficult line-drawing between different types of programmes, and threaten to leave petitioners with either no protection or rigid protection that makes it impossible for the State to respond to changing macroeconomic circumstances. The approach considered in this chapter has, however, been the one primarily followed by the Court in this area.

[81] As an example of the increased flexibility on macroeconomic matters, consider Decision C-038 of 2004, which considered sweeping changes to the laws governing workers' rights.

was difficult for its critics to dispute – it was problematic for state officials to openly deride the maintenance of a minimum level of subsistence for the impoverished. As we will see in the next section, the Court has at times used similar targeting to justify its structural interventions in the displaced persons and health realms.

V. The vital minimum and structural interventions for the poor

The Court's targeted review of austerity measures in light of the social state of law and vital minimum doctrines has played a key role in giving the State the flexibility to respond to crises while protecting its most vulnerable citizens. But in a country like Colombia, which continues to battle a serious poverty problem, protection of the poor via maintenance of the status quo is insufficient.[82] The Court has also needed to nudge the State into creating new programmes and improving existing ones. In so doing, the interaction between the vital minimum doctrine and the Court's creative use of structural remedies is critically important.

The Court has no explicit constitutional power to issue complex structural orders involving groups of people, as its listed powers are limited to reviewing laws abstractly (the public action of unconstitutionality) and revising *tutela* judgments filed by individual petitioners.[83] However, the Court has developed mechanisms stemming from its inherent powers to enforce the Constitution. The Court can aggregate *tutela* claims filed by separate petitioners for the purposes of adjudication.[84] It can also issue 'complex' orders aimed at tackling a problem systematically, rather than simply giving a remedy to the individual petitioner.[85] Most importantly,

Generally speaking, the law made the hiring, firing and regulation of workers more flexible by, for example, making workers easier and less expensive to terminate and altering the definition of a working day. See C-038 of 2004, § II (giving the text of the legal changes in question). In applying proportionality analysis, the Court noted the empirical difficulty of determining the effect of the changes in question on the economy and on the situations of workers, and thus upheld them. The case is discussed extensively in Uprimny and Guarnizo, 'Es possible una dogmatica adecuada', 11–12.

[82] See World Bank, 'Data: Poverty Headcount Ratio at National Poverty Line (% of Population)', http://data.worldbank.org/indicator/SI.POV.NAHC/countries/CO?display=graph, last accessed 15 January 2014 (showing that between 30 and 40 per cent of the population was below the national poverty line between 2004 and 2012).

[83] Constitution of Colombia, arts. 86 (*tutela*), 241 (public action).

[84] See, e.g., T-025 of 2004 (aggregating a large number of individual claims for purposes of adjudication).

[85] See, e.g., T-291 of 2009, § 9 (in a case involving 'informal recyclers' who make their living sifting through a trash dump, distinguishing simple orders dealing with the individual

in the 1990s it developed the concept of the 'state of unconstitutional conditions'. This doctrine is used when state policy on a certain issue is fundamentally flawed because of structural failures in state policy, and those structural failures have led to massive violations of constitutional rights held by large numbers of people.[86] The concept of a 'state of unconstitutional conditions' (sometimes referred to as an 'unconstitutional state of affairs') is often paired with other devices such as the aggregation of a large number of individual claims, the use of complex remedies and the maintenance of jurisdiction over a case for the purposes of monitoring and issuing follow-up orders.[87] In that sense, it closely resembles the American structural injunction used in cases like the school desegregation litigation following *Brown* v. *Board of Education*.[88]

The concept of a state of unconstitutional conditions has been used for prison conditions, pensions in parts of the country and the system of notaries, but the most famous example involved internally displaced persons (IDPs).[89] Colombia has around five million internally displaced persons – refugees from endemic violence still living elsewhere in the country, generally exiled to the big cities.[90] The Congress passed a law addressing the problem in the 1990s, but the State in practice paid relatively little attention to these groups despite their obvious and significant needs.[91]

In 2004, the Court aggregated a large number of individual *tutela* actions and held that the government's failure to have a coordinated public

petitioners from complex orders intended to give all of those in the same situation as the petitioners relief).

86 Uprimny, 'The Enforcement of Social Rights', pp. 134–5 (outlining the usage of the doctrine in the prisons and displaced persons cases). The Court has stated that this doctrine is a consequence of the 'social state of law' principle, because that principle requires that the Court act to ensure the 'effective, not theoretical, enjoyment of fundamental rights'. T-025 of 2004, § III.8.

87 For example, all of these techniques were used together in the inernally displaced persons case, T-025 of 2004, and its various follow-up orders.

88 For a classic treatment of structural injunctions in the United States, see D. Horowitz, *The Courts and Social Policy* (Washington, DC: Brookings, 1977).

89 T-153 of 1998 (prisons); SU-090 of 2000 (pensions); C-373 of 2002 (notaries); T-025 of 2004 (internally displaced persons).

90 International Displacement Monitoring Center, 'Global Statistics', www.internal-displacement.org/8025708F004CE90B/(httpPages)/22FB1D4E2B196DAA802570BB005E787C?OpenDocument, last accessed 15 January 2014 (reporting a government figure of 4.9 million and a figure from a domestic organisation of approximately 5.5 million).

91 A. M. Ibanez and A. Velasquez, *La politica publica para atender para la poblacion desplazada: Cuales deben ser las funciones de las autoridades locales?* (Bern: Brookings, 2008), pp. 4–5.

policy constituted 'an unconstitutional state of conditions' that justified a broad structural order.[92] Critical to the Court's reasoning was the finding that the State, in various ways, was failing to ensure that the right to a vital minimum was met for members of these groups by ensuring that they had access to emergency relief, housing, access to health care and work, and along other dimensions.[93] The Court also noted that the social state of law principle required that the State take action to 'correct the visible social inequalities, to facilitate inclusion and participation of weak, marginalised and vulnerable sectors in the economic and social life of the nation, and to stimulate progressive improvement of the material conditions of existence for the most depressed sectors of society'.[94]

The Court has since maintained jurisdiction over the case, issuing hundreds of follow-up orders and holding regular public hearings involving representatives of civil society and the State.[95] An important innovation in the displaced persons case was the creation of a 'Monitoring Commission' composed of different civil society groups as well as ex-judges of the Court. The Commission has played a critical role in carrying out empirical investigations, feeding the Court information and in formulating policy ideas that have subsequently been adopted by the Court.[96] Progress in the displaced persons area has been slow and uneven, but genuine advances have been made. As documented by Rodríguez Garavito and Rodríguez Franco, the Court's decision led to large increases in the budget and in the visibility of the issue in public fora.[97] Moreover, the Court cajoled the State into creating a coordinated bureaucracy on the topic. Finally, certain policy areas have seen substantial advances, although progress on others has lagged.[98]

This kind of complex structural intervention also played a key role during the more recent economic downturn, with regard to the right to health. The

92 T-025 of 2004. 93 *Ibid.*, § III.6.3.4.1. 94 *Ibid.*, § III.8.1.

95 For a list of key follow-up orders as of 2010, see C. R. Garavito and D. R. Franco, *Cortes y cambio social: Cómo la Corte Constitucional transformo el dezplamiento forzado en Colombia* (Bogota: Dejusticia, 2010), pp. 88–9. For an overview of the model, see C. R. Garavito, 'Beyond the Courtroom: The Impact of Judicial Activism on Socio-economic Rights in Latin America', *Texas Law Review*, 89 (2011), 1669–98, 1682–88.

96 D. Landau, 'The Reality of Social Rights Enforcement', *Harvard International Law Journal*, 53 (2012), 189–247, 227–8.

97 Garavito and Franco, *Cortes y cambio social*, pp. 97–100 (documenting increased visibility in the press following the decision), 211–14 (documenting huge increases in the budget following the decision).

98 *Ibid.*, pp. 247–72 (summarising the statistical impact of the decision on the displaced population).

2008 global financial crisis caused a shallower retrenchment in Colombia than in many other countries, and a much less significant slowdown than the steep decline of the late 1990s. As Figure 9.1 shows, GDP growth grew 6.9 per cent in 2007 but slowed sharply to 3.5 per cent in 2008 and 1.7 per cent in 2009, while unemployment rose somewhat and hit 13 per cent in early 2010.[99] The economy recovered fairly quickly, as growth rebounded in 2010 and 2011. Nonetheless, the crisis did have some important impacts on the Colombian economy – it exacerbated budget deficits and had at least a modest impact on social spending.[100] Further, the slowdown occurred during the administration of a president, Alvaro Uribe, who was sometimes seen as prioritising defence spending over social spending.[101]

Unlike the crisis of the 1990s, the Court did not see a sudden spike in *tutelas*, but instead a continuation of the long-term increases in its caseload and particularly in the number of cases dealing with the enforcement of socio-economic rights. As shown in Figure 9.3, the number of *tutelas* dealing with the right to health has soared in the past ten years, and the percentage of cases dealing with health rights at times reached close to a quarter of the cases filed.[102]

That system relies on the provision of health care benefits by regulated private entities (called EPSs) who are required to offer a governmentally defined package of benefits (called the POS) to their beneficiaries.[103] There are two separate systems with two distinct packages of benefits – a

[99] Departamento Administrativo Nacional de Estadistica (DANE), 'Buletin de prensa noviembre 2013: Anexos, Gran encuesta integrada de hogares' (serie mensual 01–13), www.dane.gov.co/files/investigaciones/fichas/empleo/Anexos_Comision_GEIH.pdf, last accessed 15 January 2014 (noting an unemployment rate over 14 per cent in January 2010).

[100] See A. Escobar and M. Olivera, 'Gasto Publico y Movilidad y Equidad Social' (Documentos CEDE 09, 2009), 8, fig.2 (showing that central government social spending dropped as a percentage of GDP between 2009 and 2010, although most of that drop was concentrated on pensions); World Bank, *International Debt Statistics 2013* (Washington, DC: World Bank, 2013), p. 104 (showing that debt as a percentage of gross national product increased sharply between 2008 and 2009 after falling steadily since 2000).

[101] C. G. Hernandez, 'Neopopulismo en Colombia: el caso del gobierno de Alvaro Uribe Velez', *Iconos: Revista de Ciencias Sociales*, 27 (2007), 147–62, 160, www.flacso.org.ec/docs/i27galindo.pdf, last accessed 28 September 2013 (finding that the Uribe 'democratic security' strategy had the effect of 'forcing important resources (which could have been oriented towards social spending) to be used on the intensification of the war against terrorism').

[102] Defensoria del Pueblo, 'La Tutela y El Derecho a la Salud 2011', 102, tbl. 7.

[103] For an overview of the system and its problems, see A. E. Yamin and O. Parra-Vera, 'Judicial Protection of the Right to Health in Colombia: From Social Demands to

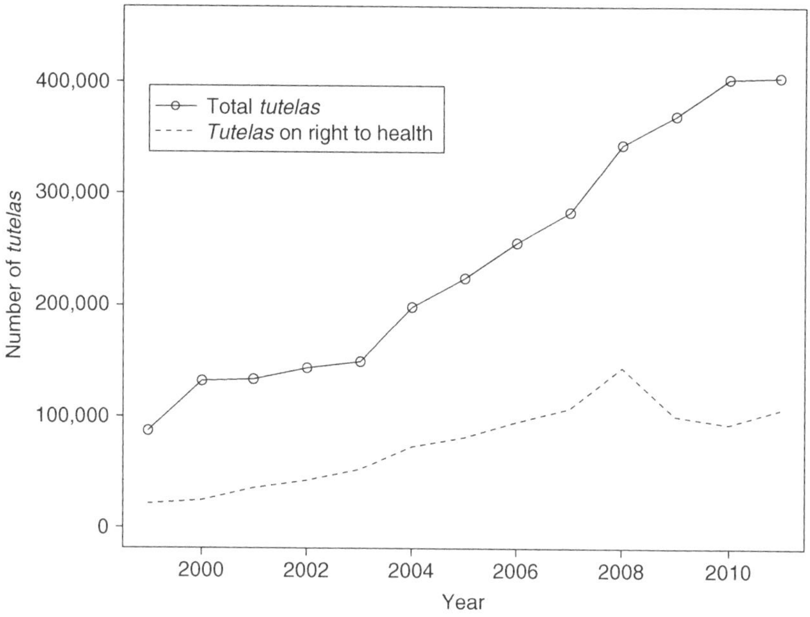

Figure 9.3 Total *tutelas* and health *tutelas* (1999–2011)

contributory system with a larger POS for those with employment in the formal sector, and a subsidised system with a smaller POS for those without it. The contributory system has always represented a minority of the population, and a large number of citizens historically belonged to neither regime, although coverage has improved sharply in recent years.[104] Although the relevant statutes indicated that the two regimes should have the same POS within a set period of time, they in fact had never been equalised, so that in practice the subsidised POS for the poor was greatly inferior to the contributory POS for those with economic resources and formal sector jobs.[105]

Individual Claims to Public Debates', *Hastings International and Comparative Law Review*, 33 (2010), 431–59, 433–45.

[104] Recent official statistics show that around 90 per cent of citizens have at least formally been affiliated with one or another of the two regimes, although critics complain that many citizens continue to lack effective access to health care. See Ministerio de Salud y Proteccion Social, 'Cobertura en salud ano 2012', www.minsalud.gov.co/salud/Paginas/CoberturasdelR%C3%A9gimenSubsidiado.aspx, last accessed 28 September 2013.

[105] Yamin and Parra-Vera, 'Judicial Protection of the Right to Health', 447–8.

The explosion in health litigation has been driven by a few major factors. First, many important but costly treatments – forms of cancer treatment, etc. – were left wholly outside of the POS, so litigants sought *tutelas* in order to compel their provision. The Court has held that necessary non-POS treatment would be paid for with state funds, rather than by EPSs. Second, the content of the POS was often unclear, so litigants and health insurers often did not know whether a given treatment was covered. Third, governmental regulation of the EPSs has been inadequate, so companies often have denied even clearly covered treatments and forced patients to accede to the courts should they want a remedy.[106]

Statistics have shown that petitioners almost always win these cases – according to the Ombudsman's office, about 80 per cent of such claims succeeded in the first instance in 2010 and 2011.[107] Further, there is a considerable class bias in the question of who sues, despite the ease of filing *tutelas*. A study by the Attorney General's Office found that more than half of all *tutelas* invoking the right to health were filed by the minority of the population that belongs to the contributory regime and thus who hold formal sector employment.[108] Furthermore, these decisions have not improved the overall management of the health care system – the health care providers often continue to deny services to affiliates and simply wait for these affiliates to decide whether or not they want to sue.[109] Thus, those who utilise the *tutela* – who are often relatively affluent – get access to services while others do not. In that sense, the flood of individual decisions has been in some tension with the concept of the 'vital minimum' aimed at prioritising the needs of the poorest.

The Court made a significant effort to respond to these problems in late 2008, when it issued decision T-760 and granted a series of general orders dealing with the health care system. On this occasion, the Court did not use the language of a state of unconstitutional conditions, but it aggregated a large number of claims, issued complex structural remedies

[106] The majority of claims were in fact for items that should have been covered by insurance. See Defensoria del Pueblo, 'La Tutela y El Derecho a la Salud 2011', 83 (finding that 65 per cent of *tutelas* on the right to health in 2010 corresponded to items included in the POS).

[107] *Ibid.*, 109, tbl. 10.

[108] Procuraduria General de la Nación & Dejusticia, 'El derecho a la salud en perspectivade de derechos humanos y el sistema de inspección, vigilancia y control del estado Colombiano en materia de quejas en salud' (2008), 171.

[109] Landau, 'Reality of Social Rights Enforcement', 214–15 (noting some systematic changes in the composition of the POS due to individualised judgments but that health insurers continued to deny a large number of meritorious claims).

and has maintained jurisdiction over the case by filing a large number of follow-up orders.[110] Among the complex orders issued in the decision, a key one required the equalisation of the POS between contributory and subsidised plans.[111] Others required the authorities to clarify and reassess the contents of the POS, and to improve the system of state financing for non-POS treatments that were needed to preserve the life or health of the petitioner.[112]

The decision is important for its reasoning about the nature of socio-economic rights. In it, the Court confirmed that the right to health could be held fundamental in and of itself and thus enforceable via *tutela* directly in many cases, without needing to be linked to other rights like the right to life or the principle of human dignity.[113] This reasoning was closely linked to the Court's conceptions of the right to a vital minimum and the social state of law principle. The right to a vital minimum helped to determine when the right would be enforceable by *tutela* – 'the grade of health that can be protected by any person immediately by the State, is the protection of "a vital minimum, outside of which, organic deterioration impedes a normal life" '.[114] Further, the Court explained that the social state of law principle required that the State take action to move rapidly towards the unification of the contributory and subsidised POS: 'The progressive nature of a right does not justify standing still nor much less forgetting the mandate to unify beneficiary plans in order to avoid subjecting persons with low incomes to inferior constitutional protection, which is openly inadmissible in a social state of law'.[115] At the very least, the Court explained, the Constitution demanded that the State develop a plan to unify the two types of POS in the near term.

[110] For an overview, see Yamin and Parra-Vera, 'Judicial Protection of the Right to Health', 445–55.

[111] T-760 of 2008, § 6.1.2. [112] *Ibid.*, §§ 6.1.1., 6.2.

[113] *Ibid.*, § 3. This argument had been made in some prior *tutela* decisions collected in T-760, see *ibid.*, § 3.2.5, but the Court's confirmation of it in a major structural case was notable.

[114] *Ibid.*, § 3.2.4. As in other areas, the economic resources of the petitioner were important to this determination. The Court noted however that health was in some ways distinct from other areas because of the often very high cost of services. For example, it noted that it 'had protected the right to health of persons with a not insignificant income and wealth, whenever the cost of the required health services disproportionately affects the economic stability of the person'. *Ibid.*, § 4.4.5.3. It gave as examples cases where the petitioner would regularly need treatments costing more than half her income, or where she would require a one-time treatment costing double her income. See *ibid.*

[115] *Ibid.*, § 6.1.2.1.1.

In the midst of the economic slowdown of 2009, the conservative Uribe government did not embrace this ruling. The decision, coupled with the economic crisis, impelled the administration to issue a declaration of a state of economic, social and ecological emergency in health, thus giving the administration the power to bypass Congress and issue decrees with force of law.[116] Some of its decrees issued during the state of emergency attempted to pump new revenue into the system by creating new taxes and by taking measures to limit fraud. But many others essentially circumvented the decision by, for example, preventing treatments outside of the package of benefits from being covered under most circumstances, redefining the POS to cover fewer services and limiting access to the *tutela*.[117]

This declaration of emergency was widely criticised by health care providers, the press and even politicians close to the administration.[118] The critics argued that the administration was trying to undermine the right to health and the Court's decision rather than complying with it, and they noted that the decrees were issued without sufficient debate or democratic deliberation. Uribe himself was forced to distance himself from some of the decrees, for example the one stating that patients should rely on their own savings rather than state funds to pay for treatments outside of the POS.[119] The Court in turn responded by unanimously striking down the declaration of a state of emergency, although a majority left the new revenues intact temporarily.[120] The Court held that the problems in the health system leading to the declaration were chronic and structural in nature

116 Yamin and Parra-Vera, 'Judicial Protection of the Right to Health', 453–5.

117 *Ibid.*

118 'Decretos de emergencia social se metieron al debate presidencial', *El Tiempo* (2 February 2010), www.eltiempo.com/archivo/documento/MAM-3820854, last accessed 28 September 2013 (giving the criticisms of various presidential candidates of the decision); 'Pese a la lluvia, en Cali se protesto por la emergencia social', *El Tiempo* (6 February 2010), www.eltiempo.com/archivo/documento/CMS-7135487, last accessed 28 September 2013 (recounting a protest march by health care providers and others in Cali); K. G. Young and J. Lemaitre, 'The Comparative Fortunes of the Right to Health: Two Tales of Justiciability in Colombia and South Africa', *Harvard Human Rights Journal*, 26 (2013), 179–216, 192–5 (recounting protests against the decree measures).

119 'Solo los estratos 5 y 7 podran usar las cesantias para salud', *El Tiempo* (6 February 2010), www.eltiempo.com/archivo/documento/MAM-3826761, last accessed 28 September 2013 (summarising a Uribe statement that only the wealthy should be forced to rely on savings to fund non-POS treatments, and that if this was not what the decree said, then it should be repealed by Congress).

120 C-252 of 2010. The Court upheld the new revenues despite striking down the emergency because it held that the 'seriousness of the facts' justified a modulated decision. *Ibid.*, § 7.3.

rather than being caused by a sudden emergency, and that the proper response to such problems was congressional legislation rather than a declaration of economic, social and ecological emergency. Even those justices who were nominated by and close to Uribe, such as his former legal secretary, voted to strike down the declaration.

In the longer term, the decision has proven even tougher for the Court to enforce than the displaced persons case. The Court has issued numerous orders dealing with the enforcement of the decision, held regular public hearings and hired a number of staffers working only on this case.[121] It has not had as much success rallying civil society behind its cause.[122] Nonetheless, the decision has achieved some real results for poorer Colombians – in 2012, the government finally unified the POS, giving all Colombians, whether in the subsidised or contributory regime, access to the same benefits.[123] The decision appears also to at least have limited the growth in the flood of individual *tutelas*, which have fallen from a peak of 42 per cent of all *tutelas* in 2008 to only 26 per cent in 2011.[124] Thus, the Court's structural remedy seems to have helped the Court to manage the large number of individual claims that was exacerbated by the economic crisis.[125]

VI. Conclusions: the value of the minimum core and the Colombian model

Judicial responses to economic crisis are contextual, and one should be cautious about extrapolating too easily from the Colombian case. There are, for example, numerous and obvious differences between the Colombian context and the European countries currently experiencing sweeping fiscal austerity. Nonetheless, there are important and

[121] Rodriguez-Garavito, 'Beyond the Courtroom', 1675. There is still a sense of 'crisis' hanging over the health care system. Young and Lemaitre, 'Comparative Fortunes of the Right to Health', 196–7.

[122] Yamin and Parra-Vera, 'Judicial Protection of the Right to Health', 459.

[123] 'Estos son los retos de la unificacion del Plan Obligatorio de Salud', *El Tiempo* (2 July 2012), www.eltiempo.com/archivo/documento/CMS-11990418, last accessed 28 September 2013.

[124] Defensoria del Pueblo, 'La Tutela y El Derecho a la Salud 2011', 102 tbl.7.

[125] In other areas, the Court has issued structural remedies on a smaller scale to aid marginalised groups. For example, in 2009, the Court issued a decision disallowing the city of Cali from barring 'informal recyclers' who make their living sifting through trash from gaining access to the trash. It also issued structural orders requiring the State to offer economic resources, training and other support to all the members of this group, which is among the most marginalised in Colombian society. T-291 of 2009.

generalisable lessons from the rich, evolving Colombian jurisprudence on socio-economic rights, and the approach adopted by the Colombian Court may be very useful as a model for courts in both the developing and developed worlds.

The Colombian case shows that courts reviewing austerity measures can adopt an approach that both has real bite and yet is politically and economically sustainable. Deferring to all cuts imposed by government may read socio-economic rights out of the constitution, while freezing the status quo and striking down all social protection cuts during a crisis may risk political backlash against the judiciary, as occurred after the Colombian salary decision. The more recent Colombian experience demonstrates a targeted form of review that allows fiscal considerations to be taken into account but also provides protection for vulnerable populations. The 'social state of law' doctrine does not coerce the State into adopting any single model of social welfare, but it does have important consequences for the way in which that model is both constructed and affected during economic downturns.

More specifically, the Colombian Court's experience with regard to the vital minimum doctrine suggests a doctrinal model for judicial review of austerity measures that may run across countries. The minimum core is a contested concept in comparative and international law. The Committee on Economic, Social and Cultural Rights in its General Comment No. 3 defined it as 'the obligation to ensure the satisfaction of, at the very least, minimum essential levels of each of the rights' and noted that 'in order for a State Party to be able to attribute its failure to meet at least its minimum core obligations to a lack of available resources it must demonstrate that every effort has been made to use all resources that are at its disposition in an effort to satisfy, as a matter of priority, those minimum obligations'.[126]

Not all courts that have enforced socio-economic rights in the context of resource constraints (which was a key element of the Colombian crisis jurisprudence) have adopted a minimum core approach. For instance, the South African Constitutional Court has rejected the use of the concept in several prominent cases in favour of a 'reasonableness' approach, holding that it would be impossible to define what the content of the minimum core is with respect to rights like the right to housing and the right to water, and that making those judgments would involve the court in

[126] CESCR, 'General Comment No. 3', para. 10.

fundamentally political judgments better left to the other branches.[127] Similarly, scholarly critics of the doctrine argue both that the minimum core is indeterminate and that it violates accepted notions of the separation of powers and the role of a court in a democracy.[128]

In contrast, the Colombian experience suggests that the minimum core can be seen, as David Bilchitz has argued, as a prioritisation device rather than as a requirement to define a set level of enjoyment of each discrete right.[129] It means that cuts to government programmes and failures to create programmes will be subject to an especially substantial burden of justification when they impact the most vulnerable citizens. Such a usage weakens the indeterminacy objection because it means that judges need not set arbitrary quantities of socio-economic goods and make those quantities intangible during a crisis. Instead, they can merely issue orders that demand higher burdens of justification for either cuts affecting the poorest or a refusal to construct programmes that would benefit these groups. Moreover, that usage weakens the separation of powers objection by showing how the use of the minimum core can restrain and target judicial power in many contexts, rather than enhancing it.

[127] See, e.g., *Mazibuko* v. *City of Johannesburg*, 2010 (3) BCLR 239 (CC), paras. 52–66 (noting that the Court has consistently rejected a minimum core approach because of textual and separation of powers concerns). For more on the South African experience, see Pillay and Wesson's contribution to this volume.

[128] K. G. Young, 'The Minimum Core of Social and Economic Rights: A Concept in Search of Content', *Yale Journal of International Law*, 33 (2008), 113–75 (arguing that the minimum core is a largely indeterminate concept); C. Steinberg, 'Can Reasonableness Protect the Poor?: A Review of South Africa's Socio-Economic Rights Jurisprudence', *South African Law Journal*, 123 (2006), 264–84, 274–6 (arguing that the South African Court's reasonableness approach is more 'democracy-promoting' approach than a minimum core approach because it leaves more room for dialogue); R. Dixon, 'Creating Dialogue About Socioeconomic Rights: Strong-Form vs. Weak-Form Review', *International Journal of Constitutional Law*, 5 (2007), 391–418, 416–17 (arguing that certain uses of the minimum core concept by courts may cut off legitimate dialogue about what it ought to mean); M. S. Kende, *Constitutional Rights in Two Worlds: South Africa and the United States* (New York: Cambridge University Press, 2009), pp. 261–5 (rejecting a minimum core approach as unworkable, contrary to the intent of the framers, and on separation of powers grounds). For an excellent overview of the debate on 'reasonableness' vs the minimum core in the South African context, see S. Liebenberg, 'Socio-Economic Rights: Revisiting the Reasonableness/Minimum Core Debate' in S. Woolman and M. Bishop (eds.), *Constitutional Conversations* (Pretoria University Law Press, 2008), pp. 303–329, p. 305.

[129] See, e.g., Bilchitz, *Poverty and Fundamental Rights*, p. 208 ('The first important point to recognize is that the minimum core approach is a means of specifying priorities'). Bilchitz argues that the correct understanding or 'priority' in this context is a 'weighted priority' giving the minimum core 'special attention' rather than a 'lexical priority' requiring that all governmental efforts be devoted to ensuring the minimum core before

The Colombian jurisprudence appears to view a minimum core approach as compatible with proportionality review, rather than, as often presented in the literature, as an opposing principle.[130] The Colombian Constitutional Court envisions the minimum core as working at a prior stage to proportionality. The minimum core plays a prioritisation function that allows the Court to give substantive content to socio-economic rights. Proportionality functions in the jurisprudence at a subsequent stage, as a way to compare the infringement of a socio-economic right to the opposing constitutional right, principle or interest that is stated as a justification for the infringement. The issue of whether the minimum core and proportionality can in fact be philosophically reconciled is a difficult one that requires further work (and which depends in part on how the minimum core is defined).[131] Further, the minimum core may not exhaust the justiciable content of socio-economic rights at all times and in all places.[132] But the jurisprudence of the Colombian Constitutional Court suggests that the minimum core can be a powerful tool for exercising effective control over state austerity measures, for ensuring that relief is targeted towards the poorest, and for keeping review within reasonable bounds that may avoid backlash.

other activities be undertaken. *Ibid.*, pp. 208–13. This conception appears similar to the Colombian understanding of the vital minimum.

130 For example, Contiades and Fontiadou argue that proportionality review is superior to the minimum core approach because a minimum core approach requires that judges first define an intangible core of socio-economic rights, which they are unlikely to be willing to do. X. Contiades and A. Fotiadou, 'Social Rights in the Age of Proportionality: Global Economic Crisis and Constitutional Litigation', *International Journal of Constitutional Law*, 10 (2012), 660–86, 670 ('Subjecting social rights in a rationale shared with civil and political rights through the use of proportionality, that is subjecting them to the narrative of proportionality which is becoming a constitutional Esperanto, solidifies the content of social rights more than a unending struggle to settle for a minimum core').

131 If the minimum core, once identified, is always protected and may not be balanced against competing rights or interests, then it is incompatible with proportionality review. *Ibid*, 661 ('Do social rights have an inviolable minimum core that may not be limited by the legislator and may not be subjected to any balancing with competing rights and interests?').

132 Some commentators argue that a minimum core approach may be under-protective, particularly in developed societies, because it gives the State room to undertake draconian austerity measures that infringe on important interests but do not touch the minimum core. See C. Bernal, 'The Structure of Proportionality for the Adjudication of Positive Socio-Economic Rights' (in draft, manuscript on file with author) (arguing that socio-economic rights, prima facie, are best understood as including a 'highest reasonable level of satisfaction', that is as more than a minimum core but less than a conceivable maximum).

A comparison between the Court's initial and later responses to the economic crisis of the late 1990s is illustrative of the targeting role that a well-defined minimum core approach can play. The Court initially undertook interventions on the housing finance and salary issues that were dramatic responses to crisis but not well-targeted in terms of the vital minimum doctrine. In the first salary case, for example, the Court invoked the right to a vital minimum to protect the real value of salaries even of government workers earning high wages. It is clear that the benefits in the housing and first salary cases were slanted towards the relatively affluent. Moreover, these are decisions that had significant macroeconomic effects and thus provoked a strong political reaction. Neither the identity of the beneficiaries nor the size of the macroeconomic effects automatically render the housing and salary decisions unjustifiable, but these factors do show the problems that can arise with excessively broad judicial interventions to protect socio-economic rights during times of austerity.

In contrast, after the Court turned over in 2000, it adopted an approach that put more emphasis on the minimum core. In the second salary and VAT tax cases, the State was given broad latitude to alter benefits and tax burdens for the relatively affluent. But it was subject to much stricter scrutiny when it tried to reduce the real value of salaries or raise tax rates in ways that would have substantial effects on the marginalised. The result of this was a way of reviewing austerity measures that protected vulnerable populations and gave the social state of law principle teeth, without preventing the State from responding to economic crisis or provoking large-scale political backlash. This kind of targeted review of austerity measures may be appropriate in the face of austerity even in different contexts, such as Europe.

Finally, the Colombian case highlights the importance of remedial creativity for effective judicial responses to economic crisis. The Court often achieved its best results when using remedies aggressively and creatively, with the 'state of unconstitutional conditions' doctrine and the use of structural injunctions. These remedies are costly and can be politically problematic, but in Colombia they also transformed substantial areas of state policy and achieved results for impoverished and marginalised individuals who rarely bring *tutela* suits on their own. In contrast, the Court's frequent use of a simpler individual remedy model, where a single petitioner receives a single remedy such as access to a medical treatment, proved quick and easy to apply but less effective at altering bureaucratic practice. More complex remedies proved necessary to deal effectively with social problems during economic crises, particularly for the benefit of the poor.

In short, the Colombian Constitutional Court has increasingly evolved towards a position where it has effectively protected vulnerable citizens and even expanded the social safety net, in the face of two economic crises and corresponding austerity measures. At the core of this effort is the vital minimum doctrine, which has served as a kind of lodestar for the Court, targeting its efforts towards the most vulnerable members of society. It has allowed the Court to review austerity measures in a meaningful way without depriving the State of the room to respond to true fiscal crisis, and it has also been used, in conjunction with bold and creative remedies, to encourage the State to spend scarce resources on improving social programmes for the poor. In comparative terms, the Colombian experience should give us at least some optimism that courts can play an effective and sustainable role in protecting and expanding safety nets during times of crisis.

10

Economic and social rights and the Supreme Court of Argentina in the decade following the 2001–2003 crisis

GUSTAVO MAURINO AND EZEQUIEL NINO

I. Introduction

This chapter examines the work of the Supreme Court of Argentina pertaining to economic and social rights (ESR) since 2001. In doing so, it focuses in particular on the way in which the Court dealt with the extreme socio-economic and political crisis of 2001–3.

Argentina included many ESR in its 1994 Constitution, which also provided for collective suits to enable such rights to be claimed, as well as incorporating human rights treaties as part of the bill of rights. The Supreme Court of Argentina's interpretation of these new provisions began in the late 1990s and, shortly afterwards, the country was confronted by a crisis which had a tremendous impact on disadvantaged communities and markedly increased inequality.

The decade or so since 2001 constitutes an important period in terms of analysing the impact of the economic emergencies on the way in which the Supreme Court constructed its approach to ESR. The cyclical dynamics of the economy provide an interesting backdrop for this study, permitting an exploration of the way in which the judiciary adapted to the rapidly changing context when adjudicating ESR. Furthermore, the composition of the Supreme Court was almost completely renewed in 2003 and 2004 after its most conservative members were impeached or forced to resign because of their extremely close relationship with the executive branch and a lack of transparency in the Court's functioning.[1]

The authors would like to strongly thank Mishkila Rojas and Andrew Lyubarsky for their invaluable help.

[1] To facilitate the descriptions included in this chapter, we will refer to this new composition of the tribunal as the 'new' Court as opposed to the 'old' or 'previous' Court.

This state of affairs allows for a comparison between, on the one hand, the Court's decisions immediately after its reconstitution during the peak of the crisis and its more recent rulings on ESR, including an evaluation of the extent to which the Court has evolved in terms of adopting an expansive or restrictive approach towards ESR suits over time and in contexts of varying resource constraint.

This chapter is structured around, first, a historical account of the central events of the 2001 social and economic crisis and the policies that were adopted at that time, contextualised in terms of the Argentine constitutional framework and the institutional configuration of its judicial branch. Second, it discusses the most significant ESR rulings issued from 2001 on. In doing so, it focuses in particular on two categories of issues. It begins by analysing the decisions of the Supreme Court regarding the scope of the ESR of socio-economically disadvantaged populations, who were more harshly affected by the crisis than anyone else. The chapter then addresses the Court's approach to restrictions on ownership and other rights of an economic nature which were affected by regulations relating to salaries, pensions, personal savings and private contracts ordered by Congress and the executive branch in response to crisis-caused resource constraints. These two jurisprudential areas encompass the most representative spectrum of cases that the Supreme Court dealt with relating to the crisis, and are of special interest with regard to evaluating this tribunal's role in the exceptional process that Argentina has undergone since 2001.

The property rights decisions are directly linked to the crisis since they concern policies that were introduced by the political branches to cut state spending just before and after the December 2001 crisis in an effort to make the country's financial situation more viable. In contrast, the Court did not explicitly address the crisis context in its decision-making in the ESR cases, leaving no express statements on the dockets that reveal the judges' view of the appropriate judicial role to be adopted to such rights in times of economic crisis. However, these judgments do provide a sense of how the Court dealt with ESR during the worst period in Argentina's history from a financial perspective, including the treatment accorded by that tribunal to people who were left behind in socio-economic terms, and its willingness to engage with such rights in periods of severe resource constraints.

This work aims to offer some analytical elements for readers in other countries who are currently facing significant constrictions and reductions in terms of state benefits and services resulting from the international financial turbulence that began in 2008. The Argentine example may be relevant for these jurisdictions, as it depicts an experience where many of the conflicts arising from a situation of economic emergency were 'judicialised', under the framework of a Constitution that accords strong recognition to ESR.

II. The 2001 crisis and the Argentine constitutional context

A. *The development of the crisis*

Between 2001 and 2003, Argentina underwent one of its darkest periods, entering an unprecedented economic, political and social crisis. During the preceding ten years, the country had adopted a 'convertibility' regime that legally bound the Argentine peso and the United States dollar to a one dollar-one peso parity, established in order to contain the hyperinflation that struck the country in the 1980s.[2]

Over the years, this model of exchange rate overvaluation produced a loss of competitiveness and a large increase in foreign debt to compensate for the trade deficit.[3] Multilateral institutions began to impose ever harsher conditionalities on the country to renew its loans, and interest rates for private debt rose to such a level that the situation became unmanageable.[4] In turn, the government's fiscal deficit exploded in the 1990s during Carlos Menem's Peronist government. The administration led by Fernando de la Rúa of the Radical Civic Union that succeeded him in 1999 adopted a growing number of fiscal austerity measures and

[2] See Law 23.928, 27 March 1991. The core of the so-called 'Convertibility Law' consisted of the Central Bank's guarantee that at any time, any resident could exchange their pesos for dollars at a rate of 1 peso = 1 dollar. In this way, the State committed itself to not devaluating its currency and to backing up any monetary emission with anti-inflationary fiscal policies. This was the system that collapsed in 2001.

[3] M. Rapoport, *Historia Económica, Política y Social de la Argentina (1880–2003)* (Buenos Aires: EMECE, 2007), p. 135.

[4] For an analysis of the inconsistency of such programmes with the substantive conceptions of social rights recognised in the Argentine Constitution and the role of the judicial branch in litigation about these rights, especially in the early twenty-first century, see H. J. Etchicury, 'Argentina: Social Rights, Thorny Country: Judicial Review of Economic Policies Sponsored by the IFIs', *American University International Law Review*, 22 (2006), 101–25.

continued taking on more debt in a restrictive economic cycle that showed no signs of improvement.[5] In the 2001 legislative elections, the governing party was defeated and lost its majority in Congress, further weakening it against the victorious Peronist party.

In the second half of that year, a sharp drop in all socio-economic indicators reflected the depth of the crisis. The poverty rate reached 55 per cent of the population and included two-thirds of those under 18 years of age – having almost doubled in less than three years – while gross domestic product (GDP) fell by 19.5 per cent between 1998 and 2002.[6] One of the main consequences of the 2001 crisis was an increase in the unequal distribution of wealth.[7] The Gini coefficient rose from 40 in 1995 to 55 in 2002, a tremendous blow for a country that had historically been one of the region's most egalitarian.[8]

By late November 2001, repeatedly poor economic results and the increasing difficulty of servicing the country's debts translated into a rapid flight of bank deposits. In this context, large companies managed to transfer significant sums of money abroad, but small and medium-sized savers were trapped under various legal provisions[9] adopted for emergency reasons which came to be known as the 'financial *corralito*' (bank freeze):[10] in early December 2001, the government established extreme restrictions on cash withdrawals of money deposited in the banking system, permitting only the withdrawal of tiny weekly sums per person. This generated a profound discontent among the middle class, which represented almost half the population of the country.[11] On 19 December 2001, massive public protests occurred, including a mobilisation in Buenos Aires' main plaza, where violent clashes left 30 people

[5] D. Rubinzal, *Historia económica argentina (1880–2009). Desde los tiempos de Julio Argentino Roca hasta Cristina Fernández de Kirchner* (Buenos Aires: Ediciones del CCC – Universidad Nacional de Quilmes, 2010), p. 84.

[6] Rapoport, *Historia Económica, Política y Social de la Argentina*, p. 238.

[7] Centro de Estudios Latinoamericanos, Resumen de estadísticas sociales, Centro de Estudios Latinoamericanos, www.cesla.com/descargas/estadisticas-sociales.pdf, last accessed 27 November 2013.

[8] See, e.g., A. F. Blanco, 'La decadencia argentina, más pobreza, más desigualdad' (Observatorio de la Economía Latinoamericana, No. 37, January 2005), www.eumed.net/cursecon/ecolat/ar/2005/afb-deca.pdf, last accessed 27 November 2013.

[9] Law 25.561, 6 January 2002.

[10] The term 'corralito' (little corral) was coined by a radio journalist in 2001.

[11] F. Ferreira, J. Messina, J. Rigolini *et al.*, 'La movilidad económica y el crecimiento de la clase media en América Latina' (World Bank, 2013), http://bucket.lanacion.com.ar/common/anexos/Informes/94/81494.pdf, last accessed 27 November 2013.

dead at the hands of the police. In turn, many poor areas saw the looting of stores, which also provoked confrontations with security forces.

The following day, the President resigned. During the next ten days, three different people succeeded each other as provisional presidents. On 24 December 2012, one of these leaders, Alberto Rodríguez Saá, declared the suspension of payments of Argentina's foreign debt, with the support of the National Congress. But several days later, he too resigned from his post.

On 3 January 2002, the National Congress designated Senator Eduardo Duhalde as President, who would remain in this position until May 2003. On 6 January 2002, Congress put an end to the legal system of convertibility between the peso and the dollar, with the direct consequence of producing a violent devaluation of over 340 per cent.[12] At the same time, the legislators passed regulations which exchanged certificates of deposits in dollars for treasury bonds with a long-term maturity date (on average ten years). From this point on, over 100,000 lawsuits were filed against both the banks that retained deposits and the national government that had adopted these measures.[13]

After the devaluation and the pesification of deposits and debts, the country began to gain competitiveness and also benefitted from the extraordinary rise in global commodity prices (especially soy, and to a lesser degree wheat, corn and other cereals).[14] In 2003, GDP grew by 8.7 per cent and continued in a similar pattern over the following years.[15] In the same year, presidential elections were held and were won by Néstor Kirchner, who after a four-year term was succeeded by his wife Cristina Fernandez de Kirchner (currently in her second four-year term). In the ensuing years, poverty, indigence and inequality all reduced significantly – at least until 2008.[16]

In terms of Argentina's contemporary economic position, 2009 saw the international economic crisis. The growth in inflation averaging over 20 per cent annually begin to significantly impact upon the Argentine economy

[12] E. Basualdo, *Estudios de historia económica argentina. Desde mediados del Siglo XX hasta la actualidad* (Buenos Aires: Siglo XXI, 2006), pp. 52–65.

[13] 'La Corte ordenó que durante quince días solo se atiendan amparos', *Los Andes* (1 March 2002), www.losandes.com.ar/notas/2002/3/11/un-35207.asp, last accessed 15 January 2014.

[14] M. Weisbrot and L. Sandoval, 'Argentina's Economic Recovery: Policy Choices and Implications' (October 2007), www.cepr.net/documents/publications/argentina_recovery_2007_10.pdf, last accesed 27 December 2013.

[15] F. Ferreira *et al.*, 'La movilidad económica'.

[16] R. Cortes and G. Kessler, 'Políticas, ideas y expertos en la cuestión social de la Argentina democrática (1983–2012)', *Revista de Indias*, 73(257) (2013), 239–64, 251.

and there is consensus that the main socio-economic variables worsened.[17] However, the executive branch's intervention in the national statistics agency has meant that trustworthy data has been unavailable over the last three years.[18] Indeed, the International Monetary Fund (IMF) sanctioned Argentina in February 2013 for not providing accurate statistics.[19]

B. *The Argentine constitutional context*

Argentine constitutionalism was consolidated in the nineteenth century in a model consisting of liberal doctrines influenced by the American system and conservative and traditionalist traditions.[20] Since then, the Argentine Constitution has included a declaration of fundamental rights and guarantees, moulded on the basis of liberal Enlightenment principles.[21] In the mid-twentieth century, successive attempts at constitutional reform resulted in the introduction of new norms which established certain social rights, although the application of these clauses remained 'dormant' for several decades.

In 1994 Argentina underwent a profound constitutional reform.[22] At that point, the country incorporated the content of various international human rights treaties into its constitutional fundamental rights structure,[23] among them the International Covenant on Civil and Political Rights (ICCPR) and the International Covenant on Economic, Social and

17 F. Gatto, 'Crecimiento económico y desigualdades territoriales: algunos límites estructurales para lograr una mayor equidad' in B. Kosacoff (ed.), *Crisis, recuperación y nuevos dilemas. La economía argentina 2002–2007* (Buenos Aires: CEPAL, 2011), pp. 307–56, www.cepal.cl/publicaciones/xml/1/32311/CapVIII.pdf, last accessed 27 November 2013.

18 R. Cachanosky, *Por qué fracasó la economía K'* (Buenos Aires: El Ateneo, 2009), p. 145.

19 S. Rastello and I. Katz, 'Argentina Is First Nation Censured by IMF for Economic Data' (2 February 2013), www.bloomberg.com/news/2013-02-01/argentina-becomes-first-nation-censured-by-imf-on-inflation-data.html, last accessed 27 November 2013.

20 Roberto Gargarella has developed this thesis in R. Gargarella, *The Legal Foundations of Inequality: Constitutionalism in the Americas, 1776–1860* (New York: Cambridge University Press, 2010) and R. Gargarella, *Latin American Constitutionalism, 1810–2010: The Engine Room of the Constitution* (Oxford University Press, 2013). His works show how this marriage has shaped the classical Latin American constitutional frameworks in the nineteenth century.

21 For an analysis of the complexity of Argentine constitutional borrowing in its foundational period, see M. Gordon, 'Don't Copy Me, Argentina: Constitutional Borrowing and Rhetorical Type', *Washington University Global Studies Law Review*, 8 (2009), 487–519, 489.

22 For a general analysis of the constitutional transformations in Latin American countries over the past 25 years and their most distinctive characteristics, see U. Rodrigo, 'The Recent Transformation of Constitutional Law in Latin America: Trends and Challenges', *Texas Law Review*, 89 (2011), 1587–609.

23 Argentine Constitution, sec. 75(22).

Cultural Rights (ICESCR).[24] In addition, the Supreme Court stated that the General Comments, General Observations and other interpretive measures of United Nations human rights treaty-monitoring bodies and the Inter-American human rights actors were authoritative interpretations of the scope and content of those conventions.[25] Finally, the new Argentine Constitution expressly recognised that, for the first time in Argentina, the Office of the Ombudsman, civil society organisations and any affected citizens could pursue collective litigation for social rights.[26] As citizens were armed with these powerful tools, the judiciary became an actor with regard to many conflicts which arose in the context of the 2001 crisis and beyond.

Before turning to case analysis, we must complete this initial synopsis of the Argentine constitutional context with a few words about the structure of the judicial branch and constitutional review.[27] In Argentina, all judges are competent to perform a constitutional review of the cases that they rule on, and the Supreme Court is the final authority in the system.[28] Formally, judges hold their office for life and can only be removed through impeachment proceedings.[29] The judges of the Supreme Court are appointed by the executive branch and require the approval of the Senate,[30] while, since 1994, lower court judges have been selected by competitive processes organised by a Council of Magistrates.

Although constitutional review in Argentina imitates the functioning of its American counterpart, the non-existence of *stare decisis* means

[24] International Covenant on Civil and Political Rights, 999 UNTS 171 (ICCPR); International Covenant on Economic, Social and Cultural Rights, 993 UNTS 3 (ICESR).

[25] L. Filippini and J. Rossi, 'El Derecho Internacional en la Judiciabilidad de los Derechos Sociales en Latinoamerica' in C. Rodríguez, P. Arcidiácono and N. Espejo (eds.), *Derechos sociales: justicia, política y economía en América Latina* (Bogotá: Centro de Estudios Legales y Sociales, Universidad de Los Andes and Universidad Diego Portales, 2010), pp. 195–214.

[26] Argentine Constitution, sec. 42.

[27] For more information about judicial review in Argentina, see A. Garro, 'Judicial Review of Constitutionality in Argentina: Background Notes and Constitutional Provisions', *Duquesne Law Revue*, 45 (2007), 409–29.

[28] See Argentine Constitution, secs. 116, 117; Act N°48 (1863) (borrowed from the American Judiciary Act). The 'Sojo' case ('D. Eduardo Sojo por recurso de habeas corpus contra una resolución de la H. Cámara de Diputados de la Nación' (22/09/1887 – Fallos 32:120 (1887)), decided in 1887, is regarded as the local equivalent of *Marbury* v. *Madison* 5 US 137 (1803). The 1994 Constitution made explicit the authority of the courts to declare that a law is unconstitutional (see. sec. 43).

[29] See Argentine Constitution, sec. 110.

[30] This procedure traditionally occurred without any opportunity for discussion or public participation. In 2003, a procedure with robust participatory spaces and citizen scrutiny of processes organised by the executive branch and the Senate was approved. This procedure was employed for the last four nominations. See Executive Order N° 222/2003 (establishing the procedure).

that a specific ruling's authority is formally limited to the case in question,[31] and that the constitutional interpretations of the Supreme Court can legitimately change for the sole reason that new judges understand the Constitution differently[32] or that the same judges change their opinions in a new context, even only a few years after ruling on a similar case. Despite the lack of a formal doctrine of precedent, the Court has in numerous opinions stated that there is a 'moral obligation' to follow its rulings for reasons of procedural economy since contradictory decisions made by lower courts would be struck down by the higher tribunal.[33] In practice, this heterodox mandate is only followed by lower-court judges in some cases and there are many tactics used by judges in order to stray from precedent without expressing opposition to this principle of moral obligation.[34]

It should finally be mentioned that the Supreme Court of Argentina, like its counterpart in the United States, has a *writ of certiorari*, under which it has broad discretion to decide which cases it will accept without providing any justification for its decision. This enables the Court to rule on only a few of the cases that are sent to it for its consideration.[35]

These features demonstrate that, compared with the American model that inspires it, the Argentine Supreme Court has greater freedom and faces fewer institutional restrictions – both in terms of procedure and substance – in exercising constitutional review. However, its rulings have much lower institutional weight in relation to the other two branches of government. Moreover, the degree of political independence from central governments has historically been very low – although this has increased

[31] If the Supreme Court declares a law to be unconstitutional in one case, the government can legitimately continue applying it to the rest of the citizenry; or if it declares that a state law is unconstitutional, other states can legitimately continue enforcing identical laws. See J. C. Rivera (H) and S. Lagarre, 'Los efectos de la declaración de inconstitucionalidad en los Estados Unidos y la Argentina', *Lecciones y Ensayos*, 86 (2009), 321–50.

[32] The impact of this characteristic is increased by the historic instability in the composition of the Supreme Court.

[33] J. C. Rivera, 'Corte Suprema. Los efectos de sus sentencias y el stare decisis vertical', *Revista Jurídica Síntesis Forense*, 125 (2008), 26–7, www.rivera.com.ar/es/assets/Uploads/Publicaciones/Los-efectos-de-sus-sentencias-el-stare-decisis-vertical.pdf, last accessed 27 November 2013.

[34] A. Garay, 'El precedente judicial en la Corte Suprema', *Revista Jurídica de la Universidad de Palermo*, 2 (1997), 51–108, www.palermo.edu/derecho/publicaciones/pdfs/revista_juridica/n2N1y2-Abril1997/02%201y2Juridica05.pdf, last accessed 27 November 2013.

[35] E. Oteiza, 'El certiorari o el uso de la discrecionalidad por la Corte Suprema sin un rumbo preciso', *Revista Jurídica de la Universidad de Palermo*, 3(1) (1998), 71–85, 74–5, www.palermo.edu/derecho/publicaciones/pdfs/revista_juridica/n3N1-Abril1998/031Juridica06.pdf, last accessed 15 January 2014.

significantly over the last decade, marking an important qualitative change in this dimension.[36]

III. The judiciary and ESR during the economic crisis in Argentina

The last two decades have seen Argentina transform from an egalitarian country with the strongest middle class in the region and a social protection network into a country with severe poverty, high unemployment, elevated rates of employment informality and poor basic services.

As Gasparini explains:

> [b]etween 1992 and 2005 around one million Argentineans (out of a population of around 40 million) crossed the USD1-a-day poverty line. When using the USD 2 line the results are also similar: poverty has dramatically increased during the last decade. The headcount ratio rose from 4.2 [million] in 1992 to 8.5 [million] in 2006, which means that the estimated number of poor increased by around two million … poverty increased 4.1 points from 1992 to 1998, 6.2 points during the stagnation of 1998–2001, around 9.1 points during the 2001–2002 crisis, and then substantially fell between October 2002 and the second half of 2006.
>
> The official poverty line in Argentina is set at higher levels than USD 2 a day at PPP, a fact that reveals that Argentina is a middle-income country. Although the level of official poverty is higher than poverty computed by international standards, the patterns shown in Tables 4.4 and 4.5 for official poverty are similar to those commented above. The dramatic increase in poverty is captured by all indicators. According to the official line, extreme poverty increased from 3.8% in 1992 to 8.2% in 1996. After a fall around 1998, extreme poverty increased again to 13.7% in 2001 and reached 27.6% in 2002. Extreme poverty has been falling since then, reaching 8.6% in the second half of 2006.[37]

[36] Over the last 60 years every new government – whether constitutional or de facto – has appointed a new majority in the Supreme Court, with Justices personally or politically close to the president. This has occurred through mass resignations, impeachments or through changes being made to the number of Justices of the Supreme Court. See F. N. Barrancos y Vedia, 'La Corte Suprema de Justicia en la historia constitucional argentina', *Anales de la Academia Nacional de Ciencias Morales y Políticas*, 28 (1999), 201–30.

[37] L. Gasparini, 'Monitoring the Socio-economic Conditions in Argentina 1992–2006', (2007), www.depeco.econo.unlp.edu.ar/cedlas/monitoreo/pdfs/argentina.pdf, last accessed 27 November 2013. The paper is an updated version of a paper with the same title published as a Working Paper by the World Bank and the Center for Distributive, Labor and Social Studies, Universidad Nacional de La Plata, in 2005. The study is part of the project 'Monitoring the Socio-economic Conditions in Argentina, Chile, Paraguay and Uruguay', CEDLAS–The World Bank.

The country's GDP fell 3.4 per cent in 1999, 0.8 per cent in 2000, 4.4 per cent in 2001 and 10.9 per cent in 2002.[38] During that time, the disadvantaged were not only affected because of the consequent reduction of their income but also because the government instituted draconian budgetary cuts in the programmes which provided for enjoyment of the basic rights to education, health, sanitation and social security. Some countries, such as Chile, implemented a stabilisation fund that increases during expansion years and can be used during crisis periods to prevent fiscal deficits and guarantee the provision of services.[39] However, the experiences in most Latin American countries showed that harsh social benefit cuts were the usual way of dealing with this kind of problem,[40] and Argentina's 2001–2 crisis was no exception.

At the peak of the social mobilisations that took to the streets at the end of 2001 and continued throughout the most part of 2002, the Court was one of the targets of the unrest. Many people saw the 'old' Court as being responsible for having failed to impede the structural reforms that made possible the privatisations, the public administration reforms that caused hundreds of thousands of layoffs, and the widespread corruption of the 1990s.[41] The 'new' Court (the Court as constituted after the 2003 and 2004 changes in personnel) came into existence at a time at which most citizens, millions of whom had fallen beneath the poverty line, believed that the tribunal had a share of responsibility for the crisis since it had not prevented governmental wrongdoing such as the irregular privatisation process that had taken place during the previous decade.[42] In this context, the 'new' Court began to take on some issues and rights that it had not dealt with before.

For the purposes of our analysis of the position taken by the Supreme Court from the explosion of the crisis in 2001–2 until the present day in

[38] Global Finance, 'Argentina GDP Data & Country Report', www.gfmag.com/gdp-data-country-reports/328-argentina-gdp-country-report.html#axzz2jp3Y8z6a, last accessed 27 November 2013.

[39] For details, see Ministerio de Hacienda, 'Fondo de Estabilización Económico y Social', www.hacienda.cl/fondos-soberanos/fondo-de-estabilizacion-economica-y.html, last accessed 27 November 2013.

[40] A. F. Giraldo, 'La crisis actual y la salud' (CEPAL Serie Población y Desarrollo No. 104, 2011), 11, www.eclac.org/publicaciones/xml/4/43194/lcl3318-p.pdf, last accessed 27 November 2013.

[41] Equipo de Justicia de Asociación por los Derechos Civiles (Argentina), 'Reformas Institucionales en la Corte Suprema de Justicia argentina', *Sistemas Judiciales*, 13 (2008), 48–58, http://sistemasjudiciales.org/content/jud/archivos/revpdf/39.pdf#page=48, last accessed 27 November 2013.

[42] *Ibid.*, 52–8.

relation to the ESR of deprived citizens, we examined the decisions issued by the Court relating to basic rights of socio-economically excluded people. Concentrating on ESR litigation, we found that the tribunal got involved in a number of cases where plaintiffs sued over a state violation of the rights to health, adequate nutrition and housing. In total, we surveyed 54 ESR cases[43] and selected the ones whose beneficiaries were Argentina's least advantaged populations, the number of whom, as mentioned above, had increased exponentially during the crisis.[44]

Our evaluation will seek to delve deeper into the impact and the messages that the Court's actions sent to other judges, public actors and the general citizenry after its reconstitution in 2003–4. This includes, for example, a consideration of whether specific interventions ordering the immediate provision of a given benefit could be considered as indicative of an assistance-based model[45] because they did not attack the structural causes of the failures that led to this state of affairs, and whether the judiciary managed to have its rulings duly implemented by the political authorities. This will involve a consideration of the Court's approach to ESR brought to its attention by means of both individual and collective judicial actions.

With some exceptions, the tribunal has resolved most of the individual ESR conflicts that have appeared before it in sparse, concise language. Thus, those judgments' main value lies in the inferences that can be drawn from the Court's choice to deal with those particular controversies (given that the Court only selects a small percentage of the cases which are presented to it[46]), the decisions themselves, and the contexts in which they were brought. In contrast, the judgments regarding collective actions feature more extensive reasoning with frequent reference to international human rights treaties and their interpretation by the Inter-American

[43] The discretion accorded to the Court means that it can discharge any case it does not want to examine without providing reasons. Thus, it is not possible to analyse all of the cases submitted that the Court decided not to consider – and therefore it is impossible to determine if these decisions were a product of some sort of substantive position by the Court about the issue at stake, an excessive workload, or some other unknown criteria. For this reason, the evaluation of the impact of the Court's interventions must be limited to those cases that the Court took on and in which it provided reasoning for its decision.

[44] See also L. Gasparini and M. Cicoviez, 'The Socio-Economic Conditions in Argentina' (2007), 1–11, www.cei.gov.ar/userfiles/cicowiez-seminario-arg-aus-v03.pdf, last accessed 27 November 2013.

[45] An assistance-based model is one that seeks to provide an immediate and concrete response to a particular situation without aiming to address the structural causes and solutions to the problems identified in the context of that situation.

[46] For more details on the certiorari mechanisms applied by the Court, see S. Lagarre, 'Una puesta al día en materia de certiorari', *La Ley*, 240 (2003), I–3.

Commission on Human Rights, the UN Committee on Economic, Social and Cultural Rights (CESCR) and other international bodies.

Methodologically, the cases are separated thematically, allowing for a focused examination of the Court's approach to each protected right.

A. *Right to health care*

Argentina has historically been a country in which access to free public health services was granted even to newly arrived immigrants. Despite this, the quality of these services has always been unequal, with better medical care available in central urban areas and in the south of the country, with the city outskirts and the north of the country significantly less well-served.[47]

As a result of the economic policies pursued by the government during the neoliberal 1990s, much of the wealthier population transferred to private health programmes and the social security benefits assigned to formal workers were deregulated, resulting in an increase in the inequality of the services received.[48] The 2001–2 crisis aggravated this process and had devastating consequences for the poor. Amongst other problems, there was an increase of morbidity and mortality rates among mothers, babies and the elderly, several outbreaks of endemic epidemics, an unprecedented deterioration in infrastructure and equipment, an increase in the demand for mental health services and an increase in the cost assumed by patients since many public hospitals and clinics started requiring contributions from patients.[49]

In this context, litigation to access urgent and basic health care provision became ever more common and judges reacted in different ways depending on their attitude towards legal activism and their receptiveness towards the changes introduced in the 1994 Constitution.[50] In such a tumultuous environment, the signals sent by the Supreme Court were highly significant.

[47] N. Perrone and L. Teixidó, 'Estado y Salud en la Argentina', *Revista de la Maestría en Salud Pública*, 5(10) (2007), 1–46, http://msp.rec.uba.ar/revista/docs/010estado_y_salud_arg.pdf, last accessed 27 November 2013.

[48] S. Belmartino, 'Una década de reforma de la atención médica en Argentina', *Salud Colectiva*, 1(2) (2005), 155–71, 160–7.

[49] J. L. Zeballos, *Argentina: Efectos socio-sanitarios de la crisis, 2001–2003* (Buenos Aires: Pan-American Health Organization, 2003), pp. 57–63, http://new.paho.org/arg/publicaciones/pubOPS_ARG/Pub57.pdf, last accessed 27 November 2013.

[50] For a specific analysis of the evolution of litigation related with the right to health care and HIV in Argentina from 1994 on, and the relationship between the economic austerity measures taken in the months before the 2001 crisis and the development of the judicialisation

Individual suits

In many cases, the 'new' Court received suits from individuals seeking to oblige a particular public administration (whether national or provincial) to provide emergency health care to people whose lives were at risk and who did not have the possibility of accessing health care through other providers (such as insurance plans or private medical companies). The tribunal, moreover, repeatedly accepted its 'original jurisdiction', which allowed cases to be presented directly to it without first going through lower courts.[51]

The *Diaz* ruling[52] is illustrative of the individual cases. In this decision, the Court ordered the Province of Buenos Aires to provide the claimant with a pacemaker for cardiomyopathy resulting from Chagas disease (a tropical, parasitic disease that is found in very low-income rural areas in the north of the country). *Sanchez*[53] involved a 51-year-old disabled woman who suffered from strangulation and entrapment of the spinal cord and who lacked any type of health insurance. She sued the Province of Buenos Aires and the national government, seeking to compel them to provide funding for the highly complex surgery. Something similar occurred in *Laudicina*[54] in relation to a claimant's asthma medication. Due to the risk that delaying a decision would entail, all these cases were

of health rights issues, see P. Bergallo, 'Courts and Social Change: Lessons from the Struggle to Universalize Access to HIV/AIDS Treatment in Argentina', *Texas Law Review* 89 (2011), 1611–41. For a general analysis of the judicialisation of the right to health in Argentina, and its evolution after the 2001 crisis, see V. Abramovich and L. Pautassi, 'Judicial Activism in the Argentine Health System: Recent Trends', *Health and Human Rights: An International Journal*, 10(2) (2008), 53–65. A more general conceptual analysis of the phenomenon of judicialisation in different instances, and the type of institutional dynamics produced in Argentina was conducted by Bergallo in P. Bergallo, 'Argentina: Courts and the Right to Health: Achieving Fairness Despite "Routinization" in Individual Coverage Cases?' in A. E. Yamin and S. Gloppen (eds.), *Litigating Health Rights* (Cambridge, MA: Harvard University Press, 2011), pp. 43–75.

51 Section 117 of the Argentine Constitution grants the Court original jurisdiction in cases regarding foreign ambassadors and consulates, and in cases where state provinces are parties. This latter clause is excessively broad, and overall it can be said that the Supreme Court has been rather selective in its decisions to intervene directly. When a citizen of a province sues his province and the federal government, the Court has shown a very inconsistent behaviour, accepting some cases and rejecting others.

52 Corte Suprema de Justica de la Nación (CSJN), 'Díaz, Brígida c/ Prov. de Buenos Aires y Estado Nacional' (25/03/2003).

53 CSJN, 'Sanchez, Norma Rosa c/ Estado Nacional y otros s/ acción de amparo' (11/05/2004).

54 CSJN, Laudicina, Ángela Francisca c/ Pcia. De Buenos Aires y otro s/ amparo' (09/03/2004).

decided with preliminary injunctions without listening to the State's arguments and without the Court giving a formal justification. Given this lack of explanation, it can be inferred that the Court takes for granted the constitutional right to the highest attainable standard of health (set out in ICESCR, which is part of the 1994 Constitution) and the consequent obligation of the State to guarantee this right.

In the *Maria* case,[55] a handicapped plaintiff sought comprehensive coverage of the expenses generated by a degenerative illness. Besides the judicial petition, an administrative claim had also been submitted and the provincial Court of Appeals held that it was necessary to wait until the claim's resolution before a legal suit could be presented. On this occasion, the Supreme Court ruled that, in general, serious health situations require the reduction of formal requirements, and militate against the application of a strictly formalistic justice.[56] The Court's decision explicitly referred to the right to health in Article 12(c) of ICESCR and Articles 4 and 5 of the American Convention on Human Rights and the right to life in Article 6(1) of the ICCPR. It added that these kinds of cases, where there are severe health issues involved, tend to be related to the principle of individual autonomy, given that a gravely ill individual is not in a condition to carry out his/her life plans.[57]

At the same time, the Court ruled in favour of providing medication in extreme circumstances for people with limited resources. (Medicines are generally not provided for those who do not have any health insurance and are partially discounted for those who have.) In *Parraga*,[58] a retiree with a minimum wage pension (around 50 USD at that time) requested that, given his lack of resources, the health insurance plan for retirees and pensioners be required to cover all of the medication costs for his chronic anxious depressive disorder, panic attacks and agoraphobia. The Court ruled that the insurance provider – a state agency that covers retirees – had the responsibility to protect its members' health comprehensively; this would not occur if the plaintiff was left without the required medications given his particular circumstances.[59] In addition, in *GME*,[60] it held that people

55 CSJN, 'María Flavia Judith c/ Instituto de Obra Social de la Prov. de Entre Ríos y Estado Provincial' (30/10/2007).

56 *Ibid.*, 2. 57 *Ibid.*, 3.

58 CSJN, 'Parraga, Alfredo c/INSSJ y P (ex Pami) s/amparo' (16/05/2006).

59 Shortly thereafter, the Ministry of Health decided to obligate health care providers to cover 100 per cent of medication costs for chronic illnesses.

60 CSJN, 'GME c/ Instituto Nacional de Servicios Sociales para Jubilados y Pensionados s/ amparo' (17/12/2011).

with disabilities and the elderly have the right to enjoy the highest possible level of physical and mental health 'without discrimination based on age or income'.[61] The Court of Appeals had required that the plaintiff's family demonstrate that they did not have the income to afford his expenses. The Supreme Court expressed the view that this requirement did not seem reasonable as a negative test would be difficult to satisfy, especially when finding an appropriate solution was urgent and when the treatment of the illness required significant, unavoidable and immediate costs. In this case, the claimant sought, and was granted, the hiring of a health care aide for a period of 12 hours daily.

Class actions

In addition to these individual cases, the Court decided to intervene in a number of collective cases, issuing favourable decisions to a class of victims of state omissions. In late 2003, the Court issued a ruling in a lawsuit presented by an association that defended patients with multiple sclerosis.[62] The government had allowed insurance companies and prepaid medical providers to exclude covering costs for patients suffering from multiple sclerosis who had not had at least two attacks or exacerbations in the previous two years. The Court considered that the plaintiffs had demonstrated the severe damage done to the class represented by the association and confirmed the sentence of the Court of Appeals that had ruled to revoke this exclusion. The primary basis of the Court's decision was the fact that the medical reports provided by both parties did not demonstrate the reasonableness of the limitation imposed by the Ministry of Health.

In the *Defensor del Pueblo* case,[63] the National Office of the Ombudsman initiated a judicial action against the Province of Buenos Aires and the national government to guarantee medications for the treatment of oncological diseases, especially Hodgkin's lymphoma. The Court held that it was evident from the administrative files that this request had been made to provincial authorities on repeated occasions without success, and, consequently, due to the seriousness of the situation, it was appropriate to issue an injunction, even without ruling about whether it would have subsequent validity as the litigants had requested.

[61] *Ibid.*, 5.

[62] CSJN, 'Asociación Esrlerosis Múltiple de Salta c/ Ministerio de Salud, Estado Nacional s/ amparo' (18/12/2003).

[63] CSJN, 'Defensor del Pueblo de la Nación c/ Buenos Aires, Provincia de y otro (Estado nacional) s/ amparo' (08/05/2007).

B. Right to adequate nutrition

Argentina has historically been regarded as the breadbasket of the world, as it is one of the main producers of wheat, corn, soy and many other grains. Despite this, the 2001–2 period saw the worst nutrition problems ever seen in the country.[64]

First, news articles started to report stories which focused primarily on specific cases of small children suffering in desperate situations. After the scandals erupted, municipalities and provinces gave notice of a situation as widespread as it was severe. For example, in 2002, a report from Tucuman province identified 17,000 cases of malnutrition, 90 per cent of them among children under six years of age, many of whom had suffered neurological damage as a result. In the province of Jujuy, there was a 24.5 per cent rate of malnutrition in children from the ages of 2 to 5 years.[65] In the tourist city of Mar del Plata, a study found that 21 per cent of all pregnant women were underweight, a number which increased to 33.8 per cent among teenage mothers.[66] In La Matanza, a suburb of Buenos Aires, a study of 6,889 births showed that 26.6 per cent of newly born babies were underweight due to their parents' nutritional problems. In the province of Buenos Aires, the country's most populous jurisdiction, a door-to-door survey produced by the provincial government showed that 56,000 out of 800,000 children had grade I malnutrition.[67]

All this was shockingly new in a country that had always been considered to be exemplary in terms of the existence of a substantial middle-class population and the extensive availability of basic services for most citizens. The Supreme Court made some forceful interventions on the issue; it examined the right to adequate nutrition with particular care, especially when linked to the malnutrition of minors, while acknowledging that it is not independent of the right to health.

[64] L. Gasparini and M. Panadeiros, 'Argentina: Assessing Changes in Targeting Health and Nutrition Policies' (HNP Discussion Paper, October 2004), 10–16, www.bvsde.paho.org/texcom/nutricion/Changes.pdf, last accesed 18 December 2013.

[65] *Diálogo Argentino*, Boletín Informativo No. 1 (Secretaría Técnica, PNUD, January 2002), www.undp.org.ar/archivos/A378_DOCUMENTO%20BASES%20PARA%20LAS%20REFORMAS%20PRINCIPALES%20CONSENSOS.doc, last accessed 20 December 2013.

[66] M. Manzanal, 'Hambre en un país con abundancia de alimentos', *Clarín* (26 April 2002).

[67] J. Zevallos, *Argentina: Efectos socio-sanitarios de la crisis, 2001–2003* (Buenos Aires: Organización Panamericana de la Salud, 2003), p. 46. Grade I malnutrition is a mild state of malnutrition where the sufferer is at 80–90 per cent of the ideal body weight. F. Gomez, R R Galvan, J. Cravioto and S. Frenk, 'Malnutrition in Infancy and Childhood, with Special Reference to Kwashiorkor', *Advances in Pediatrics*, 7 (1955), 131–69.

In 2006, in the *Rodriguez* case, an individual action, which caused great commotion in the mass media due to the seriousness of the situation that was reported, the Court issued what would be one of its most widely publicised decisions.[68] A mother with several minor children presented a case against the national government, the Province of Buenos Aires and the Municipality of Quilmes in order to oblige them to carry out the actions necessary for her children to overcome severe malnutrition, and for their progress to be overseen by the relevant authorities. She claimed that they had been fed in local soup kitchens for children which had been closed for several days since they had not received provisions from the governments in charge of their administration. She requested an injunction in order for her children to be provided with the products necessary for a healthy diet and for the evolution of the minors' health to be monitored. In doing so, she based her claim on the right to health provided for in the American Convention on Human Rights and ICESCR.[69]

The Supreme Court majority granted an injunction due to the sufficient legal credibility of the claim and the particular dangers implied by any delay.[70] It later declared that it would transfer the case to a lower circuit judge. The minority argued that neither a manifest illegality nor arbitrariness were evident, which are the necessary requirements for any protective action.[71]

In the later *Defensor del Pueblo* v. *Chaco* case,[72] the National Ombudsman requested an injunction against the province of Chaco and the national government, asking for them to be obliged to adopt the measures necessary to improve the living conditions of indigenous populations located in the southwest of the province, who, due to the defendants' repeated and systematic omissions in providing proper humanitarian and social assistance, were on the brink of starvation.

The Ombudsman indicated that the indigenous populations were in a dire socio-economic state, and that as a result of this, the majority suffered from endemic diseases which were products of extreme poverty, lacked food and did not have access to potable water or necessary medical services. The Ombudsman alleged that the defendants had failed to carry out

[68] CSJN, 'Rodríguez, Karina Verónica c/ Estado Nacional y otros s/ acción de amparo', 329:553 (07/03/2006).

[69] ICESCR, art. 11; American Convention on Human Rights, OAS Treaty Series No. 36, art. 26.

[70] Rodríguezi, *ibid.*, 2. [71] *Ibid.*, 5–6.

[72] CSJN, 'Defensor del Pueblo de la Nación c/ Estado Nacional y otra (provincia del Chaco) s/ proceso de conocimiento' (18/09/2007).

the actions necessary to reverse or resolve this situation. The complainant emphasised that, due to these health and food crises, 11 deaths had been registered in the region during the previous months. Additionally, the Ombudsman requested that the provincial and national governments be obliged to guarantee these communities a real and effective quality of life that permits them to exercise, amongst others, their rights to life, to social and medical assistance, to adequate nutrition, to potable water, to education, to general welfare, to work and to social inclusion, and that these rights be satisfied continuously and permanently.

The judges decided to issue the injunction, without providing details of the basis of the order, and ordered the national government and the Province of Chaco to supply potable water and food to the indigenous communities, as well as adequate transportation and communication to each of the medical stations which the decision ordered to be established. Meanwhile, within the framework of the public hearing procedures that the Court released in 2007,[73] it called for a public hearing between state representatives, the Office of the Ombudsman and members of the affected community.

Subsequently, the Court decided to continue monitoring the process. To date, the case is still pending and both the Ombudsman and the communities involved report breaches of the injunction adopted by the tribunal.[74]

C. *Right to adequate housing*

Section 14bis of the National Constitution, introduced in a 1957 constitutional reform, provides the right to 'adequate housing' for all legal residents of Argentina. This is one of the most debated provisions in that text. In a country with scarce resources like Argentina, with millions of people with severe housing problems and an open-border policy for migrants, universal enjoyment of this right may be regarded as an ideal not possible to achieve in the medium term. But it can also be perceived as a clear obligation that the State bears towards the most disadvantaged – one which requires the State to come up with innovative solutions (which do not necessarily or exclusively entail the disbursement of state funds) to improve the situation of people unable to access affordable, dignified housing.

[73] *Ibid.*

[74] National Ombudsman Office, '2012 Annual Report', 265–70, www.dpn.gob.ar/informes_anuales/ianual2012.pdf, last accessed 27 November 2013.

Since the mid-1990s, there has been an exponential increase in the number of people living in precarious settlements and shanty towns. In the Metropolitan Area of Buenos Aires, where almost 15 million people live according to the last census produced in 2011,[75] around 10 per cent of the population live in informal neighbourhoods, a figure which was only 6 per cent in 2001. In 2001, in Greater Buenos Aires, there were 376 shanty towns and precarious settlements; by 2006, this number had more than doubled to 796.[76] Some of the inhabitants of these areas, not previously considered to be poor, were unable to continue paying rent as a result of the crisis, while others had to leave the countryside to find work in the cities.[77]

Recently, the Court has dealt with the right to adequate housing in two instances of structural litigation.

The most complex class action decided by the Court since the inception of collective procedures in 1994 was the *Mendoza* case.[78] In this litigation, the tribunal exercised original jurisdiction over a suit presented by residents of the watershed that separates the City from the Province of Buenos Aires. This is one of the world's most polluted bodies of water and almost three million people, the majority of whom are poor or indigent, live in its surroundings. A group of residents and their representatives sued the national government, the Province of Buenos Aires, the City of Buenos Aires and 44 companies for jointly causing the situation. The plaintiffs sought comprehensive environmental remediation for the area based on the constitutional rights to a clean environment, dignified housing for part of the affected population and water, as provided in the National Constitution and international human rights treaties.

75 L. Fernández, 'Somos 14.819.137 habitantes en al Región Metropolitana de Buenos Aires' (Instituto del Conurbano, Universidad Nacional de General Sarmiento, 2011), www.urbared.ungs.edu.ar/pdf/pdf-articulos/Censo%202010.pdf?PHPSESSID=0fce44533851f68b53e527e4dcae434f, last accessed 27 November 2013.

76 M. C. Cravino, J. P. del Rio and J. I. Duarte, 'Magnitud y crecimiento de las villas y asentamientos en el Área Metropolitana de Buenos Aires en los últimos 25 años' (2008), www.fadu.uba.ar/mail/difusion_extension/090206_pon.pdf, last accessed 27 November 2013.

77 D. Adasko and A. Salvia, 'Deficit de acceso a servicios públicos domiciliarios y de infraestructura urbana' (Observatorio de la Deuda Social, UCA, 2010), http://cursa.ihmc.us/rid=1K4VPH925-1S5HVS9-1FNX/UCA%20BOLETIN%20VIVIENDA.pdf, last accessed 27 November 2013.

78 CSJN, 'Mendoza, Beatriz Silvia y otros c/ Estado Nacional y otros s/ daños y perjuicios (daños derivados de la contaminación ambiental del Río Matanza-Riachuelo)', 329:2316 (20/06/2006).

After receiving the case in 2006, the Court decided – as a preliminary measure – to order the state authorities to present a comprehensive plan that included environmental planning and monitoring of human activities in the area, a study of the environmental impact of the companies implicated in the lawsuit and environmental education and information programmes.[79] At the same time, it also mandated the formation of an inter-jurisdictional agency to deal with the measure's implementation.

Sometime afterwards, in 2008, the Court issued its final ruling. It stated that the decision was based on three objectives: first, the improvement of the quality of life of the watershed's inhabitants; second, the recovery of the natural environment of the watershed in all of its components (water, air and soil); and third, the prevention of future damage.[80]

Along with many other environmental measures, the Court issued specific orders that have a strong impact on the right to housing of those most affected by the area's pollution, including: (a) the extension of the potable water network to local residents who lack access; (b) the cleaning, extermination of rodents and conversion of the river's shores into walkable public spaces; (c) the regularisation of the area's sewer system so that watershed inhabitants would not discharge their waste informally into the river; and (d) the relocation of shanty towns that are situated in the watershed to new social housing elsewhere.[81]

Five years later, the implementation of the case is still ongoing and, even in terms of the most optimistic scenario, it will take many more years for the decision to be considered fully implemented. The Court has organised many public hearings during this period, in which it has required the defendants to provide extensive accounts of the work that has been undertaken. There have been significant advances in the extension of water and sanitation networks, but the relocalisation of shanty towns is still at a preliminary stage.[82]

The other significant case relating to the right to housing is the *Quisberth Castro*[83] decision. In this action, a homeless mother of a minor with

[79] *Ibid.*, 18–20.

[80] CSJN, 'Mendoza, Beatriz Silvia y otros c/Estado Nacional' (08/07/2008), 20–8, www.pnuma.org/gobernanza/documentos/fallo_mendoza_c._e.n._cuenca_matanza-riachuelo.pdf, last accessed 27 November 2013.

[81] *Ibid.*, 18–25.

[82] For more details on the execution of the decision, including the reconversion of industries, relocalisation of informal settlements, situation of garbage dumps, etc., see the platform created by different participant organisations, '¿Qué pasa, Riachuelo?' www.quepasariachuelo.org.ar, last accessed 5 January 2013.

[83] CSJN, 'Quisberth Castro, S.Y. c/ Gobierno de la Ciudad de Buenos Aires s/ amparo' (24/04/2012).

disabilities demanded that the City of Buenos Aires provide her with a solution for the housing emergency that they were facing. The bases for the challenge were the principles of maximum available resources and progressive realisation under ICESCR (Article 2(1)), the Convention of the Rights of the Child (Article 24(4))[84] and the UN Convention on the Rights of Persons with Disabilities (Article 7)[85]. The City had, on the one hand, a programme of night shelters, and, on the other, a limited programme of subsidies (with a maximum duration of ten months) enabling benefit recipients to rent a room in a hotel. The plaintiff argued that neither of these options was appropriate for her situation. The Superior Court of the City of Buenos Aires rejected the demand on the basis that that ICESCR (an integral part of the Argentine constitutional framework, as discussed above) only required that authorities ensure the satisfaction of minimal and essential levels of the rights it guarantees. Therefore, States 'only have the duty of guaranteeing the minimal content of the right to housing, which [the Court reasoned] is acceptable if it offers "shelters" to those who lack housing'.[86]

The Supreme Court overturned this judgment and ruled in favour of the plaintiff with very emphatic arguments. Amongst other points, it held that the budget-related defence presented by the City could not be accepted because, as the UN Committee on Economic, Social and Cultural Rights had stated, for this defence to be valid it must be in accordance with (a) 'the country's level of development'; (b) 'the country's current economic situation, in particular whether the country was undergoing a period of economic recession'; and (c) 'whether the State attempted to find low cost options'.[87]

In the case, the lower court judge had issued an injunction so that the family could enjoy a reasonable solution while the case evolved, ordering that they be provided with a monthly sum of an equivalent of approximately $400 so that they could have access to appropriate housing.[88]

[84] UN Convention on the Rights of the Child, 1577 UNTS 3 (CRC).

[85] UN Convention on the Rights of Persons with Disabilities, 2515 UNTS 3.

[86] Superior Tribunal de Justicia de la Ciudad de Buenos Aires, 'Quisberth Castro, S.Y. c/ Gobierno de la Ciudad de Buenos Aires s/ amparo' (12/07/2010), 2 (referring to the decision by the same tribunal 'Alba Quintana, Pablo c/ GCBA y otros s/ amparo (art. 14 CCABA) s/ recurso de inconstitucionalidad concedido' (12/05/2010), 17).

[87] UN Committee on Economic, Social and Cultural Rights, 'An Evaluation of the Obligation to Take Steps to the "Maximum of Available Resources" under an Optional Protocol to the Covenant' (10 May 2007) UN Doc. E/C.12/2007/1 (cited in 'Quisberth Castro, S.Y. c/ Gobierno de la Ciudad de Buenos Aires s/ bamparo').

[88] CSJN, 'Quisberth Castro, S.Y. c/ Gobierno de la Ciudad de Buenos Aires s/ amparo', 2 (describing the judgment of Court of Appeals of the City of Buenos Aires).

The Supreme Court ordered the City to intervene by providing comprehensive social assistance to the family, expressly warning that the absence of coordinated and proper planning by the City had led to a situation in which it had to pay more for a basic hotel room than the market rent of a two-room apartment in the same neighbourhood.[89]

Therefore, the judges ordered the City government to intervene with its social and health assistance teams so that the child could have the care and attention that his disability required and the mother could have the advice and guidance necessary to resolve her housing problems.[90] They also mandated that she be guaranteed, although not permanently, housing with facilities that adequately accommodated the child's illness, without limiting her possible inclusion in some sort of present or future housing programme offering a permanent solution to the situation of exceptional need presented in the case.[91]

D. *The significance of the decisions*

The cases illustrate how the Court has firmly intervened in far-reaching ESR-related public policies, often without even entering into arguments of budgetary distribution and limitation of resources. This has even been so in a crisis context.

The many individual petitions involving the right to health and the Court's decisions clearly show that it did not even consider the possible counter-argument. All the cases in the record have been favourable to the plaintiffs and many decisions were granted as a preliminary measure (without even listening to the State's position). The traditional doctrine of the Supreme Court is that it does not look at preliminary measures,[92] which makes its taking on this number of cases a statement in itself. Despite the fact that many petitions were probably not even discussed as a result of the Court's discretionary certiorari powers, the message to lower courts is clear and leaves no room for debate about what should be done in emergencies when a person's health is at stake.[93]

Overall, we find that the position of the 'new' Court has been quite different from that adopted by the previous Court, which did not tend to intervene in the defence of ESR.[94] After its composition was changed

[89] *Ibid.*, 26. [90] *Ibid.*, 27. [91] *Ibid.*, 28.

[92] Summarised in 'Grupo Clarín y otros' (05/10/2010), G 456 XLVI.

[93] F. García Pullés, *Medidas cautelares autónomas en el contencioso administrativo* (Buenos Aires: Hammurabi, 2006), p. 19.

[94] Roberto Gargarella illustrates the complexities that arise from the inclusion of social rights in liberal-conservative constitutions for the effective realisation of these rights.

in 2003–4, the Court began to create the basis for a progressive jurisprudence and to justify judicial intervention regarding issues that the majority of the previous Court considered non-reviewable public policies. It also started to hold public hearings with the highest political authorities at the national and provincial levels. Society began to see an active judiciary in this field, which was not the case during the preceding decade.[95]

One of the biggest challenges that remains is the implementation of the structural class action decisions. As the *Mendoza* case shows, the follow-up is sometimes even more complex than the original decision. Judges simply do not have a suitable police force that can enforce sensitive judgments against the political branches. Thus, they always need to be careful and strategic in order to maximise the likelihood of successful implementation.[96] A period of severe crisis is even more tricky in terms of the Court's role, given the budgetary constraints arguments advanced by the public administrations.

IV. Emergency, property rights and the judiciary

During the entire twentieth century and the beginning of the twenty-first century, the Argentine justice system has periodically had to evaluate the constitutionality of states of economic emergency declared by the government and the laws and regulations passed to overcome them.[97] In the early twentieth century, emergency norms were primarily directed

The conservative behaviour of the Argentine Supreme Court could be adequately explained based on this thesis. However, the 2001 crisis and the acute situation that it led to could also be understood as having acted as an activator for the 'dormant clauses' on ESR – at least in the most serious cases, as we evaluate in the following sections. R. Gargarella, 'Grafting Social Rights onto Hostile Constitutions', *Texas Law Review*, 89 (2011), 1537–55.

[95] For a conceptual discussion about these new dynamics of judicial intervention, see R. Gargarella, 'Dialogic Justice in the Enforcement of Social Rights: Some Initial Arguments', in Yamin and Gloppen (eds.), *Litigating Health Rights*, pp. 232–45.

[96] H. Corti, *Derecho Constitucional Presupuestario* (Buenos Aires: Lexis Nexis, 2007), pp. 745–90.

[97] For a reconstruction and critical evaluation of the role of the Argentine judiciary in relation to economic crises, including the 2001 crisis, see C. Rosenkrantz, 'Constitutional Emergencies in Argentina: The Romans (not the Judges) Have the Solution', *Texas Law Review*, 89 (2011), 1557–86. The author affirms that the judicial branch is not, in general, in a condition to supervise and monitor the exercise of emergency policies. However, we believe that his conclusion is based on an oversimplification of the magnitude of the challenge that these situations generate for the entire institutional system.

towards regulating contracts and private economic activities.[98] However, as a result of transformations in state structure and functions, and the significant fiscal impact of such, the measures directed towards containing economic emergencies over the last 50 years have also focused on the reduction of current account deficits in the public administration and social security systems.[99]

In this section, we will analyse the standards that the Argentine Supreme Court constructed and developed to conduct constitutional review in the context of economic emergency. We will look at the proliferation of suits relating to the protection of property rights – both those framed by classic civil law and those relating to public sector salaries, retirement funds and pensions. In order to do this, we will review the classical principles that guided the judiciary's responses in the twentieth century to explore the treatment of the 2001 crisis and the post-crisis period. As we will see, ESR standards have progressively come to occupy a significant role in the constitutional interpretation in these kinds of cases as well.

A. The classical standard: broad 'emergency' powers to restrict economic property rights

Historically, the Supreme Court constructed an interpretative doctrine regarding emergency powers that was extremely generous and deferential towards the public authorities – one that, it must be added, made no distinction between constitutional authorities and military governments. In a series of rulings throughout the twentieth century,[100] the following principles were established, which form the basis for the test of constitutionality in relation to these issues:

[98] Examples include exceptional regulations of rental contracts and foreclosures, controls on salary levels in the private sector, establishment of taxes or other exceptional fees on various economic sectors, etc.

[99] For instance, through the freezing or reduction of salaries in public administration or pensions, reprogramming of payments of credits on the State's or financial system's current debts, restructuring of the public debt, etc.

[100] The sequence of leading cases is composed of the following precedents: 'Hileret c/ Provincia de Tucumán' (05/9/1903 – Fallos: 98:20); 'Ercolano c/Lanteri de Renshaw' (28/04/1922 – Fallos: 136:170); 'Avico c/de la Pesa' (07/12/1934 – Fallos: 172:21); 'Inchauspe c/Junta Nac. de Carnes' (01/09/1944 – Fallos: 199:483); and 'Cine Callao' (22/06/1960 – Fallos: 247:121). In all of these, the Court upheld the constitutionality of the emergency measures. See Secretaría de Jurisprudencia, CSJN, *Emergencia económica I*, 1st edn (Buenos Aires:

a. *Constitutional rights are not absolute*, but rather must conform to the general interest of the community and are subject to regulations towards these ends.
b. In periods of emergency, defined as *social and economic perturbation*, the State is authorised to exercise its policing powers in a *more energetic fashion* than would be admissible in periods of calm and normality.
c. In these contexts, judicial review of reasonableness and proportionality is *less demanding*, and governmental interventions are constitutionally valid unless they imply a deprivation, suppression, or an irremediable denaturalisation of rights.
d. When evaluating governments' exercise of emergency powers, the Court should act by 'interpreting the Constitution in a manner such that its limitations do not destroy or block the efficient exercise of the powers attributed to the State for the ends of meeting its noble goals and purposes in the most beneficial fashion for the community'.[101]

On the basis of these principles, which require that the standard applied to evaluate the constitutionality of state action should be less stringent in extreme situations so as to facilitate the exercise of state power, various Supreme Courts have historically endorsed practically all of the economic measures adopted in the exercise of emergency powers when these have been challenged by individuals whose property rights were affected.[102] Furthermore, even if the cases in question involved the evaluation of laws and administrative actions undertaken by both constitutional and de facto governments, the Supreme Court never established procedural requirements for decision-making regarding emergency measures.

In the first half of the 1990s, the Supreme Court ruled on several cases which questioned harsh fiscal austerity measures that severely impacted upon the economic rights of large cross-sections of society.

CSJN, 2009). See also J. Miller, S. Cayuso and M. A. Gelli, *Constitución y Poder Político*, 2 vols. (Buenos Aires: Astrea, 1992).

101 *In re* 'Inchauspe c/Junta Nac. de Carnes' (01/09/1944 – Fallos: 199:483), 8–9.

102 For a historical and comparative analysis of the relationship between the political branches of government and the Supreme Court, and the influence of the doctrines of the Supreme Court of the United States, with a special emphasis on the constitutional review of emergency measures prior to the 2001 crisis, see W. C. Banks and A. D. Carrió, 'Presidential Systems in Stress: Emergency Powers in Argentina and the United States', *Michigan Journal of International Law*, 15 (1993), 1–76; J. Miller, 'Judicial Review and Constitutional Stability: A Sociology of the U.S. Model and its Collapse in Argentina', *Hastings International and Comparative Law Review*, 21 (1997), 77–176.

In *Peralta*,[103] the Court constitutionally legitimated an executive decree,[104] issued for reasons of 'necessity and urgency' – with the National Congress in session – which, in a context of growing inflation and rising interest rates, ordered that existing fixed-term deposits in the financial system would be 'returned' through ten-year public debt bonds. This ruling, along with a disproportionate use of the so-called Decrees of Necessity and Urgency by the executive branch, led to the inclusion of a clause in the 1994 constitutional reform that formally recognised the emergency legislative powers of the President, while at the same time limiting them constitutionally.[105]

In 2000, when Argentina had already embarked on its third year of economic stagnation, over-indebtedness and fiscal deficits, the Supreme Court ruled on the last case involving tensions between rights and emergency norms before the outbreak of the 2001 crisis. In the *Guida* decision,[106] the Court constitutionally endorsed another presidential Decree of Necessity and Urgency which dated to 1995.[107] This decree had ordered the reduction of public employees' salaries by between 5 per cent and 15 per cent for an open-ended and indeterminate period, together with other measures directed towards containing and reducing public spending.

[103] 'Peralta c/Estado Nacional' (27/12/1990 – Fallos: 313:1513).

[104] Executive Decree N° 36/1990.

[105] See Argentine Constitution, sec. 99(3):

> The Executive Power shall in no event issue provisions of legislative nature, in which case they shall be absolutely and irreparably null and void. Only when due to exceptional circumstances the ordinary procedures foreseen by this Constitution for the enactment of laws are impossible to be followed, and when rules are not referred to criminal issues, taxation, electoral matters, or the system of political parties, he shall issue decrees on grounds of necessity and urgency, which shall be decided by a general agreement of ministers who shall countersign them together with the Chief of the Ministerial Cabinet. Within the term of ten days, the Chief of the Ministerial Cabinet shall personally submit the decision to the consideration of the Joint Standing Committee of Congress, which shall be composed according to the proportion of the political representation of the parties in each House. Within the term of ten days, this committee shall submit its report to the plenary meeting of each House for its specific consideration and it shall be immediately discussed by both Houses. A special law enacted with the absolute majority of all the members of each House shall regulate the procedure and scope of Congress participation.

[106] 'Guida, Liliana c/Poder Ejecutivo Nacional' (02/06/2000 – Fallos: 323:1566).

[107] This was issued in the context of the global financial crisis labelled the 'tequila effect'; sparked by a sudden devaluation of Mexican peso that severely affected the financial conditions of emerging markets. For more information, see J. Sachs, A. Tornell and A. Velazco, 'Financial Crisis and Emerging Markets: Lessons from 1995', *Brookings Papers on Economic Activity*, 27 (1996), 147–215.

When the 2001 crisis broke out, the century-old jurisprudence of the Supreme Court and its two most relevant decisions about limitations on economic rights in emergency contexts from the previous decade, *Guida* and *Peralta*, seemed to predict how conflicts that the emergency triggered would be resolved.

B. *The 2001 crisis, public policies and judicial review*

A few months before the crisis exploded, the national government tried a new and unprecedented fiscal austerity measure, called 'deficit zero'.[108] A congressional law enabled the executive branch to carry out various measures in order to ensure a monthly financial balance in the public accounts. These measures included the reduction of public employee salaries and retirement plans by 13 per cent. The president implemented the salary reductions in July, and resigned in December.

In turn, among the measures that Congress (and the new President that it appointed) adopted from December 2001 to January 2002, was the rescheduling of the maturities of fixed-term deposits in dollars. In a context of devaluation, this implied a significant loss of purchasing power of the amounts deposited.

The Court's traditional jurisprudence suggested that such measures would be endorsed by the judiciary. However, perhaps motivated by the seriousness of the institutional crisis that had broken out – in which the justices of the Supreme Court themselves were confronted with impeachment procedures promoted by the acting president[109] – the years 2002 and 2003 saw a series of significantly heterodox jurisprudential decisions which declared the main economic measures unconstitutional, on the grounds that they implied a *denaturation* of property rights, beyond the scope of constitutional regulation.[110]

108 Law 25.453, 30 July 2001, www.infojus.gov.ar/legislacion/ley-nacional-25453-ley_deficit_cero.htm;jsessionid=1btpu29494tew161plno8k0bz3?0, last accessed 16 December 2013.

109 These procedures were based on different irregularities that had taken place in the Supreme Court during the 1990s. See 'Argentine leader calls for Impeachment of the Supreme Court', *New York Times* (6 June 2003), www.nytimes.com/2003/06/06/world/argentine-leader-calls-for-impeachment-of-the-supreme-court.html, last accessed 20 December 2013.

110 In 'Tobar, Leónidas c/E.N. - Mº Defensa - Contaduría General del Ejercito - Ley 25.453 s/ amparo - Ley 16.986' (22/08/2002 - Fallos: 325:2059) the Court declared that the 13 per cent cut to public sector salaries carried out in 2001 was unconstitutional, rather poorly explaining the consistency of this decision with the principles that justified its ruling in

By late 2003, while the economic crisis was still pounding Argentina, the country had a new popularly elected President in office; and four of the justices that formed the majority in the Supreme Court's 2002 decisions had been impeached or had resigned.

Cases on emergency measures and the property rights of bank depositors and mortgagees

The new Supreme Court attempted to proceed quickly to the judicial review of the norms that had delayed and recalculated the devolution of the amounts of bank deposits.[111] In 2004, with a narrow majority and concurring votes which complicated the understanding of the decision, the Court ruled on the *Bustos* case,[112] in which it annulled the doctrine of the 2002/3 cases – *Smith* and *Provincia de San Luis* – and endorsed the emergency regulations' constitutionality, as a legitimate regulation of property rights. However, several lower courts, which had hundreds of thousands of cases to resolve, rejected the Supreme Court's doctrine and adopted decisions that offered greater protection to savers.[113]

Only two years later, in late 2006, the Court ruled once again in a case relating to the recalculation of deposits (the *Massa* case),[114] and managed to consolidate a unanimous doctrine. In this decision, the Court made financial adjustments to the relevant norms to protect savers with regard to the disputed legislation[115] and, with these safeguards in place, endorsed

'Guida', which had been decided only two years earlier. In February 2002 (in 'Smith c/ Poder Ejecutivo Nacional' (Fallos: 325:28)) and March 2003 ('Provincia de San Luis c/ Estado Nacional' (Fallos: 326:417)) the Court declared the rescheduling of bank deposit payments unconstitutional, trying equally weakly to explain the consistency of this ruling with that of the 'Peralta' case, in which it endorsed a substantially similar emergency measure in 1993.

[111] Horacio Spector analysed the principal legal theories available for the protection of property rights linked with financial activities in emergency situations, and their use in Argentina, concluding that none of them were adequate to deal with the situation the country faced. H. Spector, 'Don't Cry for Me Argentina: Economic Crises and the Restructuring of Financial Property', *Fordham Journal of Banking and Financial Law*, 14 (2009), 771–823.

[112] 'Bustos c/Estado Nacional' (26/10/2004 – Fallos: 327:4495).

[113] Among others, two prestigious Chambers of the Buenos Aires Federal Appeal Court openly expressed their rejection of the ruling of 'Bustos'. see 'Reali Alejandro Juan Ruben c/PEN' – CNACAF – SALA IV – 07/11/2006; 'Roger Martín Raúl c/EN-PEN' – CNACAF – SALA I – 11/09/2004. Some federal courts around the countries took the same path.

[114] 'Massa c/Poder Ejecutivo Nacional' (27/12/2006 – Fallos: 329:5913).

[115] Primarily the interest rate and the time period for which it applied in relation to the capital of the original deposit in dollars, which had been converted to pesos by the legislation.

the constitutionality of the norms in question, setting a precedent that was accepted by lower courts.

By this time, the economy had stabilised relatively and the exchange rate depreciation had recovered partially in comparison to the previous years, so depositors' capital losses due to this legislation were comparatively lower than in 2002.[116] This factor, together with the Court's patience in waiting to rule on the issue after the ill-fated attempt two years before, the significant increment that the tribunal adopted to improve what depositors would receive in relation to what the contested regulation granted, and, last but not least, the unprecedented unanimity that the Supreme Court judges reached after painstaking efforts to support the adopted solution, created a successful and unprecedented innovation in terms of the Court's intervention in the constitutional review of emergency measures from a property rights perspective.

In *Massa*, while emergency powers and a 'flexibilisation' of economic rights to meet the regulatory requirements of the emergency were upheld in general, the Court adopted remedies which tended to minimise the sacrifice of these rights and increased the proportionality of the restrictive measures up to the furthest point it could without 'co-legislating'. In its decision, the tribunal sent a convincing message about its own internal institutional unity as a body committed to a fair consideration of citizens' rights together with state needs.

A year later, the Court took on another serious problem stemming from the economic crisis: the situation of mortgagors with dollar loans outside of the banking system, following the more than 400 per cent devaluation of the Argentine currency.[117] Mortgagees demanded payment in dollars as had been agreed in the contracts, and mortgagors demanded that their debts be converted into pesos. The executive authorities approved various norms aimed at containing the situation and alleviating the mortgagors' situation. This led to thousands of cases being taken to the courts by the mortgagees.

At the time that the Court decided to intervene in the matter, legislation established a solution that was broadly protective of debtors when the credit capital was less than 100,000 dollars and the mortgage was for the debtor's sole family residence, through the provision of an 'escape clause' of equitable readjustment when the result of this legislation was deemed

[116] L. Di Matteo, *El Corralito* (Buenos Aires: Editorial Sudamericana, 2011), pp. 105–23.
[117] *Ibid.*, pp. 145–8.

to be disproportionate according to the circumstances of each case.[118] In *Rinaldi*,[119] the Court sanctioned this legal solution as a principle, interpretatively establishing criteria for the application of the 'escape clause' in the recalculation of the funds owed in order to guarantee proportionality in the application of the relevant legislative standards.

The Supreme Court's reasoning in this case had a novel and significant element: it was the first case in which the 'reasonableness analysis' of the emergency legislation was presented as not only a matter of permissible restrictions on property rights – as in the classical approach – but also as a tool which aimed to balance creditors' property rights with debtors' right to housing. This latter right had been enshrined in Section 14bis of the Constitution since 1957 (albeit with little practical effect), and was reinforced in its effectiveness after the 1994 constitutional incorporation of international human rights conventions discussed above.

In other words, this was the first time when social rights played a role in the legal reasoning on property restrictions in emergency situations.[120]

Cases on economic rights relating to social security benefits and public sector salaries

As we have described, regulations over social security benefits have been one of the basic variables of fiscal control in Argentina over the last several decades. The country has had a constitutional provision which guarantees social security benefits since 1957, among these retirement benefits and 'adjustable pensions'[121] – meaning that there should be a constant proportionality between pensions and wages of active workers in similar positions. However, on many occasions this adjustability was suspended by laws adopted in situations of economic crisis.

118 Law 25.798, 6 November 2003, and Law 26.167, 8 November 2006, established the conversion of debts to pesos at a rate of 1 US dollar to 1 peso and the application of a coefficient of capital in pesos in relation to the devaluation, that only neutralised the devaluation very partially, to the detriment of the creditor.

119 'Rinaldi c/Guzman Toledo' (15/03/2007 – Fallos: 330:855).

120 The situation of debtors – mortgagors or renters – at risk of losing their housing has been the subject of consideration in various rulings relating to emergency measures, but the evaluation of constitutionality has been typically conducted with an exclusive analysis of property rights and the reasonability of restrictions imposed for reasons of general well-being. It is possible that the traditional interpretation may have opened the scope for state action over rights so broadly due to the fact that the non-existence of social rights prevented the cases from being framed as a conflict between rights of prima facie equal constitutional hierarchy.

121 See Argentine Constitution sec. 14bis.

The so-called Convertibility Law[122] that regulated the economy during the 1990s prohibited the application of indexing mechanisms to debts, while retirement laws had established different mechanisms for updating the value of benefits for decades, as a reflection of the constitutional principle of adjustability. When the Convertibility Law was applied to the calculation of pensions and retirement funds, freezing assets in relation to the evolution of the salaries of active employees, thousands of retirees turned to the justice system for relief.

The Court had to rule on this issue in 1996, less than two years after the ratification of the new Constitution that had incorporated the recognition of social rights into its fundamental rights structure. In the *Chocobar* decision,[123] the Court held that the reference to available resources found in the constitutionally incorporated international human rights conventions was a suitable guideline for the purposes of determining the economic content of the constitutional principle of pension adjustability in making judgments about readjustments of benefits.[124] On this basis, the Court decided that the application of the new legislation, inspired by the protection of general welfare, did not violate the Constitution, even though it made retirement funds and pensions non-adjustable.

In 2005, after the Convertibility Law was repealed, and when the economic situation began to brighten, the (new) Court issued a ruling in the *Sánchez* case[125] which overturned the 'Chocobar' doctrine. The Court based its decision on a robust interpretation of the right to social security in general and to the adjustability of retirement funds and pensions as a constitutional guarantee in particular.

This same interpretation led the Court to issue two momentous decisions in 2006 and 2007 in a case in which a retiree demanded that his pension be adjusted in accordance with the general evolution of wages, accusing the legally adopted mechanisms of not doing so adequately. In the *Badaro* case,[126] the Court considered that the Argentine economic situation had modified substantially over the last several years as the

[122] Law 23.928, 27 March 1991. See n. 2.

[123] 'Chocobar, Sixto Celestino' (27/12/1996 – Fallos: 319:3241).

[124] See 'Chocobar, Sixto Celestino', majority vote, para. 11, concurring opinion of Justice Boggiano, para. 8.

[125] 'Sánchez, María del Carmen' (17/05/2005 – Fallos: 328:2833).

[126] 'Badaro, Adolfo Valentín' (resoluciones de 08/08/2006 – Fallos: 329:3089 y de 26/11/2007 – Fallos: 330:4866). In the first determination, the Court urged Congress to adequately regulate the adjustability of retirement funds, and in the second it found that the regulation that Congress had made did not adequately guarantee this adjustability in the case of Mr Badaro.

country recovered its economic and fiscal stability, and that the regulations regarding pension and retirement adjustability issued after the *Sánchez* precedent were no longer reasonable in terms of guaranteeing retirees' rights.

In 2013, more than a decade after the *Guida*[127] and *Tobar*[128] decisions, the Court again examined the constitutionality of an emergency law that had provided a reduction in public sector remuneration during the 2001 crisis.[129] The development of ESR interpretation standards and their progressive influence on the evaluation of emergency laws were definitively crystallised in this judgment.

In its argumentation in *ATE* v. *Municipalidad de Salta*,[130] the Court established that public sector workers' salaries had constitutional protection as social rights and that this protection rendered applicable the principles of progressive realisation and non-retrogression, which implied that any regressive measures affecting these rights carried a 'strong presumption' of unconstitutionality. With regard to emergency measures, the Court found that their reasonableness and consistency with the 'general welfare in a democratic society' (the wording of the American Convention on Human Rights)[131] required that they be directed by the priority of protecting the fundamental rights of the most disadvantaged sectors of society. With this as a foundation, citing expressly the principles of paragraph 9 of the CESCR's General Comment No. 2,[132] the Court concluded that 'the weight of the crisis cannot ultimately fall on working families'.[133] Within this interpretive framework, commenting only on ESR norms and making no reference to property rights, the tribunal concluded that the reduction of salaries was unconstitutional. 'Guida c/Poder Ejecutivo Nacional' (02/06/2000 – Fallos: 323:1566).

The Court has been dealing with the restrictions to property rights established by the emergency rules sanctioned after the crisis for over a

[127] 'Guida, Liliana c/Poder Ejecutivo Nacional' (02/06/2000 - Fallos: 323:1566)

[128] *Ibid.*

[129] See 'ATE v. Municipalidad de Salta' (6/18/2013). In this case, the constitutionality of an executive order enacted by the mayor of the city of Salta in 2003 ordering a reduction in the salaries of municipal employees for emergency reasons was challenged.

[130] See *ibid.*, paras. 9–11.

[131] See American Convention on Human Rights, art. 32.

[132] UN Committee on Economic, Social and Cultural Rights (CESCR), 'General Comment No. 2' in 'Note by the Secretariat, Compilation of General Comments and General Recommendations Adopted by Human Rights Treaty Bodies' (27 May 2008) UN Doc. HRI/GEN/1/Rev.9 (Vol. I).

[133] See *ibid.*, para. 11.

decade. The traditional interpretational rules admitted a wider deference towards state action to restrict those rights in exceptional circumstances, without any consideration of distributive justice. Despite this, in the years following 2001, particularly after the worst period of the crisis had passed, the Court continually refined its analysis to include that class of considerations and protect the property rights of the most vulnerable social groups more intensively, incorporating robust ESR-based interpretative standards.

V. Comparative analysis and conclusions

This review of cases relating to ESR and property rights, which were resolved by the Supreme Court of Argentina after the 2001 crisis, allows us to draw some conclusions about three key issues: (a) the challenges and opportunities that an economic crisis can generate for the construction of the judicial authority in countries where independence and impartiality are not taken for granted by the community or the institutional actors; (b) the impact of ESR on constitutional interpretation and the significance of such for the protection of the groups most affected by the crisis; and (c) crisis and the potential for countries to reaffirm strong constitutional commitments to ESR during periods of fiscal limitations.

A. Crisis as a risk and as an opportunity for the legitimacy of the courts

When dealing with the legal consequences of the 2001 crisis, the 'new' Supreme Court of Argentina adopted a very different approach to that of its predecessors on the 'old' tribunal, who held a very firm, restrictive view of ESR and were strongly opposed to the government's policies on property. The 'new' Court adopted a minimalist approach, undertaking patient and unhurried decisions, leaving room for other solutions through the political process, including legislative and regulatory measures to channel the impact of the crisis. The Court also tended to correct the deficiencies of government policies instead of simply invalidating them, and to demonstrate a priorisiation of groups who were particularly disadvantaged or in extreme conditions of socio-economic vulnerability.

In the years following the crisis, many ESR cases were strategically selected by the Court as deliberative processes that could serve to demonstrate critical social conditions, alert the political branches to the need to adopt adequate remedies and reinvigorate the role of the tribunal as a last resort for human dignity. The public hearings held in relation to the cases *Mendoza*, *Defensor del Pueblo* v. *Chaco* and *Quisberth Castro*, which had enormous public impact, were the most significant examples of this strategy.

In the Argentine context, it was evident that the response that the Court would have to the crisis and its impact on rights would not only involve the delineation of relevant aspects of constitutional law but would also establish the tribunal's own identity within the broader institutional framework. Thus, in the cases relating to property, bank deposits and mortgages, the Court had to decide not only what limitations were acceptable in terms of the rights in question and the impacts that its decisions would have in the political and social turmoil of that crisis context. It also had to reflect the fact that the Constitution of 1994 had incorporated the widest promises of rights ever made to citizens of Argentina.

B. ESR, constitutional interpretation and the protection of the most vulnerable groups in the face of the crisis

The rulings on ESR described up to this point are undoubtedly protective of such rights, particularly those of the low-income populations who were hit hardest by the 2001 crisis. The 'old' Court's jurisprudence in the 1990s was based on a purely formalistic analysis, and, as a consequence, was characterised by frequent rejections of complaints for not fulfilling some of the formal legal requirements supposedly envisaged for such situations (for instance, administrative remedies).[134] One of the most common reasons for the 'old' Court refusing to deal with ESR cases was the argument that a request for a protective injunction was only permissible in cases which did not require further clarification of the facts through extensive evidence presentation or where an in-depth consideration was not necessary.[135]

The cases examined here, however, demonstrate that from 2003–4 on, the Court adopted an entirely different stance and now can be classified as part of the select group of national superior courts which have been especially active in the defence of ESR – a group which includes India, South Africa and Colombia.[136]

[134] For a general analysis of the role of formalism in the legal culture of 'civil law' countries and its progressive decline over the last decades, see J. H. Marryman and R. P. Perdomo, *The Civil Law Tradition*, 3rd edn (Stanford University Press, 2007).

[135] This is a requirement of the 'amparo' (injunction) law (Law 16.986, 18 October 1986).

[136] For an overview of the Colombian and South African constitutions and ESR, see the contributions by Landau and Pillay and Wesson to this volume. For further information

Our analysis also demonstrates that the Argentine Court has not provided many clues to its theory of the justiciability of ESR. Of course, regarding health care and medications, urgency was the driving force behind its interventions and this in turn served as an obstacle to the detailed elaboration of a justification. Several other cases were also treated with injunctions, and, therefore, the interpretation of such arise more from the facts and the measures adopted than from the reasoning of the decisions. (Indeed, the most obvious principle that can be extracted from these decisions is that, given a potential for serious damage, the benefit or economic payment should be granted, and only later should the legality of the claim be discussed.)

In relation to the economic and social crisis, it is clear that – although it has never stated so explicitly – the severe situations that reached the Court (among the most significant of which were the malnutrition cases) appear to have influenced the expansive approach that it adopted in relation to ESR. Overall, the Supreme Court has been most generous towards the rights of the populations who are in the worst economic situations.

In the context of cases dealing with other groups, however, the Supreme Court has demonstrated more cautious behaviour. Faced with structural financial constraints, it ultimately upheld the measures imposed by the political authorities, although lower courts had ruled in favour of depositors who wished to collect the entirety of their deposits in dollars. In this category of cases, the Court's attitude was marked more clearly by an economic analysis of the consequences of its decisions. But, at the same time, it did not adopt decisions requiring the return of the deposits that thousands of savers had managed to withdraw thanks to decisions of lower court judges. Its approach was marked by the idea that waiting to rule on cases would improve the possibility that the situation would become less conflictual – what one of the Court's judges called 'chronotherapy'.[137]

After a decade (the 1990s) in which the Court had undermined the primacy of human rights over governmental regulatory measures, the subsequent decade represented significant progress in terms of the Court's approach. However, ESR activists continue to advocate for a position

on these jurisdictions and India, see M. Langford (ed.), *Social Rights Jurisprudence: Emerging Trends in Comparative and International Law* (New York: Cambridge University Press, 2008). For more, see International Commission of Jurists, 'Courts and the Legal Enforcement of Economic, Social and Cultural Rights' (2008).

137 See R. Á. Ugarte, 'Pesificación: el tiempo trajo la solución para los ahorristas', *Iprofesional* (28 December 2006), www.iprofesional.com/notas/38275-Pesificacion-el-tiempo-trajo-la-solucion-para-los-ahorristas.html, last accessed 27 November 2013.

which is even broader on structural cases and to seek significant improvement in the execution of the Court's rulings.

C. *Economic crisis and robust constitutions for ESR*

When the crisis started in 2001, ESR were just written words in the Constitution and the general understanding was that the government would have free rein to deal with the crunch. Ten years later, the Court affirmed in *ATE* that the rights of the most disadvantaged should be prioritised and accorded protection by public policies when the State is confronted with an economic crisis, and that those rights significantly limit the margins of state action, according to the principle of non-retrogression contained in ICESCR.

It is possible that in the case of a new crisis, any future government of Argentina would not be accorded unlimited discretion in terms of its response to such. Like Ulysses' pact when he crossed the sea to hear the Sirens' song, public policies would be tied to a strong mast, formed by ESR under the Constitution. Ultimately, however, the best case scenario would be not to have to examine whether this hypothesis is correct or not.

11

Recession, recovery and service delivery: political and judicial responses to the financial and economic crisis in South Africa

ANASHRI PILLAY AND MURRAY WESSON

I. Introduction

This chapter discusses the effects of the global financial crisis on South Africa. It considers the economic effects of the crisis and the government's response. It also assesses whether the crisis has had any impact on the judicial enforcement of economic and social rights. South Africa provides an interesting case study for two main reasons. First, because its transformative Constitution includes directly enforceable economic and social rights and, second, because the Constitutional Court has produced an influential body of case-law giving effect to these rights.[1] For these reasons, the South African experience might seem to hold valuable lessons for the role that economic and social rights can play as the financial crisis continues to unfold in other parts of the world.

However, there are factors that complicate our inquiry. For a start, South Africa had high levels of economic deprivation and inequality prior to the financial crisis. Thus, the crisis has served mainly to highlight and exacerbate these pre-existing problems. As well as this, the recession in South Africa has been relatively shallow compared to that experienced by some other countries. At the time of writing the South African economy had returned to modest growth and although the South African government was operating in conditions of fiscal constraint it had not

[1] The key provisions of the Bill of Rights are Section 26 (housing), Section 27 (health care, food, water and social security) and Section 29 (education). The Constitutional Court's decisions are discussed in the body of the chapter. For a general overview see S. Liebenberg, 'South Africa: Adjudicating Social Rights under a Transformative Constitution' in M. Langford (ed.), *Social Rights Jurisprudence: Emerging Trends in International and Comparative Law* (Cambridge University Press, 2008), pp. 75–101.

felt compelled to implement the type of austerity measures seen in many European countries.

The result is that it is difficult to discern a distinct turn in the Constitutional Court's case-law in 2009, the year in which the South African economy entered recession, or to establish a direct causal link between the global financial crisis and any developments in the Court's jurisprudence. Nevertheless, given that all of the South African cases have been decided in circumstances of deprivation and inequality – problems now gripping many other parts of the world to various degrees – we hope that our discussion can shed some light on the role that the judicial enforcement of economic and social rights can play in times of economic crisis.

II. A crisis prior to a crisis? South Africa 1990–2007

In order to properly understand the effects of the global financial crisis on South Africa, it is necessary to provide some background and historical context. It is well-known that South Africa emerged from apartheid in the early 1990s with extremely high levels of poverty, inequality and unemployment, following decades of discriminatory provision in health, education and infrastructure across population groups. The South African economy had grown at an average of only 0.8 per cent from 1985 to 1994,[2] and the African National Congress (ANC) inherited a substantial budget deficit and burgeoning debt.[3] The new government was therefore faced with the daunting task of embarking on a project of social transformation in line with the new Constitution while also ensuring the sustainability of state finances.

In response to this challenge, the government adopted a broadly orthodox macroeconomic policy, focused on fiscal deficit reduction through expenditure restraint and tight monetary policy, coupled with trade liberalisation. This approach was embodied in the Growth, Employment and Redistribution Programme (GEAR), a five-year programme adopted in 1996.[4] The objective of GEAR was to create the conditions for higher levels of economic growth, thereby addressing South Africa's unemployment crisis and generating the resources necessary to provide health care,

[2] S. Du Plessis and B. Smit, 'South Africa's Growth Revival After 1994', *Journal of African Economies*, 16 (2007), 668–704, 670.

[3] T. Ajam and J. Aron, 'Fiscal Renaissance in a Democratic South Africa', *Journal of African Economies*, 16 (2007), 745–81, 746.

[4] See 'Growth, Employment and Redistribution: A Macroeconomic Strategy', www.treasury.gov.za/publications/other/gear/chapters.pdf, last accessed 20 August 2013.

education and other services. According to John Weeks, it was predicted that GEAR would generate average growth of 4.2 per cent for 1996–2000.[5] Weeks observes that this figure may seem modest but was in fact ambitious given the anaemic growth of the preceding years.[6]

GEAR largely set the agenda for the ANC's subsequent economic policy. As Stewart Ngandu *et al.* note, there has been considerable debate about the advantages and disadvantages of South Africa's macroeconomic policy.[7] On the one hand, there is no doubt that the South African economy achieved increased rates of economic growth, averaging 3.1 per cent from 1995 to 2004 and reaching 5 per cent in 2004–6.[8] The government made significant progress in reducing the budget deficit, even achieving a surplus in 2007–8.[9] Progress was also made in reducing government debt, to just 27.1 per cent of gross domestic product (GDP) in 2006–7.[10] Finally, the adoption of inflation targeting in 2000 meant that from 2003 to 2007 the inflation rate fell within the 3–6 per cent target range.[11]

For defenders of the ANC's macroeconomic policy, these figures represent significant achievements that allowed for a sustainable expansion of social spending, especially through the system of social grants. As we shall see, defenders also argue that the government's 'countercyclical' economic policy – whereby surpluses are run in good years – meant that South Africa was in a stronger position than it would otherwise have been when the waves of the global financial crisis reached its shores. The net result was that South Africa did not need to seek external financial support from the International Monetary Fund. Nor has South Africa had to adopt austerity measures, although in its 2013 budget the government

5 J. Weeks, 'Stuck in Low GEAR? Macroeconomic Policy in South Africa, 1996–98', *Cambridge Journal of Economics*, 23 (1999), 795–811, 796.

6 *Ibid.*

7 S. Ngandu, M. Altman, C. Cross, P. Jacobs, T. Hart and I. Matshe, 'The Socio-Economic Impact of the Global Downturn on South Africa: Responses and Policy Implications' (2010), xvi, www.hsrc.ac.za/en/research-outputs/view/5390, last accessed 20 August 2013.

8 Du Plessis and Smit, 'South Africa's Growth Revival After 1994', 670.

9 Department of National Treasury, 'South African National Budget 2008: Overview of the 2008 Budget', 4, www.treasury.gov.za/documents/national%20budget/2008/review/chap1.pdf, last accessed 9 January 2014.

10 Department of National Treasury, 'South African National Budget 2007: Overview of the 2007 Budget', 16, www.treasury.gov.za/documents/national%20budget/2007/review/chap1.pdf, last accessed 9 January 2014.

11 J. Aron and J. Muellbauer, 'Review of Monetary Policy in South Africa since 1994', *Journal of African Economies*, 16 (2007), 705–44.

indicated that fiscal constraints mean that growth in spending will be 'moderated' over the next three years.[12]

On the other hand, for many commentators South Africa is a prime example of the failure of neoliberal economic policies. It is not difficult to find fault with the ANC's economic track record. For a start, even though the South African economy achieved a prolonged period of growth, many observers have noted that the figures are not especially impressive by global standards.[13] As well as this, only modest progress was made in addressing South Africa's deep-rooted structural problems of poverty, inequality and unemployment. The 2011 census reveals that although the income of black households increased by 170 per cent over the preceding decade, their annual income is still only one-sixth of that of white households.[14] In respect of income inequality, South Africa remains one of the most unequal societies in the world.[15] By some standards, the country has even moved backwards since 1994. For example, from 1995 to 2003 the unemployment rate rose from 17 per cent to 28 per cent on a narrow definition and from 29 per cent to a staggering 42 per cent on a broad definition.[16] In late 2007, even before the effects of the financial crisis had reached South Africa, unemployment had reduced somewhat but still stood at 24 per cent on a narrow definition. Although the government has increased social expenditure since 1994, this has not always yielded better outcomes. Education accounts for one-sixth of government spending but in the World Economic Forum's Global Competitiveness Report

[12] Department of National Treasury, 'South African National Budget 2013: Fiscal Policy', 32, www.treasury.gov.za/documents/national%20budget/2013/review/chapter%203.pdf, last accessed 9 January 2014.

[13] See, e.g., Du Plessis and Smit, 'South Africa's Growth Revival After 1994', 670. The authors note that East Asia, for example, achieved growth rates of 6.2 per cent during 1994–2004. See also H. Marais, 'The Impact of the Global Recession on South Africa' (17 July 2009), www.realinstitutoelcano.org/wps/portal/rielcano_eng/Content?WCM_GLOBAL_CONTEXT=/elcano/elcano_in/zonas_in/cooperation+developpment/ari115-2009, last accessed 9 January 2009.

[14] 'South Africa's Census: Racial Divide Continuing', BBC News (30 October 2012), www.bbc.co.uk/news/world-africa-20138322, last accessed 20 August 2013.

[15] 'Over the Rainbow', *The Economist* (20 October 2012), www.economist.com/news/briefing/21564829-it-has-made-progress-becoming-full-democracy-1994-failure-leadership-means, last accessed 20 August 2013.

[16] The narrow definition of unemployment applies a job search test whereas the broad definition accepts as unemployed those who did not search for work in a four-week reference period but who report being available for work and say that they would accept the offer of a suitable job. See G. Kingdon and J. Knight, 'Unemployment in South Africa, 1995–2003: Causes, Problems and Policies', *Journal of African Economies*, 16 (2007), 813–48, 814.

South Africa ranks 132nd out of 144 countries for its standard of primary education and 143rd for the quality of its mathematics and science.[17]

It is therefore no exaggeration to say, as Isobelle Frye does, that 'the crisis in South Africa existed long before its more recent international counterpart'[18] and that the term 'economic crisis' might be said to 'permanently characterise' the lives of many South Africans.[19] As we shall see, the effect of the global financial crisis has been to amplify and entrench these pre-existing problems.

III. The global financial crisis reaches South Africa: denial, response and muted recovery

There was initially a view that the South African economy would emerge from the global financial crisis largely unscathed. For instance, Finance Minister Trevor Manuel asserted confidently in 2008 that 'we are not looking at a recession in South Africa'.[20] The reasons for this view are complex and, in retrospect, difficult to fathom. However, Hein Marais argues that a narrative of impressive growth and economic stability had taken hold in government and business circles, with much emphasis placed upon 'sound economic fundamentals' and South Africa's well-regulated financial sector.[21]

Others were less sanguine. Early in 2009, *The Economist* ranked South Africa as the most vulnerable of the larger emerging economies, taking into account South Africa's large current account deficit, short-term debt as a percentage of foreign exchange reserves and the ratio of banks' loans to their deposits.[22]

As it happens, the South African economy tipped into recession in the same year. But it is important to see that the triggers for recession were very different in South Africa to developed countries in North America

[17] 'Over the Rainbow'.

[18] I. Frye, 'Responses and Alternatives: South Africa's Response to the Crisis', in *Perspectives: Political Analysis and Commentary from South Africa* (2009), 8–12, 8, www.boell.org/downloads/Perspectives_3-09.pdf, last accessed 20 August 2013.

[19] *Ibid.*, 11.

[20] W. Roelf, 'Manuel Sees No Recession but Inflation to Fall', *Mail & Guardian* (18 November 2008), http://mg.co.za/article/2008-11-18-manuel-sees-no-recession-but-inflation-to-fall, last accessed 20 August 2013.

[21] Marais, 'The Impact of the Global Recession in South Africa'.

[22] 'Domino Theory: Where Could Emerging-Market Contagion Spread Next?', *The Economist* (26 February 2009), www.economist.com/node/13184631, last accessed 20 August 2013.

and Europe. The South African banking sector had only limited exposure to international financial instruments and the United States sub-prime mortgage market. The economic downturn in South Africa was therefore not caused by a banking crisis. Nor was the downturn caused by unsustainable state finances. Instead, according to Ngandu *et al.*, the impact in South Africa mostly resulted from contagion effects from developments in international markets, which took the form of decreases in private capital inflows and commodity exports and a consequent reduction in trade revenues.[23] The mining and manufacturing sectors were the hardest hit by the changes in trade induced by the global downturn, while there was a sharp outflow of foreign portfolio capital in late 2008 – an especially worrying development given that South Africa is highly reliant on private capital flows to finance its current account deficit.[24]

The net result of these developments was that GDP fell by 0.7 per cent in the fourth quarter of 2008 and then by 7.4 per cent in the first quarter of 2009.[25] These two consecutive contractions in the growth rate of GDP meant that South Africa entered a recession for the first time in 17 years.[26] In total, from the fourth quarter of 2008 to the second quarter of 2010, the South African economy shed 1.1 million jobs as a result of the recession.[27] Given that South Africa had made only incremental progress in addressing unemployment since 1994 there is no doubt that job losses of this magnitude served only to deepen a pre-existing problem while also representing a 'significant setback' for the country.[28]

Unsurprisingly, the effects of these developments on vulnerable sectors of society were especially severe. Frye notes that many of the jobs lost have been in the semi-skilled sectors of trade, transport and mining. Statistically, such workers tend to live in households that have fewer employed persons. It follows that the number of people dependent on the income of these workers tends to be higher than in households made up of skilled persons.[29] The financial crisis also reached South Africa following a period of high food and oil prices, resulting in a 'compound crisis'.[30] From 2002 to 2007 there was a sustained decrease in food insecure households. However, by 2008 the intersection of high food prices and the

[23] Ngandu *et al.*, 'The Socio-Economic Impact of the Global Downturn on South Africa', 20.

[24] *Ibid.*, 21. [25] *Ibid.*, 22. [26] *Ibid.*

[27] *Ibid.*, 32. [28] *Ibid.*, 32.

[29] Frye, 'Responses and Alternatives', 8.

[30] Ngandu *et al.*, 'The Socio-Economic Impact of the Global Downturn on South Africa', vii.

recession resulted in an increase in food insecure households, especially amongst lower-income households.[31] Female-headed households in traditional huts and informal settlements were disproportionately affected, with roughly 20 per cent of female-headed households reporting that adults in the family had experienced hunger in the last year compared to 15 per cent of male-headed households.[32]

After some initial denials, how did the South African government respond to these unfolding problems? At a fiscal level, the government's response was to initially increase spending, coupled to lower increases in spending in the years thereafter in an attempt to ensure sustainability. Some of these spending increases had been planned in advance. In 2007 the government had already committed to increasing the value and scope of the various social grants.[33] The 2010 budget therefore extended the eligibility criteria for the child support grant, resulting in an increased allocation of R9.4 billion over a three-year period.[34] Other spending increases were in keeping with the government's countercyclical economic policy and represented an attempt to stimulate the economy. For example, the 2010 budget allocated R52 billion for an expanded public works programme.[35] Overall, the 2010 budget resulted in government's share of GDP rising from 28.5 per cent in 2007–8 to 34.1 per cent in 2009–10. The budget as a whole increased by 8.6 per cent with social services receiving 54 per cent of government spending, an increase of 9.3 per cent relative to 2009–10.[36] For Finance Minister Pravin Gordhan, this was testament to the government's prudent macroeconomic policy: 'We entered the recent recession with a healthy fiscal position and a comparatively low level of debt. This allowed us to maintain government spending despite a sharp deterioration in revenue.'[37]

However, questions can be raised about the sustainability of government spending in the years ahead. In the 2009 financial year, revenue

[31] *Ibid.*, 66. [32] *Ibid.*, 70. [33] *Ibid.*, 147.

[34] Department of National Treasury, 'National Budget Review' (2010), 104, www.treasury.gov.za/documents/national%20budget/2010/review/default.aspx, last accessed 20 August 2013.

[35] Minister of Finance, 'Budget Speech 2010' (17 February 2010), www.treasury.gov.za/documents/national%20budget/2010/speech/speech2010.pdf, last accessed 20 August 2013. Although by the Minister of Finance's own admission public works create only 'short-term job opportunities'.

[36] Ngandu *et al.*, 'The Socio-Economic Impact of the Global Downturn on South Africa', 129.

[37] Minister of Finance, 'Budget Speech 2011' (23 February 2011), www.treasury.gov.za/documents/national%20budget/2011/speech/speech2011.pdf, last accessed 20 August 2013.

decreased by 9 per cent or R34 billion while expenditure increased by R127 billion.[38] The result was that the budget balance swung from a surplus of 1 per cent of GDP in 2007–8 to a deficit of 7.3 per cent in just two years.[39] The 2013 budget estimated that the budget deficit had reduced to 5.2 per cent of GDP.[40] Nevertheless, it should be clear that the South African government is acting in a tight fiscal environment. Indeed, in the 2013 budget the government announced that growth in spending would be curbed by R10.4 billion over the next three years and its contingency reserves would be reduced by R23.5 billion over the medium term.[41] Although no longer in recession, South Africa continues to be plagued by weak economic growth, with a recent report from the African Development Bank ranking the country 48th out of 52 countries in terms of economic outlook.[42] Should there be a further downturn the ability of the South African government to stimulate a recovery would be severely limited.

As far as monetary policy is concerned, prior to the crisis the South African inflation rate had exceeded the target range of 3–6 per cent, reaching a high of 13.7 per cent in 2008.[43] The Reserve Bank therefore raised the repurchase (repo) rate to a high of 12 per cent in an attempt to contain inflation.[44] However, with the onset of the recession in 2008 the Reserve Bank adopted a more accommodating monetary policy and lowered the repo rate to 7 per cent in December 2008.[45] The repo rate currently stands at 5 per cent while the inflation rate is just within the target range of 3–6 per cent at 5.3 per cent.[46] Given the low exposure of South African banks to United States financial instruments, the Reserve Bank has not had to engage in policies such as 'quantitative easing' whereby central banks inject money into the economy.[47]

[38] Ngandu *et al.*, 'The Socio-Economic Impact of the Global Downturn on South Africa', 127.

[39] Minister of Finance, 'Budget Speech 2010'.

[40] Department of National Treasury, 'South African National Budget 2013: Fiscal Policy'.

[41] *Ibid.*

[42] 'South Africa's Economy, Muddle through Will No Longer Do', *The Economist* (1 June 2013), www.economist.com/news/middle-east-and-africa/21578692-slow-growth-and-sliding-currency-are-alarming-symptoms-deeper, last accessed 9 January 2014.

[43] South African Reserve Bank, 'Targets and Results', www.resbank.co.za/MonetaryPolicy/DecisionMaking/Pages/TargetsResult.aspx, last accessed 9 January 2014.

[44] South African Reserve Bank, 'Rates', www.resbank.co.za/Research/Rates/Pages/Rates-Home.aspx, last accessed 9 January 2014.

[45] *Ibid.*

[46] South African Reserve Bank, 'Targets and Results'.

[47] Ngandu *et al.*, 'The Socio-Economic Impact of the Global Downturn on South Africa', 134.

A final aspect of the South African response to the global financial crisis that should be mentioned is that, in early 2009, the government, organised labour, business and community organisations established the *Framework for South Africa's Response to the International Economic Crisis*.[48] The Framework prioritised 12 areas of work including a training layoff scheme for workers at risk of retrenchment, support for distressed sectors of the economy and an expanded public works programme.

The South African economy emerged from recession in 2010 and achieved modest growth rates of 2.3 per cent in 2012 and a projected 2.1 per cent in 2013.[49] In a sense, South Africa has therefore been fortunate. South Africa has not had to recapitalise its banks or cut spending on social programmes. However, the position remains precarious. Although the European Union is no longer South Africa's main trading partner – that position is now occupied by China – a further European crisis would have highly detrimental knock-on effects for the South African economy.[50]

It is also important to emphasise the point made earlier in this chapter. Even before the financial crisis reached South Africa, the country suffered from exceptionally high rates of poverty, inequality and unemployment. South Africa might have been spared the worst of the global financial crisis but there is no doubt that these underlying structural problems have been deepened and entrenched, with fewer resources available to the South African government for such issues to be addressed and decreased prospects for economic growth. Indeed, the global financial crisis limits South Africa's possibilities at a time when the country has been described as being in a state of malaise, resulting from industrial strife, failure of government services and ineffective political leadership.[51] The question is to what extent, if any, the negative repercussions of the global financial crisis have filtered through to the economic and social rights case-law produced by the courts. It is to this issue that we now turn.

[48] 'Framework for South Africa's Response to the International Economic Crisis' (19 February 2009), www.info.gov.za/view/DownloadFileAction?id=96381, last accessed 20 August 2013.

[49] H. Nyambura-Mwaura, 'South Africa Slashes 2013 GDP Growth Forecast to 2.1%', *Reuters* (21 October 2013), www.reuters.com/article/2013/10/23/safrica-budget-growth-idUSL5N0ID2FL20131023, last accessed 9 January 2014.

[50] N. Bauer, 'It Gets Worse: SA Economy Headed for Troubled Waters', *Mail & Guardian* (14 June 2012), http://mg.co.za/article/2012–06–13-sa-economy-headed-for-troubled-waters, last accessed 20 August 2013.

[51] 'Over the Rainbow'.

IV. Adjudicating economic and social rights in a recession: case-law from 2009

The South African Constitutional Court has produced a well-known series of cases – *Soobramoney*,[52] *Grootboom*,[53] *Treatment Action Campaign*[54] and *Khosa*[55] – dealing with the positive obligations imposed by economic and social rights. Early commentary focused on defining the Court's approach and suggesting more robust alternatives to that approach. Some scholars praised the jurisprudence as evidence that courts may play a useful role in implementing economic and social rights whilst, at the same time, respecting the expertise and democratic mandate of the other branches of government.[56] Others saw the Court's reasonableness-based approach as a weak device which stood little chance of fulfilling the transformative promise of the key economic and social rights provisions.[57] Even these commentators, however, expressed approval for aspects of the Court's reasoning.[58] Concerns about the practical effect of the judgments were rife but, for most commentators, and for civil society organisations thinking about strategies to implement the rights, these concerns highlighted the fact that courts are only one tool in the struggle to fulfil rights.

In some later cases, the Court indicated that it saw its role as a managerial one, that creative judicial remedies were possible and appropriate and that the goals of participatory democracy would inform judicial approaches to the rights.[59] In *Olivia Road*,[60] for instance, the Court had issued an interim

[52] *Soobramoney* v. *Minister of Health (KwaZulu-Natal)* 1997 (12) BCLR 1696 (CC).

[53] *Government of the Republic of South Africa* v. *Grootboom* 2000 (11) BCLR 1169 (CC).

[54] *Minister of Health* v. *Treatment Action Campaign (No. 2)* 2002 (10) BCLR 1033 (CC).

[55] *Khosa and Others* v. *Minister of Social Development* 2004 (6) BCLR 569 (CC).

[56] See, e.g., C. Sunstein, *Designing Democracy: What Constitutions Do* (Oxford University Press, 2001), p. 221. See also C. Steinberg, 'Can Reasonableness Protect the Poor? A Review of South Africa's Socio-Economic Rights Jurisprudence', *South African Law Journal*, 123 (2006), 264–84; M. Wesson, '*Grootboom* and beyond: Reassessing the Socio-Economic Jurisprudence of the South African Constitutional Court', *South African Journal on Human Rights*, 20 (2004), 284–308.

[57] See, e.g., D. Bilchitz, *Poverty and Fundamental Rights: The Justification and Enforcement of Socio-Economic Rights* (Oxford University Press, 2007), ch. 5; M. Pieterse, 'Coming to Terms with Judicial Enforcement of Socio-Economic Rights', *South African Journal on Human Rights*, 20 (2004), 383–417, 407.

[58] See D. Bilchitz, 'South Africa: Right to Health and Access to HIV/AIDS Drug Treatment', *International Journal of Constitutional Law*, 1 (2003), 524–34, 530–1; Pieterse, 'Coming to Terms with Judicial Enforcement of Socio-Economic Rights', 402–3.

[59] See *Port Elizabeth Municipality* v. *Various Occupiers* 2005 (1) SA 217 (CC), para 39.

[60] *Occupiers of 51 Olivia Road, Berea Township and 197 Main Street Johannesburg* v. *City of Johannesburg and Others* 2008 (3) SA 208 (CC).

order that the City of Johannesburg should engage meaningfully with some 400 people that it wished to evict from unsafe and unhygienic buildings. The judgment affirmed the principle that where people face homelessness due to an eviction, public authorities should engage reasonably and in good faith with the occupiers with a view to finding solutions to their dilemma. Objectives of the engagement process should include, for instance, determining what the consequences of the eviction might be and whether the City could help in alleviating those consequences.[61] In *Olivia Road* the engagement process was marked by good faith on both sides[62] and resulted in a significant amount of agreement between the parties on the issues in the case. It is possible to see this as yet further evidence of an approach fixated with procedure rather than the substantive content of the rights. But commentators have seen the potential value of the meaningful engagement idea. Both scholars and activists were quick to suggest ways in which the remedy could be usefully developed – through combination with a supervision order, for example.[63]

Two cases decided in 2009 – *Joe Slovo*[64] and *Mazibuko*[65] – attracted criticism of a more serious kind. The hope that the Court could develop its reasonableness model of economic and social rights adjudication to interrogate governmental action more closely and the early participatory promise of meaningful engagement orders were both severely undermined by these decisions. The principal concern for this chapter is to assess whether these cases represent a judicial response to the global economic and financial crisis. The timing is significant – *Joe Slovo* was decided shortly after the President had officially acknowledged that the South African economy had entered into a recession. *Mazibuko* was heard and decided some months after this.[66] We begin this section of the

61 *Ibid.*, para 14 (*per* Van der Westhuizen J).

62 Stuart Wilson refers to the 'almost comprehensive surrender on the City's part' when it came to framing the settlement, which was the product of the engagement process ordered by the court. See S. Wilson, 'Litigating Housing Rights in Johannesburg's Inner City: 2004–2008', *South African Journal on Human Rights*, 27 (2011), 127–51, 150.

63 See B. Ray, 'Proceduralisation's Triumph and Engagement's Promise in Socio-Economic Rights Litigation', *South African Journal on Human Rights*, 27 (2011), 107–26; A. Pillay, 'Toward Effective Economic and Social Rights Adjudication: The Role of Meaningful Engagement', *International Journal on Constitutional Law*, 10 (2012), 732–55.

64 *Residents of Joe Slovo Community, Western Cape* v. *Thubelisha Homes and Others* 2009 (9) BCLR 847 (CC).

65 *Mazibuko and Others* v. *City of Johannesburg* 2010 (3) BCLR 239 (CC).

66 *Nokotyana and others* v. *Ekurhuleni Metropolitan Municipality and Others* 2010 (4) BCLR 312 (CC) may be included in this group of cases but is not discussed here as it does not add anything to the analysis below. For a detailed examination of the case,

chapter with a brief analysis of the two cases. We then move on to discuss the Court's subsequent jurisprudence with a view to considering how, if at all, the crisis has impacted the Court's model of economic and social rights adjudication.

A. *Meaningful engagement diluted*

In *Residents of Joe Slovo Community, Western Cape* v. *Thubelisha Homes and Others*, residents of the Joe Slovo settlement in the Western Cape resisted their eviction on several grounds. Government had targeted the settlement for reconstruction as part of its Breaking New Ground housing policy aimed at eliminating informal settlements country-wide.[67] The residents complained that government had breached an agreement that 70 per cent of the new houses in the development would be allocated to eligible Joe Slovo residents. Furthermore, rentals in the first phase of the development were considerably higher than the governmental estimates.[68] Residents also objected to moving to Delft, the area designated for temporary relocation, because of reports of a high crime rate, poor transport services and few employment prospects in the area.[69] The applicants wanted the Court to hand down an order for further engagement between the parties, rather than eviction, at this stage.[70]

The Court handed down a unanimous order, allowing for the eviction of the Joe Slovo residents. The eviction was made conditional on their relocation to temporary residential units which had to comply with certain specifications regarding size and quality. The parties were ordered to engage meaningfully with each other to try to reach agreement on the scheduling of the relocations and the respondents agreed to set aside 70 per cent of the houses yet to be built to eligible Joe Slovo residents.[71]

see J. Dugard, 'Urban Basic Services: Rights, Reality and Resistance' in M. Langford, B. Cousins, J. Dugard and T. Madlingozi (eds.), *Symbols or Substance: The Role and Impact of Socio-Economic Rights Strategies in South Africa* (Cambridge University Press, 2013), pp. 275–309, p. 33. See also Ray's comments on *Abahlali Basemjondolo Movement SA and another* v. *Premier of KwaZulu-Natal and others* 2010 (2) BCLR 99 (CC) in 'Proceduralisation's Triumph and Engagement's Promise in Socio-economic Rights Litigation', 108.

67 *Residents of Joe Slovo Community, Western Cape* v. *Thubelisha Homes and Others*, para. 25 (*per* Yacoob J).

68 *Ibid.*, paras. 32–33 (*per* Yacoob J).

69 *Ibid.*, para. 31 (*per* Yacoob J), para. 222 (*per* Ngcobo J).

70 *Ibid.*, para. 316 (*per* O'Regan J), para. 401 (*per* Sachs J).

71 *Ibid.*, para. 7.

All the judges acknowledged that there were serious deficiencies in the process of engagement.[72] Justice O'Regan actually held that there had been no meaningful engagement.[73] But they found that these flaws were not so serious as to render the governmental action unreasonable.

One of the main reasons why the residents were arguing for a further process of engagement was that they wanted the upgrade to be conducted whilst they remained on site, allowing them to avoid the distress of relocation. *In situ* upgrading was stressed in the government's Breaking New Ground housing plan and was consistent with international best practice,[74] but the judges held that it was reasonable for government to opt for relocation in this case, noting that this was a matter over which the government exercised a wide discretion.[75] There is little explanation for the choice of relocation in the judgment – simply a contention by the respondents that *in situ* upgrading would not be feasible.[76]

The Court's approach was problematic in a number of respects. For one thing, the delays, rising costs and miscalculations[77] associated with the N2 Gateway housing project were not primarily a consequence of a lack of cooperation by the residents. These problems arose directly from flaws in the project.[78] The judges allowed the State's nominal acceptance of the need for meaningful engagement and the overall worthiness of the project[79] to outweigh concerns about its impact on the residents. The argument that other, affected parties – particularly those who had already moved to Delft and were waiting to be allocated permanent housing – had also to be considered was, on the face of it, very convincing.[80] However, the idea that an order allowing for eviction of the residents would speed things up rested on the assumption that the primary cause of the delay was the residents' unwillingness to move. As discussed above, this was not the case.

On 24 August 2009, the Court decided to stay the execution of its eviction order in *Joe Slovo* until further notice.[81] The decision was a response

[72] *Ibid.*, para. 167 (*per* Moseneke DCJ), paras. 113, 117 (*per* Yacoob J), para. 247 (*per* Ngcobo J), para. 301 (*per* O'Regan J), para. 378 (*per* Sachs J).

[73] *Ibid.*, para. 301. (*per* O'Regan J).

[74] *Ibid.*, paras. 364, 367 (*per* Sachs J).

[75] *Ibid.*, para. 113 (*per* Yacoob J), para. 174 (*per* Moseneke DCJ), para. 253 (*per* Ngcobo J), para. 295 (*per* O'Regan J), para. 367 (*per* Sachs J).

[76] *Ibid.*, para. 253 (*per* Ngcobo J).

[77] *Ibid.*, paras. 371–2 (*per* Sachs J).

[78] *Ibid.*, paras. 371–2 (*per* Sachs J), para. 295 (*per* O'Regan J).

[79] *Ibid.*, para. 302 (*per* O'Regan J), para. 380 (*per* Sachs J).

[80] *Ibid.*, para. 303 (*per* O'Regan J), para. 392 (*per* Sachs J).

[81] P. de Vos, 'Sanity and Humanity Prevails – For Now', *Constitutionally Speaking* (8 September 2009), http://constitutionallyspeaking.co.za/sanity-and-humanity-prevails-for-now/, last accessed 20 August 2013; A. Majavu, 'Evictions Suspended: Shack Dwellers

to the Western Cape government's acknowledgement that the relocation of Joe Slovo residents could end up costing more than the *in situ* upgrading of the settlement. Furthermore, the N2 Gateway Project would not offer enough houses to accommodate all the original Joe Slovo residents and there was no plan for those people left behind in the temporary relocation area.[82]

It is possible to read the *Joe Slovo* decision as a narrative of success for the notion of meaningful engagement – after all, the government's ultimate capitulation resulted from the further engagement ordered by the Court. And the conditions imposed on the evictions by the Court highlighted the flaws in the project. From the perspective of the development of the Court's jurisprudence, however, it is difficult not to see this case as a retreat from an engagement remedy informed by the values of accountability, equality and participation.[83] The case made it clear that meaningful engagement was not a condition for governmental action. And the Court refused to attach the requirement of further engagement to a supervision order. Consequently, whether or not governmental bodies comply with the meaningful engagement requirement depends on factors like the extent to which the community involved is supported by a well-resourced, powerful civil society organisation with the wherewithal to place continued pressure on governmental bodies.[84]

B. Mazibuko*: reasonableness redefined?*

The litigation in the *Mazibuko* case arose in the context of Johannesburg Water's Operation Gcin'amanzi ('to save water') Plan.[85] Johannesburg Water decided to overhaul the system of water provision, starting with Phiri Township in Soweto. The plan was not directly prompted by the recession but its aims – 'to reduce unaccounted for water, to rehabilitate the water network, to reduce water demand and to improve the rate of

Reprieved', *The Sowetan* (4 September 2009), www.sowetanlive.co.za/sowetan/archive/2009/09/04/evictions-suspended, last accessed 20 August 2013.

[82] Majavu, 'Evictions Suspended'. See also Q. Mtyala, 'New Bricks for N2 Gateway', *IOL News* (2 March 2011), www.iol.co.za/news/south-africa/western-cape/new-bricks-for-n2-gateway-1.1034716, last accessed 20 August 2013.

[83] Pillay, 'Toward Effective Economic and Social Rights Adjudication'; S. Fredman, *Human Rights Transformed: Positive Rights and Positive Duties* (Oxford University Press, 2008), p. 103.

[84] Pillay, 'Toward Effective Economic and Social Rights Adjudication'.

[85] *Mazibuko and Others* v. *City of Johannesburg*, para. 13 (*per* O'Regan J).

payment'[86] – have clear resonance in the aftermath of the financial crisis, both in South Africa and elsewhere. The Phiri applicants alleged that the City's policy of allocating 6 kilolitres of free water per household per month (amounting to approximately 25 litres per person per day in areas such as Phiri where households are large) was unreasonable. The applicants wanted the Court to quantify the amount of water that would be considered 'sufficient' under Section 27(1)(b) as 50 litres per person per day, and to determine whether the State had acted reasonably in seeking to achieve the progressive realisation of this right.[87]

The Court stated that fixing a quantified content to the right of access to sufficient water could be a 'rigid and counter-productive' way of dealing with the right. An approach based on reasonableness, in contrast, allowed for the Court to take account of variations in context and time in adjudicating economic and social rights.[88] According to O'Regan J, for a unanimous court, the government's duty in respect to these rights was to take reasonable and progressive action to secure the 'basic necessities of life' to all citizens.[89] And rights-holders were entitled to hold government accountable for the manner in which it chose to do this.[90] The content of the right had to be determined in light of the content of the obligations set out in Section 27(2).[91] The parameters of a reasonableness-based approach were defined most clearly in this case – and the definition was consciously very narrow.[92]

One of the main considerations weighing against acceptance of the applicants' argument in the Court's decision was the finding that the expert evidence did not provide a single, clear answer to the question of what constituted 'sufficient water' in the context of this case. This was a debate the Court felt ill-equipped to settle.[93] But the disagreement was based on the fact that the amount of 50 litres per person per day included water-borne sanitation, which was relevant to the case. Furthermore the

86 *Ibid.*

87 For a summary of the arguments that the applicants made against the Plan, see *ibid.*, para. 44. The facts of the case are complex – for a more detailed discussion see M. Wesson, 'Reasonableness in Retreat? The Judgment of the South African Constitutional Court in *Mazibuko v City of Johannesburg*', *Human Rights Law Review*, 11 (2011), 390–405.

88 *Mazibuko and Others* v. *City of Johannesburg*, para. 60.

89 *Ibid.*, para. 59. 90 *Ibid.*, para. 59. 91 *Ibid.*, para 68.

92 Sandra Liebenberg notes that the court's approach, as described in *Mazibuko*, is primarily a 'process-oriented approach to reasonableness review'. See S. Liebenberg, *Socio-Economic Rights: Adjudication under a Transformative Constitution* (Claremont: Juta, 2010), p. 471. See in particular *Mazibuko and Others* v. *City of Johannesburg*, paras. 67, 71.

93 *Mazibuko and Others* v. *City of Johannesburg*, para. 62.

experts relied upon by the State indicated that the amount of 25 litres per person per day entailed a '"high" level of health concern'.[94]

Justice O'Regan found that, based on average household sizes, the existing free basic water allocation was sufficient for 80 per cent of households in Johannesburg, even if 'sufficient water' were taken to mean 50 litres per person per day.[95] But, as she recognised in the judgment, the average household size in the townships of Johannesburg was higher than that in the rest of the city. Often, more than one household relied on the same water connection. Sometimes, this meant that 20 people, rather than the average of 3.2 people, were dependent on one source for their supply of water.[96]

The applicants also challenged government's decision to install pre-paid meters for the applicants and others in their position. There were three levels of service provision under Johannesburg Water's Operation Gcin'amanzi Plan: 'The first level is the most basic and consists of a communal tap and communal ventilated pit latrines; the second level is a yard standpipe and a sewer connection or shallow communal sewer system with a pour-flush toilet; and the third level is a full metered water connection on each stand and a conventional water-borne sewerage system.'[97] Residents of Phiri Township were not given the option of a credit meter system.[98] There were disadvantages associated with the credit meter system: customers with credit meters paid higher tariffs for water supply than those with pre-paid meters; interest could be charged for arrear payments; defaulters' names could be registered with the credit bureau;[99] and, of course, water supply could be cut off, as a consequence of non-payment. However, the discontinuation of the water supply could only be effected after officials had complied with a range of requirements ensuring a fair procedure.[100] With the pre-paid connections, water supply would stop once the free basic water supply had been exhausted, unless and until the consumer purchased credit for further water supply.[101]

The Court ruled that the municipality did not need to provide pre-paid customers with reasonable notice and an opportunity to be heard before their water supply was stopped. Affected customers would be aware of the

[94] See 'Heads of Argument Submitted by the *Amicus Curiae*, the Centre for Housing Rights and Evictions', para 83, www.wits.ac.za/files/res922904ce301243159e1c40e81148b21c.pdf, last accessed 20 August 2013.

[95] *Mazibuko and Others* v. *City of Johannesburg*, para. 89.

[96] *Ibid.*, para. 87. [97] *Ibid.*, para. 107.

[98] *Ibid.*, para. 155. [99] *Ibid.*, paras. 141, 152–3.

[100] *Ibid.*, para. 116. [101] *Ibid.*, para. 117.

fact that the water would be cut off once the supply was exhausted and '[t]o require the City to provide notice and an opportunity to be heard each time a pre-paid allowance is about to expire ... would be administratively unsustainable and in most cases serve no useful purpose'.[102]

The Court relied on the municipality's indigent persons policy as a kind of safety net.[103] In terms of this policy, an additional 4 kilolitres per month would be provided free of charge to those households registered as indigent.[104] In response to arguments that the extra amount should simply be extended to all, the Court held that such an approach would benefit people who did not require the excess water, which would be costly and wasteful.[105] But the fact that only one-fifth of the households eligible to be registered as 'indigent' were actually on the register[106] is an indication that the introduction of the indigent persons policy was ineffective. The burden of knowing about, and following, a complex application procedure to be included on the register should not be placed on vulnerable people with few resources.

However one analyses it, Johannesburg Water's plan to overhaul the system of water provision in Phiri Township resulted in people with pre-paid meters being limited to the free basic water allowance for potentially months at a time while they tried to somehow find the money to pay for additional water. As was pointed out by the *amicus curiae* in the case, this policy applied regardless of how dire the need for water was.[107] It is submitted that the Court's treatment of the equality dimension of the case is also unconvincing, given that the City's plan was to introduce pre-paid meters solely in poorer, predominantly black areas, and not in more affluent, predominantly white areas.[108]

But perhaps the most concerning aspect of *Mazibuko* is the exceptionally deferential standard of review applied by the Court. We have noted already that the objectives underlying Operation Gcin'amanzi – for example, to reduce water demand and improve the rate of payment – have clear relevance in the aftermath of the financial crisis, not only in South Africa but in other jurisdictions where governments are attempting to deliver services in circumstances of fiscal constraint. On the facts of the case, the City's

[102] *Ibid.*, para. 123. Compare the court's reasoning on the notice requirement related to default judgments in the National Credit Act in the later *Sebola and another* v. *Standard Bank of South Africa Ltd and another* 2012 (5) SA 142 (CC); 2012 (8) BCLR 785 (CC).

[103] *Mazibuko and Others* v. *City of Johannesburg*, paras. 92–3.

[104] *Ibid.*, para. 93. [105] *Ibid.*, paras. 99–102. [106] *Ibid.*, para. 98.

[107] See 'Heads of Argument Submitted by the Centre on Housing Rights and Evictions'.

[108] For further discussion, see Wesson, 'Reasonableness in Retreat'.

objectives appeared to be legitimate given that the decrepit state of the existing water infrastructure meant that much of the water pumped into Soweto was unaccounted for, and given the culture of non-payment for services originating in the apartheid era that exists in many parts of Soweto.[109]

However, there is little consideration in *Mazibuko* of whether these objectives might have been pursued through less restrictive means. For example, the Court did not consider whether the City's objectives might have been achieved through installation of conventional credit meters, coupled with rehabilitation of the water network and more serious attempts at debt recovery. Nor did the Court consider whether a universalist approach to providing the extra 4 kilolitres a month would be more cost-effective than keeping an indigent persons register, given that the City's representative had indicated that the universalist system would be cheaper to administer.[110]

Governments must generally of course economic and social rights within the scope of their available resources. In this regard, it is difficult for courts to determine the quantum of available resources, given that this may implicate issues such as levels of taxation and borrowing where judicial legitimacy and expertise are limited.[111] It is also difficult for courts to second-guess policies adopted in response to resource constraints. However, courts can be vigilant to ensure that such policies do not impact disproportionately on vulnerable sectors of society, especially where less restrictive alternatives exist. In *Mazibuko*, the vulnerability of the group in question, and the fact that Operation Gcin'amanzi implicated not only the right of access to sufficient water but also the right to equality, means that the reasonableness standard should have hardened so as to include an element of proportionality.[112]

However, as with *Joe Slovo*, the outcome of the litigation does not provide a complete picture regarding the vindication of the right to water in the *Mazibuko* case. In fact, following the case, the City of Johannesburg decided to raise the amount of water provided free to the poorest households in the city to 50 litres per person per day and took other steps to

[109] *Mazibuko and Others* v. *City of Johannesburg*, paras. 10–12, 166.

[110] *Ibid.*, para. 99.

[111] See M. Pieterse, 'Coming to Terms with Judicial Enforcement of Socio-Economic Rights', *South African Journal on Human Rights*, 20 (2004), 383–417, 394–5; K. McLean, *Constitutional Deference, Courts and Socio-economic Rights in South Africa* (Pretoria University Law Press, 2009), pp. 195–6; M Tushnet, 'Social Welfare Rights and the Forms of Judicial Review', *Texas Law Review*, 82 (2004), 1895–919, 1896–7.

[112] This argument is made at greater length in M. Wesson, 'Disagreement and the Constitutionalisation of Social Rights', *Human Rights Law Review*, 12 (2012), 221–53.

soften the impact of the installation of pre-payment meters on relevant households.[113] The litigation played a role in achieving this result because of the publicity it generated. But the litigation was only one feature in what Jackie Dugard refers to as the 'politicisation of the ongoing process of engagement and contestation between civil society and government'.[114] Other aspects of the 'legal mobilisation process' included 'meetings, marches, media exposure and bypass, a form of civil disobedience that entails removing the offending technology ... and connecting to the main water supply, thereby restoring the unlimited water supply'.[115] Residents were supported in this process by the Anti-Privatisation Forum and the new, affiliated Coalition Against Water Privatisation.

Dugard and others point out that, whilst the ANC is still able to depend on convincing victories in national elections, the ANC government is not insulated from public protest.[116] In fact, some studies indicate that the country has 'one of the highest *per capita* rates of protest action in the world'.[117] Protests over failures in service delivery and communication, particularly at the level of local government, have become an important feature of the political landscape since 2004 and mushroomed in 2009.[118] And sustained protest action has, in combination with litigation or threatened litigation, influenced governmental policies and decisions.

Returning to the assessment of *Mazibuko*, then, a wider lens provides evidence of the value of litigation where that litigation is used as one of the tools in the struggle for rights implementation. Where local communities can draw on organised assistance and advice to place various forms of pressure on government, judicial decisions are more likely to have an important and sustained impact. But the principles articulated in the *Mazibuko* judgment suggest a court distancing itself from the possibility of a more substantive, robust approach to reasonableness review in the context of economic and social rights.

C. *Assessing the cases: recession jurisprudence?*

As noted earlier, the Constitutional Court's 2009 decisions in the area of economic and social rights have attracted concerns about a possible retreat to an approach that is much more deferential than that suggested

[113] Dugard, 'Urban Basic Services', 31. [114] *Ibid.*
[115] *Ibid.*, 28. [116] *Ibid.*, 12–18.
[117] Marais, 'The Impact of the Global Recession on South Africa'.
[118] Dugard, 'Urban Basic Services', 12.

in earlier cases and one that is not warranted by the judicial obligation to balance protection of the rights with respect for governmental decision-making. For our purposes, these concerns raise two questions. First, did the 2009 cases mark a departure from the Court's earlier jurisprudence and second, if so, is this shift connected to the financial and economic crisis?

For many commentators, the cases were not a departure from the Court's established approach but what Brian Ray refers to as the 'culmination of a strong trend towards the proceduralisation of socio-economic rights'.[119] Scholars have consistently argued that a reasonableness-based approach is, by its nature, process-driven and overly deferential.[120] But some arguments have focused on the potential of a reasonableness-based approach to protect the values underlying economic and social rights and to interrogate governmental action in a robust way. Some analysis of the meaningful engagement idea suggests that even an ostensibly procedural remedy may give rise to substantive protection.[121]

Whilst the Constitutional Court did, in its earlier jurisprudence, sometimes adopt a stance more deferential than was warranted, its reasoning left open the possibility for more serious interrogation of governmental policy. In cases like *Treatment Action Campaign* and *Khosa*, the Court was responsive to arguments based on the disproportionate adverse impact on individuals when weighted against the governmental objective. The Court indicated that it would enquire into the weight of submissions regarding limited resources, not simply take them at face value.[122] The dicta in *Mazibuko* closed down the space available to make such arguments. *Mazibuko* was not just a highly deferential decision on the facts of the case. It amounted to a statement of principle, a redefining of the Court's general approach to economic and social rights adjudication as light touch review.

The next question for us is whether what we have argued to be a departure from the Court's earlier approach may be attributed to the economic and financial crisis. There are several reasons why this is a difficult

[119] Ray, 'Proceduralisation's Triumph and Engagement's Promise in Socio-Economic Rights Litigation', 107.

[120] See Bilchitz, *Poverty and Fundamental Rights*; Pieterse, 'Coming to Terms with Judicial Enforcement of Socio-Economic Rights'.

[121] See Pillay, 'Toward Effective Economic and Social Rights Adjudication'; Ray, 'Proceduralisation's Triumph and Engagement's Promise in Socio-Economic Rights Litigation'.

[122] *Minister of Health* v. *Treatment Action Campaign (No. 2)*, paras. 65–6; *Khosa and Others* v. *Minister of Social Development*, paras. 60–2.

assessment to make. First, there are no overt indications in the cases that the judgments were informed by concerns about the country being in a recession. Second, resource scarcity is usually relevant in South African economic and social rights cases anyway. The two pivotal sections of the Constitution – Sections 26 and 27 – require the State to act 'within its available resources' and the State has made submissions based on resource scarcity in nearly all the cases decided in terms of those provisions thus far. In the later cases, those submissions have not been linked to the specific economic climate of a recession. Third, as the jurisprudence has developed, and government responds to its obligations, as defined in the Constitution and by the Court, a greater level of complexity and more serious resource implications are to be expected whether the State is operating in an economic recession or not. Thus, for instance, *Olivia Road* involved housing plans for a relatively small group of people whereas *Joe Slovo* concerned a massive housing project with a corresponding huge potential impact. Finally, as noted earlier in this chapter, the extreme levels of poverty in South Africa pre-dated the financial and economic crisis. The number of people living in poverty has increased and this is due, partly, to the economic crisis. The dire living conditions of the most vulnerable have been exacerbated by the economic downturn. But the crisis has served mainly to highlight pre-existing problems with governmental responses to poverty.

In terms of what this means for the Constitutional Court's model of economic and social rights adjudication, the Court has always had to balance its obligation to give effect to the economic and social rights with respect for the more democratic nature of governmental decision-making and the greater expertise of certain governmental officials and bodies. Neither the recession nor a global climate of economic insecurity and resource scarcity changes this fact. It does raise the question of whether the Court is getting the balance right. For the reasons described above, our argument is that the Court got it wrong in the 2009 cases. We turn now to examine post-2009 cases and consider the implications of this case-law for the Court's general approach to economic and social rights. Our focus in the discussion below is on how the Court has treated arguments about resources and how it has developed the meaningful engagement remedy. The post-2009 jurisprudence reinforces the point that the financial crisis has had no real impact on how the South African Constitutional Court approaches economic and social rights cases. However, the Court's treatment of arguments about limited resources contains valuable lessons for how courts adjudicate such rights in a general context of resource scarcity.

V. Post-2009 developments in the case-law

The *Blue Moonlight*[123] decision was handed down on 1 December 2011. The case considers *inter alia* the impact of resource constraints on housing policy. Like *Mazibuko*, *Blue Moonlight* is therefore clearly relevant to the post-recession issue of how the State should deliver services in circumstances where resources are limited, and the role that judicial review can play in this regard. However, the case holds more constructive lessons than *Mazibuko* on both counts.

Blue Moonlight was a private company which, in 2004, had purchased several buildings in a state of considerable disrepair with the intention of redeveloping them.[124] The buildings were occupied by some 86 people who had been living on the property for more than six months, some of them for a considerably longer period. Between 1999 and 2004, they had also paid rent to a caretaker claiming to act for the owner, and to two different letting agencies. By 2005 the buildings were in a shocking condition and the City of Johannesburg issued notices warning Blue Moonlight to deal with the safety and health issues. The company then posted notices in the buildings giving residents approximately a month to vacate. The notices also claimed to end any lease agreement that may have existed. Blue Moonlight began eviction proceedings in the High Court in 2006. At this stage, the occupiers of the buildings asked that the City be joined to the proceedings because of their obligations with respect to housing – the City did not object and became a party in the case. When the case eventually came before the Constitutional Court, one of the main legal issues was whether the City's policy of excluding people evicted from private property from consideration for temporary housing was constitutional.[125] The fact that the occupiers would be homeless if evicted from the buildings was undisputed in the case.[126]

The City sought to argue that its obligations with respect to emergency accommodation were limited to applying to the provincial government for assistance as and when the need arose. Its application for such assistance had been unsuccessful and it therefore had no further duties with respect to the occupiers.[127] In response, the Court held that there was nothing in the *Grootboom* decision or in Chapter 12 of the Housing Code to indicate that local government's capacity to provide emergency accommodation

[123] *City of Johannesburg Metropolitan Municipality* v. *Blue Moonlight Properties 39 (Pty) Ltd* 2012 (2) BCLR 150 (CC).

[124] *Ibid.*, paras. 1, 8. [125] *Ibid.*, para. 14.

[126] *Ibid.*, para. 47. [127] *Ibid.*, paras. 48–9.

was conditional on provincial funding. Indeed, when the Housing Code was read in light of the broader constitutional and statutory framework, it was clear that the City was both entitled and obliged to allocate resources in the sphere of emergency housing.[128] In essence, this aspect of *Blue Moonlight* makes clear that the central finding of *Grootboom* – that those in immediate and desperate need of housing should not be neglected – applies to all levels of government.

From the perspective of this chapter, an especially important argument advanced by the City was that it simply lacked the resources to provide emergency accommodation for the occupiers if they were evicted.[129] The City submitted that it could not budget for emergency accommodation due to the element of unpredictability, and that it was 'not obliged to go beyond its available budgeted resources to secure housing for homeless people … [r]esources not budgeted for are not available'.[130] The City argued further that although a budget surplus had been projected it was now in a budget deficit.[131]

The Court acknowledged that it would be wholly inappropriate for a court to order an organ of state to do something that was impossible and that the City's assertion about a lack of resources therefore deserved serious consideration.[132] However, the Court rejected the submission that unpredictability precluded budgeting for emergency housing. This is because 'the budgetary demands for a number and measure of emergency occurrences are at least to some extent foreseeable'.[133] Furthermore, it was not good enough for the City simply to assert that it had not budgeted for something, where it was legally obliged to do so.[134] The City had also not provided any documentary evidence to support its claims of a deficit.[135] The evidence provided related to the City's housing budget, rather than its overall financial position.[136] The Court was not prepared, in the light of this limited information, to overturn the Supreme Court of Appeal's finding that the City had not demonstrated that it could not afford to provide the relevant emergency housing.[137]

The Court went on to assess the constitutionality of the City's policy of distinguishing between those relocated by the City and those evicted by private landlords, and providing for only the former in its temporary accommodation programme. In its analysis, the Court noted that state resources are limited in any country and that this was especially

[128] *Ibid.*, para. 53 [129] *Ibid.*, para. 71. [130] *Ibid.*, para. 72.
[131] *Ibid.*, para. 73. [132] *Ibid.*, para. 69. [133] *Ibid.*, para. 63.
[134] *Ibid.*, para. 74. [135] *Ibid.*, para. 73. [136] *Ibid.*, para. 74. [137] *Ibid.*, paras. 74–5.

so for South Africa. Section 26(2) recognises that resource constraints are relevant for an enquiry into the validity of housing policies and programmes.[138] The question was whether the differentiation between those evicted by private landlords and those evicted by the City could stand.[139] The Court held that the distinction was unreasonable inasmuch as it obscured the individual situations of the persons at risk and therefore did not meaningfully take their needs into account;[140] the City's duty arises not on the basis of who carries out the eviction but rather the fact that the eviction may result in homelessness.[141]

The Court thus dismissed the City's appeal. It ruled that the occupiers could be evicted but that the City had to provide them with temporary accommodation 'on a date linked to the date of eviction'. The Court ordered that the temporary housing be as close as possible to their current location and that it be provided 14 days before the eviction to allow the occupiers enough time to make the necessary moving arrangements and give them the security that the housing was, in fact, available to them.[142] Although the occupiers had asked for a structural interdict in their written submissions,[143] the Court did not grant this, noting simply that the written arguments were not persuasive and had not been seriously pursued during the oral argument.[144]

Nevertheless, the importance of *Blue Moonlight* lies in the Constitutional Court's consideration of the relationship between constitutional obligations and resource constraints. The Court emphasised that resource constraints must be taken seriously. However, the Court will not simply accept assertions that, for instance, a public authority has a deficit. The State is required to provide evidence supporting its assertions regarding resource limitations. Furthermore, even where resources are constrained, the State must budget so as to fulfil its constitutional duties. The State cannot evade its obligations to those who are most vulnerable simply by failing to allocate resources. The Court will not prescribe exactly how much should be budgeted for a specific purpose. But the Court will ensure that

[138] *Ibid.*, para. 86. [139] *Ibid.*, para. 86. [140] *Ibid.*, para. 92. [141] *Ibid.*, para. 92.

[142] *Ibid.*, paras. 99–101. For the court order, see *ibid.*, para 104.

[143] A structural interdict is a type of supervisory jurisdiction –'an injunctive remedy that requires the party to whom it is directed, to report back to the court, within a specified period, the measures that have been taken to comply with the court's orders'. See D. Davis, 'Socio-economic Rights in South Africa: The Record of the Constitutional Court after Ten Years', *Economic and Social Rights Review*, 5(5) (2004), 3–7, 4.

[144] *City of Johannesburg Metropolitan Municipality* v. *Blue Moonlight Properties*, para.101.

those constitutionally entitled to the State's assistance are not neglected or excluded from the State's social programmes.

In two cases immediately following *Blue Moonlight* – *Pheko*[145] and *Schubart Park*[146] – the State did not raise any arguments regarding budgeting decisions and resource constraints. In contrast to *Blue Moonlight*, the Court's remedy in each of these cases included court supervision of the order.[147] In *Pheko*, the local authority involved, Ekurhuleni Metropolitan Municipality, sought to use the provisions of the Disaster Management Act 57 of 2002 to evict over 700 residents of the Bapsfontein Informal Settlement.[148] The key question was whether the Municipality could do this without first getting a court order.[149]

The Court held that Section 55(2) of the Act did not allow for eviction or demolition of homes without a court order – only evacuation, which is limited to cases where temporary action is necessary for the preservation of life.[150] Here, there was no need for urgent evacuation. The circumstances which gave rise to the declaration of a disaster area – the presence of sinkholes – were first evident in 2004. Several reports were commissioned in 2005 but no action was taken until 2009 when another report was commissioned. It was only in 2010 that the municipality started to relocate residents. The eviction of the residents and demolition of their homes therefore constituted a violation of Section 26(3) of the Constitution.[151]

The Court made a declaratory order that the removal was unlawful. It also held that the municipality had a duty to provide the residents with temporary accommodation on suitable land.[152] The municipality was under an obligation to engage with the applicants meaningfully regarding the identification of this land. The municipality had to report to the Court about its progress in approximately one year.[153] In ordering supervision, the Court noted that it was 'uncertain how long it will take for the Municipality to identify land for purposes of affording the applicants access to adequate housing. Supervisory relief is thus necessary in this

145 *Pheko and Others* v. *Ekurhuleni Metropolitan Municipality* 2012 (2) SA 598 (CC); 2012 (4) BCLR 388 (CC).

146 *Schubart Park Residents Association and Others* v. *City of Tshwane and Others* 2012 ZACC 26.

147 *Pheko and Others* v. *Ekurhuleni Metropolitan Municipality*, para. 50; *Schubart Park Residents Association and Others* v. *City of Tshwane and Others*, para. 51.

148 *Pheko and Others* v. *Ekurhuleni Metropolitan Municipality*, paras. 1, 4.

149 *Ibid.*, para. 3. For the factual background, see *ibid.*, paras. 5–11.

150 *Ibid.*, paras. 38–40.

151 *Ibid.*, paras. 41, 45.

152 *Ibid.*, para. 53 (on what 'suitable' temporary accommodation would amount to).

153 *Ibid.*, para. 50.

case to enable the Municipality to report to this Court about, amongst other things, whether land has been identified and designated to develop housing for the applicants'.[154] The Court's reason for ordering supervision in *Schubart Park* was similar. In this case, residents of three buildings who had been removed from their homes sought an order for re-occupation. The buildings in question were state-owned and, by 2011, they were occupied by many people not known to the City authorities. Conditions in the buildings had deteriorated significantly. In response to the City cutting off the water and electricity supply, some residents engaged in protest action – including the lighting of fires. When two fires broke out in one of the blocks, the police removed the residents from that block and did not allow them to return once the fire had been extinguished. Some weeks later, residents of the other two blocks were also removed. Ultimately, about 3,000–5,000 people were either living on the streets or in temporary shelters by the end of September 2009.[155]

The High Court handed down what the Constitutional Court referred to as a 'tender implementation order'. This provided that the City had a duty to assist the affected residents by, amongst other things, providing temporary accommodation, beginning a process of refurbishment of the buildings and subsequent relocation of the residents to the buildings, and, if technical advice showed this was not possible, providing habitable alternative buildings which had to allow for 'shelter, privacy and the amenities of life'.[156]

The only defence presented by the City was that re-occupation was impossible because of the life-threatening conditions the High Court had found to exist, as a matter of fact, in the buildings. The City conceded before the Constitutional Court that this defence only applied for as long as it was actually impossible to return the residents – in other words, 'immediate removal on grounds of safety and temporary impossibility' could not 'result in the permanent lawful deprivation of the occupation of their homes'.[157] The Court pointed out that any other understanding would be inconsistent with previous case-law.[158] The Court agreed with the High Court's findings that the removal was not a lawful eviction but action made temporarily necessary to preserve life, and that the residents were entitled to re-occupation once it was safe for them to return. But the

[154] *Ibid.*,

[155] *Schubart Park Residents Association and Others* v. *City of Tshwane and Others*, paras. 1–8.

[156] *Ibid.*, para. 12. [157] *Ibid.*, para. 20. [158] *Ibid.*, paras. 19–20.

judges objected to the lower court's finding that if the buildings could not be made safe, those who had accepted the City's tender must be provided with alternative accommodation. At that stage, the action would amount to eviction, rather than temporary removal, and eviction could not be effected without a court order.[159]

The Court also held that the High Court should have explicitly recognised the residents' right to eventual restoration of their occupation, provided the buildings could be rehabilitated.[160] The Court noted that a meaningful engagement order was appropriate, not just as a means of securing acceptable temporary accommodation for people facing eviction but also in circumstances where possible restoration of occupation was at issue.[161] Perhaps most importantly, the Court held that the City's tender or offer of temporary accommodation was an 'inadequate basis for a proper order of engagement' because '[i]t proceeds from a "top-down" premise, namely that the City will determine when, for how long and ultimately whether at all, the applicants may return to Schubart Park'.[162] Thus, the Court ordered that the City and the applicants had to engage meaningfully broadly in order to achieve restoration of the applicants' occupation. The parties were given slightly under two months to report to the High Court on their plans and progress. The Court held that this supervision was needed because of the uncertainty regarding how long the process of re-occupation would take.[163]

On the face of it then, the decision to order supervision in the latter two cases and not in *Blue Moonlight* rested on the quality of argument put forward regarding supervision and the level of uncertainty with regard to when the Court's order could be implemented. At the same time, the supervisory element of the Court's orders in *Pheko* and *Schubart Park* highlights the capacity of the Court to hand down more robust remedies where resource constraints are less of a concern. Importantly, the cases suggest that, where there is evidence of serious resource scarcity – whether linked to a global financial crisis or not – the courts may still play a role in, at least, holding government to account for its decisions. Thus, resource scarcity may influence a court's choice of remedies, rather than act as a reason for non-justiciability of economic and social rights.

159 *Ibid.*, para. 41.
160 *Ibid.*, para. 49.
161 *Ibid.*, para. 42.
162 *Ibid.*, para. 50.
163 The courts specified certain issues with respect to the subject matter of engagement. See *Schubart Park Residents Association and Others* v. *City of Tshwane and Others*, paras. 51, 53.

VI. Conclusion

It is still too early to measure whether the experience of recession will result in any real changes to political and economic conditions in South Africa. The crisis highlighted the pre-existing structural problems which have resulted in extreme poverty and inequality. But, in its fundamentals, the government's economic policy remains unchanged. And the ANC's electoral dominance suggests that a shift in that economic policy is extremely unlikely.

The increase in organised resistance to governmental policies and the manner in which those policies are implemented – particularly when it comes to basic services – is perhaps the most interesting development of the 2009–12 period in terms of the current and future prospects for ESR realisation in South Africa. As noted above, it is difficult to establish a direct link between the kind of protest action now common in the country and the financial crisis. The protests are an expression of dissatisfaction over continued lack of access to basic services, and frustration over the government's failure to properly engage with communities about their needs. These issues pre-dated the recession but were exacerbated by it.

Organised resistance has resulted in identifiable gains with respect to the protection of economic and social rights.[164] And litigation has proved to be a valuable element in the struggle for access to goods such as housing and water. The capacity of courts to effect social change is limited. For one thing, the social and economic rights cases decided in the courts represent the tip of a very large iceberg. And, most importantly, judicial decisions in this context have proved to be truly useful only when reinforced by community pressure for enforcement and further engagement. But, taking these considerations into account, the development of judicial principle continues to be an important element of social and economic rights discourse in South Africa.

Notwithstanding the fact that South Africa entered a recession in 2009 as a result of the global financial crisis, it is difficult to discern a distinct impact on the Constitutional Court's economic and social rights jurisprudence. It is true that two of the cases decided in that year – *Mazibuko* and *Joe Slovo* – have been criticised for diluting the requirements of reasonableness and meaningful engagement. However, the seeds for these developments were present in the Court's earlier decisions. And, whilst

[164] See, further, Dugard, 'Urban Basic Services'; H. Marais, *South Africa Pushed to the Limit: The Political Economy of Change* (London and New York: Zed Books, 2011), pp. 455–7.

Mazibuko appeared to signal a more fundamental shift in the Court's approach, subsequent developments suggest a quiet retreat from the deferential assumptions of that decision. The finding in *Blue Moonlight* that government had not provided adequate support for the claim that what was being asked for was beyond its resource capacity is significant. It is possible to argue that the difference in the cases was really one of scale: *Mazibuko* and, for that matter, *Joe Slovo* dealt with far greater numbers of people and the resource implications were therefore more serious. But the Court's finding in *Blue Moonlight* that the City could not exclude people who had been evicted by private property owners from its temporary housing programme has quite wide-ranging implications.

The Court has also adopted a more robust approach to the meaningful engagement remedy. Evacuation or eviction had already occurred in the later cases dealing with engagement so the question of whether removal should be made conditional on engagement did not really arise. However, in the *Schubart Park* case, the Court's declaratory order that the residents were entitled to re-occupy their homes in the buildings concerned, combined with the engagement order about the details of temporary accommodation, etc., meant that a future eviction (if the buildings could not be restored) could not take place in the absence of meaningful engagement. Furthermore, the addition of supervision orders to the engagement remedies in *Pheko* and *Schubart Park* was a step toward more careful scrutiny of governmental action that the Court had previously refused to take.

Taken as a whole, the jurisprudence of the Constitutional Court since 2009 – both the more restrained and interventionist elements – cannot be seen to be a direct response to the economic downturn. Nevertheless, we should not conclude that the South African experience holds no lessons for the role that economic and social rights can play in times of economic crisis. As we have emphasised throughout this chapter, all of the Constitutional Court's economic and social rights decisions have been reached in a context of deprivation and inequality. In a sense, all of the Court's judgments are a response to the ongoing economic crisis that characterises the lives of many South Africans. Decisions such as *Grootboom* and *Blue Moonlight* demonstrate that, at its best, the reasonableness approach is capable of holding even resource-constrained governments to account for the steps that they have taken to realise economic and social rights, while also respecting the expertise and democratic credentials of executive and legislative decision-makers. The difficulty is that the reasonableness standard is capable of lapsing into overly deferential review, as illustrated by the *Mazibuko* decision. However, there is now a considerable body of literature about how the reasonableness standard can be strengthened so as to avoid this eventuality.[165]

The case-law on meaningful engagement likewise emphasises the central importance of the values of accountability, equality and participation in circumstances where people face eviction, and possibly more broadly where the State threatens to deprive people of enjoyment of economic and social rights. Of course, there are limitations to the Court's meaningful engagement jurisprudence, some of which have been canvassed above. Perhaps the most damning critique is that some government officials may use, and have used, the remedy in a cynical way. Wilson has written about the City of Johannesburg's use of '"engagement" to narrow the scope and content of its obligations toward the poor significantly'.[166] To some extent the problem has been recognised by the Constitutional Court in their orders in cases such as *Blue Moonlight*, where details were included about the conditions appropriate for temporary accommodation. The cases decided in 2011 and 2012 are also of some assistance because of the newly introduced court supervision of engagement orders. Supervision will go some way towards ensuring that engagement does not descend into a top-down exercise in information provision by governmental officials. The principles elaborated in the cases following the 2009 Constitutional Court term have yet to be tested in the context of large-scale projects in the nature of the government's Breaking New Ground housing policy or Operation Gcin'amanzi (to save water) Plan. They are, however, a promising development of the Court's economic and social rights jurisprudence. These cases add strength to the argument that adjudication is an important tool for organisations and individuals seeking to vindicate economic and social rights.

Moreover, given the fact that the South African experience of economic and social rights adjudication is located with a context of continuing economic insecurity, the jurisprudence speaks to the kind of demands that may be placed on governmental bodies in situations of very serious resource scarcity such as a global financial crisis. Even when not attached to court supervision, a detailed meaningful engagement order may contribute to the protection of interests in housing, water provision and so on. And court supervision is a useful way of ensuring the integrity of meaningful engagement. This is not to advocate a process-driven

[165] For general discussion, see the articles cited in notes 57–8. For a recent contribution, see Wesson, 'Disagreement and the Constitutionalisation of Social Rights'.

[166] Wilson, 'Litigating Housing Rights in Johannesburg's Inner City', 150.

approach to the implementation of economic and social rights in general. Importantly, the jurisprudence also does not suggest that resource scarcity, however extreme, allows government free rein in deciding on best practice when it comes to economic and social rights. Rather, the cases discussed here show that the political and economic complexity, whether due to the nature of a particular project or the global financial climate, may demand that courts apply a level of creativity in deciding on appropriate remedial action.

INDEX

Lightning Source UK Ltd.
Milton Keynes UK
UKOW06f0414050816

280024UK00001B/105/P

9 781107 618428